"MAN OVER MONEY"

The

FRED W. MORRISON

Series in Southern Studies

"MAN OVER MONEY"

THE SOUTHERN POPULIST CRITIQUE
OF AMERICAN CAPITALISM

Bruce Palmer

The University of North Carolina Press

Chapel Hill

© 1980 The University of North Carolina Press

Manufactured in the United States of America

Library of Congress Cataloging in Publication Data

Palmer, Bruce, 1942–
"Man over money".

(The Fred W. Morrison series in Southern studies)
Bibliography: p.
Includes index.
1. People's Party of the United States.
2. Populism—United States—History. 3. Southern
States—Politics and government—1865–1950.
4. United States—Politics and government—1893–1897.
I. Title. II. Series: Fred W. Morrison series in
Southern studies.
JK2372.P34   329'.88'00975   79-24698
ISBN 0-8078-1427-X

To: Mother, Dad, David, Ann, and Ralph—

and Leah, whose timing was excellent.

CONTENTS

Chapter 10. The Logic of a Metaphor 126

Part Three: The Political Price

ACKNOWLEDGMENTS

At one time or another over the last ten years I have used a large number of libraries and state archives, particularly in the South. I received important help from the staffs in the archives, manuscript, and newspaper divisions of the libraries at Yale University, the University of Virginia, the University of North Carolina at Chapel Hill, the University of Georgia, the University of Alabama, Louisiana State University, Tulane University, and the University of Texas at Austin, and the Alabama and Georgia State Departments of Archives and History, the Texas State Library, the Tennessee State Library and Archives, and the Arkansas History Commission. Tom Bates of the University of Houston at Clear Lake City library deserves special mention for his willingness to try and his considerable ability in finding often strange interlibrary loan requests.

Thinking about it I realize that not only in the research and writing of this book have I acquired debts; I owe thanks to friends who never knew, and may very well never know, about this book. I hope they do not underestimate their contribution. Jim Burnett, Curt Lamb, Bambi Brown, Tom Roberts, and Mike Lerner assisted in ways only real friends can. Ralph Palmer and Bob Greenberg helped at critical stages to clarify my ideas and writing. Grace and Sam Oren graciously took time off from visiting their daughter and new granddaughter to help me proofread the final copy of the manuscript.

In the Student Nonviolent Coordinating Committee I first learned of the South and the Southern Populists. To the amazing people I knew there, particularly Mike Sayer, Walter Tillow, Rick Manning, James Bond, Frank Minnis, and Laurence Guyot I owe a considerable debt, intellectual and otherwise, including the germination of this book. To Sarah Jones, Lou Medvene, and Kathleen Hynes of the Rochester Action for Welfare Rights I owe as considerable a debt of education and friendship. They helped me learn something of what it must have meant to be an Alliance lecturer or a Southern Populist editor. Organizing is an exhilarating but exhausting physical, emotional, and intellectual business; I learned invaluable lessons.

In a more strictly academic sense I am deeply indebted to C. Vann Woodward, not only for the inspiration of his own work but also for his

Acknowledgments

support of what must have seemed to him, at least at its outset, a rather dubious undertaking. As many Woodward students can attest, living up to his standards is perhaps the most difficult, and rewarding, lesson learned from Professor Woodward. From Professors Eugene Genovese and Sanford Elwitt and their students, especially in a fall 1971 seminar on the rise and expansion of capitalism, I learned for the first time what a rigorous and critical Marxism means. The impact of that seminar appears all through the book, and continues today. Professor Genovese has since been a strong supporter of the book. As others know, his encouragement and help are often as invaluable as his intellectual example.

Finally, I owe the greatest debts to two people. Larry Goodwyn followed this manuscript on the long road from dissertation to book. His friendship and untiring efforts to keep me from condescension and errors of fact and interpretation did not always meet with success, but his honesty and frankness in agreement and disagreement improved the final product immensely. To Laura Oren I am indebted beyond possible thanks. Over the last ten years she probably read every page at least once, and many of them more often. She certainly heard every thought and idea I ever had about the Southern Populists more than once, along with every complaint and enthusiasm. Each page and idea shows her outstanding ability as an historian, editor, and friend.

Introduction

> *The conditions which*
> *surround us best justify our cooperation;*
> *we meet in the midst of a nation brought to*
> *the verge of moral, political, and material ruin.*
> *Corruption dominates the ballot-box, the legisla-*
> *tures, the Congress, and touches even the ermine*
> *of the bench. The People are demoralized; most of the*
> *States have been compelled to isolate the voters at the*
> *polling-place to prevent universal intimidation or bribery. The*
> *newspapers are largely subsidized or muzzled; public opinion*
> *silenced; labor impoverished; and the land concentrating in the*
> *hands of the capitalists. The urban workmen are denied the right of*
> *organization for self-protection; imported pauperized labor*
> *beats down their wages; a hireling standing army, unrecog-*
> *nized by our laws, is established to shoot them down,*
> *and they are rapidly degenerating into European condi-*
> *tions. The fruits of toil of millions are boldly stolen*
> *to build up colossal fortunes for a few, unprece-*
> *dented in the history of mankind; and the posses-*
> *sors of these, in turn, despise the republic and*
> *endanger liberty. From the same prolific*
> *womb of governmental injustice we*
> *breed the two great classes—tramps*
> *and millionaires.* [1]

So begins the preamble to the 1892 Omaha platform of the Populist party, "the Second Declaration of Independence." For the Southern Populists this preamble remained, at least through mid-1896, the single most comprehensive statement of what was wrong with America. [2] In their

1. For the Omaha platform, see Norman Pollack, ed., *The Populist Mind*, pp. 60–66.
2. Historians have generally overlooked the message contained there, and consequently disregarded what the Populists themselves said they were doing. The result has been the frequently ahistorical tone to much of the debate over Populism since World War II. Populists have been labeled everything from protofascists to proto-Marxists. The debate probably reached its public nadir at the 1964 Southern Historical Association meeting in

own terms the Populists described a society which teetered on the brink of chaos, "on the verge of moral, political, and material ruin." They called on the American people to recreate American society "upon the love of the whole people for each other and for the nation" by expanding "the powers of government—in other words, of the people . . . as rapidly and as far as the good sense of an intelligent people and the teachings of experience shall justify, to the end that oppression, injustice, and poverty shall cease in the land."

But most of the Southerners who supported the Omaha platform were farmers, and behind Southern Populism lay the condition of southern agriculture in the late 1880s and early 1890s. The low prices for agricultural products, especially cotton, railroad rate discrimination, the lack of adequate marketing facilities, and the increasingly unfavorable ratio between crop prices and the cost of manufactured goods[3] taught southern farmers what it meant to be excluded from America's new industrial society. Their rapid decline into debt peonage through the crop lien made the threat even clearer.[4] In the eleven former Confederate states plus Kentucky, the percentage of farmers who were tenants in 1880 was 37.0 percent. In 1890 that figure had climbed to 39.1 percent. By 1900 it reached 47.2 percent and in 1910 48.6 percent. Tenancy grew at an even faster rate in the Deep South states of North and South Carolina, Georgia, Alabama, Tennessee, Mississippi, Arkansas, Louisiana, and Texas.[5] In both groups of states the biggest jump came in the Populist decade. The 1890s saw increases from two to four times greater than those of either the 1880s or the first decade of the twentieth century.

Southern farmers first responded to these conditions with the Alliance's cooperative crusade.[6] Designed to release them from the lien system, by the early 1890s it had failed, but the defeat taught many of the Alliance reformers, especially the more radical ones, not to limit their solutions

Little Rock, where, among others, Norman Pollack used the Populists to suggest that the intellectual temper of the late 1940s and the 1950s in America was fearful and part of the same McCarthyite trend it purported to deplore. Irwin Unger, in rebuttal, found the resemblance between Father Coughlin and Ignatius Donnelly "uncanny." The papers presented at the meeting were published in *Agricultural History*, 39 (1965), pp. 59–85.

3. Fred A. Shannon, *The Farmer's Last Frontier*, chap. 5.

4. Lawrence Goodwyn, *Democratic Promise*, pp. 25–31; Robert C. McMath, Jr., *Populist Vanguard*, p. 35; Michael Schwartz, *Radical Protest and Social Structure*, p. 13.

5. The tenancy figures for those southern states excluding Kentucky, Florida, and Virginia were: 1880–39.7 percent, 1890–43.7 percent, 1900–52.9 percent, 1910–55.1 percent. The data on tenancy came from Theodore Saloutos, *Farmer Movements in the South, 1865–1933*, p. 237.

6. For the cooperative crusade, see Goodwyn, *Democratic Promise*, chap. 5; McMath, *Populist Vanguard*, pp. 48–58; Saloutos, *Farmer Movements*, pp. 88–96; Schwartz, *Radical Protest*, chaps. 13, 14, 16.

simply to building alternative structures for farmers within the American economic system. It was time to move their organization beyond the farmers' interest and turn it into a political party capable of mounting a wide-ranging attack on the whole late nineteenth-century American political, economic, and social order. Beginning with the Southern Alliance's St. Louis platform in late 1889, the radicals among the reformers promoted a national political program through which they hoped to achieve this end.[7] The Omaha platform of 1892 was the announcement of their challenge, their call to action, and their program for change. Leveling the final, most comprehensive attack of nineteenth-century reform on the new society they found growing up around them, the Omaha platform represented to its southern adherents, whatever else they believed, a battle cry in their last ditch fight to prevent America and Americans from being overwhelmed by the steamroller we now call American capitalism.

It did not work any better than the cooperative crusade. In 1896 the Populist party collapsed in a disorderly commitment to fusion and sectional politics. By the admission of most of their historians and some of the Southern Populists themselves, free silver spelled disaster for both the national and state parties. In the 1896 campaign to elect Bryan the Southern Populists abandoned many of the reforms considered more important in the Omaha platform and their early campaigns—the subtreasury plan, government ownership of the railroads, telephone, and telegraph. Why did these Southerners, who in the early 1890s risked a great deal to identify themselves as Populists, by 1896 reject much of the Omaha platform in favor of free silver?

The answer lay in what the Southern Populists thought they were doing and what they actually wanted. If the commitment to the Omaha platform had been total in 1892, how can 1896 be explained? Some of the reasons, such as race, were functions of southern society and history. Others lay in the structure and organization of the National Farmers' Alliance and Industrial Union. But serious contradictions and inconsistencies also existed in the thought of the antimonopoly greenback radicals who created the Omaha platform to destroy what they perceived to be the primary source not only of the plight of the southern farmer but also of all the other multitudinous ills of American society—the maldistribution of wealth. Just as importantly, Populists whom I have called the more moderate financial reform Populists did not share their more radical brethren's understanding of the Omaha platform. Farm problems and prices concerned these moderates more than antimonopoly and the general inequities of wealth distribution. While the enthusiastic opti-

7. Goodwyn, *Democratic Promise*, chap. 8.

mism of 1891 and 1892 concealed these tensions, the stresses and strains of four years of politics revealed analytical failures and differences of interpretation.

While we know quite a bit about the politics of southern reform between the 1890 Ocala demands of the Alliance and the fall of 1896, without comprehending how these people thought we will never understand what happened in 1896. Political activity is governed not only by demands made on individuals by their surroundings, but also by what the actors believe and think about themselves, their world, and what they feel they are trying to do.[8] These ideas and beliefs can only be found in statements such as the preamble to the Omaha platform, and in the speeches of Southern Populist orators, the editorials in Southern Populist newspapers, the letters to these papers from the leadership and the rank and file of the party,[9] and the material preserved in a few manuscript collections. We have no other sources. Large parts of these letters, speeches, and editorials often contained little on specific economic and political grievances. Its preamble makes up nearly half of the Omaha platform, never mentioning particular issues. It describes a society gone bad. It explains why the demands that follow are necessary. It implies that more than particular economic and political complaints are troubling the Populists. That whole speeches and editorials sometimes consisted entirely of this kind of discussion suggests that it was more than an ornamental flourish designed to please audiences.

Few Populists, including the leaders of the southern movement, gave much *direct* thought to these ideas. Every speech and editorial made implicit or explicit mention of them, yet, with few exceptions, they were never considered in their own right. Most of the Southern Populists, including the lawyers and editors, were disinclined by training and experience to reflect long on such attitudes alone. But since the Populists had to draw heavily on these ideas to attract voters and to explain their positions, they can be discovered indirectly from the Populists' speeches, letters, and editorials.

These ideas and beliefs furnished the intellectual scaffolding which supported particular issues. They revealed the fundamental beliefs an individual held about his or her physical and social environment. These ideas varied from person to person, for ultimately human experience is always and individually unique. Nevertheless, what is true for an individual is also true, to a more limited extent, for any society or for particular groups and classes within it. While differences on specific reforms and the way they should work existed among the Southern Populists, and

8. See Appendix A, Method.
9. See Appendix B, Populist Newspapers as Source Material.

were of major importance to what happened in 1896, neither free silver, the subtreasury, nor even government ownership of the railroads created the hostility which led to the death of fifteen blacks and several whites in the 1892 Georgia elections.[10] What did, and what has gone generally unrecognized, were the ideas and attitudes about society which almost all Southern Populists shared, and which lay behind the issues and gave them their meaning. Over and above their individual and collective differences, the beliefs from which these issues sprang gave to the Southerners their reasons for risking social ostracism, physical violence, and even death by declaring themselves Populists.

In the effort to understand the Southern Populists' thought and its effect on their politics, this study begins with the large areas of agreement which, despite differences on issues or political strategy, they shared. They all believed that material self-interest made human beings run and that the production of tangible wealth ought to be society's first concern. They all wanted the material benefits of industrial development; they broadly shared a commitment to a competitive, private property- and profit-oriented market economy; they generally concurred on the nature of human law and government. Even more basically, they all agreed that serious disparities existed between the way the world was and the way it should be, and that the source of these discrepancies lay with America's emerging industrial order.

From this perception flowed the Southern Populists' specific proposals for reform—the abolition of land monopoly, the subtreasury plan, government ownership of the railroad, telephone, and telegraph systems, free silver, the issue of legal tender fiat greenbacks—all of which were intended to make America the society it should be. Major disagreements on the importance and meaning of these issues existed, however, especially between those Southern Populists who came out of or adhered to an antimonopoly greenback tradition and made a more throughgoing critique of American society, and those who came from a more limited tradition which focused on monometallism as the source for much of what was wrong with the country. Believing in the necessity of expanding the money supply, for instance, meant to Tom Watson in both 1892 and 1896 that free silver was an insignificant reform.[11] Marion Butler, the 1896 national chairman of the People's party, also wanted expansion, but rarely did the columns of his paper, the *Caucasian*, ever intimate that free silver might be less than the most important Populist demand.[12] Beyond these differences, however, lay a more significant difficulty. None

10. C. Vann Woodward, *Origins of the New South, 1877–1913*, p. 259.
11. Atlanta *People's Party Paper*, 31 Dec. 1891; 24 Apr. 1896.
12. For an example, see Raleigh *Caucasian*, 12 Mar. 1896.

Introduction

of the Southern Populists ever resolved the basic dilemma of their reform critique—how to retain the benefits of industrial development while preserving from their rural experience and their Jeffersonian, Jacksonian, and evangelical Protestant heritage the values they felt would prevent the social disaster industrial capitalism so obviously represented for them and many others.

The story of their political efforts is the story of this failure. Not all the Southern Populists followed the same path to defeat. The Populist party in Texas, from 1891 through 1896, consistently maintained a radical antimonopoly greenback position and emphasized the entire Omaha platform above any one specific issue. The Texas Populists, along with the greenback Georgia reformers, remained hostile to fusion with either of the two old parties, though in both states Republicans sometimes supported them.[13] The Populist parties in North Carolina and Alabama, where the more moderate financial reformers dominated party councils, quickly came to emphasize what they called "the money question"—free silver, abolition of the national banks, and sometimes a demand for an increase in the currency in circulation by adding greenbacks—rather than land monopoly, the subtreasury, a legal tender fiat monetary system, or government ownership of the railroads. The party in these two states also much more openly favored fusion, with either the Republicans or Democrats. By 1896, however, antimonopoly and the rudimentary class politics of biracial cooperation had failed the radicals as surely as fusion and sectional politics had the moderates. Neither succeeded in making Populism a viable political alternative on a national scale.

Though their analysis could not go far enough and their political efforts came to nothing, the Populists mounted in the 1890s the last major mainstream political attack on capitalism and its business culture in America. This was perhaps even more true of the Southern Populists than their western brethren, for the Southerners proved generally more thoroughgoing in their assault than did most of the Westerners.[14] The Southern Populists took a received tradition and did the best they could with it. We propose to do the same by them, examining the terms of their attack as the Southern Populists discussed and thought about them in order to learn what explains the ultimate failure of their assault, and what, if anything, the attempt still has to say to us.

13. John D. Hicks, *The Populist Revolt*, pp. 246, 330, 371.
14. See Woodward, *Origins*, p. 286.

PART I

THE PROBLEM: SOCIETY, ACTUAL AND IDEAL

INTRODUCTION

The Southern Populists shared certain important ways of thinking which gave to the whole body of their thought a coherence that particular attitudes about issues, society, and government often lacked. These were assumptions about the way things worked and were in the world, rather than specific ideas about specific things. They were, in a sense, axioms which the Southern Populists accepted, though not always without question, and upon which they built their notions about what ailed American society and what would cure it.

The first, although not necessarily the most important, such axiom was that what was most real and most important in the world was that which was most tangible, that which could be seen and touched. In a society entranced by the physical manifestations of reality, where a vast expanse of waistcoat swung with a heavy gold watch chain stood for personal success, where smoking factories, mighty engines, vast prairies, miles of railroad and the solid ring of "hard cash" not only symbolized but were Progress, the Southern Populists, too, believed that the weight and heft and size, their visible and physical attributes, made things real. All the Southern Populists, for instance, believed that any stable and worthwhile society depended on the people they called, often indiscriminately, the farmers, producers, or laboringmen. These people produced what the rest of society, in order to exist, consumed. On the products they created rested all else—society's laws, government, medium of exchange, the welfare of the entire social order. The tangibility of such production gave it its importance and its social validity. Wealth had little to do with money; wealth meant tangible produce. Money ought to enable people to obtain more easily than through barter what they needed to live, but remain preeminently a tool, not an end in itself.

The strength of this attitude was the attention it called to the basic human importance of material goods for sustenance and the promotion of a decent life. Its weakness was that, except for a few antimonopoly greenbackers, the Southern Populists never understood the importance of intangible factors in the production and distribution of wealth in an expanding industrial and financial capitalism. Most of them suspected credit. That money, only the representative of wealth, could increase

3

The Problem

faster than actual tangible production had to be untrue or the result of a monstrous fraud. Either way American society faced nothing but disaster, as the impact of the furnishing merchant and the crop lien on rural life had demonstrated to almost every southern farmer. On a wider scale, the Southern Populists never really understood the relationship between industry's increasing power and importance and their enjoyment of an increasing number of benefits of industrial society. Most of them also missed the growing significance in this new social order of the conflict between employer and employee, a failure which had serious consequences for their ultimate success.[1]

A second such quality or axiom of Populist thought emphasized the personal as opposed to the impersonal. That something could happen which no one willed was impossible. In a proper society, and, in fact, in the society in which most of these Southerners had lived and grown up, people made things move, and if some people were moved more than movers, it was because others, more powerful, moved them. The idea of a bureaucracy with a life of its own was, as to most Americans, unknown to the Southern Populists. The essential social relationship was between individuals, not between people and organizations. The worker ran the machine. That it could be the other way around rarely occurred to them, and when it did, they considered the situation unnatural and wrong. Those who ran the corporations knew that they were shooting down innocent workers at Coeur d'Alene. The owners of the railroads knew they were gouging the life out of the farmers.

As a result, the Southern Populists sometimes argued that America did not need structural, qualitative modifications of the country's social, economic, or political organization, but a change in people's behavior. For similar reasons, Southern Populists could at times maintain that government ought to be small, economical, and efficient while they demanded that government own and operate the railroads. Moreover, since they considered the social order at bottom a network of personal relations between human beings rather than impersonal relations between people and social organizations such as the government, labor unions, courts, and corporations, they cast their judgments of good and bad in American society and its parts in terms of a personal morality borrowed from their religious background. The use of the metaphors of personal morality could obscure distinctions between the relative importance of their issues to the Southern Populists themselves. It helped not a few of them overlook differences in substance between free silver and the sub-treasury scheme, for instance. When they perceived President Cleveland and his administration, Wall Street, or even free silver as a basic evil, and this became an issue in itself, attention turned away from a wide-ranging

4

reform program and toward using whatever issue appeared most likely to defeat such opposition.

On the other hand, this emphasis on the personal supplied one of the most basic strengths of Southern Populist thought—their belief that the only decent society was one in which each person looked out for every other one, a society in which *all* people enjoyed equal rights and the benefits of their labor. The same attitude also enabled them to understand that suffering caused by the way the system worked was as immoral, and as personal, as the suffering caused by individual acts. It helped them realize that if people starved and froze while the prices of wheat, corn, and cotton dropped below production cost, the issue was not overproduction but underconsumption. People did not have enough. It also pushed them toward the conception of an America in which each individual accepted a personal responsibility for every other, rather than a society in which each watched out for his or her own interest and the Devil took the hindmost. The belief that society was basically, and properly, a network of individual human relations in which personal morality and responsibility continued to play a central role gave the thought of these Southerners, and their critique of the social and human costs of an expanding industrial capitalist society, the power that it had. Ironically, of course, it also often undercut their analysis of the inner workings and dynamic of that society and impeded their political attack on it.

Neither of these axioms, which supplied the warp on which the Southern Populists wove the woof of specific ideas and attitudes to make the whole cloth of their thought, appeared in pure form in Southern Populism. The tangibility of the world and its personal and moral aspects were not always paramount. To a certain extent, especially among the antimonopoly greenbackers, the Southern Populists began to move toward the notion of a society which exhibited intangible factors and in which impersonal and essentially amoral considerations and distinctions had to be made. The steps taken were hesitant, but significant, because they indicated that for most Southern Populists the use of their past represented not blind nostalgia but an effort to make creative use of what they knew best in order to reflect upon and organize their contemporary experience. In general, however, they did not question these qualities of their thought, and usually assumed them as fixed points in their analysis of how society operated and how it ought to operate.

The tangibility and the personal and moral qualities of Southern Populist thought originated in and were reinforced by their experience and their inheritance from the thought of the past. Almost all Southern Populists were rural people. If their leaders sometimes came from the professional classes of small towns—country lawyers, preachers, and editors—

the bulk of the members of the party lived in rural, farming communities. What little direct experience they had of manufacturing came from their exposure to the local cotton gin and mill, if there was one, and from their perhaps once-in-a-lifetime visit to Atlanta, Birmingham, New Orleans, Raleigh, or Dallas. Some Southern Populists knew the city better, but none knew it well, for the "city" as yet could not readily be found in the South.

While those fortunate enough to ship their own crops had experienced freight rate discrimination, and a few others had witnessed the effects of railroad money in the state legislatures, for most Southern Populists the physical reality of the railroads—the tracks, the cars, the locomotives—provided their most immediate and visible experience of American industrial capitalism. Their contact with the financial apparatus of the same industrial organization came through the local banker at best, and usually through the supply merchant. The Southern Populists lived physically, and to a considerable extent experientially, outside of urban, industrial America. To be sure they felt its tentacles invading their lives through the furnishing merchant and the lien system. They saw the physical signs of its growing domination of the whole country in the expansion of railroads and telegraph lines and the establishment of cotton mills. But their world did not include the huge smoking factories and crowded commercial districts, the vast city slums, the expanding stretches of middle class housing and increasingly opulent upper class residential sections, the urban density, confusion, and chaos of industrial society's urban heartland.[2]

Their communities most often focused on the rural church, which might be served once or twice a month by a circuit rider or itinerant pastor, often untrained. They usually held their regular community meetings, religious or political, at the church. Many local Alliances gathered here, where revivals also met, and the South in the last two decades of the nineteenth century experienced more revivals than ever before, more than any other section of the country.[3] They might also gather at a crossroads store or in town on some Saturdays to purchase supplies or market their crop, or once a month for court day. These people perceived their community as being more homogeneous than even town society. Aside from the furnishing merchant, whose disappearance would not have dismayed any Southern farmer—Populist or Democrat, black or white—men were big farmers, small farmers, tenant farmers, or sharecroppers, but they were all farmers. Fewer extremes of wealth than might be expected existed in the countryside which most Southern Populists knew best because the main source of their strength lay in the white counties, the poor piedmont and mountain areas, rather than in the black belt, home of the rich southern planter and often absentee landlord.[4]

In a rural community like this the wealthiest producer (not landlord or merchant) was usually the one who had the best and highest producing farm. Relations being personal among most people, including the farmers and the furnishing merchants, people judged each other and their actions on a moral standard, as questions of right and wrong, good and evil. The close contact with the church as one of the few focal points of the community did nothing to discourage this way of judging people and social organizations. Finally, although technology might change farming some, credit sources might alter, the railroad might come through, and the local town might grow a little, the basic pattern of life remained the same outside the cities and larger towns. The essential activity of the community that the Southern Populists knew best, farming, changed little in its essence, despite the rapidity with which industrial and financial capitalism spread into the countryside.[5]

Not all of the elements of this rural community, however, exerted their pressure in one direction only. The Southern Populists read about the New South and industrial progress in the big city dailies or in their little country weeklies, and very few of them entirely opposed the idea that manufacturing and industrial growth could benefit their communities and the South.[6] The railroad and the local cotton gin, mill, and bank gave the southern farmers some experience in relating to impersonal organizations. This experience, and the failure of the Alliance cooperative efforts, demonstrated to many farmers the power and influence of those who did not necessarily produce a tangible product. The benefits that railroads brought, the lack of adequate marketing facilities for their crops, the need for more money and easier credit, required these farmers to examine the world around them in terms not only of people and their motives but also in terms of more impersonal conditions. The substitution of the subtreasury plan for a failing cooperative movement meant that Southern Alliancemen planned to use the federal government in a new way, as an active agent in the promotion of the farmers' interest.[7] The requirements of third party politics subsequently pushed many Southern Populists to expand this idea to a conception of using the federal government to promote the general welfare of all of American society. Finally, the need to explain how specific demands like the subtreasury or government ownership of the railroads would work forced some of the Southern Populists, particularly the more radical, to begin developing an analysis of American society and its proper organization which transcended their limited experience to include some of the complexity of modern American industrial capitalism.

Like their experience as rural people, the Southern Populists' intellectual inheritance, which they shared with their Democratic opponents, cut two ways. From Jefferson many of the Southern Populists learned the importance of a rural community of yeoman farmers; only these enjoyed sufficient moral virtue to guarantee the continuation of the American republic. Although this virtue was the key to the importance of these farmers, their relationship to the land was its source.[8] Building on this idea, many Jacksonians, and others who later made use of Jeffersonian thought, expanded the notion of republican virtue to include the working classes and small businessmen.[9] In order to explain the relationship among the three groups, these people dropped the idea that civic virtue grew from a close attachment to the land and substituted for it an emphasis on the producer of tangible wealth. The moral excellence which Jefferson supposed to inhere in the farmer's situation became closely tied to the fact of production itself. Those who produced became the most important element in the social order, not only economically but also socially.

Like other elements of Southern Populist thought, this tradition had its drawbacks when called on to help explain the social and economic realities of the new American industrial capitalism. But like them it also encouraged the reformers' critique of that society. The democratic element in the tradition supported the Southern Populists' demand for equality and an end to the exploitation of the many by a wealthy few. For the very reason that it described a relatively homogeneous society, the Jeffersonian-Jacksonian tradition called attention to the vast and growing maldistribution of wealth, of work and its rewards. And although this tradition suggested that the best government governed least, its antimonopoly strain provided the Southern Populists with a tradition of criticism of great concentrations of economic wealth and power.

This duality in Southern Populist thought has often been considered a sign of weakness. In fact, the apparent confusion was a sign of strength, evidence of a serious intellectual effort being made to formulate responses to the ills of American society in which the strengths of received tradition and experience were cut away from their limitations and put to use in an attempt to build a more adequate, decent society. Their contemporary and historical experience and their intellectual heritage, complicated affairs whose influence did not all tend in one direction, underlay the specific ideas the Southern Populists held about the proper society and their criticism of the existing one.

CHAPTER 1

Material Self-Interest and the
Moral Society of Producers

When a Virginia reformer wrote in 1891 that there was "a principle pervading all human nature, however civilized and cultured, that invites the individual to grasp all that is attainable and utilize every opportunity for personal gain not interdicted by law,"[1] very few Americans would have disagreed with him. The Southern Populists, as much as their contemporaries, accepted the Lockean formula which equated acquisitive behavior with human rationality.[2] Unlike most of their contemporaries, however, the reformers discovered some liabilities in allowing self-interest full freedom to function uncontrolled in an industrial society. Millionaires, corporations, and trusts, "in their insatiate greed," charged a North Carolina Populist, had plundered the wealth of America and driven many laboring people and farmers into debt slavery to stay alive.[3] The Southern Populists, with firsthand knowledge of freight rate discrimination, business hostility to their cooperative efforts, and the spread of the lien system over the southern countryside, spoke with good authority.

Yet the Southerners remained unwilling to abandon the notion of material self-interest, despite the problems it caused. They shared with their contemporaries a faith in the market system, and like them, as we will see in greater detail later, believed the success of a market society depended on the material incentives which profits provided. To attack the operation of individual material self-interest in American society would be to question the efficacy of the market system, competition, and profit.[4]

To resolve their dilemma, the Southern Populists often sought to eliminate the contradiction. The railroads, argued a Texas Populist, "capable of such gigantic gains and so intimately bearing upon every interest of every man in the land cannot be safely entrusted to the hands of a few private men combining in a few corporations for private gains and private ends." The people had to control them. Equity would be served only if everyone's self-interest was considered.[5] Others, usually but not always the more radical antimonopoly greenbackers, sought to define what right and justice should guarantee every workingman and his family. They joined a Texas Populist in maintaining that God "never intended there should be one man or one woman on this broad earth without the comforts of life equal to the demands of his being. It was never intended that poverty and suffering should be the general conditions and wealth and happiness the exception in this life."[6] These people did not argue that the proper society would no longer encourage everybody to work for their own material gain. But without abandoning the idea as a touchstone for their analysis of human behavior, they strove to resolve the problems it presented either by limiting its legitimate scope or by expanding its narrow definition to include the interest of others in society.

At its best, this effort to reconcile individual material self-interest with the welfare of the community led to the abandonment of the core of the former idea—that society was held together and progressed because of the action of each person's material self-interest—and moved toward the consideration of society as a group of people rather than a collection of individuals. "Selfishness," wrote a North Carolina Populist in late 1892, "is the impelling force in nearly every action we now perform." When each person considered his or her own interest primary to the "general weal of society," the constant conflict which resulted gave rise to much bitterness. "Life would pass more pleasantly and we accomplish many needed reforms, if, instead of being governed by selfish considerations, we permitted ourselves to be controlled by that higher principle which regards the welfare of society as of greater importance than individual good." No longer would selfish people, in pursuit of their own material gain, impose suffering upon others.[7]

As with so many other things, the experience and inheritance of the Southern Populists clearly affected their analysis, whose source of power was often identical with the source of its limitations. Their learned commitment to a competitive market society prevented them from clearly challenging the idea that people had to be driven by material self-interest to create a successful society, while their experience of privation and their basic decency taught them the dangers of not setting limits on such activity.

Another reason the Southern Populists never rejected the necessity for individual material self-interest, however, originated in their conception of America and their ideas about the ends any properly organized society should serve. For most nineteenth-century Americans, including the Southern Populists, the success of the American experiment and the happiness of its people depended on the proper exploitation of the potential productivity of the country's rich environment and active population.[8] Full of optimism, no American doubted that all the wants of humanity could be fulfilled by a prosperity which, as a Texas Populist editor maintained, depended upon seeing that "every natural agency of the country may be utilized in the production of wealth."[9]

Production, for the Southern Populists, meant most often the creation of what they had the most experience with, foodstuffs and raw materials, although it could also include manufactured products. Work was the physical labor needed to produce a tangible product. "Labor," in the words of an Arkansas reformer, "is man's proper function."[10] Aside from an appeal to obvious common sense—without productive labor no society, however crude, would be possible[11]—the Southern Populists most often offered divine decree as a rationale for the importance of productive labor: "'In the sweat of thy face thou shall eat bread.'"[12] And the Southern Populists interpreted the Lord's word literally; sweat came from physical labor. The Lord said nothing about the sweat of managers, merchants, or moneylenders.

Their notion of value tied the Southern Populists' ideas about the importance of tangible production and work to their conception of the proper organization of society. They usually spoke of labor as the creator or measurer of wealth and value.[13] The combination of a labor theory of value with the notion that, in justice, the producers should receive the full value of their labor,[14] meant for one Georgia Populist that the capitalist was completely unnecessary, simply "an encumbrance."[15] Most often, however, it did not result in a rejection of a competitive market society. That the more radical antimonopoly greenback Populists, whose economic analysis was usually more sophisticated, often hedged on this issue indicated something more was involved. In 1896 W. M. Walton, a Texas Populist, stated that labor made wealth, but explained himself by arguing that "therefore when the non-laboring man accumulates more than he could, were he to labor, he becomes a robber of the laboring man."[16] Through the opening allowed the nonproducer to earn as much or less than the laboringman the Southern Populists slipped most of the market economy they desired to maintain.

In a speech given in March 1891 to the Brotherhood of Locomotive Engineers in Augusta, Georgia, Tom Watson made the relation between value and labor more explicit. He maintained that labor created all wealth, but because of his commitment to a market system and private property, he also had to argue that "without capital accumulated in the hands of some citizen there could be nothing but the simplest manual labor—there could be no manufactories, no railroads, no steamboats, no foundries, no merchants and no bankers." While he might have liked to eliminate the last two categories—Watson urged the engineers to copy the farmers' efforts in cooperation—he clearly realized some of the difficulties in balancing the needs of capitalists and the rights of producers in a market economy. What was labor's "fair share," asked Watson? "No man can be more definite than this: 'It should get all it makes after due allowance for material and the use of capital.'"[17]

While not as explicit, others of the more radical Southern Populists came down on the same side as these two when choosing between the implications of a labor theory of value and a market economy.[18] Most Southern Populists, however, never made the choice; they never felt it necessary. From the greenbackers, if not from John Locke,[19] they learned that property was simply the product of nature or of labor applied to natural resources.[20] Nothing in their experience called for a more intricate analysis of labor, profits, and surplus value in a capitalistic society. Indeed, the traditions of Jefferson, Kellogg, and Campbell gave the Southern Populists an entrepreneurial ideal which their experience tended to support. As producers who employed little if any hired labor, a labor theory of value looked to them quite uncomplicated and fair. They wanted to be free of the merchant and the crop lien. With the necessary credit they believed they could achieve their independence, the essence of which was to receive all the benefits of their labor. Their cooperative experience reinforced their belief in the desirability of being independent producers, and the subtreasury plan, by freeing farmers of having to consider private sources for the credit they needed, would eliminate for them any conflict between the realization of a labor theory of value and the maintenance of a market system and private property.[21]

What the Populists never fully realized, ironically, was quoted in the 24 August 1892 issue of the Tarboro, North Carolina, *Farmers' Advocate*. "'Labor,' says Karl Marx, 'is bought at its exchange value and sold at its use value. Exchange value is the least amount that will permit the laborer and his family to live, while the use value is all the employer can squeeze out of it.'"[22] The Southern Populists were usually self-employed, often considering themselves, in the words of the editor of the *Wool Hat*, "the yeomanry of the country, the small landed proprietors."[23] And if they were tenants, they aspired to independence. They did not yet clearly move in an advanced capitalist society. They lived at the fringes of it, where it seemed that if only things would go right, they could all become independent producers and maintain a just distribution of wealth while preserving a market economy, profit, and private property.

In fact, this vision of the ideal economic order corresponds almost exactly to what C. B. MacPherson, in *The Political Theory of Possessive Individualism*, calls a "simple market society." Such a social organization is essentially a capitalist society in which "the production and distribution of goods and services is regulated by the market but in which labour itself is not a market commodity." All members of society retain control of "their own energies and skills" and exchange only products and services. Since no market in labor exists, no person's gain comes at the expense of another. MacPherson designed this model of society less, he says, because it reflected an "historical reality" than because it served as a convenient analytical tool for discussing modern possessive market societies, where labor is a commodity.

The most important differences between a simple and a possessive market society are that land or other resources on which to get a living are available to all, and that "the satisfaction of retaining control of one's own labour is greater than the difference between expected wages and the expected returns as an independent producer."[24] Certainly in theory, and perhaps also in fact, in many areas of seventeenth-, eighteenth-, and early nineteenth-century America these preconditions obtained. Jefferson's ideal society of independent yeoman farmers, based on an almost inexhaustible supply of land, posits a simple market society. Elements of this kind of society crop up later among Jacksonian labor leaders, among radical Republicans and free laborites, and among the post-Civil War greenbackers.[25]

The Southern Populists inherited this ideal. This is why their version of the labor theory of value seems so limited. In a simple market society a simple labor theory of value works for each owner, and none suffer. Each producer enjoys the total value of his or her labor in direct exchange with other producers. All receive the full value of their labor because, since a market in labor does not exist, people cannot accumulate more than they actually produce with their own hands. The rural setting in which most Southern Populists lived and had been raised suggested that, with some reform, this kind of society could indeed exist, and it certainly would be more just than the poverty and exploitation experienced by most of the farming population in the South. The Populists remained unwilling, of course, to give up their right to buy another's labor[26] and never really understood the connection between the benefits of industrial society which they enjoyed and the accumulation of surplus value in a labor market which made those benefits possible within a market society. But their dream was real, and makes sense if properly understood.

A last qualification of the Southern Populists' labor theory of value came from their religious heritage and experience.[27] Divine decree, as we have seen, commanded human labor. It made the production of wealth morally right and just. The value given productive labor in this manner tinged it with the notion of right and wrong, and value tended to become as much a function of the moral order of society as a function of the relation of labor to the production of tangible wealth. When used in this sense by the Southern Populists labor put value into a commodity in good part because productive labor was humanity's proper activity, and because tangible production was a godly affair beneficial to human beings and their society.

The Southern Populists, in fact, rarely used the words "economic" or "economy." The words appear nowhere in the Omaha platform. Words such as "moral," "robbed," "stolen," "injustice," "enslave," "wrongs," "plunder," "corruption," "evils," and "virtuous" set the preamble's tone.[28] The Southern Populists did not normally distinguish as we do between economics and questions of right and wrong, moral questions. There were some exceptions. Watson spoke of the election of 1896 as "a battle of economic doctrines."[29] The editor of the *Texas Advance* stated that Populism meant, among other things, "the abolition of all manner of false systems of economics."[30] Most often, however, the reformers quite clearly associated moral attitudes with economics. Under "ethical economic conditions," one North Carolina Populist argued in 1895, workingmen would have benefited far more from the introduction of new machinery into manufacturing.[31] The editor of the *Caucasian* that same year had maintained that preachers would command a wider respect from the laboring people if they studied sociology and became "teachers of human and Christian-like public economics."[32] Economic problems were usually perceived within a moral or even overtly religious context, becoming in that sense only one part of the question of right and wrong which helped define people's social, economic, and political relations with each other and their environment.[33]

It should be added that the tendency to cast economic problems in a moral context had roots other than the Southern Populists' religious heritage. Jefferson had endowed the farmer with a special rural virtue closely related to a view of society as a moral order.[34] The Jacksonian Democrats who expanded the notion of republican virtue to include working people explained that virtue by relating it to the productive function of both groups.[35] The Southern Populists inherited with this combination of Jeffersonian virtue and Jacksonian producerism the moral tone which often accompanied it, and which their religious experience reinforced.

The Southern Populists used the relationship between productive labor and wealth to analyze the social order. Since labor "produces all the wealth of the country," reasoned an Alabama Populist, "it should be respected above all things."[36] So it was, wrote a Texas Populist in 1892, "except in a perverted and corrupted state of society."[37] On this basis the Southerners divided society into groups: farmers, workingmen, merchants, professionals, manufacturers, and bankers, financiers, capitalists, and speculators. The closer any group came to actual production of tangible goods, the more socially useful and virtuous the Southern Populists considered it.

The standard of measurement, buttressed by their rural background and experience and their Jeffersonian-Jacksonian heritage, meant that the Southern Populists invariably considered farmers the most important group in society.[38] "[T]hey who labor in the earth are chosen people of God."[39] His southern brethren shared widely and repeated often this North Carolina reform editor's beliefs.[40] Borrowing an old but apt Granger phrase, the Southern Populists lauded agriculture as "the art of all arts, the science of all sciences, and the life of all life, the true basis of all wealth and of substantial progress."[41]

A few of the Southern Populists described more carefully how this worked. In a speech in early 1892, Georgia state senator and Populist C. H. Ellington explained that when farmers did not do well, they purchased few manufactured articles. Because of the decline of demand from the farming population, manufacturing, and thus the working people, suffered hard times. In turn, working people and farmers having less to spend hurt the merchants, whose well-being depended on what others bought from them. When the farmers profited from production, the whole process was reversed, and the manufacturers, merchants, and working people all prospered.[42] The farmers, because they produced the food and raw materials indispensible to organized society, were, in the words of a Virginia Populist, "the master wheel of all business and the foundation of every nation's prosperity."[43]

After the farmer, the southern reformers talked most often about the merchants, probably because they had more contact with them than with any other of their social groups. Almost always[44] the Populists considered merchants nonproducers.[45] The farmers being the most important group, the merchants' interest should always be identical to theirs.[46] This view of the relationship between merchants and farmers gave the merchants a distinctly subordinate and dependent role to play, and showed not a little hostility, well-deserved if most recent studies are at all correct.[47] The southern farmers or tenants most often saw merchants, with their control over needed credit, standing between them and the rewards economic independence promised. At best, the southern reformers allowed merchants a convenience role, facilitating farmers and laborers in their work.

The Southern Populists mentioned and discussed the professional group less often than merchants or farmers, again reflecting how their rural environment influenced them. They disliked this group, particularly lawyers and politicians (often the same people in the South), almost as much as merchants. They almost always regarded lawyers as a worthless group, despite the number of Populist leaders recruited from this profession. Like merchants, professionals, especially the oft-mentioned lawyers, produced nothing. The merchants, however, might aid the producers; lawyers never did.[48] Although at times the Populists exempted doctors and teachers from as harsh a judgment as some editors, many preachers, and almost all lawyers received, the Southerners rarely found distinctions necessary, perhaps because with the exception of lawyers and preachers, they had little contact with this group.

Even lower in social value and usefulness were a number of related occupations generally, but not always, lumped together—bankers, financiers, speculators, and moneylenders. The Southern Populists almost never expressed qualifications about the desirability of banks and bankers.[49] "Who are these bankers, anyway?" angrily demanded a North Carolina Populist after the repeal of the Sherman silver purchase clause. "What do they produce? What do they distribute? What moral right have they to cumber the earth?"[50] The Southerners' experience with their cooperative exchanges taught them that even if the local merchants and their crop liens could be avoided, the bankers still stood between the farmers and economic independence because they ultimately controlled access to credit.[51] The reformers' response to this realization came in the financial sections of the Ocala demands and the St. Louis and Omaha platforms, something which we will discuss in more detail later. Suffice it to say here that these platforms suggested that the bankers' control of credit was directly related to their control and manipulation of the country's currency, which allowed them to use high interest rates to siphon off the profits of the farmers.[52] So not only did the bankers produce nothing, they threatened the whole social order. In the words of a Texas greenback editor: "The banking business is an evil. Bankers are leeches on the business body. Bankers prosper when the people mourn. Banking destroys more wealth than any other business. The bankers produce no wealth, but rather consume it. . . . There is no doubt but that the people would be much more prosperous and contented if there did not exist a solitary bank in the land."[53] Worse than useless, bankers and their ilk threatened to destroy the central pillar of American society, the production of tangible wealth.

Although they mentioned the working people less frequently than merchants, lawyers, and bankers,[54] the Southern Populists felt that the working people's social value and usefulness exceeded all of these groups, and came from the same source that the farmers' did. They produced tangible wealth. A North Carolina editor asked the railroad workers who really owned the railroad and supported the railroad workers. "Did the stockholders throw up the embankments? Did they make the ties, lay the rails, or string the wires? Do they run the trains, keep up repairs, collect receipts, or run the engines?" No. "Labor built the road and in return labor received barely enough to live upon while the road was building. It now receives the means of a meager existence for operating it."[55] Although the specific topic for this Populist was low wages, he implicitly assumed that the most important aspects of the railroads were physical—the embankments, ties, rails, wires, rolling stock, engines. The physical labor involved in building and maintaining the road became the most valuable contribution of people to the railroad. Without the workers, there would be no railroad.

About the identity of the working people, however, the Southern Populists, like most Americans, showed some confusion, evident in the varied terms used to describe them. Those who worked in factories and shops they most commonly called workingmen or laboringmen. Most Southern Populists, including antimonopoly greenbackers, usually did not even distinguish between skilled and unskilled workers,[56] and sometimes labeled working people "mechanics,"[57] or, less often, "artisans."[58] Borrowed from the Jeffersonians and Jacksonians, these last terms described the workers of an earlier era, the independent, small-scale, self-sufficient, and self-supporting middle-class artisans and mechanics so especially praised by the Locofoco wing of Jacksonian Democracy. Such workers were not the unskilled or semiskilled factory operatives of the industrial capitalism of the 1890s who continually faced conditions which threatened to throw them out onto an overcrowded labor market where they had no assurance of being able to work at all, much less earn a living.

Sympathy by the Southern Populists for the plight of industrial workers, especially by the more radical antimonopoly greenbackers, appeared whenever labor trouble broke out in the South, from the great Southwest strike of 1886 to the northern Alabama miners' strike of 1894.[59] But most Southern Populists could hardly be expected to understand the situation of the Pullman striker who confronted directly a new industrial capitalism that the farmers knew only by hearsay. S. D. Dennington, editor of the Ozark, Alabama, *Banner* in 1894 and member of the typographers' union, understood a major part of the reason. "The Southern People have not the remotest idea of the trying times experienced by the poor in the big cities of the North."[60] Lacking experience with labor's changed role in American urban-industrial society, little prevented the Jeffersonian-Jacksonian view of the working people from heavily influencing most southern reformers' perception of them.[61]

The Southern Populists discussed manufacturers least of all. Most reformers never explicitly attacked manufacturers or factories,[62] and on several occasions spoke of the need for them.[63] Watson's statement in 1891 that the manufacturers made themselves "a necessity" to the country and "absolutely essential to national welfare" by "working up into finished fabric the cruder material of a simple laborer" was rare among Southern Populists, if not unique.[64] Interestingly, Watson's metaphor for the manufacturing process—working crude material into a finished product—suggested that he drew his image of manufacturers and factories from the Southern cotton mills, the one example with which larger numbers of Southern Populists might have had some experience. In general, however, the reformers did not assign manufacturers any clear position in the social order. Sometimes they rated explicit producer status;[65] more often whatever social value they enjoyed came from their association with the production of tangible wealth.[66] Their social value and usefulness undoubtedly exceeded that of speculators, moneylenders, or lawyers, but ranked lower than that of the working people.

The confusion about exactly who and what the manufacturers were and what role they played in the social order resembled the confusion over the working people. It was not as evident, however, because Southern Populists rarely mentioned the manufacturers and never considered their proper role at any length. This omission itself indicated the source of the confusion. A North Carolina Alliance editor, discussing the effects of high protective tariffs, established a hypothetical mid-ocean island composed of "farmers, mechanics of all trades, laborers, with a suitable sprinkling of doctors, lawyers and ministers." Later on foreign manufacturers came to the island to help the islanders build up their manufactures.[67] Interestingly, laborers and mechanics of all trades lived and worked on the island without the existence of factories. For most Southern Populists the laboring classes consisted largely of the skilled, independent, middle-class village artisan and the local day laborer. Although the Populists acknowledged the value of manufacturers, they remained a foreign and somewhat ambiguous element.

This North Carolina editor proved a good example of the problems their Jacksonian and Jeffersonian heritage brought the Southern reformers. This heritage gave them a social ideal which reflected their aspirations and helped reinforce their experiential isolation from some of the central realities of American urban and industrial capitalism. For the most part Southern Populists continued to view human nature as basically selfish, although they argued, in keeping with their Enlightenment predecessors, including Jefferson, that the social environment in which people found themselves could have a great influence on the extent to which that selfishness dominated every other human emotion. Their explanation of the proper function of all human beings and their organization of the social order in terms of the production of tangible wealth also reflected the Southern Populists' tendency to analyze people and society in terms of material problems. This made agriculture "the very foundation of all industries,"[68] with the other groups of society described by and following in importance according to their relationship to this referent. Much of this analysis filtered through a religious heritage which gave a distinct moral cast to questions of economics and politics. It also clearly reflected the rural community and experience of most of the reformers.

None of these influences on the Southern Populists provided adequate means or information for understanding American industrial and financial capitalism. References in the Southerners' rhetoric to capitalist overlords and the power of aggregated capital, while indicating that the reformers had begun to target the proper enemy, did not mean that they understood its internal workings. Such references did show, however, an increasing awareness of the source of the social havoc and destruction the reformers saw around them. The extent and sophistication of this perception will become clearer when we talk about the kind of society the Southern Populists thought America ought to be, and was not.

CHAPTER 2

The Middle Class and the Distribution of Wealth

For the Southern Populists any properly ordered society required what might best be called balance, though they most often used the words "harmony," "equilibrium," and sometimes "homogeneity." "When He multiplied the loaves and the fishes," wrote a North Carolina Allianceman, "none went away hungry. God does not create disparities."[1] Despite their positions at opposite ends of the Populist political spectrum in the South, North Carolina Populist Senator Marion Butler and radical Texas organizer H. S. P. "Stump" Ashby could agree that in a society properly ordered "the merchant and farmer, lawyer and artisan . . . [would] dwell together, not as warring enemies, but as kind friends, joining willing hands in the beneficent work of production."[2] Rather than serve as a battleground on which selfish people fought each other for personal advantage, society should be the arena in which everyone worked together for what most benefited each—the production of tangible wealth.

The distance between the ideal and the actual social order, those real disparities which existed in America, made this idea pivotal in the Southern Populist demand for reform. L. L. Polk, president of the National Farmers' Alliance and Industrial Union for a little less than three years, noted that the country had not witnessed the "peace, contentment and plenty" that should have been expected from America's tremendous post-1865 expansion in railroads, manufacturing, towns, and cities. Instead, the result had been hard times. "The greatest industrial revolution of the ages" had one more goal to reach: "To restore and maintain that equipoise between the great industrial interests of the country which is absolutely essential to a healthful progress and to the development of our civilization."[3] A balanced and harmonious development did not mean America's thousands of homeless and hungry families, thousands dressed in rags. America's social development, concluded Helen W. Post, a *Peo-*

ple's Party Paper contributing editor, "is deformity, monstrosity; it is not symmetry; it is dropsy and not good healthy substance; and it means premature death."[4]

At the center of the Southern Populists' notion of social balance lay their concept of the "middle class": "the great and noble middle farming and laboring class" to which a Georgia Populist declared the southern reformers themselves belonged.[5] This class consisted solely of the producers of tangible wealth and drew its members neither from the rich nor the poor. These people provided "the bone and sinew of the country,"[6] those who supported the government,[7] "the bulwark of any social system."[8] But in America these people of "moderate means" were fast disappearing, wrote a Texas Populist, "leaving only the two classes, the two extremes, the very rich, who live in idleness, extravagance and luxuriousness, and the destitute poor, who are compelled with their families to labor incessantly for a subsistence."[9]

More clearly than anything else this growing imbalance signaled a major injustice in American society. God had made the bounty available and ruled that it be distributed properly, to all people. "Larger equity in the division of labor—in the distribution of the products of labor, must obtain," wrote a North Carolina Populist. "Anything short of this is contrary to the teachings of the Holy Writ."[10] At issue were not the productive abilities of American farmers and laborers. "There is plenty of wealth in this country," wrote a Georgia Populist. "It is not that we are kicking about. The trouble is that the people who produce all this great wealth are robbed of it by bad laws made in the interest of an idle, do-nothing class of people."[11] To correct the situation the producers demanded enjoyment of the fruits of their own toil, fruits which heretofore the Rockefellers, Carnegies, Goulds, and others had stolen from them to create their gigantic fortunes.

The worsening depression of the 1890s substantiated the Southern Populists' fear that social and economic disaster would follow the growing injustice. Nor was the issue at hand purely secular. The wealthy few's accumulation of riches, stolen from the producers, flew in the face of a righteous and wrathful God. "False systems," created by "false legislation," meant that labor no longer enjoyed what it produced, millions of children starved, and thousands of women were forced into prostitution. It was the work of the Devil, and the millionaires were warned by Arkansas editor W. S. Morgan that "it is only a matter of time when [the people] will turn upon you and rend you. Again we say, beware. Get back to the righteousness of God."[12] Whether the problem was a secular or a moral and religious one, however, the result was the same. "Millionaires make paupers," declared a Texas Populist; "paupers make anarchists and anarchists destroy nations."[13]

Southern Populists often drew on a specific Biblical image, the Belshazzar story, to express their sense of outrage at the material and moral disaster they saw flowing from the growing maldistribution of wealth. One part of the image juxtaposed riches and poverty to emphasize the injustice of the widening chasm between rich and poor. Watson in early 1892 described a postelection dinner of the Georgia Democratic leaders in Atlanta using the image to make his point, contrasting the elaborate preparations and food inside the hotel with the "millions of toilers going to rest in their squalid homes, amid all the gloom, the cold and the hunger of their hard lot."[14] The second element of the image made the threat to the wrongdoers explicit. Disaster awaited the rich who robbed and plundered the producing masses. Blind to what was happening, they wined and dined on their last evening, Watson wrote, "the tread of Cyrus and his Persians without. The pampered Aristocrats will listen to no warning, until Daniel strides into the Hall and the laugh of the voluptuary freezes on the lips of the quaking coward."[15] The situation could not continue. Retribution would be had, justice be done.

Historians should not dismiss religious images and metaphors as routine political appeals to which no special consideration need be given, or as rhetorical banalities, or as evidence of irrationality. If these same statements had come from an evangelical pulpit in 1894, they would be taken seriously. Why should what people believed in a rural church Sunday morning be disbelieved when heard in the same church on Sunday evening? To discount it in the evening is to fail to understand the intimate relationship between politics and culture, especially between political and social thought and culture. Such imagery and metaphor was part of the Southern Populists' culture, and part of what many of them believed. That is why they used it.

Another reason for believing much of what was said is that most of the Southerners were new to politics. They sought to make politics more, not less relevant to people's lives. In this sense they could be considered political innocents in a way the major party leaders were not. What they said ought to be taken more seriously than what politicians say normally. After all, the southern reformers were fighting against the vapidity and emptiness of traditional politics.[16]

Nor does it follow from such statements and images that the Southern Populists were irrational. Their religion, and their belief in it, made them no more irrational than Calvin's religion made him. The Southern Populists turned to religious metaphor and imagery to express to their listeners, in language they all understood, the danger in allowing the maldistribution of wealth to become much greater. When they used such metaphors, however, they always faced a tendency to emphasize purely religious and moral solutions for serious social and economic problems. The difficulty faces any person advocating change. Metaphor and imagery imbedded deeply enough in a culture to have real power and meaning can sometimes work to guide the advocate, and his or her audience, away from change at the same time it expresses the tremendous need for it. The image of the hand of God, predicting the demise of the sinners with strange signs understandable only to the elect, could suggest to its users and hearers that waiting for the cataclysm might be more viable than working for change to relieve the suffering of the just. The very extremity of such a solution, however, reflected both the extent of the Southerners' concern as well as the difficulty they had expressing that concern in an understandable way.

The Southern Populists, however, did not always picture the danger from growing extremes of wealth in such stark terms. The maldistribution also caused disorders and immorality on a lower but increasing level of intensity. The extremes of wealth and poverty bred disease, vice, and sensuality—the extremes of human personal and social behavior.[17] The producing middle class—quite literally in the middle between rich and poor, debauched and degraded, idler and slave—furnished the moderate virtues which sustained a harmonious and balanced society. The same class which concentrated wealth was destroying had, as Populists, to save the country from both the rich and poor by restoring the proper distribution of wealth.[18] Politically this achievement required returning equality to the social order. Inherited from the Jacksonians, the motto which ran at the head of Watson's *People's Party Paper* from 1891 through 1896 read "Equal Rights to All, Special Privileges to None." His southern brethren agreed completely with him on his choice. They did not intend, as a North Carolina editor pointed out, an actual material equality for everyone, for "people are not born equals, neither physically, mentally nor morally." They did share "natural rights" to life, liberty, and happiness, however, which implied "a right to the means of comfortable existence, the right to the conditions that produce happiness."[19]

To what area did this demand for equal rights refer? "The Omaha platform has but one principle," wrote a Georgia Populist, F. J. Ripley, "that wealth belongs to him who creates it, rather than to those who by chicanery, legislation and fortuitous circumstances manage to get possession of it." The platform favored the distribution of "wealth, prosperity and happiness," and opposed their concentration; it called for "such legislation as will give every man a fair chance to obtain and retain a competency."[20] If that fair chance were provided, observed a North Carolina editor, there would be but one class, "those who do honest work and enjoy the fruits of their labor. Of course some of these will be richer than others in worldly goods, for God has given to some men more talents than to others, but all of this class will be equally as rich in contentment and happiness."[21] No one who worked would be poor.[22] The major problem of imbalance in society would be solved, social and economic justice served.

Their religious experience gave the Southern Populists, like most Americans, a tool for explaining and understanding American society. One of the best examples of its usage appeared in the southern reformers' attempt to deal with their own relation to American politics in the 1890s. An Alabama Allianceman, in mid-1892, expressed his hopes and concern for the reform movement with an elaborately mixed metaphor built around the flight of the Jews from Egypt. "The children of Israel," he wrote, had at last escaped Egypt, and would regain the promised land if they did not hesitate at the Red Sea or linger to hear "the syren [sic] song of the money power Delilah, and the lying entreaties or menaces of the Benedict Arnolds of American Independence, and the Judases to the cause of justice, liberty and righteousness."[23] Although they had turned toward the land of milk and honey, the reformers, open to the blandishments and threats of their enemies and faced with the seeming impossibility of defeating them, had yet to win their struggle. The metaphor served to define, in terms the Populists' listeners would understand, the difficulty of the reform struggle, the enemies it confronted, and the promise victory held. And it gave all the importance that only the guiding hand of God could provide for the faithful.

Often their choice of terms indicated that the Southern Populists perceived the mission of their party as analogous to the task of religious salvation. Many believed, with one Georgia Populist, that "the People's Party is the political Savior of this country."[24] The southern reformers often used Christ to link religious salvation with Populism. Their Christ was not, however, a savior who told people to repent of this world to win salvation in the next. "Christ did not come, as our theological quacks are so fond of saying, to prepare men for another world," wrote a Texas Populist, "but to teach them how to rightly live in this."[25] Christ was a reformer and a radical. The Southern Populist demand for equal rights to all and special privileges to none urged nothing new. "Years ago the Man of Galilee used it," wrote Watson, "as the chief plank in His platform. 'Whatsoever ye would that I do unto you do ye even so unto them.'"[26] Like the Populists, Christ was born a workingman, a producer,[27] and His Sermon on the Mount, argued a North Carolina Populist editor, showed that He understood that "the unduly rich were the worst sort of criminals, because it is they who are responsible for the social conditions which make all other crimes possible or necessary."[28]

Their attitude toward the institutional church, as opposed to Christian doctrine, emphasized the Southern Populists' commitment to a Christianity which measured public as well as private morality. They openly criticized the church, and although such criticism was not frequent, it remained constant and its content rarely changed. Their censure aroused the greatest controversy in North Carolina. In a speech in 1895 to a state Alliance meeting, Dr. Cyrus Thompson, a prominent churchman and Populist leader, criticized the institutional church, though not Christianity, for constantly siding with oppression against human aspirations toward freedom. The North Carolina Democrats, having lost the previous state election to a fusion ticket of Republicans and Populists, seized upon the remark and used it in an effort to stir up religious opposition to the Populists. The progress of the controversy and its outcome are not of interest to this study,[29] but the attitudes of the Populists involved are, for their willingness to criticize the very institution which many of them considered the most important in society outside the home underscored the strength and extent of the break they made with their contemporaries in their thinking about society and its proper order.

In subsequent articles in the *Caucasian*, Dr. Thompson elaborated on his comments in an attempt to clarify what he had meant. He asserted that for 1900 years the church had failed to follow Christ's teachings. "Christianity is the very genius of human freedom,"[30] but the institutional church of the temporal world, with buildings, staffs, rules, regulations, and creeds had always been "the ready handmaiden of monarchy, aristocracy, and tyranny; of gorgeous greed and human oppression. . . . [T]he care of wounded humanity, the application of Christianity to the world, has been the task of the sceptic of his time who reverenced Christ more than Creed."[31] No one, he maintained, could understand and serve God and Christ "save by doing, in a Christly way, service to His children here." Christ cared for humanity's "temporal welfare."[32] Dr. Thompson called for a reorientation of the church's role in American society, away from the notion that the church existed only to save souls for the hereafter—the "scripturalist" view that was stronger in the southern churches than anywhere else in the country—and toward a more active involvement of the church in the life of this world. To do so he appealed to the historic Christ, Christ the Reformer, a tradition which the Southern Populists felt the established churches in the South did not reflect.[33]

Just before Dr. Thompson made his famous remarks, a Texas Populist, in a letter to the *Southern Mercury*, asked "if the church properly represents the Kingdom of Christ on earth; if there is more God in it than in any other institution, why has it not defended the oppressed as Jesus did? On the contrary, it is noted fact that with very few exceptions, it has stood with the oppressor all the time."[34] The failure of the church to care for humanity's temporal condition gave the lie to its claim to be of Christ, who had worked with the poor all His life.[35] The blame for the failure of the church's social conscience lay with the familiar sin of ava-

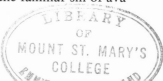

rice. "Plutocracy," remarked an Alabama reform editor, "has bribed the church with fine buildings and big salaries and many churches and ministers are now working for the devil."[36] These Southerners wanted a church which gave up the formal moral delineations of creed for a less formal contribution to the immediate needs of human beings. They called for practical Christianity at its simplest. "A 'christianity' that cannot go down to the root of causes from which poverty and oppression come is a stench in the nostrils of Jesus Christ," wrote Marion Butler. Most Christians organized charities and took up collections for the poor, but made "no organized effort to eradicate the evils" that made these necessary. A religion that failed to work toward ending poverty would "not command respect from men who think about men." A religion "which cannot mingle with such politics as looks to the betterment of the part of mankind which is oppressed and driven to poverty and desperation is none of Christ's religion."[37] Religion and politics became two sides of the same coin. If true Christianity involved preaching the politics of the Populists, then Populism meant the spreading of true Christianity.

The Southerners took their religion seriously. They took literally what they heard from the pulpit or read in their Bibles about the wrongs of oppression and the responsibility of all for their neighbors. The Populists, a Texas reformer asserted, "led mainly by men who are Christians in principle, but like the late Judge Nugent, not members of any so-called orthodox church," were "leading the industrial millions out of slavery into freedom. The church that professes to be the light of the world under Christ is not doing it. We plead for the rights of man and the old-fashioned gospel of the brotherhood of humanity as Christ preached it and lined [sic] it."[38] In this real sense, for many southern reformers the Populist party obviously came very close to replacing the church, at least in this world. As the use of the religious metaphors and imagery indicated, for these the authority of the church in society belonged to the People's party.

While their own experience taught them about the injustice of a growing maldistribution of wealth, the Southern Populists often used religious metaphors and imagery to organize and articulate that experience, to give it more universal meaning, and to explain both the process and solutions they proposed utilizing to eradicate that social and economic injustice. The southern reformers, of course, had another frame of reference available—their Jeffersonian and Jacksonian intellectual and political heritage—which they often closely tied to their moral and religious referents. One Alabama editor called Populism "the morals of Christ and the politics of Thomas Jefferson."[39] The religious framework lent divine sanction to the Jeffersonian and Jacksonian formulations, while

The Middle Class and the Distribution of Wealth

Jeffersonian and Jacksonian ideas often served to particularize God's commandments as they affected politics, economics, and society.

The Southern Populists cited not only God's commandments but Jefferson's authority for the injustice of and solutions to the great inequalities of wealth in American society. Not only was equal rights to all and special privileges to none a Jeffersonian doctrine, but so was the idea to which the Southern Populists tied it, equal opportunities for each person in the race of life.[40] The notion of Jeffersonian simplicity highlighted for the Southern Populists the evils of the growing extremes of wealth. Regarding the costly paraphernalia and the elaborate ceremony surrounding President Cleveland and his entourage, Populists in North Carolina, Georgia, and Texas could only regret the passing of the "days of Jeffersonian simplicity."[41] The concentration of wealth from which this extravagance flowed threatened to destroy American society. The extravagance itself signaled impending destruction.[42] Jeffersonian simplicity, in the same way, reflected the ideal society out of which it grew, a society balanced and homogeneous, where all enjoyed a relatively equal amount of the total wealth of the country.

The analysis of society based on the function of tangible production allowed the Southern Populists to elaborate an ideal society which consisted of the interaction of several groups—working people, manufacturers, bankers, merchants, and some professionals. Religious metaphors and images affected the range of this elaboration little, although they helped to explain some of it. The Southern Populists drew most of the content of this ideal society from their own rural and reform experience, although they often interpreted it through the metaphors and images their Jeffersonian and Jacksonian heritage provided them. While their background as post-Civil War southern farmers taught them, with the sharp lessons of experience, that the most central injustice in American society was the growing maldistribution of wealth, they used their religious heritage, and the metaphors and images offered, to explain the extent and import of this injustice, to predict what would happen if the wrong were not righted, and to explain the importance of the means to be used by the reform movement in correcting it. As their religious heritage had played a secondary role in their elaboration of a producer-oriented society, so their Jeffersonian and Jacksonian heritage, while it identified some of the more particular elements of society that needed change, played a secondary role in explaining what had gone wrong with America. It was contact with the specific society around them, however, that forced the Southern Populists to make the choices which ultimately governed their reform program.

CHAPTER 3

The Economic Order

As late nineteenth-century Southerners, the Populists encountered a conception of the proper economic and social order which owed little to Jefferson and Jackson. When the South emerged in the late 1870s from the turmoil of Reconstruction and depression, among some young urban Southerners talk began of a way to solve the problems of southern backwardness, poverty, and the region's burdens of race and sectional isolation. Henry Grady, Richard Edmonds, Henry Watterson, Daniel Tompkins, and others like them outlined a plan for sectional development which, they called the New South and which Paul Gaston has noted "bespoke harmonious reconciliation of sectional differences, racial peace, and a new economic and social order based on industry and scientific, diversified agriculture—all of which would lead, eventually, to the South's dominance in the reunited nation."[1]

In the 1880s a small but vigorous southern "new middle class"[2] adopted this creed as its own, and as this commercial, professional, and land-owning class grew stronger in the cities and towns of the South, the New South gospel matured with it. Although in order to win political control in most southern states the new middle class had to wait for the Populists and the Redeemers to destroy each other,[3] by the 1890s their creed of industrialization and urbanization had spread widely in the small towns and cities of the South.[4] The New South advocates were the middle class regional representatives of America's maturing industrial society. They rode to sectional power on the direct penetration of American capitalism into the southern towns and countryside, and the New South creed furnished them with an ideology to explain and justify both their struggle and their victory. The Populists, challenging the Redeemers and the Redeemers' temporary middle-class allies in the 1890s,[5] also had to confront the New South creed.

Although the New South advocates paid only spotty, and usually critical, attention to the farmers,[6] Southern Populists did not remain entirely immune to the plans and promises of the new order. Walter Hines Page

28

had a wider readership in North Carolina than many historians have credited him with.[7] "We regret," wrote a North Carolina Allianceman, "that we have a good many old fogies in the State, but are glad that North Carolina is keeping up with what is known as the New South."[8] They often supported the New South's largest advertising vehicle, the local, state, or regional fair.[9] Almost every Southern Populist newspaper, and all the major ones, at one time or another carried a column from the *Manufacturers' Record*, a Baltimore-based paper and major exponent of the New South gospel, noting the start of manufacturing and other enterprises in their states, and sometimes in the whole South. On rare occasions editorial paragraphs distinctly reminiscent of the heyday of Grady and Dawson appeared in southern reform papers. In an otherwise critical response to an editorial in the Brooklyn *Eagle* praising the North, the *Progressive Farmer* in 1892 commented that Northerners were, in fact, "full of business; they read, they study, they plan. They put business into politics, where we of the South put sentiment. We must change. We must have some business ideas. Our people must read and get posted."[10] The *Farmer* continued the advice, four years later urging farmers to visit "some prosperous manufacturing establishment" to learn techniques of regularity and efficiency.[11]

Like most Southerners, the Populists uncritically accepted certain other accoutrements of the New South order which were often alien to their rural-centered life. The business college was one,[12] and while the reformers frequently opposed them,[13] even land development and town building schemes, close to the heart of the New South gospel of progress, could get support. Watson's paper in early March 1892 began carrying a full-page advertisement offering land for sale in Nantahala, a town planned for western North Carolina. Although he was careful to observe that such "town-booming" schemes could be risky, Watson also noted that "more fortunes have been made out of new built towns of late years than in any other way." Having found that the officers and stockholders were "substantial," "cautious," and "reliable" Georgia businessmen and that a demand existed for Nantahala's mineral and timber resources, Watson in an editorial praised it as "one of the very best investments now offered" and "a grand opportunity."[14] Three years later he gave editorial support to a similar development in Atlanta, a "speculation" in town lots in Inman Park that would beat "even farm lands" for investment.[15]

Nor was Watson alone in his advocacy. The county-city booster edition of the Dallas, Georgia, *Herald* could have been printed in any town or county weekly within the last ninety years.[16] For the growth it promised, Populist editors in North Carolina and Texas urged their readers to fight for railroads through their counties and towns.[17] The Ozark, Alabama, *Banner-Advertiser* mounted a two-year campaign of varying intensity, starting in early 1895, to get a cotton factory started in the town.[18] W. S. Morgan constantly advertised the benefits and desirability of Arkansas for farming and business.[19] Progress, development, and town growth sometimes mattered as much to these Populist papers as they always did to their many Democratic, New South rivals.

But while they supported the New South goals of progress and prosperity—few Southerners would not have done so[20]—and even some of that creed's techniques, the Southern Populists were never happy with the new society envisaged by the New South adherents. In the heart of the northern Alabama coalfields, location of one of the proudest examples of the New South, Birmingham, an Alabama Populist editor wondered whether the new era would blend with the old to prevent "the undesirable surroundings too often produced in a 'development' whose only object is the sordid desire for the accumulation of wealth."[21] Even the *Progressive Farmer*, which generally responded more positively than other Populist papers to New South sentiments, knew the reality of the New South. "A few cities like Atlanta, Birmingham, Chattanooga and other smaller places have grown up quite rapidly, factories have multiplied with gratifying rapidity," wrote the editor in 1893, "but the great agricultural sections of the South have made no progress." A very few farmers had prospered, but most of them were worse off than in 1880. Until the farmers benefited the "New South" would remain "rather more vapor than anything else."[22] The New South was an urban and industrial ideal, the ideology of a new southern small town and city merchant and professional class which led the opposition to the Alliance and later to Southern Populism.

The Southern Alliance and its Populist issue spoke, as much as any group in the late nineteenth century, for the victims of the penetration of Northern industrial and finance capitalism into the South. The new southern middle class climbed to power on that penetration, and used the New South gospel of urban and industrial development to sell the new order and to justify their efforts toward political and social dominance. Despite some talk of making the farmer an efficiency expert, the Southern Populists knew that a victory for this class and its creed would come at their expense. They did not object to southern prosperity; they found advantage to the producers in the development of manufacturing and processing industries. But they wanted everyone to benefit, and had second thoughts about the effects of New South boosterism and development on the rural society to which they remained firmly attached. They wholeheartedly endorsed economic development for the South, objecting only to what now appear to be the necessary concomitants of that development. They never succeeded, however, in separating the one from the other. By accepting the same basic economic system which the New

South advocates did, the Southern Populists chose to fight on territory not only far more familiar to their New South opponents, but also where they were outmanned and completely outgunned. The choice made, the reformers were bound to lose.

That they made this choice was evident whenever the Southern Populists discussed the kind of economic system America ought to have. Almost all of them accepted what they understood to be the basic American economic system—a simple market society with private property, profit, and economic competition among small producers. The Populists, wrote a Virginia Populist editor, were not "destroyers of private property" and did not desire "to uproot the existing order of things and start a brand new arrangement of our own."[23] Populists elsewhere echoed his demurrer.[24] At issue was not private ownership of wealth and property but their concentration in a few hands. A wider distribution of private property through equalization of opportunities would correct this basic injustice.

Since a chance to accumulate wealth remained important to their argument, most southern reformers, although they equivocated about it, could not spurn economic competition.[25] The Populist party, stated Watson, "stands for the doctrine that the whole world's stock of wealth and opportunity belongs to all mankind—to be won or lost on the basis of merit and demerit." Accumulated wealth should not be permitted to protect itself from the risks of "competition" through legislation giving special privileges to the wealthy few.[26] Other southern reformers agreed.[27] Marion Butler, defending government ownership of the railroads, argued that the men who wrote the Constitution "took the position that any business that affected all or a great portion of the people, under circumstances where there could be no successful competition by men of small capital, was a *government function* and should be owned and operated by the government, at cost, for the benefit of all the people alike."[28] He justified an apparent violation of America's economic system in terms of preserving one of its essential qualities. According to Judge Nugent, the Populists wanted a society where "strictly public or social functions shall be turned over to the government, and the private citizen left in undisturbed freedom to achieve his own destiny in his own way by the exercise of his own individual skill and industry, and the legitimate investment of his own capital."[29] The Southern Populists accepted competition between small, individual, relatively equal economic units and, within this context, the individual accumulation of wealth.[30]

The southern reformers' attitude toward socialism provided a counterpoint to their adherence to a private enterprise market economy. When they spoke as producers or as landowners or aspiring landowners, most of them wanted no part of what they felt to be the socialists' commitment to ending private ownership of property and profits. This opposition was a good deal more vocal during the 1895 and 1896 debate between the right and left wings of the party, although so few reformers advocated socialism before 1895 that there is little reason to suspect large numbers of Populists had suddenly deserted it.[31] Certainly Watson had not. A committed though more articulate Lockean than most other Southern Populists, he maintained that the Populist party protected those who profited justly from their exertions and skills by supporting "the constitutional rights of the individual—individual liberty, individual enterprise, and individual property. She (the party) does not believe in Socialism, with all its collective ownership of land, homes, and pocketbooks."[32] An Alabama Populist found communism "fascinating" but "impracticable" and "evidently unwise" because it was based on a yet unreachable "individual perfection."[33] Without the incentive provided by profit and private ownership, people, no longer driven by their material self-interest, would stop working, production would cease, and society would collapse.

A just and equitable society did not require eliminating the existing economic order. While the unequal distribution of wealth was the "menacing evil of the times," the way to distribute it more evenly, argued Judge Nugent, was not to grant every person an equal share, but to give everybody "fair opportunities for the exertion of their faculties." The creation of a "community" with "no material waste, no check in production" and a general sharing among the producers of the wealth they created required only the destruction of "monopoly in these things which productive labor must have for practical use. Protect these things from the speculative greed of men, disembarrass trade of arbitrary legal interference, give free play to competition within the proper sphere of individual effort and investment, and steadily oppose those extreme socialistic schemes which ask by the outside pressure of mere enactments or systems to accomplish what can only come from the free activities of men—do these things and you will have achieved the real genuine and lasting reforms which labor and capital equally need, and which, in fact, are the only practicable reforms lying within range of party action."[34] Socialism could not accomplish what control and reform of the existing economic system would. With the assurance of profits and private ownership and some governmental control, "individual effort and investment" would assure ceaseless production and a fair distribution to all who worked.

When not talking about practical political and economic problems, however, the Southern Populists, antimonopoly greenbackers and financial reformers alike, often had positive things to say about socialism. Many agreed with the Alabama editor who thought socialism too ideal to be a workable way of organizing society, with the qualification that "if the whole world should be converted to practical Christianity . . . thus rendering socialism possible, so much the better."[35] Some even felt that there might be some good in the doctrine in the here and now.[36] This was particularly true of the antimonopoly greenback Populists. One Texan maintained that although the People's party was not socialist, its platform did contain "a few of the underlying principles of socialism," a necessity for destroying "the infernal industrial monopolistic system which we have upon us." Such principles included demands for a national currency, an income tax, a postal savings bank, and government ownership of the railroad, telephone, and telegraph systems.[37] "There is socialism in all governments that are not purely despotic," stated the editors of the *Arkansaw Kicker*.[38]

In fact, two Austin, Texas, Populist papers openly adopted socialism during the period—the *People's Advocate* and the *Argus*. Neither paper stopped backing Populist candidates. The editor of the *People's Advocate*, G. W. Mendell, in 1894 served as chairman of the Travis County (Austin) People's party executive committee.[39] The call to socialism, the call to get rid of private property, proceeded from the same perceptions of the ills in existing society that other Populists held—millions unable to work, the growing chasm between the poor masses who produced the wealth and the wealthy few who consumed it, the same contrasts of poverty amid plenty, starvation alongside wealth.[40] The *Argus*, discussing the Pullman strike and its lessons, shared with Watson, Marion Butler, Judge Nugent, and the rest of the Southern Populists the idea that government ownership would solve the railroad crisis. Unlike them, however, it extended the reasoning behind such a solution and came up with something a little different. If the government had owned and operated the coal mines, the railroads, the oil wells, the sugar refineries, and the banks, then coal millionaires, Pullman, Gould, Rockefeller, Havemeyer, a sugar Senate, and a financial panic would not have been possible. "The only remedy, the only means of abolishing wage-slavery, poverty, and the unendurable despotism of the money kings is the collective ownership of all the means of production and distribution."[41] These papers, with a slight extension of Southern Populist ideas, became socialist, albeit very moderate. Both papers, however, continued to advocate the whole panoply of Populist reform, including the Omaha platform.[42]

The ease with which it was ideologically possible to move to socialism meant that the Southern Populists often had to make a conscious decision to avoid it. In some cases political expediency helped draw the line. As Watson pointed out, "do you believe that the People's party in Georgia would have a corporal's guard left, if it were generally understood among Populists that the platform opposed individual ownership of homes and money?"[43] There was, however, more to it, as Watson's statement itself hinted. Their desire for a better society could propel them in the opposite direction. "Every living man who has a spark of human sympathy in his chest is socialistic to some extent," wrote W. S. Morgan in the *National Reformer.* "Socialism, in its literal sense, means a better state of society, and as the world gets better it 'drifts' nearer to socialism."[44] Their experience with poverty and exploitation, combined with a sense of human sympathy reinforced by their religious background and tradition, tended to push the Southern Populists toward some sort of socialism as the only decent and humane alternative to the society they found around them. But their political heritage and their class position as landowners or aspiring landowners suggested both the decency and possibility of a market society of independent producers. The latter influence, reinforced by political considerations of the kind Watson stated so bluntly,[45] prevented them from moving into socialism, a move which would seem to have been an easy one for them to make, given their adherence to government ownership of various large industries and a basic commitment to a society made more decent by a more equitable distribution of wealth. Some of the Southern Populists, though, particularly the antimonopoly greenback radicals, came close. How close we will discuss further at a later point.

Anarchy, socialism's nineteenth-century radical American counterpart, had no appeal at all, although the reformers used the term quite as often, applying it most frequently to those whom they regarded as the most serious enemies of the social order, the anarchistic politicians, plutocrats, and corporations.[46] Their condemnation of anarchy or anarchists concentrated on the order imposed on society by its laws. The Southern Populists, believing as they did in the importance of private property, had no reason to regard with equanimity the social upheaval anarchy promised. The producing middle classes, wrote a North Carolina Populist in 1892, "are not enemies of law and order, they do not envy or hate those who have acquired property by honest methods."[47] The reformers carefully supported strict adherence to the law, good or bad, until it was changed. Walter E. Grant, running for Congress on the Populist ticket in Virginia's third congressional district, told the voters that despite inequitable laws his party did "not blame anyone for using the law to accumulate a large fortune;" the Populists would, if necessary, "aid him in keeping whatever he has lawfully acquired."[48]

Because they associated the rule of law with a stable, orderly society, the Southern Populists often expressed concern over the violence of labor strikes. Few of them, however, censured strikes quite as completely as did the North Carolina Populists, who announced in their 1894 platform: "We sympathize with the oppressed everywhere, but we are opposed to all lawless combinations of men, whether representing capital or labor. We believe in peace and strict obedience to law." The platform urged that, instead, labor use the ballot to defeat monopoly peacefully.[49] The political orientation of the Knights of Labor and its minimal strike activity in the state during the late 1880s and early 1890s,[50] the financial reform stance of most of the state Populist leadership, and fusion with the Republicans had much to do with the attitude of the North Carolina party. In Texas, Alabama, and Georgia, Populists more often directed their antistrike hostility at the owners and the capitalists.[51]

On the other hand, most Southern Populists advised laboringmen to vote right instead of striking.[52] This was not the case usually only where the Populists had some contact with working people and strikes. In Alabama, in the Birmingham area, Populists worked in 1894 to keep the miners' strike going at least through the fall elections.[53] In Texas the massive 1886 railroad strike played a role in energizing the Alliance radicalism which led to the Omaha platform and the Populist party.[54] Connections like these made the attitudes of some Southern Populists toward working people more complex.[55]

In general, however, most Southern Populists regarded strikes and labor violence with concern. Part of the reason was their lack of contact with industrial labor and the absence of a thorough education in working class problems such as the mass of Texas Alliancemen received in 1886. They also differed with working people on how best to win the goals labor wanted. "Quicker than dynamite, more effective and more lasting than revolution, more far-reaching in its sweep than strikes, and more terrible to plutocracy than all is the ballot," argued the socialist editor of the Austin *Argus*.[56] This advice had a strong element of practicality, for strikes often seemed to work badly for the strikers. Nevertheless, the Southern Populists, even those who had a better understanding than most of their brethren of the working people's lot, often failed to appreciate either the desperation of strikers like those at Pullman or the tactical pressures which labor union leaders like Debs faced when a strike broke out. In neither case did the participants have much choice. Certainly the option of ballot or strike was not available in the spring of 1894 to workers living in Pullman, Illinois.[57]

Both of these commitments—to America's basic economic order and to a stable, orderly society—also revealed a side of Southern Populism about which we have not spoken. Their conception of themselves as the middle class was not rooted exclusively in their Jeffersonian-Jacksonian heritage. The economic revolution after the Civil War created, even in the South of the 1890s, a new kind of middle class. Ragged Dick and Andrew Carnegie often replaced the yeoman farmer and Daniel Boone as cultural heroes.[58] Independence shaded into cleverness in the search for the main chance; simple abundance became the security of success; hard work acquired overtones of diligence and tenacity in search of profits; and a business education became more important than a farm upbringing for social mobility. This new urban middle class, a white-collar, professional, clerical, storekeeper, management middle class, had its own ethos of success and failure[59] which the Southern Populists did not escape any more completely than they did other parts of the middle class' New South creed. While they questioned the actual existence of equal opportunity for success, the reformers shared with most other Americans a firm belief in the beneficial effect of such equal opportunity for all who would work.[60] The concern for law and order, the careful opposition to socialist and anarchist, was more familiar in the late nineteenth century than in Jeffersonian or Jacksonian America. The yeoman farmer and artisan worried about threats to private property from anarchist and labor violence far less than did the new middle class, or the Southern Populists. Jeffersonians and Jacksonians would not have given corporations, finance capitalism, and town-booming quite as clean a bill of health as the Southern Populists sometimes did, even though the latter's certificate always contained many more qualifications than those handed out by most of their contemporaries.

At times the religious metaphors and imagery used by the Southern Populists reflected a more recent middle-class concern for purity than did the Biblically based religious morality of a younger America. An Alabama Populist spoke of the need for "wholesome" reform legislation.[61] A favorite crusade of this new middle class, the prohibition movement, occasionally touched the Southern Populist party around its edges, although demon rum never became an important party issue.[62] Another North Carolina man identified himself as a "Bryan Populist" for three reasons, the first being that, like himself, Bryan was a good moral man, affiliated with the church, and did not smoke, chew, swear, or drink.[63] The Southern Populists rarely denied the propriety of prohibition. Many obviously felt that temperance might be a good, if not important, ingredient in a better society.

The Southern Populists' concern with respectability also disclosed some affinity with the new middle classes. The complaint against the influence of riches in society, especially in regard to personal integrity and character, was rather widespread. "Honest labor," blessed by God, and not the accumulation of money, made men "truly great," wrote a Texas reformer. "Therefore, men should seek rather to be upright, honest and true rather than to be rich."[64] The increasing importance of money in determining one's respectability furnished another excellent example of the evils of the growing maldistribution of wealth. But the concern with this change, although rare, also reflected the impact on the Southern

Populists of the social code of new middle class society, where men were respectable as often as independent, pure-minded as often as rational, and as virtuous in the service of blue laws as in the preservation of republican government. The Populists did "not wish to be rich," maintained a North Carolina reformer, "but only want a reasonable chance that we may be able to go decent and respectable and educate our children. Surely no enemy could say anything against such doctrine as this."[65] No one could; the wish was only for a decent life. A more even distribution of wealth and the opportunity to enjoy the fruits of their toil, however, promised not only a more productive, harmonious, and balanced society, but also an increased portion of a new town and city middle class respectability.

Finally, the Southern Populists also shared with other nineteenth-century Americans, including their new middle class, success-oriented contemporaries, a belief in the social and personal value of industry and frugality. "Nothing in this life can be gained without hard work. . . . If you are industrious, your work, even though hard, will be a pleasure."[66] But the Southern Populists, having experienced for a generation the seemingly inexorable advance of rural poverty, knew that the existing organization of society failed to reward properly hard work and frugality.[67] A Georgia Populist speaker in 1892 pointed out that in the last twenty-five years Georgia farmers had grown millions of dollars worth of cotton, yet remained poor. The farmers were "intelligent, economical and industrious," but under the existing system these qualities went unrewarded.[68] Since the seventeenth century hard work and saving had been supposed to guarantee at least a fair share of wealth to those who practiced them diligently. When the Southern Populists found this ideal at odds with reality, however, rather than question their own personal worth, as the success ethic and their middle class contemporaries told them to do,[69] they questioned the organization of society and found it unbalanced and unjust, favoring not those who worked but those who were clever enough to get more than they needed without working.[70]

The Southern Populists found themselves in a difficult situation in the 1890s. They and those around them were sliding quickly into a poverty and dependence from which it became more and more difficult to escape. At the same time certain aspects of the new world encroaching upon their lives—machinery, railroads, economic development, and new markets— seemed beneficial, apparently representing possible gains for them and their neighbors. In response to the unfavorable elements of this new American industrial society, the Southern Populists tried to elaborate a social order which would preserve what they wanted to keep and get rid of what they did not. In doing so they drew on the material available to them—their rural Southern experience, their evangelical Protestant heritage, and their Jeffersonian-Jacksonian tradition. Of course, these elements supplied the basis for their critique of the new world they faced as well as their response to it.

Sometimes the Southern Populists' experience and heritage distorted their perceptions of capitalist America, particularly when, as in the case of manufacturers or the new industrial labor, these two things gave them no way to develop an accurate analysis of this new society. On the other hand, in some cases their class position or contemporary experience overrode the dictates of their heritage, as occurred in their response to the New South gospel or in their affinity for a socialist ideal of society. In the areas of conflict between their heritage and their experience lay the sources of change in the Southern Populists' response to American industrial and financial capitalism.

To this theme—the complicated interaction between past and present in the southern reformers' recognition of and response to the new social and economic order—we will return more than once. These first three chapters, and to a certain extent the two that follow, identify some basic components of and influences on that response, and ought to have established that the Southern Populists cannot be easily labeled as would-be Jeffersonian yeomen, as protosocialist agrarian and economic radicals, or as harried rural small businessmen. At times they considered themselves, and appeared to be, each of these. At other times they wrote and spoke as if they were all of them at once, or none of them at all. We will continue to see examples of this. We shall also see how their perception and analysis of themselves, of the society around them, and of its proper and ideal alternative, were changing in important ways. Before we deal with these changes, however, we ought to consider in greater detail how the Southern Populists felt they could resolve the conflicts they perceived between their own historical experience and heritage and the new American society they found growing up around them and its ideal alternative.

CHAPTER 4

Law and Goverment

The Southern Populists' concern with orderly change in part reflected their belief, which reached back to their Enlightenment predecessors, in a world essentially structured and regulated by law. For the southern reformer, as for Jefferson and many of his eighteenth-century contemporaries, law—general and specific, human, natural, and divine—outlined the proper society, limned in its details, and provided the means for its realization.[1] In this capacity, for the Southern Populists the law served a dual function as both map and vehicle for the reform of society.

The Southern Populists, as the Jeffersonians and Locke before them, discerned three distinct levels of the law governing the world and the human society within it, each with a different source.[2] Human society existed within a framework of fundamental and unchangeable law which God authored and which extended outside and beyond the human world.[3] God, for instance, had never intended His world to be given over to the control and enjoyment of only a few individuals;[4] to prevent it He had declared that every man eat bread only by the sweat of his own face, and that to the laborer alone belonged the fruits of his toil.[5]

To discuss particular arrangements and reforms of the social, economic, or political order, however, the Southern Populists usually referred to natural law. As their Jeffersonian and Lockean predecessors, however, they did not divide the two. "Nature is the handwriting of God," stated an Arkansas Populist editor.[6] Natural law, like divine law, blessed tangible production and dictated its necessity,[7] and the reformers traced the maldistribution of wealth to its violation.[8] The operation of the market system depended on natural law, which, as one Alabama Populist put it, "decrees that the price of anything wanted depends on the supply of it and the demand for it."[9] The president of the Tennessee Farmers' Alliance defended the subtreasury plan to a Mississippi audience by arguing that it would place farmers, like merchants and manufacturers, under "'the natural and just law of supply and demand.'"[10]

The Problem

Consistent with their Lockean and Jeffersonian heritage, the Southerners believed that the closer human laws correlated with natural and divine law, the closer human society came to its proper order.[11] The Southern Populists were often quite explicit on this point. "[I]f we could ascertain the Divine Law, and then put it on the Statute Books and observe it," maintained a Georgia Populist in 1891, "the people would be in a far better condition than that which they are in today. . . . Then the people would enjoy equal rights. Then the laborer would enjoy the profits of his labor, and the idler would suffer for his idleness."[12] Human laws, however, often served exactly the opposite purpose. Like many of his brethren, one Texas Populist did not blame the "strangely disjointed times" on poor soil, bad weather, or people who were not "industrious, temperate and economical." "[T]hey were and are the inevitable results of vicious class legislation."[13] Human laws could, and did, disrupt God's intentions for human society because, unlike divine and natural law, the ends served by human laws determined their value.[14] They could either destroy or heal. So, ironically, a major cause of America's ills became the source of its relief. Laws had to be passed which, like divine and natural law, assured each person of "a free and equal opportunity to work out his own prosperity, and to enjoy the fruit of his own labor,"[15] which regulated human society by the rule of "Equal Rights to All and Special Privileges to None." In such a society injustice would end. The extremes of rich and poor would disappear. Society would be balanced, harmonious, and relatively homogeneous, dominated by the producing middle class, the class which worked hard, saved carefully, and was sober and temperate.

Government, for the Southern Populists, implemented and enforced the law, particularly human law. They would have agreed with a North Carolina reformer that it shared with the law a natural or divine model to which it should conform. "We learn from divine writ that government is an institution ordained of God."[16] They would also have agreed that government should serve the same particular functions that the law did. It should guarantee each person a relatively equal share of the wealth created by providing everyone equal opportunities to enjoy the fruits of their productive labor.[17] What kind of government did this? "Give us," wrote W. S. Morgan, the editor of the Arkansas *National Reformer*, "a government of the people, by the people, and for the people."[18]

Government as the agent of the people was only one aspect of an idea which colored a great deal of Southern Populist thinking about the relationship between government and society—"the right of the people to govern themselves."[19] Often this meant that the distinction between the people and their government disappeared. Only in his explicit statement of this idea did Evan Jones of Texas differ from most of his Populist brethren: "We . . . recognize the fact that the government is not something separate from the people, but, when properly administered, is simply the people governing themselves."[20]

That the government should be the agent of the people, that laws could be passed and implemented by government to improve the conditions in society, suggested a need for at least some active participation of government in American society. The Southern Populists agreed with their conservative opponents that the government should serve a protective function.[21] They differed in wanting the government to go beyond policing society and guaranteeing contracts. While a few Southern Populists qualified their advocacy of a more active government—having caused the depression of the 1890s, argued an Alabama Populist, the national government unfortunately had to take aggressive corrective action[22]—most had fewer reservations about the government's duty to protect the welfare and prosperity of all its citizens. "All this racket about paternalism is bosh," wrote an Alabama Alliance editor, pointing out that the state government supported colleges and helped to support the public school system, established a railroad commission, financed an agricultural department to teach and disseminate information and maintain experiment stations, and organized and paid a state militia. All exhibited paternalism, and all were "necessary, advantageous and beneficial, and have not and will not destroy the government; but make it better, stronger and more advantageous to the people who pay taxes to support it."[23]

Among the antimonopoly greenbackers the idea of a positive role for the government in the social and economic order emerged most strongly. According to the editor of the Lampasas *People's Journal*, "if the government has a right to punish men for idleness it has an equal right to furnish them with work to keep them from starving."[24] The *Southern Mercury*'s editor argued that "the only reason for establishing government is to utilize human effort to the advantage of the governed. . . . It is the duty of every government of, by and for the people to provide for the constant and profitable employment of its people."[25] Many Texas reformers felt that a government which did not concern itself in their social and economic lives was of little good to them.[26]

As in other areas, however, influences from the past confused, although did not compromise, this commitment to an active central government. The Southern Populists found their model for the legal structure of the proper society in a fixed and timeless divine or natural order. They referred much less to Jefferson or Jackson. With government the importance of these two referents was reversed. The reformers used Jefferson's philosophy and principles of government to develop their criticism of existing government and to outline their concept of its proper alternative. Their demand for a more economical government, for instance, they drew directly from him.[27] Even the editor of the *Southern Mercury*, advocate extraordinary of a more active government, wanted "to reduce our state and national governmental expenses to an economical basis."[28]

Jeffersonian inroads were even more marked in a related and more fundamental area. The Southern Populists almost all agreed with Jefferson's hostility to the central government and with the historical states' rights stance of the South before and after the Civil War.[29] In general, their opposition to government centralization meant an opposition to the growth of federal power in the hands of the plutocrats and wealthy who used that power to oppress the producers.[30] But this point often remained implicit, partly because the Southerners used states' rights and the Jeffersonian demand for a small, limited, and economical government to justify and explain their opposition to the power of the plutocracy. States' rights could and did mean far more than the demand that the federal government be taken out of the hands of the plutocrats and returned to the control of the mass of people in the country. Historically it entailed a very limited and minimal role for the national government. The result was a conflict in Southern Populist thought between the Jeffersonian ideal and the reformers' demand for a central government increasingly active in the social and economic life of the nation. The latter did not govern best because it governed least.

The Southern Populists never resolved this conflict successfully, although they tried. Some denied the conflict by equating government with the governed.[31] Most, however, eventually had to admit that the national government was actually an entity separate from the entire population of the country, that government ownership of the railroads, for instance, was not simply each American owning and operating the railroads. Others chose to argue, like a Tennessee Populist, that an increasingly active government was the lesser of two evils. The tremendous economic power of the railroads made them more dangerous centralized under private ownership than under government ownership.[32] The commonest form of this argument appeared all over the South. In the words of A. P. Longshore of Alabama: "The way to avoid railroad ownership of the government is to have government ownership of the railroads."[33] For reformers who felt this way, the immediate threat overruled considerations of the conflict with Jeffersonian ideas and their sectional heritage. But although this argument might be effective for a short time and for a certain group of people, particularly those who already felt that government ownership furnished the only viable solution, to sell the issue to a wider electorate the Southern Populists had to eliminate some of the internal inconsistency. Both the Democrats and Republicans could too easily attack it.

Another attempt to permit some positive government participation in society set off a few special public areas in which government involvement was permissible. The public nature of certain social functions—transportation, the distribution of currency, sometimes public utilities—made private monopolies of them detrimental to society and put them legitimately within the power of the national government to own or control for "the general good."[34] Beyond these few areas, however, private enterprise should hold sway.

Unfortunately Jefferson had opposed the increase of power in the central government that ownership or control would involve. And even if Jefferson's demand for a weak central government could be ignored or reasoned around, a further problem remained. What was to be done with Jefferson's dictum about government not interfering with the rights of the individual? Watson fell back on the lesser of two evils argument. "We favor individualism wherever the individual is chiefly concerned—just as Jefferson did." In "the present railroad system," however, individualism had no chance. On local questions the Populists stood for states' rights, but when it came to creating a "national currency" or an adequate and just national transportation system, "we believe the government should act for all and thus give uniformity and impartiality to the system."[35] Getting Jefferson on the side of government ownership of the railroads took considerable hedging. Beyond that, invoking states' rights augured further difficulties. The states' rights argument was based on a strict construction of the Constitution, and nowhere did that document give the federal government power to own and operate the railroads. Watson did not deal at all with this problem, the third aspect of the Jeffersonian conflict.

Some Texas antimonopoly greenbackers tried to create what would sound like a strict constructionist argument for increased government involvement in the life of the nation. Two efforts particularly stand out, both built on complex distinctions between implied and delegated powers. One argument worked only by assuming an identity between the government and its citizens, ignoring the fact that the subtreasury was not just seventy million Americans distributing needed currency to themselves.[36] The other finally relied on the idea that since the federal government had the power to coin and borrow money, it had the power to distribute currency.[37] The escape was more apparent than real. Opponents and other Southern Populists could point out that the power to coin money only implied the power to distribute it. Besides, to use strict construction to argue for a widening of the government's role in society seriously violated a sectional historical tradition which neither the Southern Populists nor their audience could ever really forget.

Evidence of the remarkable tenacity of this memory was the extremely rare appearance of an easy and readily available solution to the Southerners' dilemma. They might have clearly and unambiguously discarded all pretext at retaining a Jeffersonian, states' rights, strict constructionist format in any argument for increasing the activity of the central government. Such an argument was not out of reach. A North Carolina editor defended the constitutionality of the subtreasury plan by pointing to precedents for it in congressional subsidies for railroads and steamship lines, pensions to civilians, the formation of national banks, and government aid for irrigation. He found that "nearly all legislation is at the present time based upon what is not found in the constitution, but its implied powers."[38] For Southerners of a strict constructionist, states' rights, Jeffersonian background, however, this remained quite a statement to make, especially since it was completely unqualified.

That preeminent Jeffersonian, James H. "Cyclone" Davis, in his book *A Political Revelation* undertook perhaps the most extensive effort to resolve the conflict with Jefferson. He, like a few other Texas reformers, premised his major argument for expanding the role of the government in society on the preamble of the Constitution.[39] Every power granted the federal government by the Constitution, Davis contended, was given it to secure to the governed the benefits named in the preamble. Not that Congress could do anything it pleased to promote the general welfare, "but it can and must do everything named in the Constitution." He suggested, for instance, that the commerce clause be invoked to empower the government to own and operate the railroads "for the good of the people. It is the only reasonable and logical manner of carrying the power into execution."

To this point, Davis used a constitutional interpretation based on only the implied powers to build a case for increased government activity in the social order. But Jefferson always intruded in Southern Populist thinking on this issue, and Davis was no exception. He proceeded to cite Jefferson, among others, to prove that because the Articles of Confederation had given the national government too little power "to regulate trade," the Constitution had increased the federal power, "as Jefferson said, to act directly on the people and not through the States." Davis made it clear that he believed in states' rights, but cited Madison to argue that while the states "were first sovereign" in agreeing to the Constitution, they had "surrendered their sovereignty in certain matters to the general government." For the federal government to delegate or "'farm out'" these powers to any state or individual was "to betray the trust of the people" and violate the Constitution. With continual asides to states' rights, Davis used a very Whiggish interpretation of the origin of the Constitution to emphasize at every point possible the power of the central government to act. But the states' rights argument obviously confused his approach to the problem.

Davis was probably aware of this confusion, for he did not base his main effort to connect Jefferson and increased government activity on this low key states' rights argument. He needed the states' rights disclaimer, but, as we have seen already, this route had its full complement of potholes for the traveler. Rather, Davis tried to dodge the question of the implied powers by using an interpretive route outlined by Jefferson.

> [W]hile Jefferson was president, in 1807, in writing to Governor Cabell, of Virginia, officially, in passing on some questions that arose in some military laws and regulations, in Jefferson's Works, vol. 5—259, we find that he says, "in the construction of law, even in judiciary cases, where the opposite parties have a full right and counter right in the words of the law, the judge considers the intention of the law given as his guide and gives to all the parts and expressions of the law, the meaning which effects instead of defeating its intentions. But laws, merely executive, and where no private rights stand in the way, and the public object is the interest of all, a much more free scope of construction in favor of the intention of the law ought to be taken, and ingenuity should be exercised in devising constructions which may save to the public the benefits of the law. Constructions must not be favored which go to defeat instead of furthering the principle object of the law."

Applying this method to the commerce clause, Davis pointed out on the one hand that Congress had the power to regulate interstate commerce, and on the other that government existed to establish justice, insure domestic tranquility, provide for the general welfare, and secure the blessings of liberty to all citizens. Government ownership and operation of the railroads would establish justice by requiring all to pay the same rates, would insure domestic tranquility by ending strikes, would provide for the general welfare by ending the preference for a few men and increasing the benefits to the producing classes. And so he went, on through the preamble.[40]

Davis's arguments easily constituted the most ambitious attempt made by any Southern Populist to get Jefferson on the right side. His was also one of the more ambitious uses of the general welfare clause and implied powers argument. But Jefferson, strict construction, and states' rights historically were tied very closely together. For this reason Davis's resolution was not very smooth. When he quoted Jefferson in favor of a looser construction of the law—"where no private right stands in the way, and the public object is in the interest of all"—Davis tended to overlook the first phrase for the second. Many would have disagreed with him that no private right stood in the way of government ownership of the railroads.

In law, the railroads were privately owned, and this might be construed by many to be an eminently private right. Indeed, with the similar questions raised by the Slaughterhouse cases, Supreme Court Justice Field's dissent paraphrased Jefferson's Declaration of Independence to argue in favor of private rights.[41]

Moreover, not many of Davis's contemporaries, friend or foe, would have recognized the Jefferson whom he connected with increased governmental activity. Davis managed to keep Jefferson at the expense of the philosophy of government most Southerners identified as Jeffersonian. Jefferson, however, had to be present. Davis, with the overwhelming approval of his Populist brethren in the South, called Jefferson the "grand authority" in all such matters, and his presence helped prevent Davis and his southern brethren from elucidating a really thoroughgoing, unqualified, and clear exposition of the need for a general government which involved itself in American society as the agent of the producers and laboring classes.

All the Southern Populists who wrestled with this Jeffersonian contradiction lost. Watson, Nugent, the *Southern Mercury*, and the *Texas Advance* had no more success than the rest of the southern reformers avoiding charges of advocating centralization, because for all of their emphasis on individual rights and freedom from government, for all their pronouncements in favor of states' rights and local self-government, they never could concur completely with Jefferson's dictum that the best government governed least without giving up many of their demands for reform. Their testiness on the issue indicated awareness of their dilemma. The charge that they opposed Jefferson's idea of small and minimal national government always stung them into loud protestations to the contrary. The Southern Populists remained, even in their own eyes, vulnerable to the charge of advocating a centralized government which threatened the Jeffersonian ideal to which most of them clung. In the last analysis, they failed to have their cake and eat it, although they never stopped trying, being unable to relinquish either their Jeffersonian heritage or their commitment to a government which acted in the interests of the producers.

The difficulty with Jefferson reflected another fundamental problem. The Southern Populists never dealt adequately with the implications that their reforms had for change in the traditional structure and function of American government. While their critique of society related past standards to their contemporary situation, they often formulated their ideal alternative in a realm divorced from the world they found around them in the 1890s. What might government ownership of the railroads, for instance, mean for the actual structure of, and ways of thinking about, the federal government and its relatively small bureaucracy? The Jeffersonian ideal provided little impetus even for asking such questions, much less for analyzing the problem of government this way. Jefferson could not have taken into account developments about which he never dreamed, such as American industrial and financial capitalism, but with which the southern reformers had to contend. The religious metaphor provided no more incentive and even less framework for any fundamental reanalysis of the role of government in society. The Southern Populists knew that laws had to benefit those who worked and produced tangible wealth rather than reward those who did not, and that the central government had to play a more active role to insure a decent and just distribution of wealth. But they never really entertained the notion that the structure of government might have to be altered to accomplish these ends. Of their inherited traditions and their more contemporary influences only socialism could have suggested the advisability of doing so, and the southern reformers had mixed feelings about socialism, particularly on the level of practical political implementation. So although to one degree or another all the Southern Populists realized that American society had changed markedly and demanded some innovative responses to its problems, their dedication to Jefferson's thought, which had provided many of their standards for analyzing the ills of American society, helped blind them to the possible need to rethink his ideas about government.

As a result, while the Southern Populists gave various answers to the question of why "this government has grown corrupt, and the noble purposes of our forefathers have been in great measure defeated and our liberties endangered,"[42] most generally agreed with a Georgia Populist editor that "government . . . in the hands of a combination of men whose purpose and selfish instincts are to live in luxurious idleness upon the toil of the masses, invariably leads to a system of laws which rob the producer in the interest of the non-producer."[43] On the other hand, good men brought good government. As an Alabama Populist declared: "We must have men to represent us who fear God, and who will put this government in harmony with God's government."[44]

Since government was, or should be, the rule of the people, a prime requisite for an elected representative was his responsiveness to the people who elected him. Some cited Jefferson as an authority in this matter;[45] others referred to the Biblical injunction that "the servant is not greater than his Lord." Elected public officials, however, had become masters, not servants, of those who elected them.[46] One reason was the lack of elected officials with the highest moral qualifications, individuals whom Georgia Populist W. L. Peek described as "men of high morals, integrity and common sense."[47]

Background provided the most important kind of educational preparation an officeholder could have. Another Georgia Populist desired as leaders only men "who have experienced the sweat of the brow in earning their daily bread. They, and they alone, can sympathize with the workingman and provide for his needs."[48] A Texas Populist advocated making at least ten years of such experience mandatory for holding public office.[49] A North Carolina man claimed he was a Populist because he wished "to be governed by the laboring class of our people, those whose interests are our interests."[50]

The Southern Populists' assumption that farmers and laboringmen would represent them better than Democratic lawyers and politicians was, up to a point, correct. Farmers and laboringmen would know the needs of the producers and would be more apt to try to meet them than would Democratic lawyers and politicians. On the other hand, partly because they lacked experience in government but also because they did not analyze closely the relationship between the structure of government and the goals that the government was to serve, the southern reformers did not realize that the government was not designed to serve the purposes of farmers and laborers, or of any kind of radical reformer. Any good politician knew that the Alliance's 1890 victories within the Democratic party would not give them control of the party or the state legislatures. George Washington Plunkitt, their contemporary and a good Tammany Democrat, could have told the Alliance why. "The fact is that a reformer can't last in politics. He can make a show for a while, but he always comes down like a rocket. Politics is as much a regular business as the grocery or the dry-goods or the drug business. You've got to be trained up to it or you're sure to fail."[51] Those who ran the southern Democratic state machines, not farmers and laboring people, had been "trained up" for American politics and government, and American politics and government fit their needs and ends. The Southern Populists challenged the whole ethos and structure of a society in which industrial and financial capitalism and its business culture were developing their domination of politics and government, and failed to appreciate the extent to which this had already occurred.

The Southern Populists criticized American government in the 1890s for failing to fulfill its proper functions. Government did not serve its citizens adequately. It oppressed most of them, and in doing so threatened the stability of the whole society. What prevented the proper solutions to the problems which threatened to destroy the Republic lay not in the structure of government, or in its functional relationship to American capitalist society in the 1890s, but with the people who ran it. Good government could not exist without good people, and any government would be all right with good people in it. A North Carolina Populist summed up the problem and the solution in one sentence in August

1892. "Men must in their political conduct be governed by the same moral laws that control individual actions."[52] Most of the time, and for most Southern Populists, the basic concern of governing was a question of the personal morality and background of their elected officials.

As their ideas about government and governing indicate, the very same standards which the Southern Populists used to diagnose and describe the ills of American government in the late nineteenth century often helped prevent their development of a cure for the disease. They used their Jeffersonian heritage, for instance, to criticize a government which did not serve most of its citizens adequately, but Jefferson's notion of the ideal form of government remained to help prevent the reformers from creating a conception of government which would, in the context of the 1890s, serve better their needs and those of their potential supporters. Most of the reformers failed to distinguish between Jefferson's standards for a decent, just society and his elaboration of the proper form and function of government. The former retains its validity today; the latter was dated by the 1830s. The failure to separate the two often caused considerable confusion in their efforts to realize the very society which the standards outlined for them—witness the conflict of Jeffersonian ideas with the need for a more active central government.

Seen in this light, the movement of a few antimonopoly greenbackers toward some form of socialism becomes more understandable. Only where the Southern Populists made clearer distinctions between the standards of government and its duties, as in the antimonopoly greenback demand for an increased involvement of government in the social and economic life of the country, did this confusion tend to decrease. The issue of the proper form of government, however, looked like it could wait, because it involved possibilities rather than immediate demands. The Southern Populists would learn by 1896 that delay might not have been wise, but other problems appeared to press more insistently for attention.

CHAPTER 5

Blacks as a White Problem

Race pressed harder than any other problem they encountered when, in late 1891 and early 1892, Southern Alliancemen turned to insurgent third-party politics to realize their dream for a better society. Although outcasts, black people in the South were mixed inextricably in the social and economic life of the region, and in every state but Mississippi, and perhaps Georgia, they could still vote in considerable numbers. Reconstruction and the history of independent politics in the late 1870s and early 1880s had amply demonstrated the power of black votes, whether cast for or against the Democratic party.[1]

The way in which the Southern Populists reacted to the challenge of this black population to the realization of their reform program revealed how much impact the reformers' heritage and experience had on their thought. As with their other reform issues, one of the most significant variations in the Populists' response to the blacks paralleled the split between the antimonopoly greenbackers and the financial reformers. The former tended to support more strongly black participation in the party and to be less racist. None of the Southern Populists escaped their history, however. Even the best of them were weak on lynching, and none ever questioned the need to avoid "social equality" and the possible end to complete black subordination that this issue involved. Their ultimate inability to reconcile these kinds of racial attitudes with their demands for reform measured a serious weakness in Southern Populist thought and in the analysis that grew from it.

Despite these ambiguities and weaknesses, however, the Southern Populists' approach to the problem of race had some strengths. A few reformers broke far enough with the color line and the strictures of white supremacy to allow some communication and respect between black and white. Even the most racist implicitly questioned the hard-line white supremacy position by joining the third party. And whatever strengths existed, the Southern Populists had created them in the face of all they knew and had learned. They measured the degree to which the southern reformers were fighting for their existence as a class and the importance of human decency and justice in their dream of a better society.

The Southern Populists knew what to expect when they challenged the social order through political action. They remembered how the conservative appeal to white supremacy had helped defeat the earlier Greenback and Independent movements.[2] "Listen to old false Democracy in his dying hours," wrote a Georgia Populist. "See him swell up till his lungs are fit to burst, and stand on his tip-toes and hollow [sic] at the top of his voice, 'N-i-g-g-e-r Equality,' until his breath is gone." This reformer reflected the inclination of many of the rest of the Southern Populists by adding that "we have heard that till we are tired, and we have answered to the party lash long enough."[3] The cry of "nigger" may have gratified "our feelings for the wrongs we have suffered," wrote W. J. Peele, a North Carolina Populist, but the monopolists were far more gratified. They had used race to divide "those who ought to be united against them."[4]

To assert that race was not the preeminent issue, however, did not mean that the Southern Populists could forget about the blacks. If only because of their potential as voters, the reformers had to consider them. By and large, they chose to approach black voters with the same appeal they made to white—according to a Georgia greenback editor, "the general promise that by a united vote on the part of those who 'earn their bread by the sweat of their face' their freedom and independence can be maintained and their condition in this life improved by enactment into law of the principles put forth in the Populist platform."[5] Individual material self-interest defined and justified this particular approach to blacks, and explained why whites would overlook racial fears to cooperate with them. Their material self-interest would drive black and white producers together to cooperate in the reform fight to free themselves. "The white people" of Oconee County, Georgia, after organizing their local party in April 1892, asked "the cooperation of the colored people in this, our effort to free our country from its present depressed condition and put in office men who will legislate for the masses and not the classes." They explicitly disclaimed any "visionary" offer of "forty acres and a mule," but told the "colored people" of Oconee that "your race today, like ours, is groaning under the oppression of taxation and the low estimate placed on labor, and . . . under the present administration, the fruits of your labor, like the fruits of ours, instead of going to make our homes happy and comfortable, go to pay tithes to the money lords of Wall street. We also come telling you that our interest is one, and to better our condition means to better yours. So, as true citizens, let's work together harmoniously for the redemption of our country."[6] Watson repeated this idea over and over,[7] and the same arguments came from other places in the South.[8]

A few of the southern reformers, however, remained unsure of the efficacy of an appeal made solely to material self-interest, acknowledging in the process that blacks might have certain desires which did not fit precisely into the Omaha platform. The Populist position on equal political rights for black voters was "exceedingly plain," their gubernatorial candidate told Georgia Populists in 1894. "These people have been given the rights of citizens. We contend that they ought to be permitted to exercise them, and that they can exercise these rights well and wisely."[9] Except for Watson, the least grudging admission that blacks deserved equal political rights came from Texas, the center of antimonopoly greenbackism. The editor of the *Texas Advance*, in July 1894, argued that the Populist party was "the only great political organization that . . . cannot draw the color line in its party organization, because its fundamental principle is 'justice to all and exclusive privileges to none.'"[10] Equal rights to all included, at least for Watson and a few of his compatriots elsewhere, a commitment to ending the color line around the ballot box.

Some black participation in the party indicated a response by black voters. Watson's leadership seems to have meant greater black participation in the Georgia party than elsewhere. Certainly more evidence of it appeared in the Georgia papers. Black delegates attended the state Populist conventions in Georgia in 1892, 1894, and 1896. In 1892 a black man seconded the nomination of W. L. Peek for governor.[11] At the convention for 1896, held in December 1895, twenty-five blacks, out of five to seven hundred delegates, were reported in attendance, and two were elected to the state executive committee.[12] Georgia blacks also participated in county mass meetings and even held official party positions at this level.[13]

In Texas blacks participated in state conventions and on the state executive committee.[14] A third of the delegation Gonzales County sent to the state convention in 1892 was black, and in ten or fifteen counties blacks were reported active and numerous in the party.[15] Blacks were involved in the 1894 and 1896 state conventions, and local participation continued to be strong.[16]

Besides Texas and Georgia, evidence of black participation at high levels in the party was rare, although reports of local Populist meetings in North Carolina in the late spring and summer of 1892 sometimes included mention of "black and white" participation. In August 1892, the *Progressive Farmer* admitted that blacks had attended the state convention, but defended the fact by asserting that these came from overwhelmingly black counties.[17] After the 1892 election evidence of any black participation in the party disappeared completely from all the North

Carolina Populist newspapers. While this did not mean that there was none, it did imply that there was very little, and that the North Carolina Populists did not want it publicized.

In Virginia the Populists seem to have tried to involve blacks in the party during the campaign leading up to the 1892 fall elections. The call for a state convention in late June 1892 included an invitation "to both white and colored citizens" to participate in the mass meetings to elect representatives.[18] In July 1892 the secretary of the state executive committee instructed all county organizations to have at least one black representative on every precinct committee "to look after the colored vote."[19] July, August, and September saw indications of special efforts to organize black voters,[20] and the *Virginia Sun* noted some response.[21] Following 1892, however, and a very poor Populist vote in Virginia's black belt counties,[22] little evidence appeared of much continuing effort to reach black voters, and some Virginia Populists expressed hostility toward the blacks for not voting with them.[23]

From the Alabama Populist press came even less evidence of black participation in the party. The only two references came from the same county, Choctaw. The *Choctaw Alliance* reported in October 1892 that blacks had taken part in the third-party primary elections. In 1894 it noted that at the county nominating convention eight or ten "colored friends" had joined about seventy white Populists to nominate the county's candidate for the state legislature.[24] In Louisiana only one statement indicated that blacks had played any part in the party. "In the State election of 1892," wrote the editor of the *Louisiana Populist*, "the white Populists of that parish [Grant], unfortunately for all concerned, invited the colored Populists into their primary for nominating a parish ticket."[25]

None of the Southern Populists had forgotten ideas and attitudes learned earlier. It remained easy for some Southern Populists to use "nigger" in public discourse with no apparent consciousness about what the use of that term by whites might signify to black people.[26] Angered by black voters accused of voting fraudulently, the editor of the Gracewood, Georgia, *Wool Hat* referred to one of them as a "coon."[27] The difficulties into which this kind of insensitivity could lead white Southern Populists appeared in the efforts of the Dahlonega, Georgia, *Signal* to refute the charge that "the People's Party candidate said that a 'negro had [sic] no soul.'" The report, the editor continued, was completely "false . . . for we are a strong believer in the negro being descendants [sic] of Ham." He wrote the refutation, the editor concluded, "to set us right before the colored people, whom we have always been one of their best friends morally, politically and educationally, and if elected, their interests will be guarded the same as all other free citizens."[28]

Southern Populists could even at times qualify black humanity. The author of a short article in the *Progressive Farmer* in 1893 on a black Baptist camp meeting commented on the "great amusement" provided him there by the blacks' "apish qualities" of mimicry.[29] It could get worse. "The nigger" was, according to an Alabama Populist, at least "half-kin" to a mule, since he had half as many legs, and since "in all other traits of their characters they resemble very much. . . . It is claimed that the nigger is a descent [sic] of Ham but I dout [sic] it for two reasons. . . . Ham's mother and father were both white folks. And . . . I don't believe God would a sprung such a joke as that on the community."[30] Certainly any Populist who shared his sentiments would have difficulty supporting Watson's solution to the race problem in the South, treating blacks as people.

In fact, some Southern Populists explicitly repudiated Watson's commitment. The editor of Kolb's *People's Weekly Tribune* felt it necessary to assert in 1896 that "no negro was ever promised any political position by the Populists. . . . No negro ever held a seat in any Populist convention in Alabama." The Alabama Democrats, on the other hand, had sinned on both counts.[31] Twice in 1893 the Jeffersonian Democrats in Alabama[32] offered to cooperate with the state Democratic party in holding white primaries to nominate candidates for state office. The *Alliance News* criticized the second offer not for disfranchising blacks but for allowing too much latitude for Democrats to cheat.[33] The Populists in Louisiana's fourth congressional district in 1894 maintained that for many years "the question of white supremacy . . . has held the white people together often against needed reforms" and proposed to the Democrats a white primary to "insure white supremacy, and the election of a white man's ticket in the 4th Congressional District."[34] The Democratic rejection of the offer proved to the Populists that they were the only party of white supremacy in Louisiana.[35] When the DeSoto parish Democrats in 1895 invited blacks to participate in their primary, Hardy Brian, editor of the *Louisiana Populist* and secretary of the state party, wrote that by allowing the "Africanization" of their party these Democrats had done "what no decent man can put up with, and every Democrat and Populist in this district should denounce its action as unjust and disreputable, if not undemocratic."[36] Louisiana Populists left little room for blacks to take an equal part in the political process. They attacked the Democrats for doing precisely what Watson and a few other Southern Populists advocated.[37]

All the Southern Populists, however, at one time or another used race as a partisan weapon. In May 1895 Watson called his readers' attention to J. Van Allen, accused of buying an ambassadorial appointment from President Cleveland, noting that he had established a bicycle club at Newport and made "a negro byclicist [sic]" the instructor. The black instructor kept the "upper-tendom [*sic*] females . . . from falling there-from by steadying them around the waist; while the fair maidens work the pedal propellers. That's Van Allen and Newport."[38] Most appeals to racial feeling, however, concentrated on what the Southern Populists rather ingenuously called the Democratic assault on the color line in politics. The editor of the *Progressive Farmer*, for instance, in 1893 noted that "President Cleveland has appointed H. G. Smith, a 'democratic nigger,' U.S. Consul to Madagascar. . . . The nig's face looks like an ordinary round two gallon pot, and since his appointment his eyes stick out about an inch, which represent the legs on the pot."[39] The underlying attitudes of many Southern Populists toward blacks sometimes came to the surface with small irritation. Even the editor of the *Texas Advance* could write that "Grover Cleveland's nigger Taylor desires white lady stenographers for his thirty nigger clerks in the office of recorder of deeds for the District of Columbia. Southern parents desiring good positions for their daughters will endorse Cleveland by applying to Taylor for situations for their girls."[40]

One of the more popular issues used by the Southern Populists in this manner was a statute that Cleveland had signed as governor of New York and which provided that strictly "colored schools" in New York City, and their teachers and officers, be made ward and primary schools within the public school system and "'be open for the education of pupils for whom admission is sought without regard to race or color.'"[41] Watson joined many other Southern Populists in arguing that the law effectively created "mixed schools throughout the State. To the average Georgia Democrat, who affects to dread social contact with the negro more than cholera, it is commended, with the assurance that it fully illustrates Mr. Cleveland's position on the race problem."[42] Cleveland's invitation to Frederick Douglass and his white wife, and their subsequent attendance at the reception for Cleveland's wedding in June 1886, also presented a perennially popular issue to the southern reformers.[43] The editor of the Hickory *Mercury* added his own special touch to the story by noting that Jefferson Davis's wife had not been invited.[44] All who used the story agreed with the editor of the *Virginia Sun* that "here you have negro social equality and miscegenation both condoned and patron-ized by a Democratic President of the United States."[45]

Although Watson could occasionally make it appear that he was de-fending the interest of black people by, for instance, protesting mixed schools,[46] he did not normally do so. In early 1895 the Democratic governor of Virginia, Charles T. O'Ferrall, invited a delegation of Mas-sachusetts state legislators to the executive mansion, and, according to the Populists, shook hands with its black member and later, with the whole delegation, ate dinner with him. "Fact is fact, you know," Watson wrote, "and we guess the truth about this case will have to be that O'Ferrall has invited a negro into his house, dined with him at his table, bestowed upon him the usual courtesies of Southern hospitality, and sent him forth to herald to the world the great discovery that 'White Supremacy,' like all the balance of Democratic campaign goods has a wonderful knack of changing color after the election."[47] The editor of the *Progressive Farmer* was more blunt. "The good people of North Carolina," he wrote, "all bow their heads and sympathize deeply with the good people of Virginia in the disgrace that Governor O'Ferrall has brought upon that State." No one, he maintained, would deny "a colored citizen a single right given him by our Constitution," but O'Ferrall had "ruthlessly" obliterated "social," not constitutional, lines, and there it was "time to call a halt."[48]

Exposing Democratic hypocrisy on racial matters clearly served more than one purpose. The Southern Populists themselves obviously felt vulnerable to accusations of advocating "social equality," and used attacks on the Democrats to highlight their own orthodoxy. Nor did they stop at this oblique sort of proof. The first of the Jim Crow railroad laws in the South coincided with the beginnings of the Populist movement, and when they did not play their part in the passage of such laws, some southern reformers made clear their support for them. In early 1892 the Mount Olivet Alliance of Franklinton, North Carolina, resolved, among other things, "that we are in favor of the Georgia railroad system, separate cars for white and colored, with the same accommodations and a uniform traveling rates [sic] for each."[49] In Georgia, in 1894, his authorship of the state's Jim Crow railroad law was cited in support of the Populist candidate for Congress in the eleventh district.[50]

Almost every Southern Populist who discussed the race problem denied advocating social equality. That most of these denials came from Georgia, the most articulate ones often from Watson, made sense, for the public professions and activities of the Georgia Populists, especially Watson, left them more vulnerable than other southern reformers to charges of attempting to break down the barriers to social equality. The Democrats, wrote the editor of the Gracewood, Georgia, *Wool Hat*, treated the Negro "as a brute," crying Negro domination while purchasing black votes by "the most debasing means." The Populists, on the other hand, "recognize that the negro is a man and a citizen." They felt that the ballot was a sacred trust given the blacks and would not see it purchased with money or whiskey. "On the question of social equality," however, the Populists stood "where all other sensible men stand, irrespective of party or race, for to invade the sanctity of home and family by legal enactments would be the ruin of both races." They invited black political cooperation in the struggle for "equal and exact justice for all men," but they explicitly denied offering social equality.[51]

Of course, not all such explicit denials came from Georgia.[52] One of the most interesting came from an Alabama Populist in 1896. He used Booker T. Washington's famous Atlanta Exposition address to prove that interracial cooperation was a question of material prosperity and not social equality. But, he wrote, the talk of entering the Republican party or "leaning towards social equality bothers no intelligent Populist." The reason was a very old one in the South. Unlike that of state Democratic leaders, the Populists' objection to social equality "does not relax at the going down of the sun. We have got no children at the Tuskegee school or kindred there."[53] Southern whites, in their running battle over who was more orthodox, Democrat or Populist, sometimes testified eloquently to the ambivalent relations between classes and races running through all levels of southern society.

What was this "social equality" that the Southern Populists so carefully rejected? At its most fundamental, "social equality" seemed to be perceived as a threat to the domestic arrangements of southern whites, often in a way particularly related to sexual behavior. How else to explain the emphasis so often laid on the privacy of the home and personal social relationships, the ambiguous attitude toward lynching, and the implicit references to the horrors of sexual contact between black and white?[54] It would probably be fair to say that the Populists feared "social equality" for most of the same reasons their Democratic opponents did. Both sides desired a continuation of the subordinate status of blacks in southern society, particularly in any area in which extensive personal or social intercourse might occur. The opinion of the white South, even before the Populist challenge, seems to have been more and more in favor of carefully isolating black and white from anything but the most necessary and strictly controlled economic and social contact.

But the southern reformers had put themselves in a difficult spot with this issue, and their straddling here, unlike on the land issue or government ownership, was transparent. They tried to deny what, within white southern society in the late nineteenth century, all of their activities affirmed. Most southern whites presumed that any effort which might directly or indirectly benefit the South's black population promoted social equality. By merely advocating a third party the Southern Populists challenged the black people's inferior status in an area which, while it in practice had proven since Redemption to be of little danger to white supremacy, most white Southerners continued to feel constituted a real danger to the color line—black voting. For this reason Populist appeals for black support brought charges of advocating "social equality." Most

Southern reformers preferred to deny the charge flatly. This method allowed its users to continue soliciting black votes without admitting that their activity challenged the color line. On the other hand, when considering questions of white supremacy most Southerners gave much more weight to actions than to words. Simply denying that black voting threatened to bring social equality convinced few whites.

A very few Southern Populists, Watson in particular, in essence admitted the truth of their opponents' allegations. To allow all blacks to vote freely and have their ballots counted fairly did amount to a breach in the wall of white supremacy as it was currently defined. These few reformers sometimes redefined slightly the meaning of "social equality." In this effort even Watson ventured little that was new, however. His treatment of the Cleveland affair with Douglass and the O'Ferrall incident indicated that in social intercourse—eating, socializing, entertainment, education—he wanted a complete separation of the races. "Never in my life," he told an Atlanta audience in May 1894, "have I advocated social equality." It would "ruin" both races. "Let the blacks stay to themselves in their own social life and have peace and happiness. Let the whites dwell to themselves and have peace and happiness." "What you want," he told the blacks in the same speech, "is to have a fair share of the school money and to have your schools where your children can be taught by your own teachers and thus elevated into a higher citizenship. You want your own churches and worship [sic] God according to the dictates of your own consciences, in your own tabernacles."[55]

Other Southern Populists often implicitly or explicitly attributed to the black people a hostility to social equality. "The nigger don't want social equality but he wants better pay for his work," asserted one Georgia reformer.[56] A few even decried the threat of black rule over whites by turning the Democratic charge that black participation in politics would bring back black rule and miscegenation into a Democratic admission that whites were not, indeed, the superior race. "It struck me," commented a North Carolina Populist, "that the Anglo-Saxon who calls for protection acknowledges himself a very inferior creature—a rather emasculated specimen of that noble line of people."[57] Whites could protect themselves easily from inferior blacks, unless their superiority was not real, an idea no white Southerner, Populist or otherwise, would ever admit entertaining.

Other southern reformers used this argument to belittle the threat of blacks taking power and instituting social equality; Watson alone used it to support demands for equal political and legal rights for blacks. In his Douglasville speech of 4 July 1893, Watson summed up many of the various arguments we have been following about the role of blacks in the Southern Populists' ideal society.

I yield to no man in my pride of race. I believe the Anglo-Saxon is stronger, in the glorious strength of conception and achievement, than any race of created men. But from my very pride of race springs my intense scorn of that phantasm, manufactured by the political boss, and called "Negro domination!"

Socially, I want no mixing of races. It is best that both should preserve the race integrity by staying apart. But when it comes to matters of law and justice, I despise the Anglo-Saxon who is such an infernal coward as to deny legal rights to any man on account of his color for fear of "Negro domination."

"Dominate" what? "Dominate" how? "Dominate" who?

It takes intellect to dominate; haven't we got it?

It takes majorities to dominate; haven't we got them?

It takes wealth to dominate; haven't we got it?

It takes social, financial, legislative, military, naval, ecclesiastical and educational establishments to dominate; haven't we got them?

For a thousand years the whites, the Anglo-Saxons, have had all these advantages. Armed with the garnered wealth of ten centuries, equipped with all the mental advantages of school systems hoary with age; holding all the land, all the avenues of commerce, all the sources of political power, outnumbering the blacks eight to one, and continually gaining on them, what words can paint the cowardice of the Anglo-Saxon who would deny "equal and exact justice" to the ignorant, helpless, poverty-cursed Negro in whose ears the clank of chains have scarcely ceased to sound—upon the ground that he feared

"Negro domination."

Away with such contemptible timidity of counsel![58]

The conflict between Watson's realization that blacks deserved better than they received in the South and his essential commitment to white supremacy paralleled his political perception that while the blacks would demand improvement in their social condition in exchange for their votes, the whites would withhold their support if they felt white supremacy was being compromised. Without the support of both, Watson knew that Populism would fail in the South. His struggle with this personal and political dilemma resulted in the most positive approach of Southern Populist thought to the problem of race in southern society. Most Southern Populists realized the dilemma they faced, but few made the effort Watson did to resolve it. When pressured by their opponents, they opted for white supremacy.

Ultimately Watson, too, could not solve his problem. Unwilling to accept completely the strictures of white supremacy, he tried paying to

Peter what came from Paul. He gave to the blacks a little of what they wanted by taking from the whites little of what they demanded. So, ironically, the Southern Populists based the best of their thought on the place of blacks in southern society on the presumption of their inferiority. The reformers could safely redefine the color line to include black voting because the racial superiority of the whites guaranteed black subordination.

The reformers' stance on a specific issue like lynching demonstrated the difficulty involved in attempting to guarantee a white man's country in which blacks had a chance to improve their lot. The goals of both groups were incompatible. In general Watson deplored both lynching and whitecapping,[59] but not always.[60] While the Georgians' 1894 state platform condemned "white-capping,"[61] the Dahlonega *Signal*, a north Georgia Populist paper, advocated lynch law consistently over a period of years, in the harshest of terms. The editor commented in March 1891 that as long as "negroes continue to make assaults on white women throughout the South . . . white men continue to lynch the scoundrels." He proceeded to describe the latest assault and lynching in Georgia, observing that "it takes some negroes a long time to learn that death follows swiftly every time they perpetrate a crime of this kind."[62] Two years later his opinion had not changed. The paper continued to run stories detailing alleged assaults by black men on white women and predicting an early lynching for the assailant.[63] While the *Signal* was an extreme case, other Southern Populists tolerated lynching.[64] This attitude reflected the persistence of real racial hostility upon the part of white Southern Populists, and demonstrated that any offer made to blacks automatically presumed their constant subordination to the complete control of any white man.

A more subtle evidence of this presumption ran all through the reformers' thought. Although a few Southern Populists might admit that the blacks had come a long way in a short time, none would deny that whites still knew what was best for them. Considering that they had been slaves only twenty-seven years earlier, and had been "forced to the rear since," the editor of the *Progressive Farmer* thought that blacks had made "remarkable progress." The Populists, he promised, "will oppose anything that has a tendency to retard this progress and are willing to do anything reasonable to increase their welfare, but the fact remains that the Anglo-Saxons must rule this country and we believe all honest, intelligent negroes know the importance of this."[65] Judge Nugent told a Texas audience in 1894 that the blacks themselves had begun to see that they suffered mainly from the enslavement of labor through plutocracy's manipulation of the economic system, and had joined with the white reformers, "whose superior intelligence has long since enabled them to see the central fact of the economic situation."[66] A Georgia Populist speaker in 1893 was reported to have asserted that "the People's party had done much to make the negroes better."[67]

The clearer a Southern Populist's commitment to working politically with blacks, the more likely this paternalist tone would appear. In the part of his speech given in Thomson, Georgia, in 1892 which Watson directed specifically at the blacks present, he asserted that he had always handled the cases of blacks in court just as he would "the whitest white man. Has there ever been a time since you supported me and helped elect me," he asked them, "that the poorest black man in the county, if he had me representing him, would not trust me as quickly and as fast as any white man in the county?" As evidence of the justice with which he treated blacks, Watson revealed that "on my plantation there are some black men working to-day who were my grandfather's slaves, and the foreman on my grandfather's farm was my foreman, and remained there in that position until the old man was too feeble to hold the hoe,—to lead the gang." Beyond that, he asked them if they did not know "that every colored man living on my place feels just as secure when I pass my word for any thing as if I had drawn up the bond and signed the paper?"[68] Be he L. Q. C. Lamar, J. L. M. Curry, or James Alcorn, no one could have said it better.

In order to offer the black people an improved role in southern society without casting serious doubts on their sincerity, and yet retain the dominance of white over black demanded by a belief in white supremacy, Watson and a few other Southern Populists borrowed heavily from the paternalistic tradition of the conservatives. This philosophy of race relations, generally associated with the class of men Wade Hampton symbolized, regarded blacks as less capable and distinctly inferior but deserving of the same consideration and justice as other people. Black inferiority to whites made the question of black equality moot.[69] The Southern Populist who used this approach enjoyed some latitude in advocating rights for blacks because of the assumption of black inferiority which underlay it.

Even in their efforts to involve the blacks in the party the Southern Populists revealed the essential premise of their approach to the race issue. They argued, as did the conservatives, that given the superiority of white over black, duty obligated whites to make sure that the more unfortunate blacks made as much progress as possible and enjoyed all the benefits rightfully and legally theirs. But since the paternalistic argument allowed a few Southern Populists to offer an improved position in society to black people from the safety of an assumed superiority, blacks clearly would have to be content with most of the substance of their inferior position in the South.

At times, however, the efforts of the few Southern Populists to deal differently with the race problem showed a remarkable absence of the normal strictures of southern racial thinking. Not always did they qualify their approach to the blacks to the extent that has been indicated. While Watson, as we have seen, usually took a back seat to no one in affirming his pride in his Anglo-Saxon racial identity, "marvelous" was the only word he could find to describe the situation in India, where one hundred thousand Englishmen ruled over one hundred million "Hindoos." With a religion "strikingly like" Christianity, an older civilization, and "Cities, Temples, Libraries, Monuments far surpassing anything we have achieved, they yet fell an easy prey to the rapacity of the Anglo-Saxon Cannon and that remorseless vulture which always follows the Cannon, the Anglo-Saxon Capitalist."[70] Probably not by accident did the only Southern Populist who ever questioned the complete superiority of the Anglo-Saxon race over any and all comers also promise the blacks more improvement in their condition than any of his brethren.

Watson committed a similar sin against the Anglo-Saxons in September 1892 by praising the victory of "a bright people's party darkey" over a local white Democratic lawyer in a political debate.[71] To celebrate the victory of a black man over a white in an intellectual contest could also be regarded as a serious breach of white supremacy discipline. To suggest that a black man could best a white in political debate was tantamount to admitting that white supremacy was not completely secure. The blacks might once again rule, might once again destroy good government, might once again threaten white women with impunity. To cast doubt on white supremacy and its continuation, for most southern whites at this time, evoked all the images of Reconstruction's horror. If, because of his inferiority, the black man's right to vote was questionable, how much less did he have the right to debate politics with a white man? And how could a white man go so far as to celebrate a black man's victory in such a contest, for whatever reason?

Nor was Watson alone in his occasional failure to observe strictly the dictates of white supremacy. The editor of the Dallas, Georgia, *Herald* in April 1896, while writing of the Cubans' struggle to free themselves from the oppression of the Spanish aristocracy and Rothschild bonds, called attention to one of the Cuban generals—Maceo—who was "fighting for freedom and independence" and was "actually 'a nigger.'" At least, "nigger" was what the American plutocrats, under Cleveland's leadership, called him. "[W]hat," the editor asked, "will the colored people think of it?"[72] To praise a revolution for independence was perfectly correct; to call attention to a black general was not; and to hold up the actions of that leader as a possible example to American blacks could easily be construed in 1896, only twenty years after Redemption, as evidence of a

Populist appeal to blacks to reassert themselves and try once again to gain an equal role with whites in society.

In both Georgia and Texas belief in the necessity for black and white political cooperation sometimes overcame white racism and resulted briefly in praise of black Populists and voters in which the absence of racism or paternalism challenged white supremacy attitudes. In 1894 Watson appealed to the Populist state convention to assure the blacks a free ballot and a fair count. They had earned it. "These colored people were our friends in the times when we needed friends two years ago. They stood by us through thick and thin. They stood by us when they knew their pockets could be lined with money by going with the Democratic party."[73] The greenback editor of the Dallas, Georgia, *Herald* several times praised black voters in his county, particularly after the county Populist election victory in 1894. "[I]n the thickest of the fight," alongside white Populists, stood "many intelligent and patriotic colored men." In a second editorial on the same day, he added that "the People's party colored men did splendid work at the polls last Wednesday, and thereby gained the respect of every citizen regardless of his politics. It proved an independent and honest citizenship."[74]

After the 1892 elections in Texas, antimonopoly greenbacker H. S. P. Ashby of the Populist state executive committee wrote that despite their "comparatively small number," with "rare courage" black Populists had stood with the white "in the fight for principle. Some of them even at the risk of their lives, hesitated not to unfurl the banner of reform and boldly champion the cause it represents in the presence of the enemy."[75] Watson, Ashby, and a few other more radical Southern Populists understood the courage it took to be a black Populist and that, if anything, it was more dangerous than being a white Populist. Their appreciation of the fact, in spite of their devotion to white supremacy, indicated how they tried to move, albeit often unconsciously, against the pressure of the rest of the South and most of their Populist brethren.

Even the hard-line white supremacy Populists, however, made a critical change in their attitude toward race by deciding that reform took precedence over the strictest observance of absolute white supremacy.[76] As a result, simply by choosing to be Populists and threatening to split the white vote, these reformers joined with their more liberal brethren to challenge the very supremacy they demanded. In this sense, whatever their views on the proper position of the blacks in southern society, every Southern Populist contributed to the attack on absolute white supremacy and participated in holding out to the blacks a possibility, however slim it often was, for improvement in their social, economic, and political condition.

But beyond this unavoidable advocacy, for most of the Southern Populists blacks simply presented a problem which had to be neutralized in order to forward most effectively the Populist cause. Only a minority of the southern reformers, mostly antimonopoly greenbackers, understood as the editor of the *Texas Advance* did, "that the negro has been a patent lever to squeeze down prices of labor in all lines of production. . . . To emancipate white labor, black labor must also be freed. Hence, the people's party must do as much for the negro in this regard as it would do for the whites."[77] Very few Southern Populists realized the intimate connection between social reform and a solution of the race problem in the South, that if the whites freed only themselves, their opponents would soon drive them back into financial slavery by undercutting their position with black labor and black votes. Black and white would have to be freed together to free either.

But while the most discerning Southern Populists realized that any new social order would have to benefit both whites and blacks, they never understood how far this might have to go to assure the ultimate success of reform. One reason lay in the southern reformers' belief that increasing the production of tangible wealth provided the *raison d'etre* of any decent society and that material self-interest insured the cooperation of individuals in maximizing this production. Except in a narrowly defined political sense, to the Southern Populists white supremacy did not appear to impair the production of tangible wealth, nor preclude the cooperation of white and black, on the basis of individual material self-interest, to further that goal. Behavior not obviously in a person's material self-interest they often overlooked or discounted.

If their adherence to racial superiority remained more important to most whites in the South than their poverty, however, then racial cooperation would run into trouble. Watson realized it. "You might beseech a Southern white tenant," he wrote in 1892, "to listen to you upon questions of finance, taxation, and transportation; you might demonstrate with mathematical precision that herein lay his way out of poverty into comfort; you might have him 'almost persuaded' to the truth, but if the merchant who furnished his farm supplies (at tremendous usury) or the town politician (who never spoke to him excepting at election time) came along and cried 'Negro rule!' the entire fabric of reason and common sense which you had so patiently constructed would fall, and the poor tenant would joyously hug the chains of actual wretchedness rather than do any experimenting on a question of mere sentiment."[78] People did not prove as rational as Watson would have liked; he never successfully resolved his dilemma and the spectre of race dogged his political career until he died.[79]

Watson and a few others realized, imperfectly, that an end to the lynching of blacks at the will or whim of whites in many places in the

South meant more to most southern blacks than all of the gains promised by the Omaha platform. For this reason they offered blacks political equality and, while they promised the whites their supremacy, a few even tried to prove their allegiance to their promise. Watson and some other Populists, especially the antimonopoly greenbackers, seem to have convinced some blacks of the sincerity of their intentions,[80] but by and large the Southern Populists said little and tried to prove it less.

Nor did the white Southern Populists always given the blacks an equal showing within their ideal economic order. The more perceptive of the greenbackers like Watson or the antimonopoly Texans usually appeared to define the place of blacks in a properly organized society as separate from but the same as theirs, as producers in a simple market society. The less radical among the reformers often seemed to expect blacks generally to continue as employees or tenants of the white farmers. This was particularly clear in the reaction of North Carolina reformers to the proposed cotton pickers' strike of late 1891.[81] The editor of the Tarboro *Farmers' Advocate* could see "no reason on earth why the colored man should aim a blow at the white farmer, who gives him employment and pays the best wages he can afford."[82] As with the land issue, only more clearly in this case, when the chips were down at least some of the Southern Populists remained unwilling, despite their own adherence to a simple market society of producers, to relinquish actual or potential class advantages the existing system afforded them, including the employing of black labor for their own profit.

Even, however, when they accepted the blacks as producers, all of the white Southern Populists, including Watson, were further trapped in their own racism than they needed to be, in part because of this very orientation on the simple market society of producers and their belief in the primary importance of individual material self-interest. They failed to discern that blacks might want more than the promise of a possible end to their poverty, and that for any successful realization of the extensive social change that they wanted, the blacks would have to participate equally. In this matter their producer orientation served them ill.

It must be added, however, that they had little else available in their background to help them deal with the problem. Jefferson, to say the least, equivocated on the question of black inferiority.[83] The record of the white southern churches on white supremacy[84] and the Populists' past as Southerners certainly gave them few reasons and little direction for rejecting their racist positions. While the paternalistic approach to race, from which some southern reformers borrowed heavily, allowed a greater degree of flexibility in rearranging relations between black and white, it was based ultimately on a racism as strong as the other more explicitly racist approaches contemporary with it.

The Problem

Whatever break the Southern Populists made with their past was largely their own doing, owing little to their simple market society ideal and much to their human perception of the need for a society from which all and not just a few would benefit. "All," a very few of them realized, had to include blacks. Even if it was a qualified inclusion—almost completely qualified by many Southern Populists—it was more than white Southerners, or most of the rest of the country for that matter, would be willing to consider for at least a couple of generations.

In 1892 Watson, at great risk to himself, sat on and spoke from the same platforms as the black Populist, Reverend H. S. Doyle, and quickly offered him protection and aid when the stands he took in favor of Populism endangered Doyle's life. When Doyle appeared at Watson's door during the fall campaign to accept his offer, however, Watson put him in a "Negro house" in the yard.[85] Doyle, for all his courage and ability, would always have to stay in the Negro house. While it would be as unfair to castigate the Southern Populists for not having been color blind as it would be to describe them as typical southern racists, the racial attitudes of most of them remained indistinguishable from the overwhelming majority of southern whites. Only a few made any break with their past. But these few, particularly Watson,[86] in their rare moments moved against the tide and offered a limited improvement to the blacks which could not be classed as merely expedient and which would not be offered again for at least another fifty years.

PART II

THE DILEMMA OF REFORM

INTRODUCTION

The Southern Populists intended the specific reforms mentioned in the Omaha platform not only to meet specific and discreet problems, but also to be the cutting edge of a program designed to make America a simple market society where all had the chance at realizing a decent living from productive labor, and none had the right to ill-gotten gains. We have already seen, however, the tension between the Southern Populists' vision of a just and decent society and their commitment to a competitive, private property- and profit-oriented market economy. When they turned to the specific issues of the Omaha platform, this dilemma became more apparent, and more intractable.

On the land and railroad planks of the Omaha platform the Southern Populists generally agreed. They meant the land plank to destroy land monopoly and give Americans once again access to the cheap land they needed to create a society of independent producers. Government ownership of the railroads was necessary to make them accessible to the producers for the exchange of wealth. On the other hand, to determine land ownership by use threatened the Southerners' position as landlords or aspiring landlords, while government ownership of railroads raised the specter of socialism and an attack on private property and profits.

The Populists also intended their financial reforms to give the producers the tools they needed to create and exchange their wealth. On the surface, financial reform appeared easier to reconcile than the land and railroad issues with a commitment to a competitive market society. A split, however, existed among Southern Populists on the financial issue. The greenback position, focusing on a legal tender fiat currency and the subtreasury rather than free silver, led to an increased commitment to government activity in the social order, raising questions about monopoly and economic control. These questions forced the greenbackers into an unsatisfactory effort to balance private property and competition with government involvement in the social and economic order.

So even here the dilemma of reform was present. In fact, the radical greenbackers who best understood the country's currency problems and had the most sophisticated comprehension of the need for wide-ranging and basic changes were most clearly caught in the dilemma. As their greenback position led them into a thoroughgoing antimonopoly stance, they, too, stumbled on their commitment to America's basic economic system. Compounding the difficulty, for the radicals as well as all the other Southern Populists, not only the specific issues but the Southerners' very language underlined and contributed to their failure to solve the contradiction between their goal of a just and decent America and their desire to retain a competitive, private profit- and property-oriented market economy.

CHAPTER 6

Land and Transportation

The land, including
all the natural sources of wealth,
is the heritage of the people, and should not
be monopolized for speculative purposes, and
alien ownership of land should be prohibited. All land
now held by railroads and other corporations in ex-
cess of their actual needs, and all lands now
owned by aliens, should be reclaimed by
the government and held for
actual settlers only.
The land plank of the Omaha platform, July 1892.

Because it suggested to some the need for a thoroughgoing redistribution of land, this plank was potentially one of the most radical demands that the Southern Populists made. Its very radicalism, however, highlighted one of the most troublesome conflicts between the Southerners' perception of and their response to late nineteenth-century America. The unwillingness of most Southern Populists to abandon the possibility of becoming landlords pushed them, over the land issue, to one of their clearest denials of the simple market society ideal. As a result of the conflict the reformers usually left this demand much less well developed than the others.

Conditions unique to Texas—extensive immigration after the Civil War, often bloody conflict between large ranches and land companies and westward-moving small farmers, and a state policy which gave over thirty-two million acres of land to the railroads by 1882[1]—meant that concern with the land plank tended to be greatest in Texas. That did not mean, however, that reformers elsewhere paid no attention to the land question. Populists all over the South cited statistics on the growth of land monopoly in this country, and although many came up with somewhat different totals for the land held by aliens and corporations, their

71

figures most often concentrated between 230 and 250 million acres.[2] The conclusions drawn from these calculations did not vary much, either. To the editor of the Lampasas *People's Journal* this land represented "a sufficient amount, if reclaimed by the government, to provide a comfortable home for every man, in the United States who is without a home."[3] "Everyone," maintained a Georgia Populist, was "entitled" by virtue of his birth to, among other things, as much land "as is necessary, not only to his existence, but for a comfortable living provided he will exert himself towards that object."[4] Production required easy access to land, and corporate and alien land speculation threatened to make that access impossible for the producer.

The Southerners defined land speculation most often in terms of use. Merely selling land was not speculation, wrote the editor of the *Southern Mercury*. A speculator purchased and held land "without any effort to utilize it for production, letting it lay wild as a bar to progress or improvement."[5] Although large capitalistic agricultural units would fit under this definition of acceptable use of the land, since they, too, fully employed the productive power of the soil, this possibility did not occur to the Southern Populists any more than it did to most of their contemporaries. An end to land speculation and the establishment of a regime of home-owning producers seemed natural concomitants, an idea which their southern experience and their Jeffersonian heritage reinforced.

The relative importance of use in determining the just distribution of land, however, also caused some conflict among the Southern Populists, generally pitting the antimonopoly greenbackers against the financial reformers. The antimonopoly Texans consistently emphasized the idea of use in determining the proper distribution of land.[6] All people had a right to the land necessary to support themselves, and the needs of corporations, speculators, and large landowners came second. Logically, however, under this rule tenants also had more right than their landlords to the land they needed.

Although this emphasis on use as the only determinant for landownership appeared a couple of times east of Texas,[7] the Ozark *Banner-Advertiser* printed in early 1896 a short debate over its implications. A letter on land speculation touched the debate off. Like the rest of the Southern Populists, the author, a Mr. Barefield, condemned alien ownership of unused land by large corporations and foreigners. He wanted the government to redeem all this unused land and let it out "to such people as will use it for the purpose of making a living by cultivating it. Only such." Not this, but the first part of the letter triggered the controversy. Barefield had begun by pointing out that "our little home farmers, those who claim to be so opposed to speculation," frequently held more land than they could use and were among those who often charged a less fortunate man one-half of his crop "for the use of what is naturally his own"—the land he worked. Others called it rent; Mr. Barefield called it "legelized [*sic*] highway robbery. The land including all natural sources of wealth is or should be the heritage of all the people and should not be held by a man above his actual needs [for that] is robbing some one else by preventing him from using the land he is holding idle." For example, Barefield wrote, if one hundred men in his county owned one thousand acres apiece, and one hundred owned none, "how much better it would be for this one hundred thousands [*sic*] acres to be divided equally between them all and stop land renting and rowing. . . . Better still let no man lay claim to more land than he would actually use, and that would give every person who wants to work and is willing to work a chance to earn a living. This would be a long step toward conquering hard times. The above is an important factor in the oppression of the common people."[8]

A response came quickly from another Alabama Populist. He agreed with Barefield's argument as it applied to railroads and land companies, but "possession and occupancy" as an individual's "only protective title" would lead to constant war over developed land. This objection concerning title determination, an explicit one, was surmountable. The second objection was more implicit. Barefield's opponent warned him that "I haven't got but 145 acres and I am not going to let you hook me off of it, even if you do call me a thief and a robber for not dividing it with you. . . . [T]hink of your friends, even our [*sic*] aged parents," he asked. "[A]sk your baby if you are not wrong." He called on Barefield to "modify your most unreasonable demands on the government and against your fellow creatures."[9]

This was a more difficult objection. Following to its logical conclusion the idea that use ought to determine ownership, Barefield argued that neither the Southern Pacific railroad, nor any local landlord, used all the land they held, and in so doing contributed to the creation of a class of landless and homeless tenants. Barefield's opponent did not contest the assertion that people had a right to work their own land without having the rewards of such labor taken from them. That was a cardinal rule for all the Southern Populists. But many southern reformers, including perhaps Barefield's opponent, were landlords, or aspiring landlords, and Barefield's reasoning directly threatened that position. The tenant lost when a competitive, private ownership, profit-oriented system was applied to the use of land for farming. To allow some people to own more land than they could use themselves meant that God's rule for the good society—that all people had the right to the value of their labor—could not be fully realized. The Southern Populists, however, whatever the implications of their ideas, would never accede to ending that economic system, especially in their rural communities. Here again appeared the conflict between the reformers' design for the proper social order and their essential commitment to the basics of the existing one.

The *Banner-Advertiser* took no stand on the issue at all, and neither did most of the Southern Populists. Watson, however, did. As early as September 1894 he denied that the Populists taught that "no man is entitled to more land than he can cultivate for his own private uses."[10] By 1896, worried about a socialist threat to the Populist party, Watson wanted to drop the land plank of the Omaha platform because he felt it implied that the Populists advocated landownership by use alone. He contended that such an idea contradicted the private ownership of property. The person who developed the land had all rights to ownership of as much as he or she had improved. Without the developer, the land would have remained an unproductive wilderness.[11]

Nor were more firmly committed antimonopoly greenbackers willing to go as far as Barefield did. Judge Nugent, one of the few Southerners besides Watson to try coming to grips with the land issue, argued that "what a man produces by his labor, exerted upon land and aided by his legitimate surplus wealth, i.e., capital, he has the right to by the law of natural justice." This right, however, included the privilege of charging rent for land improved. Use remained the key to determining speculation, but Nugent defined speculation very narrowly as doing absolutely nothing with the land but waiting for its value to rise, excluding any form of renting or taking advantage of another's improvement.[12] Despite his avowal that "natural justice" guaranteed the fruits of a person's toil to that individual, Nugent said nothing about landlords who rented their land to tenants at exorbitant rates, receiving all the profits of their tenants' labor.

Of the few Southern Populists who tried, none really solved the conflict between demands for a home for everyone and an end to land speculation while retaining a competitive, market- and profit-oriented economy, even in its simple market form. A simple market society like that which Southern Populist thought usually implied, with no market in labor, allowed all to receive the full value of their toil. With no market in labor, landownership could easily be determined by use, since no one could rent land to another. Faced with the choice which the land issue so clearly demanded, the reformers rejected even their own ideal order, although most of them failed to grasp the contradiction and continued to insist that all producers receive the full value of their labor. A few of the more perceptive, like Watson and Nugent, did realize that when forced to choose between the landowners who feared the loss of some of their land and the tenants who had already lost theirs, most Southern Populists would, and did, side with the landowners.

That choice did not make the land question any less important, however. Since "all wealth is produced by the application of labor to land," wrote the editor of the *Southern Mercury*, the land "should be so guarded by law that any one desiring to produce wealth can secure the land as an adjunct of accomplishing this end."[13] More than enough land existed if the major land speculators could be put out of business.

> [A]s the commerce of civilized society consists of the production and distribution of what is known as wealth . . . there should be no monopoly of land. That vast tracts of land held either by individuals or corporations, without being occupied either as a home or used in the production of wealth, is contrary to divine law, in violation of every principle of civil liberty and justice known to Republican or Democratic government, and retards the advancement of civilization, disinherits posterity and creates an aristocracy of its holders and their offspring. A home and some portion of the earth from which to produce comforts, and upon which to rest our weary limbs after a day's toil in production; a home around which lingers a halo of endearment to every human being; a home, the absence of which tends to make man an alien to his God, an alien to his country, and to convert him into a vagabond, a wanderer and an outcast; is so essential to human happiness that the decay of liberty, the downfall of society and the wreck of happiness in every age and every country have been measured by the homeless numbers within her borders. Our platform contemplates a civilization in which the sacred rights of home in a reasonable amount of acres, and the production and enjoyment of comforts are held inviolable.[14]

This was the vision behind the land plank, the just, prosperous, middle-class, producer-oriented society. But of their major issues, the Southern Populists, even in Texas, discussed the land issue least. The inability of the Southerners to come to grips with a basic contradiction in their approach probably caused this neglect. While not so serious because it did not call for a repudiation of even their ideal order, a similar difficulty existed in the solution the Southern Populists proposed for the railroad problem and resulted in a similar, although less complete, lack of attention.

The Dilemma of Reform

Transportation being a means of exchange and
a public necessity, the government should own and operate
the railroads in the interest of the people.
The transportation plank of the Omaha platform, July 1892.

The Southern Populists entertained no doubts about the need for or advantages of the railroads. "It is not the railroads of which the people complain," said the radical Texas Allianceman Evan Jones, "but the abuses of their power, chartered rights, and privileges."[15] The Populists' historians have already covered well the long and detailed list of what the reformers meant by "abuses": stock watering, rebates, drawbacks, preferential rates, concessions to large shippers, legislative bribery, free passes, etc.[16] To these particular charges, however, the Southern Populists added some more general but equally important violations which their historians have not detailed as adequately. As the biggest single landowner in the country, for instance, the railroads were intimately involved in the land question.

The reformers also spoke of the oppression of the working people, especially railroad employees. The accident rate for workers, wrote the editor of the *Texas Advance*, declined significantly in countries where the government owned and operated the railroads.[17] The *Progressive Farmer* estimated that with government ownership the workers would receive the nearly $500,000 a day "now going into the pockets of railroad wreckers."[18] Behind the desire to improve the lot of railroad employees, however, often lay another consideration. Except for the socialist papers in Texas, the benefits accruing to the working people from government ownership and operation usually remained a necessary but secondary consideration.[19] Especially after Pullman the reformers considered ending the social disorder brought by strikes a more important goal. The Southern Populists wanted peaceful change. Deeply attached to the idea of an orderly society and to the safety and security of personal and private property, they frowned on the threat of violence and social upheaval presented by the Pullman strike's riots, federal troops, and nationwide rail tieup.[20]

Not that they were hostile to the strikers only. The fear of an alliance between the military and monopoly, as in the Pullman strike, provoked as much concern as any activity of the strikers.[21] Cleveland and company often bore the brunt of denunciations the Southern Populists made of the events surrounding the strike. But little indicated that the reformers understood the conditions with which the Pullman workers dealt or the pressure on Debs and his American Railway Union to join the strike. Lacking good information, and with little in their experience to help them sympathize with a situation so different from their own, the reformers often denounced the strikers, too, out of their concern with social order. Both sides appeared to threaten disaster, and government ownership promised to end the threat from both. It "would remove the causes of the hatred of the people to the Roads and harmonize all interests," wrote Watson. "It would equalize all avocations and shippers; and would take away the power the Roads now have to destroy a business, a section or an individual. . . . It would be a giant strike in the direction of equality and manhood rights and to the destruction of our Class System of Special Privilege, Shoddy Aristocracy based on Commercial Spoils and advancing through the dirty lanes and perils of bribery and corruption."[22] In a word, government ownership of the railroads would go far to help realize the Southern Populists' conception of the proper society and in the process eliminate some of the most serious threats of social upheaval.

The most important reason for controlling the railroads, however, involved their connection with production. The American producer created more of the "abundance of everything necessary to the content and comfort of mankind" than any other ever before, stated North Carolina Populist Pat Winston. Yet there were "more than 4,000,000 of our countrymen without sufficient food, raiment and shelter." Why? Because private ownership of the railroads hampered production and prevented an equitable distribution of wealth both by allowing a few individuals to charge rates that ate up the legitimate profits of the producers and by making the cost of their produce so high that many could not afford to buy it.[23] Such an argument implied that the railroads were not ordinary property because they had qualities which made them, in some ways, public institutions. Arguing for government ownership, Marion Butler attempted to pin down why railroads should not be considered ordinary private property with which the owner could do anything he pleased. "[A]ny business that affects all or a great portion of the people, under circumstances where there could be no successful competition by men of small capital," he wrote, "[is] a *government function* and should be owned and operated by the government, at cost, for the benefit of all the people alike." He opposed allowing "private individuals and corporations to have charge of or control any business that was a monopoly *per se*," because private individuals would not run such monopolies "for the benefit of the people, but would take advantage of their monopoly to bleed the people for the benefit of a few."[24] Others agreed with him.[25] Because of the importance to everyone in society of an equitable distribution of wealth, and because of the ease with which the railroads could distribute that wealth unfairly, they had to be considered essentially public utilities. In private hands they threatened the public interest because competition failed to keep them responsive to the needs of the people who used them. With the rejection of regulation by government commission,[26] government ownership became the only alternative to the continued robbery of the many for the benefit of the few.[27]

The argument for the essentially public, unavoidably monopolistic nature of the railroads was of great importance to the Southern Populists. Unless the railroads could be defined primarily as public utilities, their opponents could accuse the reformers of demanding that the government take over private property, which clearly looked like socialism and an attack on the existing economic order. If, however, railroads were and always had been natural monopolies like the mail service and were wrongfully in private hands, then these charges could not be made so easily and the threat to private property rendered less potent an attack.

The antimonopoly greenbackers, however, sometimes explicitly asserted that in certain cases, the railroads in particular, considerations of the public interest took precedence over questions of private rights. "Government is instituted," wrote one Texan in 1892, "on the idea that private rights must yield to the general good. It is pursuant to this principle that the railroads obtained their franchises, and pursuant to the same principle they must yield back the right in turn to the higher right and sovereign well-being of the country."[28] Where most southern reformers urged government ownership because the existing danger of the railroads to society demanded such an extreme step, these people argued that the beneficial idea of government ownership might best be applied to the railroads because of their importance to society. Underneath the difference lay the antimonopoly greenbackers' greater ease with the need for increased government participation in the social and economic life of the country.

The great number of Southern Populists were never so cavalier with private interests and rights. They remained unable openly to place the public welfare before private rights like property ownership, although most of them implicitly made this argument since the railroads in the 1890s were privately owned and operated. The efforts to disguise the conflict between public and private rights which lay at the center of the issue considerably blunted the force of the railroad demand. While the reformers eventually supported government ownership, the commitment to private property and their intellectual and sectional heritage prevented them from working out a clearer rationale for their railroad plank. The most radical of them, the antimonopoly greenbackers, came closest to resolving the conflict only by rejecting some of their heritage and their affection for the fundamentals of the existing economic system.

Efforts to skirt the issue of private versus public rights almost always led the Southern Populists back to law and the Constitution. We discussed most of the general problems that the reformers faced with the

Constitution in chapter 4, but we have not yet considered several such efforts related specifically to the railroads. Watson chose one popular way to avoid the clash with private rights yet fit government ownership into the American legal structure by arguing that "the evolution of modern society" had made railroads replacements for waterways and highways as means of public transportation. In the "public interest" the Constitution made waterways public, and Congress later did the same for roads. "Should not the railroads also be made public property, in the public interest, especially considering the danger to that interest poised by private ownership?"[29] Of course, this argument said nothing about states' rights and strict construction, and ignored the question of the private rights of the existing owners to their property.

To solve both these last two problems, some southern reformers turned to the right of eminent domain, guaranteed to the federal government by the Constitution.[30] James Davis stated that the right of eminent domain established the government's right to build any form of highway for the public good and argued that, by extension, it established the government's right to own and operate such highways, including railroads.[31] One drawback, of course, was that the land granted to the roads was overwhelmingly public land and eminent domain had played little role. Such grants could be construed much more easily to be direct subsidies by the government to what remained all along private enterprise and property. Also, while eminent domain allowed seizure, it did not necessarily imply the ownership and operation of the seized property.

A third rather roundabout and debatable constitutional argument used by a few southern reformers involved the idea that the government could not legitimately permit the exercise of power that the government itself did not possess. The opponents of government ownership did not realize, maintained one Texan, that the railroads in private hands exercised power which no government in America possessed: the power to levy and collect taxes without permission from the people. If the government could not exercise such power, how could the government allow a private individual or group of men to do so?[32] To call levying rates a species of taxation, however, stretched a point. This argument could be used to demand federal control of any national necessity. It might be maintained that the government ought to control the price of food, or even own the farms and the processing industries, a situation with which the Southern Populists undoubtedly would not have been very happy. They might like to set these prices themselves, but to have the government do it could not really be welcome.

The effort to fit the demand for government ownership of the railroads into a coat of constitutional respectability was limited largely to Watson and the Texans. Except for the few antimonopoly greenbackers,[33] most

Southern Populists remained unwilling to break at all with inherited intellectual and sectional political traditions and begin to argue from the general welfare clause and a loose construction of the Constitution for an expanded role of the government in society. The effort to make Jefferson, strict construction, and states' rights fit government ownership, as we have seen, generally ended looking like a clever exercise in word juggling rather than a solid interpretation of the Constitution. Much more easily and effectively the opponents of government ownership could point out that Jefferson never said anything about the issue, and that his dictum about the best government governing least proved his opposition. Even Davis's considerable efforts to get Jefferson behind government ownership resulted in a Jefferson unrecognizable to the majority of Southerners including, it seems reasonable to say, many Populists.

In an effort which rejected both Jefferson and constitutional arguments, a few Texans tried to solve the problems of government ownership by arguing that in some cases the public good ought to override private rights. But even among the antimonopoly greenbackers a solid commitment to private property and profit paralleled their tentative questioning of the absolute primacy of private rights. None of the rest of the Southern Populists accepted even the limited questioning of private rights. Besides ignoring Jefferson and traditional constitutional references, this argument sounded too much like socialism, the label which most Americans, including the Southern Populists, put on any threat to everyone's right to their own property, pocketbook, and possible advantage over their neighbors.

These two influences, one from the past and one from contemporary society, reinforced each other and prevented most Southern Populists from even trying to work out a more adequate philosophy of government to suit the needs of their demand for government ownership of the railroads. Only the efforts of a few of the more radical kept the demand, like the land plank, visible. The rest avoided long or substantive discussions of the issue, never devoting much time or attention to it. Such was not true, however, of their financial demands.

CHAPTER 7

Money and the Financial System

"**M**oney, our tool of exchange; money with which we cultivate our farms; money, the very life blood of our industries," wrote a Georgia Populist in the spring of 1892, and his brethren all over the South echoed his sentiments.[1] Money and financial reform attracted more of their attention than any of the Southern Populists' other issues. Although the financial reformers and the antimonopoly greenbackers disagreed on the ultimate import of financial reform, both agreed that the right starting point for an attack on the problems of American society lay with the correct ordering of the country's financial system. Because of the importance of this issue, the strengths and weaknesses of the Southern Populists' analysis and experience often showed quite clearly in their discussion of the proper financial system.

The ambiguities surrounding the Southern Populists' short political history showed clearly here as well, including the central one: Why did the Southern Populists first break with the Democrats over the subtreasury plan, only to accept fusion with them in 1896 on a free silver platform? More than practical politics dictated the switch from the subtreasury, a radical issue, to free silver, a moderate or conservative one. Practical politicians, as the experience of the Progressives later showed, would not have left the Democratic party in the first place. More importantly, the Southern Populists failed to create an unambiguous alternative to American industrial and financial capitalism. This failure was not primarily one of politics, but of analysis. Politics was merely its more visible public manifestation. Understanding this means first understanding in some detail exactly how the Southern Populists thought about the place of money in late nineteenth-century American society.

"Money is not, in itself, a curse," wrote a Louisiana Populist. "It is only the wrong use of it that becomes a 'root of all evils.'"[2] The ends it served determined its effect on people and society. Money used in the production of tangible wealth, for instance, was used correctly and to the people's benefit. Money used otherwise, or not used at all, was bad.[3]

Only a correctly ordered financial system could assure the proper use of money. The correct monetary system had certain qualities which reflected the Southern Populists' commitment to a simple market society of producers. To facilitate the exchange of wealth between individual producers money could not interfere with those exchanges. In order to represent the exchange value of different commodities, in order to reflect accurately the relative amount of labor put into the two products being exchanged, money itself could not be a commodity. To facilitate adequately the exchange of commodities money also had to be readily available and cheap. The easiest way to guarantee all these qualities, a way sanctioned by the reformers' greenback heritage, was to give the federal government control of the currency. This greenback monetary system was, in fact, a quite sophisticated idea, considerably more accurate in its basic assumption of a quantity theory of money than the Southern Populists' opponents' defense of an intrinsic value, redemption, specie standard monetary system. Unfortunately, however, this sophistication meant that very few of the Southern reformers ever integrated all their requirements for a proper monetary system into a coherent whole.

On the other hand, all the Southern Populists were familiar with at least several parts of it. Among the reformers the most widely known characteristic of the proper financial system was the importance of the amount of money in circulation. "The civilization, christianity, integrity, morality and prosperity of any country and the degree of intelligence of the people," wrote a Florida Populist, "could safely be gagued [sic] by the amount of money in circulation, not the quality of the money but the quantity."[4] Like any other commodity, the supply and demand for its use determined the value of money. When the supply of money fell but the demand for it remained the same, or when the supply of money stayed constant and the demand for it rose, each unit of currency, each dollar, had to go further and so became worth more in terms of a fixed unit of any commodity. Its price had gone up and, according to the Southerners, it had become more valuable.[5] For this reason both Watson and the editor of the *Southern Mercury*, when speaking of commodity prices, postulated that any decline in the money supply violated "the natural laws of supply and demand." In the proper financial system this did not occur. "With a sufficient per capita circulation of money," the editor of the *Mercury* stated, "prices would be absolutely or only subject to supply and demand and the laws and customs of trade," and money would not, as it should not, "influence values one way or the other."[6] The Southern Populists intended their demands for financial reform, among other things, to prevent money from affecting market values of other commodities.

When the quantity of money in circulation did affect market values serious consequences followed. Contraction of the money supply brought hard times for the producers, benefiting only creditors, the moneylending and nonproducing classes. As a dollar gradually bought more and more products, loans undertaken by producers appreciated in value, as did the interest due on them, and each dollar borrowed required more and more labor to repay it.[7] Some Southern Populists, remembering back thirty years to the immediate post-Civil War era, could provide evidence that the prices of goods they had to buy had fallen much less than those of the produce they offered for sale, not to mention the increased cost of credit.[8] The panics of 1873 and 1893, argued the editor of the *Randolph Toiler*, grew from the same bad seed, the "scarcity of money." A reduction of the currency in circulation had "reduced the prices of products and the people could not meet their obligations and that is what caused hard times then and the same thing is causing it now."[9]

Most, although not all of the broader discussions of the adverse effects of contraction on the health of society came from the antimonopoly greenbackers, and subsequent developments have proven the general, if not always specific accuracy of their arguments. In 1895 Judge Nugent told the Texas Farmers' Alliance that those producing the wealth, if they had enough money, in large part consumed what they created. But insufficient currency in circulation kept prices ruinously low, the producers had no way to buy, and business suffered.[10] Worse, wrote the editor of the Austin *Argus* in mid-1894, contraction had made money so valuable that those who held it could make more by putting it into nonproductive areas than by investing it in building new factories and railroads, opening new mines, and cultivating new land. Without money "actively seeking investment" there could be no "enduring prosperity," for the production of wealth could not increase.[11]

Expansion of the money supply would not only improve the debtor producer's position, but rising prices would also bring back that general confidence the conservatives wanted so badly. In this matter of the "cause" of the depression and the approach ultimately necessary for recovery, these southern farmers had the better of Cleveland and the goldbugs. Both Judge Nugent and the editor of the *Southern Mercury* maintained that after the Civil War, when prices were high and the promise of profits great, "the spirit of enterprise and speculation pervaded all ranks of society; money sought investment in useful industries; labor was employed and tramps were unknown."[12] These antimonopoly greenbackers knew that declining investments in the United States did not come from a fear that the country would not pay its debts in gold. They knew that investors did not care whether money was gold, silver, or paper; investors wanted dividends and profits. These Populists argued that with an increase in the per capita circulation, profits would reappear, the business world revive, and investment rise again.[13]

The solution to the evils of contraction proceeded from the Southern Populists' quantity theory. To prevent contraction the supply of dollars had to match the demand for their use. While their language would not have been as precise, almost all Southern Populists agreed with the editor of the *Texas Advance* that the purchasing power of the dollar "depends on the quantity of money in circulation as compared with the transactions that have to be paid in money." To keep the purchasing power of the dollar reasonably uniform in relation to commodity prices—to keep the variation in the price of any commodity determined solely by the market's supply and demand mechanism—the volume of money had to increase at the same rate as the population and commerce increased.[14] This definition of commodity price stability, of course, ruled out calling for a specific policy of continued inflation.[15] The Southern Populists often made quite explicit their opposition to inflation. The "honest dollar," fair to debtor and creditor and defended by a North Carolina Populist, preserved "a constancy in purchasing power as near as may be to commodities in general . . . [and] does not fluctuate materially either way up or down."[16] Then only the prices of commodities, determined by supply and demand, would change.[17]

While literally all the Southern Populists, however, knew that to increase the quantity of money would increase prices and quite a few of them knew that to keep prices steady when the number of transactions increased, the amount of money in circulation had to expand, very few understood the last necessary component of a quantity theory of money, velocity. Only in this area did the sophistication of the southern reformers' monetary theory fail to match or exceed that of their conservative opponents. They did not realize that a dollar which circulated through ten hands did ten times the work of one which changed hands only once during the same interval.[18] This meant a whole range of ideas remained unavailable to them, particularly the use of credit to keep the money supply expanding at the necessary rate. For other reasons which will be discussed later in this chapter, they opposed credit and the idea of credit as money. Nevertheless, ignorance of this element of the quantity theory helped preserve the opposition. In addition, it meant that the Southern Populists could not explain any increase in prices not due to an increase in the quantity of money in circulation or a decline in the number of transactions, leaving a serious weakness in their arguments for an expansion of the money supply. Unfortunately, in certain areas of the United States, particularly the Northeast, a rapid development of credit and banking facilities after the Civil War had greatly increased the velocity, and thus the quantity, of money in effective circulation.[19]

Next to their belief that the quantity of currency in circulation determined the value of the dollar, the most widespread idea about money among the Southern Populists concerned its fiat nature. Like the greenbackers before them they considered money a creation of the law, nothing more and nothing less. They agreed with the Louisiana reformer that "as a basic proposition . . . there is no money except that created by law and . . . it is not the material out of which it is made that gives it the character of money but it is the law behind it and without that law nothing would be money."[20] As a consequence many of the Southern Populists rejected the notion, almost universal in the rest of American society, that money had to have an intrinsic value. They joined the Alabama Populist editor who pointed out in mid-1893 that although only one hundred million dollars in gold existed to redeem three hundred and fifty million in greenbacks, a greenback dollar was worth the same as a gold one in purchasing power, "not because they are redeemable in that metal, but because they are a legal tender for all debts between citizens."[21] Fiat money already circulated as good money in the United States. Money's purchasing power depended only on the government stamp which made twenty nickels, ten dimes, or one silver dollar worth the same amount as one gold dollar, although the market value of the metal in each, the intrinsic value, amounted to less than that of the gold in the gold dollar.[22]

Many of the Southerners' opponents claimed that gold in fact acted as "international money" and thus should be America's money in order to facilitate exchange with and investment from foreign countries. A few Southern Populists, like the editor of the *Texas Advance*, used the fiat nature of money to counter accurately that countries dealt with each other not by exchanging money but by exchanging commodities, which could be corn, wheat, iron, or cotton as easily as, and more frequently than, gold or silver. The gold and silver used in foreign trade were not so employed as money, for to be money they depended on the authority of the United States government to enforce their legal tender aspect. The American government could not force an Englishman in London to accept an American dollar in payment for a debt, nor did any international authority exist that could enforce it.[23]

Finally, fiat money required no redeemer. That the stamp of the government on silver worth fifty cents or gold worth eighty cents gave them both a purchasing power of one dollar, made the redemption of a gold dollar with a dollar's worth of gold, or a silver dollar with a dollar's worth of silver, as ridiculous as it was expensive.[24] Only a few Southern

Populists, however, distinguished clearly between the commodity value of coin and its monetary value, although all their discussions of fiat money implied this. We will consider later, when we discuss free silver more specifically, the results of the failure to make clearer distinctions and work out implications in this matter.

The third major defining quality of money entailed its proper use. "Mere barter" would not sustain "a highly civilized community."[25] Money was necessary "to facilitate trade and to effect exchanges and sustain commerce within a country."[26] This made it a key, of course, to the development and maintenance of the proper social order. "[A]s the representative of everything produced," wrote a Georgia Populist, money helped distribute produced goods. Money was only "a counter" which improved on the method of "swapping a sow and pigs for a suit of clothes."[27] The exchange of produced goods for each other, not goods for money, constituted the commerce of society.[28] The sharpest of the southern reformers realized that this was why the commodity value of the substance out of which money was made should never be confused with money itself. As "a medium of exchange and a measure of value" only, money had no "intrinsic value." The editor of the *Texas Advance* felt that money should be made from the cheapest material available to help prevent confusion between the legal tender fiat value of money and its value as a commodity, its "intrinsic value," determined by the supply and demand for the commodity on the market.[29]

Money was not wealth. The "real wealth" of a nation, stated a North Carolina Populist, "is the capacity to produce something, hence the wealth of a nation is land and men." Money was only "the legal representative of wealth" which enabled different produced commodities to be measured against each other and exchanged.[30] It had an important role vis-à-vis production, but production and productive labor always remained more important.[31] As southern reformers pointed out, "men could live on the products of labor, such as grains, the meats, and cotton without a cent of money."[32] Money's proper use reflected the simple market ideal from which the analysis of it sprang. In such a society money existed only to allow a comparison of the value of two or more kinds of tangible wealth, thus facilitating the exchange and increase of wealth in an America of independent producers.

The relationship between the Southern Populists' ideal social order and the proper financial system was intimate, the latter emerging from and depending on the former. As with the land and transportation issues, the reformers' critique of the country's problems and the solutions for them grew out of an often implicitly held social and economic alternative. The complexity of the financial issue, however, meant that only a very few

Southern Populists attempted to combine their ideas about the quantity theory of money or its fiat nature with their conception of money's role in the simple market society which America ought to be. Watson applied the idea of the proper function of money to the quantity theory several times. In July 1892 he pointed out that contrary to what many people thought, God did not make money like He made air and water. Human beings created money to avoid the inconvenience and effort of bartering, and it should have no other use. To accomplish this end "the amount of money in use" had to maintain a constant ratio with the need for it. Then the market alone determined the price or value of a particular commodity and money played no role but that of easing its exchange for other produced commodities.[33]

While Southern Populism offered numerous examples of the connection between the proper function of money and its fiat nature, few Southern Populists, all of them antimonopoly greenbackers, combined all three of the basic ideas about money. "Money," insisted the editor of the *Southern Mercury*, "is not a substance. It's a law, a decree." Its fiat nature dictated that "money is not a value within itself; it is simply a medium through which wealth is exchanged from hand to hand."[34] In order, however, for money to reflect only the comparative values of any commodity as determined by demand (often called "usefulness") and supply (often called the "labor cost"), the quantity of money in circulation must match the need for it. If the quantity of money grew progressively smaller while the demand for it increased, or the reverse occurred, the quantity of money affected the prices (often called "values") of commodities sold and bought, and thus did more than merely facilitate exchanges. It interfered with the market's setting the proper relationship in value between any two or more commodities. While such comprehensive attempts to link any of the three ideas into a logical whole were rare, the failure to do so attested to the complexity of the financial issue, not to the absence of a simple market ideal among the reformers. To one degree of complexity or another, all three ideas formed a common currency in the Southern Populists' discussions of money.

Beyond questions of what money was or ought to be, the Southern Populists also had several particular ideas about the financial system, about what money ought to do. The first of these appeared as a widespread demand which, as other of their historians have noted, grew directly out of the southern reformers' experience as farmers and their aspirations to economic independence.[35] The idea, while not entirely original to them, the Southern Populists made important in greenback monetary theory. They wanted "a flexible medium of exchange" which contracted and expanded "to meet the contraction and expansion of the demand for money caused by the great bulk of the crops being placed upon the market in the fall and winter months."[36] C. W. Macune, a major figure in the Farmers' Alliance, estimated that prices varied as much as forty percent between the time that the farmers had to sell and when they provisioned themselves for the coming year.[37] The Committee on the Monetary System, which first announced the subtreasury plan to the Alliance at St. Louis in 1889, pointed out that a large per capita circulation was not enough by itself. If the supply of currency remained unresponsive to the need for it, half the year there still would be too much money and the other half too little, both of which conditions "cut against the producer." The producers needed a financial system "conducted in such a manner as to secure a certain augmentation of supply at the season of the year in which the agricultural additions to the wealth of the nation demand money, and a diminution in such supply of money as said agricultural products are consumed." A high average amount would not suffice. The producers required a system "that adjusts itself to the wants of the country at all seasons."[38] A financial system in which the volume of business and the growth of population controlled the amount of money in circulation had to be flexible enough to provide short-term as well as long-term price stability.

The second widespread demand made by the Southern Populists on the financial system they also linked closely to their quantity theory. They wanted cheap money issued directly by the government. If "government is, or should be, the will of the majority for the greatest good to the largest number," asked an Alabama reformer, "why should not the government supercede avaricious men and blind nature in the creation and distribution of money?" As "a convenience to commerce and trade," it should be accessible to all "at first cost."[39] Without a cheap, readily accessible supply of currency, production and trade would eventually decline for lack of money.

The "avaricious men" referred to above were bankers, especially national bankers.[40] Since supply and demand regulated interest rates, money's price, by keeping the supply of money short while the demand for it from producers remained constant or increased, bankers could and did force up interest rates and appropriate to themselves a greater and greater part of the wealth created by productive labor. They perverted for their own advantage money's true function as a representative of wealth.[41] Money had to be kept in circulation to promote productive labor. Prosperity depended on the freedom of the currency from control and concentration in a few hands. Money ought to be fiat and representative in function, and in supply abundant. The financial system which governed money's distribution had to be flexible in response to varying demands for it in the economy, had to provide it cheaply enough for the producers to have easy access, and had to protect it from the control of a few individuals or groups, leaving it free to circulate widely and easily among the people. Such was the form taken and function played by money in the proper society.

This analysis, of course, was not particularly new in America. Both Alexander Campbell and Edward Kellogg, the intellectual fathers of the greenback monetary analysis, had argued for similar monetary systems, although the Southern Populists shared more with Kellogg than with Campbell.[42] Again, as in their elaboration of a labor theory of value, the Southern Populists' analysis of money reflected their class position, even though that position was deteriorating rapidly. They still spoke for a simple market society of producers who exchanged among themselves the wealth they created with their own labor and who remained free of capital, though not money. The Southerners, whether tenants or land-owners, whether trapped in the crop lien or not, aspired to the position of independent producers and elaborated a rough social philosophy which reflected this aspiration. This may not have been the most effective way to oppose the expansion of American industrial and financial capitalism, and as we will see actually conflicted with some of that society's rewards which the southern reformers wanted. It did, however, as we shall also see, provide the base, along with the Southerners' evangelical Protestant heritage, for a remarkably accurate analysis of the injustice and human toll the advance of American capitalism took.

The Southern Populists' opposition to credit and interest, mentioned earlier, in part grew from the same roots as their monetary theory—their class position, their simple market ideal, and their greenback inheritance. Since labor, not money, created wealth, interest had a tendency to stifle productive activity and enrich a few idle plutocrats, especially when, according to one Georgia Populist, "the usual interest drain upon the producer is greater than the annual production of wealth minus the cost of living."[43] Normally the Southern Populists did not oppose interest completely. Watson, for instance, felt that everyone had the right to charge for the use of anything which represented their "stored up labor," such as their horse, their land, or their money. "Tyranny" began only when people were forced to pay "a royalty" on the money needed to effect their exchanges, for at that point "the man that has the money has the advantage over those who have the produce with which to pay for that money."[44] Watson did not attempt to fix with any precision the point at which interest representing stored-up labor became interest representing a royalty on the use of money. He would have been hard pressed to do so. Maximum interest laws had failed conspicuously in the South.[45]

Watson also realized, perhaps better than many other of his compatriots, that the reformers could not reject interest while clinging to the basic assumptions of a market economy. But he was not alone. Judge Nugent of Texas also saw the possible clash, but chose to deal with it in a slightly different manner. Although interest and rent had cursed the human race since its infancy, he felt that until the "millennium . . . land, labor and capital will remain . . . as the factors employed by organized civil society in the production of wealth, and as long as these remain rent and interest in some form or degree will continue to exist." What a man produced by his labor, "aided by his legitimate surplus wealth, i.e., capital, belongs to him. . . . [H]e has a right to charge for its use."[46] Nugent, even more clearly than Watson sometimes, chose what he felt to be the lesser of two evils. Because of their commitment to a market economy both chose to tolerate interest.

A few other southern reformers who sought a more precise limit for permissible interest drew upon an idea which, like their monetary theory, ran back through the Alliance and the greenbackers to the National Safety Fund scheme of Edward Kellogg. In particular they elaborated on Kellogg's idea of determining the maximum permissible interest rate by comparing it to the annual increase in wealth produced in the country. Kellogg calculated this to be about two or three percent annually.[47] The figures used by the Southern Populists varied somewhat around this figure, but the idea remained basically the same for all who used it. The editor of the *Alliance Herald* of Montgomery, Alabama, for instance, using seven percent as the average yearly interest rate and three and a half percent for the "normal accumulation of labor," calculated that by 1904 the money power would own wealth equaling all the property in the country minus the railroads.[48]

It seemed only common sense to these Populists that the legitimate interest rate had to be kept below the annual increase of total wealth, giving the producers some chance to pay off their debts, not to speak of winning some profit from their labors. Most southern reformers, however, rested content with opposing interest rates much greater than two percent annually. They either did not bother with or did not understand the connection made by a few between total wealth produced and the interest rate. And only the most perceptive tried to analyze the problem of interest in terms of what it meant for the Populists' desire to maintain what they understood as the existing economic system while at the same time trying to correct some of its basic abuses.

The southern reformers spent little effort examining interest as a monetary problem partly because much of their hostility to it sprang from a different source, opposition to usury. On a strictly theoretical basis the Alabama Populist who argued that his state's usury law had failed to work because the supply of money was short and the demand for it great, and who suggested as a solution not tightening the usury law but increasing the quantity of money,[49] stood on solid Populist ground. That almost all the Southern Populists never used this argument indicated how much the lien system outraged them and how extensively they relied on religious and moral metaphors and imagery to express this outrage. When discussing the problem of interest as interest, few Southern Populists argued for its abolition.[50] Questions of how much and what kind of interest remained important. When the discussion focused around usury, however, such questions often disappeared. Many Southern Populists agreed with the North Carolina reformer who in 1896 contrasted Christ's teaching of reform law, particularly "'Love thy neighbor as thyself,'" with the Devil's usury, "the most gigantic power for the subjection of industrial humanity that has ever appeared on earth." One did not seek an acceptable median between these two. "Usury—interest on money, in this age of scientific and commercial progress and human liberty, is not a necessary concomitant to a monetary system that shall be suitable for the commercial business of the present age of human progress."[51] Interest as usury had to go, not only to bring society into harmony with the teachings of Christ but also to assure the progress of modern America. In fact, as seen earlier, the two went hand in hand.

Most of this condemnation of interest as usury came from the Southeast, but not all of it. One of the most thorough denunciations appeared in early 1896 in the stronghold of antimonopoly greenbackism. This Texas Populist covered it all. Interest as usury stole the producer's wealth day and night, seven days a week, fifty-two weeks a year. It threatened the social order by creating millionaires and paupers, by robbing the producers of the fruits of their toil, by defying the law of God that all should eat only by the sweat of their own brows.[52] Unlike a Florida Populist who wrote that usury was not, "as some would say, interest charged above the legal rate but it is simply interest,"[53] many Southern Populists hesitated to demand the full abolition of interest because of their adherence to private ownership and profit. But when interest became identified with usury, its connection to these beliefs was far less apparent, and under the rubric of usury many more Southern Populists rejected interest. The metaphor and imagery used had a definite effect on the response of the Southern Populists to what remained in essence the same problem, that of interest taken on money.

For obvious reasons the Southern Populists' attitudes towards interest were closely related to their notions about credit. Very few Southern Populists maintained that credit was critical to the continuation of what they understood to be the proper economic order.[54] In the fall of 1894, when the Democratic Atlanta *Constitution* argued that "debt has been one of the leading factors of our progress," fighting wars and building industry, Watson took strong exception. The *Constitution*, he felt, had overlooked the poverty of "the honest toiler" and his pain upon realizing that despite his "fruitful fields" and "abundant harvests," debt prevented him from properly housing, feeding, clothing, and educating his family. "An industrial system founded upon debt is not a factor of real prosperity. It breeds the extremes of wealth and poverty, the millionaire and the tramp, a feast for the one and a famine for another. To teach that it is a blessing is un-Christian—it is untrue."[55] If debt meant suffering, even disaster to the producers, how could it be necessary to America's growth and progress? The one precluded the other. Watson did not understand what the *Constitution* meant or how credit functioned in the system in which he believed. His experience had shown him the miserable effects of high interest on southern agriculture and farmers but had not acquainted him with the operation of industrial capitalism.

The same was true of almost all the Southern Populists. They had little notion of the role credit played in maintaining and building the very economic system they accepted and defended. An editorial in the Richmond, Virginia, *Times* claimed that since most of the business of the country was done by check, little need for currency remained. This was not true, argued the editor of the *Progressive Farmer*. Even if everyone did all their business by check, he asserted, "the amount of money needed to do the business of the country would not be one cent less, for the check only represents cash. . . . We cannot believe that the Times [*sic*] is ignorant enough to believe what it writes."[56] The editor of the *Farmer* could not conceive of a situation in which a merchant wrote a check on a loan which he received from a bank whose cash reserves would not cover it completely. The creation of money out of nothing, without one lick of work producing tangible wealth, probably never caused the huge uproar it could have only because most Southern Populists knew too little about credit and banking to understand that this might take place. Even if they received evidence of it, as did this editor, they often found it impossible to believe.[57]

There were examples of opposition to all credit elsewhere.[58] A North Carolina reformer who wrote extensively for Alliance and Populist papers in his state during the period provided the most interesting example of the ironies that could attend the demand for its abolition. One of the few Southern Populists who tried to come to grips with some of the implications of industrial development for American society, James Murdock understood that the concentration of industry represented an increase in the scale of production and felt that the future economic

development of the country lay with huge industrial and business combinations, for they could produce far more and far more efficiently than
small businessmen or manufacturers. The distinct danger was that these
huge combinations which could so benefit the people could just as easily
exploit them. The combinations already did so, partly because the credit
system encouraged incompetence by levying on the diligent the cost of
the defaulting borrower, which led to "recklessness in buying" and fostered "rascality and laziness." This kind of slackness was "one of the
principle causes of our panics. Pay as you go, should be the watchword of
individuals and nations." As part of his solution Murdock proposed
"abolishment of the credit system."[59] While Murdock argued from a
relatively sophisticated perception of the importance of America's post-
Civil War industrial development, a far cry from the simple market society of independent small producers that still dominated the thinking of
most Southern Populists, he shared with them one important solution to
America's ills, abolition of credit. No more than the rest of the southern
reformers did he realize the implications of such a step for American
industrial capitalism.

Murdock and other Southern Populists who dealt with this problem
wanted to replace the credit system with one based on cash only. In a
cash system, an Alabama editor argued, the extravagance and debt, the
mortgages, foreclosures, and exploitation brought by the lien system
would disappear. "It would bring about honest and true competition in
business. It would lower prices on the goods that we buy, for the difference between what is known as a credit price and a cash price would be
taken off." By eliminating all lending at interest the reform would force
millionaires, if they wanted profits, to put their money into "developing
the resources of the country" by investing it in productive enterprises.[60]
From the Southwest came the same demand;[61] the power of the lien
system knew no bounds in the South. Not even the antimonopoly greenback editor of the *Texas Advance*, who once criticized an article in the
Boston *Arena* for claiming that by abolishing rent and interest the country could avoid panics,[62] was immune to the desire for the abolition of
credit in favor of cash. The banker, speculator, and stock manipulator
might find credit advantageous, but it brought only panic and debt to the
masses who produced the wealth. "The fact is," the editor commented,
"if there were sufficient money to do the business of the country on a
cash basis absolutely, we could, and necessarily would, have the most
systematic and economical financial system ever established."[63]

Their treatment of interest and credit once again revealed the Southern
Populists' predominantly rural, agricultural experience. It disclosed the
destructive impact of the lien system on their class and the influence of

evangelical Protestantism and greenbackism on their attempts to resist it. The confluence of these things made the Southern Populists, in the case of interest and credit, unresponsive to the needs of the very industrial system to whose benefits they all remained quite committed.

Behind the Southern Populists' demands for financial reform lay a group of generally inherited and shared ideas about money and the proper financial organization. They recognized money as fiat in nature, its value determined by the quantity of it in circulation, not by its "intrinsic value." Ideally, this kind of money served solely as a means of facilitating the exchange of produced goods. The financial system built around this kind of currency would prevent any interference by money in the valuation of goods by supply and demand and would make money available to the producers at low cost, directly from the government. Finally, the financial system created would limit drastically or abolish all forms of interest and credit.

No Southern Populist ever articulated the whole of the system outlined above. A very few developed substantive arguments for each of them or integrated two or more into a reasonably logical whole. But all the elements of this sytem were familiar to at least some southern reformers. Most of them at least knew that the quantity of money in circulation affected prices. Many understood that only government fiat created money. Fewer were conversant with what the proper function of money ought to be. All of these ideas, moreover, their proponents comprehended with varying degrees of complexity. Most of the Southern Populists did not analyze them at length or relate them much to each other, and the unrealized disagreements which resulted had important effects on the success of the reform cause, as we will see in chapters 11 and 12.

Despite the confusion, however, and primarily because of their commitment to a simple market ideal, the Southern Populists considered financial reform the most important issue facing them and the country. In 1891 L. L. Polk warned Southern Alliancemen not to be diverted from "the great and paramount issue now before the American people—FINANCIAL REFORM."[64] Alliancemen elsewhere echoed him.[65] The coming of the Populist party brought no diminution of the chorus. Right through 1896 financial reform remained for the Populists, in the words of an Arkansas man, "the issue for the people of this country to win on. In my judgment it is the salvation of our country."[66] Of course, many of the Southern Populists did not consider financial reform the only question of importance. Until 1895 most of them made clear their intention not to relinquish their demands for reform in other areas. Their ideas about the relative importance of the basic issues—land, transportation, and money—will be discussed at length later, however. In order to do so we first must turn to the financial demands themselves, the demands which received far more constant attention and detailed discussion than any other issue, or all the other issues put together, during the whole period.

CHAPTER 8

Greenbacks, Free Silver, and
the Subtreasury Plan

With the land and transportation issues the Southern Populists generally agreed among themselves on the reasons and need for the particular reform. The same was not true of the financial issue. Although until late 1895 and 1896 most Southern Populists remained in apparent agreement on particular demands for financial reform, long before that important differences existed among them, especially over the place assigned free silver in the proper monetary system. While most Southern Populists supported a fiat, legal tender monetary system, their understanding of what that actually meant often proved deficient. As a result, while they generally shared their social analysis and their conception of the proper organization of American society, they sometimes disagreed about the methods for reaching these ends. This chapter will consider their differences over three of the most important financial issues—greenbacks, free silver, and the subtreasury plan. Chapters 11 and 12 will delve more deeply into the consequences of these differences.

Greenbacks

Almost all the Southern Populists at one time or another included greenbacks, fiat legal tender paper currency, in their demand for an expansion of the money supply,[1] for they fit well with many of their specific ideas about money and the proper financial system. Greenbacks came in small denominations, which made access to them easier for most people. Unlike bonds, no one holding them received interest. They could be issued by the government in any quantity desired, at little cost.[2] Since they bypassed the bankers, greenbacks also promised to keep money where it belonged, in the hands of the producers.[3] Finally, as the editor of the *Southern Mercury* noted, since the commodity value of the paper on which they were printed was almost nil, greenbacks avoided confusion over intrinsic value.[4]

Few Southern Populists, however, could have gone through this whole argument. Although they often spoke out against intrinsic value and a redeemable money, for instance, only a few of them dealt substantively with the intricacies involved in these ideas, an important task when explaining the need for a greenback currency. Most Southern Populists tended to discuss the need for greenbacks by relating it to their more general demands for the proper structure of society. To many a greenback currency promised an end to the maldistribution of wealth. Greenbacks would replace the government bonds on which the few based their "vast fortunes,"[5] making more money available to the producing masses and giving new life to the production of tangible wealth.[6] Other reformers noted that as a completely fiat currency, the greenbacks' value depended on faith in the national government, which rested ultimately on the capacity of the country to produce tangible wealth.[7] What could be more secure than the country's ability to produce? The answer was never in question. Greenback Texans could think of no better basis, nor could Watson.[8] The greenbacks which would aid the producer rested ultimately on what the producer created with the help of the greenbacks.

To those few Southern Populists who could discuss in detail the relative merits of paper and metallic currency, the history of money in the United States, especially since 1860, provided an instructive lesson in the advantages of greenbacks. From their greenbacker mentors[9] the Southern Populists learned that the government had been forced to issue legal tender fiat greenbacks soon after the Civil War broke out because gold and silver coin had disappeared as the bankers ended specie payments. Their issue by the Republicans during the war, wrote Watson, was "a matter of self-preservation." Nevertheless, the greenbacks "sustained the army which preserved the Union."[10]

The major problem with the greenbacks during the war had been their failure to maintain parity with the gold dollar. The greenback Southern Populists argued that this disadvantage had not constituted a failure of greenback currency. The Legal Tender Acts made greenbacks legal tender for all debts, public and private, with the exception of interest on the public debt and import duties. The exemption clauses, maintained those who could deal with such intricacies, caused the greenbacks to lose value relative to gold goin.[11] A Texas Populist explained that these clauses had provided those bankers in the United States and Europe with gold on hand an extra demand for their commodity and the price of gold coin rose relative to the greenbacks. Without the exemption clauses and no extra demand for gold coin, greenbacks would have stayed at a parity with gold.[12]

Despite the exemption clauses, however, the tremendous increase in the volume of money during the war through the issue of legal tender greenbacks led to great prosperity during and right after the war.[13] In fact, for knowledgeable Southern Populists a sin far greater than the exemption clauses was the removal of great numbers of greenbacks from circulation after the war ended.[14] Watson always emphasized that contraction of the currency had not begun in 1873 with the demonetization of silver, the Crime of '73, but with the withdrawal of greenbacks by Johnson's Secretary of the Treasury, Hugh McCulloch, in 1865 and 1866.[15] The greenbacks successfully financed the war and for a few years after brought "the greatest prosperity," wrote a Louisiana Populist in 1894. "There were but three millionaires and no tramps, but everybody prosperous and happy, what a beautiful picture." But when McCulloch called in and burned greenbacks, the currency in circulation shrank drastically. National banks gained control of the issue of currency, and they used it to "absorb all the wealth of the laborer" by keeping money short and interest high. "[W]ages were reduced below the cost of living. The price of produce was reduced below the cost of production. . . . The people worked harder, economized more, and grew poorer and poorer." The destruction of the greenbacks formed "the blackest page in American history."[16] For Watson, some of the Texas Populists, and a few other scattered southern reformers who discussed the intricacies of the history of fiat legal tender paper money, greenbacks made a great deal of sense, and unlike many southern reformers they continued to believe in their superiority right through the 1896 election.

These same few also faced a problem which did not concern even the other Southern Populists who demanded greenbacks. How were they to be distributed? Given their adherence to a market society, albeit different than that which they found around them, and given their belief in the value of productive labor, they rejected straight per capita distribution, "giving people money."[17] The Populist greenbackers were at no loss for solutions, however. They suggested that greenbacks be used to retire the federal government's debt.[18] The national government could also pay off the country's foreign debt by buying surplus cotton and wheat with greenbacks and selling them in Europe for gold.[19] Government expenses, including public works, could be paid for in greenbacks.[20] Greenbacks could be used to buy and build railroads,[21] pay government pensions,[22] provide low interest land loans to producers,[23] and put the unemployed to work.[24] Those southern reformers, especially in Texas, who dealt with the intricacies of the greenbacks most thoroughly tended to be the strongest advocates of a more active central government. Requiring the federal government to print and issue the country's money supply and regulate its volume, greenbackism proved conducive to demands for a national government which fostered the growth and development of society and the welfare and prosperity of its members.[25]

The demand for a completely legal tender fiat greenback system also correlated with the degree of sophistication shown in handling the greenback issue itself. The greenback editor of the Dallas, Georgia, *Herald* recalled that during the years following the Civil War, when east of California only irredeemable, fiat legal tender greenbacks had circulated, prosperity—good farm prices, good wages, plenty of work—had been general. "Why not return to a sensible and scientific system of currency and restore the prosperity and happiness of the people?" he asked.[26] Gold currency had been an improvement on "cow" money. Adding silver to gold "as an equal partner" accomplished "another step in progress.... [T]he step forward, which is inevitable, over all is the greenback— the money of the people; the progressive step in the upward trend of civilization."[27]

From a few other scattered places in the South came calls for an end to metallic currency and the establishment of a purely legal tender fiat paper money system.[28] Texas, however, was a different matter. Texas Populists had far more greenbackers among them. The *Southern Mercury* supported free silver in 1894 only as the better of two evils. Until "the old ideas of barbarism that money must be composed of a valuable metal" disappeared, better the currency be redeemable in two metals rather than only in one.[29] A greater number of Texas reformers understood the relation between greenbacks and the elimination of redemption money. Many reasoned, like one Texas Populist, that a completely greenback currency "would entirely eliminate the little understood question of a ratio between the two metals, and give us a currency that could not be increased or decreased in value only by limitation in quantity, which legislation could regulate."[30]

Outside Texas commitment to a completely fiat legal tender, irredeemable paper money system remained weak. Very, very few of the North Carolina Populists made it unequivocally. Isolated instances of this sort of greenback sentiment appeared in Alabama, particularly in the Ozark *Banner-Advertiser*, although they were not, except in one instance, the sentiments of the editor. In Georgia only the editors of the Dallas *Herald* and the Gibson *Glascock Banner* approached the fervency of the Texans' advocacy of an entirely greenback currency. The *Herald* editor's first paper and the only one he published before the *Herald* he had established in Missouri in 1872 and run as an independent reform paper in support of the Greenback party.[31] Watson continued throughout the period to lean toward the hard-core greenback position, but a pair of events in late 1893 and early 1894 illustrated the difference between his commitment to a greenback system and that of the Texans. The *Texas Advance* held a contest to find the best solution to the problem of how to meet the current treasury deficit; Watson ran a subscription contest for his *People's Party Paper*. The prize in the *Advance*'s contest was a five-dollar greenback; in Watson's it was a twenty-dollar gold piece.[32]

Free Silver

The Southern Populists discussed the free coinage of silver at a ratio of sixteen to one with gold more widely than any of their other specific demands. Technically, free coinage meant that all silver presented to the United States Treasury had to be minted, stamped as legal tender, and returned to the owner to be circulated. The silver would be valued at a ratio of sixteen to one with gold; sixteen ounces of silver would be worth, for the purposes of minting coin, the same as one ounce of gold of the same fineness.[33]

Milton Friedman and Anna Jacobson Schwartz, who have examined America's monetary history since the Civil War more closely than anyone else, maintain that the adoption of free silver in 1879 would have prevented the price deflation of 1879 to 1897 but would not have led to inflation. This, ironically, would have meant stable *general* price levels, one of the things the Southern Populists wanted a great deal.[34] Silver, of course, would not have met many of the other requirements of the reformers, particularly those of the antimonopoly greenbackers. It would not, for instance, have solved the problems of short-term currency flexibility, or rural credit, two things even more important to Southern Populists than the per capita currency circulation. Friedman and Schwartz, in company with many other historians of the period and of the Farmers' Alliance and Populist party, did not realize that greenbackism was not simply a program for currency expansion. It was part of a more wideranging critique of and response to American industrial capitalism as the southern reformers experienced it.[35]

Every Southern Populist, nonetheless, understood that free coinage of silver would increase the quantity of money in circulation.[36] Like the editor of the *Southern Mercury*, even the most committed greenbackers admitted that while "the advantage to result to this country from the free coinage of silver . . . is greatly over-estimated by the free silver advocates," such legislation "would tend to increase the volume of money in circulation."[37] Although not as many Southern Populists agreed, to most of them free silver also promised to reduce the control of money by the few. The few who held all of the gold did not hold most of the silver.[38] According to a Tennessee reformer their control of the circulating currency allowed bankers to contract the currency at will. With a free silver stone the reformers could kill two birds, contraction and control.[39]

Beyond these two basic notions, however, the Southern Populists rarely agreed when they discussed free silver, differing over what it meant, what it was supposed to do, and precisely how important it really was compared to the whole range of Populist financial and social reform. Sometimes they shared the sentiments of a North Carolina editor who maintained after the defeat of the free silver bill in Congress in early 1892 that "we do not claim that free coinage of silver is the great panacea. But it was a beginning."[40] Many other times, however, they talked of saving the country with free silver alone, making no mention of legal tender fiat paper currency and leaving no room for it. Free silver was the one reform, stated an Alabama Populist in 1893, "which, being adopted, will save not only the farmers, but the entire industrial and commercial classes of the country."[41]

Behind the disagreement over the importance of free silver reform lay some more precise disagreements over what money was. Not all Southern Populists comprehended the need for irredeemable money. Reformers advocating free silver at times spoke of a currency "based" on silver,[42] of "money of ultimate redemption,"[43] and of silver as "a primary money."[44] Even from Texas, heartland of antimonopoly greenback Populism, came a letter to the *Southern Mercury* in early 1893 attacking the demonetization of silver and suggesting that the currency ought to consist of paper money backed by gold and silver.[45] A money of ultimate redemption, a primary money, a double-standard metallic money—greenback Populists fought against these "intrinsic value" ideas constantly.[46]

Most of the failures to understand what a fiat money system really meant, however, were much less clear. "Facts which must be admitted," according to the editor of the *Progressive Farmer* in August 1896, were that silver was a more "honest measuring unit" than gold because the fall in the price of silver bullion since 1873 had remained closer than gold to the decline in farm prices. In addition the coinage of silver and gold at sixteen to one was "the only way of maintaining the rights of both debtor and creditor." The ratio between gold and silver was "self-adjusting. If the demand for either is excessive, from any cause, the burden is shifted upon the other. They are mutual burden bearers." When the editor spoke of silver as an "honest measuring unit" and gold and silver as "mutual burden bearers," he advocated a redemption money. But later in the same editorial he called money "the child of civilization—a creature of law. It is not a product of nature." The government held the exclusive right to create money and determine its value.[47] The idea that only the fiat decree of the government created money appeared in the same article with a demand for irredeemable currency.

While North Carolina proved the hotbed of this sort of thinking,[48] Populists elsewhere were not immune. The editor of the *Glascock Banner* in July 1895 maintained that the fiat of the government could put silver on "a parity" with gold by restoring it as "a money of final payment."[49] Two years earlier a Virginia Populist, while exposing the fallacy of the intrinsic value argument by distinguishing between the commercial value of the commodity from which money was made and its monetary function as a legal tender, continued, like the Georgia Populist, to adhere to a redemptionist position which should have been prevented by his legal tender fiat stance.[50] A thoroughly greenback Southern Populist could have pointed out to both these reformers that since government fiat set the value of money, and since money could be paper as well as gold or silver, worry about the parity of silver with gold was silly. Only redemptionists discussed the proper ratio of gold to silver. Fiat money advocates ignored it because it mixed up the commodity value of gold and silver with their monetary function.

With this confusion on monetary theory the attraction of free silver for some Southern Populists becomes more understandable. But many of the reformers were conversant with the fiat nature of currency and the effect of that argument on redemption money. Why, then, did some of these reformers accept free silver? The editor of the Wadesboro *Plow Boy* did. He felt that by remonetizing silver and making fifty-five cents of the metal worth a dollar merely by stamping it legal tender the government would prove to the people "what the Populists have been saying all along, namely that *it is the law that makes money, and that money is simply a creature of law*."[51]

A Texas Populist felt the same way but worried more about the effect of free silver on reform. The Greenback party had seen its effort to educate the people on the fiat nature of all money undercut and the party destroyed by the "silver cry" and compromise on the Bland Act.[52] This Texan had good reason to fear. Southern Populists often just did not connect free silver and the idea of a fiat currency. In fact, in some cases they not only failed to mention legal tender fiat paper money but also seemed to have never considered it.[53] When Watson did this the reader could assume he knew better.[54] With others it was not always so clear.[55] While the heat of the free silver campaign of the southern Democrats in late 1895 and 1896 might be blamed for the absence of greenback qualifiers in some of the assertions, it cannot be blamed for all of them.[56] If Populists considered the quantity of money in circulation the overriding issue, as many of the financial reform Southern Populists did, most likely they favored what appeared on the surface the most promising way to get it, free silver. Any appeal to some form of bimetallic standard, of course, made a greenback appeal impossible.

The situation that developed in the 1896 presidential campaign, when the national party nominated a man favoring a purely bimetallic standard, provided particularly striking evidence for the failure of many Southern Populists, despite their opposition to an "intrinsic value" redeemable currency, to understand what that really meant. Antimonopoly greenback Texans did. On the money question, according to one Texas greenbacker in late 1895, free silver Democrats and Populists had "absolutely nothing in common, save only to some extent an agreement on the result of an increase of money in circulation." In "the most vital phase of the case," the need for a "money of final redemption," free silverites and gold monometallists agreed. "Intrinsic value" had nothing to do with "populist theory."[57] A month later the editor of the *Southern Mercury* opposed fusion between the new silver party and the Populists because "reformers have long since discarded the antediluvian theory of redemption money, and do not believe in that system of bimetallism."[58] Only the Texas Populists opposed cooperation with the Democrats, including support for Bryan in 1896, on these grounds.[59]

Free silver, the antimonopoly greenback Texans contended, would not solve the most serious problems of the financial system and, indeed, might make some worse in the long run. Speaking for them Judge Nugent in 1895 pointed out the contradiction in the free silver Democrats' demand, included in their 1896 national platform, to end peacetime bond issues and expand the currency by issuing paper money redeemable in gold or silver. Expansion was good, but as long as government notes remained redeemable in coin, gold or silver, those who had note reserves would "always find it practicable to deplete the national treasury of its coin reserve." Why should they stop a practice which had been recently so profitable? "[S]o long as convertible paper exists to induce speculative raids on the metallic reserves," the treasury would need coin bonds to protect itself.[60] Thus the only way the free silver Democrats could supply a volume of currency adequate to the "wants of the country" would be to float "an enormously disproportionate quantity of convertible notes." But "with a volume of credit money out of all just proportion to the metallic base, withdrawals of coin will become all the more easy, and the difficulty of maintaining the volume of paper circulation must be greatly enhanced." The free silver Democrats could not simultaneously expand the currency, end peacetime bond issues, and have a redeemable currency. The first two goals were completely incompatible with the last. "There is in fact," stated Nugent, "no compromise between the paper system of the gold men and that of the populists." The country needed the free coinage of gold and silver at sixteen to one supplemented by inconvertible paper money, greenbacks. That alone would guarantee an adequate currency and eliminate all the problems caused by a reserve system.[61]

This kind of analysis had no counterpart elsewhere among the southern reformers. Only the Texas Populists seem to have been familiar enough with the greenback position to refute consistently the bimetallic advocates. If Watson and the other greenback Populists outside of Texas, hostile to Bryan and fusion with the Democrats for many reasons, never applied their arguments for a fiat legal tender, irredeemable currency to criticize the Democratic plank on free silver, then how much opposition could be expected from the large number of Southern Populists who never consistently advocated greenbacks and who never quite understood what a full legal tender fiat paper currency meant?[62] For these Populists Bryan's outspoken support of free silver helped remove many of the ideological and theoretical objections which might otherwise have prevented their support of him in 1896.

More seriously, the Southern Populists' failure to understand adequately the intricacies of legal tender fiat money allowed them, unwittingly, to follow Bryan and the free silver Democrats into a twentieth century where most of them saw little change but for the worse. Free silver meant nothing more than an expansion of the currency supply; legal tender fiat currency was the leading edge of an antimonopoly greenbackism that questioned the legitimacy of some of the central institutions of American capitalism, including the role of government in the social and economic life of the country. An analysis of the subtreasury plan, a purely antimonopoly greenback proposal, illustrates how empty the free silver issue really was for realizing what most Southern Populists, free silver and greenbacker alike, wanted.

The Subtreasury Plan

Members of the National Farmers' Alliance and Industrial Union first heard of the famous subtreasury plan at their December 1889 St. Louis national meeting.[63] The plan proposed that every county in the country producing over $500,000 worth of agricultural commodities each year should have a subtreasury office with facilities for storing certain non-perishable agricultural products offered it. At the time of presentation the product offered would be graded and classed, a certificate of deposit issued, and "United States legal tender paper money equal to eighty per cent of the local current value of the products" loaned to the storer at one percent interest annually. If not redeemed within a year, the subtreasury official auctioned off the stored commodity to the highest bidder to satisfy the debt. The federal government would build the subtreasury facilities on land provided by the counties.[64]

During 1891 and some of 1892 most of the southern reformers considered the subtreasury plan their most important issue. "Don't be misled," wrote the editor of the *Farmers' Advocate*, "the Sub-Treasury plan is the most essential demand in the Alliance platform."[65] At times, as in the Omaha platform, the reformers demanded the subtreasury plan "or a better system,"[66] but the basic idea, loans to farmers by the government at low rates of interest on commodities they produced, remained the same.

Southern Alliancemen and Populists had good reason to consider their subtreasury plan the vital core of the reform program. As might be expected, southern reformers understood best the plan's provision for expanding the volume of circulating currency.[67] By providing that "there be extended to the land and crops of the land the same power as is given to gold money," the subtreasury assured the country of a volume of currency adequate to the need for it.[68] The plan helped fulfill the demand for a fiat money by providing a safe way to issue it. Every dollar loaned would "be secured by a deposit of staple products which the world must have to supply its wants," so there would be no failure because of a shortage of gold, silver, or any "intrinsic value" redeemer.[69] For those reformers concerned about it the subtreasury provided another way to put the needed money into circulation.[70]

The subtreasury plan would also implement the demand for a flexible currency. In fact, according to C. W. Macune, who developed and elaborated the idea,[71] this was a major reason for its formulation. He pointed out that until the middle of the nineteenth century there was usually only one step from producer to consumer, so the sale of produced commodities little affected the money market. By the 1880s, however, the farmer sold to the carriers, the carriers sold to the manufacturers or processers, and they sold to the consumer.[72] This procedure required nearly three times as much money as the old system, since all the exchanges took place in a short time, usually within three months of the harvest. This large demand for money was made even greater because all agricultural products went onto the market at about the same time. As a result a serious shortage of currency existed in the months immediately following harvest. Only three things allowed the necessary exchanges to take place at all. The existing supply of currency turned over faster, the increase in velocity acting to expand the volume of currency in circulation. Second, the use of credit paper expanded, also increasing the effective volume of currency. Third, prices of agricultural commodities fell as much as twenty percent, enabling the available supply of currency to go farther.

The demand for currency slackened, however, by the early months of the new year, so that the farmer had to make his next year's investment in supplies and equipment with prices much higher than they had been during harvest time. Macune estimated the average difference between prices when the farmer bought and when he sold at forty percent.

The subtreasury alleviated this currency inflexibility by increasing the supply of money when the demand for it rose during and immediately after harvest and decreasing it when demand for money dropped during the other nine months of the year. In addition, the plan allowed the sale of agricultural commodities to be extended over a longer period of time, keeping the seasonal demand for money more even.[73] In this manner the subtreasury system prevented, as far as possible, the money supply from influencing the prices of commodities. This argument had widespread popularity. Watson used it on several occasions.[74] So did Populists in North Carolina, Alabama, Virginia, and Tennessee.[75] The Texans, as usual, supplied the most thorough arguments.[76]

The subtreasury plan promised to destroy credit, interest, and the lien system by providing an effective mechanism for putting the country on a cash basis and by allowing the federal government rather than merchants and bankers to furnish needed capital cheaply to the producers.[77] As a North Carolina Populist wrote, the increased currency issued under the subtreasury plan would allow the factories to sell for cash instead of on time, as they did at present because their customers lacked cash. The credit system would be undercut seriously, as would the price of credit, the interest rate. Farmers could also do a cheaper business for they would not have to depend on high priced money.[78] By allowing for the direct issue of money to producers by the government the subtreasury also destroyed concentrated control of the money supply. As long as a few men controlled the supply of money, remarked one Alabama reformer, they kept its volume low, its price high, and their profits good. With the subtreasury, however, "the expansion of the currency would be automatic, expanding as demand for money should increase in circulation, and contracting to the normal when such an exigency should pass away."[79] The profits of the few, made at the expense of the producing many, would disappear entirely.

The Southern Populists, in short, intended their subtreasury plan to replace completely the existing financial system and all of its inequities. It enabled the national government to issue a cheap and plentiful currency directly to the producers in short-term loans based not on gold and silver holdings, of which the producers had none, but on the more reliable tangible wealth produced by the people of the country. It eliminated high interest rates on the capital the producers needed to continue creating tangible wealth by taking control of the money supply from a greedy, nonproducing few and giving it to the national government, the agent of the producing masses. It facilitated the circulation of fiat legal tender paper money and free silver coinage among those people who used it to produce. It destroyed the lien system by eliminating credit as a factor in American economic life and development, enabling the business of the country to be done on a purely cash basis.

But the specific details of the operation of the subtreasury were not ends in themselves. Intended to overhaul completely the existing financial system, the subtreasury had wide ramifications for the realization of the proper social order. The plan, wrote the editor of the *Southern Mercury*, would "remove the inequality that farmers and wealth producers have been laboring under for years."[80] By raising the farmers' prices, argued a Georgia Populist, the subtreasury would enable them to pay higher wages to their hands. The farmers and laboring people would then spend more, creating an increased demand for manufactured goods. New factories would be built and old ones grow, "and the laborer's [sic] of every industry will find steady employment and will get good wages."[81] At this point the whole process started over again—demand, growth, increased wages, demand, etc. The subtreasury, by properly ordering the financial system, favored the producers over the idle speculators by guaranteeing them a fair share of the wealth they produced and encouraging them to produce even more.

The subtreasury plan also promised to undo the maldistribution of wealth created by the existing financial system. Elimination through the subtreasury of the power of a few to manipulate the currency, wrote an Alabama Populist, meant the elimination of the growth of extremes of wealth in society.[82] No country prospered, maintained a Texas reformer, when nine men worked ten to fourteen hours a day and gave up in interest all they earned to the one who never worked yet lived in luxury. The answer was the subtreasury system. Farmers could hold back sale of their crops for better prices and the consumer could wait for his needs to dictate his purchases, cutting the prices he was forced to pay. The supply and demand for goods and money, being stretched out over a longer period, would cut down on the profits of middlemen and moneylenders by eliminating much of the need for their services.[83]

Harry Tracy, a prominent Texas greenbacker, Allianceman, and Populist, made both the most persuasive and substantive argument for the subtreasury plan and the most comprehensive analysis of its critical role in the Southern Populists' demand for economic and social reform. Building on the base which Macune had provided and which we discussed earlier in this section, Tracy noted that in the new explosion of prosperity of the twenty-five years following the Civil War agriculture had not kept pace with manufacturing and commerce, even though, like these two areas, the development and application of new machinery had increased production tremendously and the transportation revolution had put the farmer into contact with vast new markets. These changes required "the substitution of a modern for an oxcart system of finance." Before the war "the demand for money to handle the products of the country" had remained tolerably constant throughout the year, but by the 1890s all this had changed. Tracy estimated in 1891 that the quantity of money available at harvest time was about half that available in the early months of the following year, resulting in price fluctuations of about forty percent, the same figure Macune used. To explain why prices did not vary in the same proportion as the volume of currency, as those adhering to the quantity theory of money most Southern Populists used might predict, Tracy pointed out that two things happened. "First, the contraction produces an acceleration in the speed with which the money circulates. Second, the inadequacy of the volume, with the downward tendency in the price of products, awakens the spirit of speculation, which floats a substitute in the shape of credit paper, which circulates as money." So prices did not drop as fast as the quantity of currency circulating did. Tracy, one of the very few among all the Southern Populists,[84] showed an awareness both of the effect of velocity and of credit paper on the effective volume of currency in circulation.

This forty percent price fluctuation, Tracy maintained, had serious consequences for the farmers, and through them, for "every useful and productive interest in the country." It was an "actual, tangible discrimination against agriculture," sapping "the foundation of this government and, by the legal sanction of absolute wrong, producing a contempt for law and government favorable to the growth of sentiments of anarchy and socialism that threaten the stability of modern civilization." The subtreasury system, by ending this price discrimination, would improve the condition of agriculture and "thereby benefit all classes of society." It created a new channel for widening the distribution of currency. More importantly, it provided for "an emergency issue that will increase the volume, so as to keep pace with the suddenly augmented demand, created by dumping the year's product of agriculture upon the market, without increasing the relative volume of money above what is the normal mean average, and provide, also, that such emergency volume shall be of such a character that it will always pass current, on a par value with gold coin." Moreover, the subtreasury allowed the government to loan money to a far greater number of people than the national banks ever served and on collateral that, "instead of being a *simple evidence of debt*" like bonds, were "a few of the leading products of the agriculture of the country . . . *positive evidence of wealth*." He countered the objection that the sub-treasury scheme would raise consumer prices by pointing out that unlike the present system, with the subtreasury the money supply remained completely flexible. The supply and demand for any particular commodity, unaffected by a fluctuating demand for money, would determine prices.

Nor did the subtreasury system violate the extremely important injunction of equal rights to all and special privileges to none. The advantage of the system lay not in its warehousing provisions but in its capacity to put money into circulation when necessary and keep prices from falling. Every class benefited from price stability, especially in so critical an area as agricultural commodities. "There are absolutely no favors extended to the farmer, but he is given a chance to help himself simply by having the present discrimination against him removed."[85]

Tracy obviously knew that the key to the subtreasury plan was its promise to release the farmer from the problem of credit. As Lawrence Goodwyn has pointed out, the subtreasury plan was designed specifically to destroy the grip of the crop lien in the South and was the fruition of years of effort.[86] It represented, however, not a monetary but a political innovation. The plan redefined, implicitly, the role of government in society.[87] No longer a mere watchdog, the government became the vehicle for releasing the farmer from a capitalist system and recreating in the southern countryside a simple market society of producers. In this sense it solved the farmers' problem much more thoroughly than the cooperative movement, which was a defensive effort to evade the implications of capitalism by matching its strength with farmer organization.[88] The cooperative effort was doomed to failure, at least on the scale the Southern Alliancemen wanted to operate, which included tenants, because power and economic control in the capitalist system lay with the possession of capital, one item the farmers, organized or unorganized, lacked. In an effort to regain control of their own world they intended to bypass the institutions of capitalist America, obtaining needed capital from the federal government and keeping the profits of their labors for themselves, minus a minimum charge to maintain the government. Through the subtreasury and the greenback monetary system it promoted, the government would create and maintain the southern reformers' simple market society of independent producers.

The subtreasury plan did not, however, provide an answer for the working people.[89] It promised them, according to the Southern Populists, better wages. But it did not give them control over their own labor, as it did for the farmers. By giving access to the necessary capital to all the farmers, the subtreasury theoretically eliminated the market for labor in the countryside (provided, of course, that farm land remained relatively plentiful, accessible, and cheap to begin cultivating). Without a social order, however, where independent artisans and mechanics did the nonfarm work, nothing ended the market for labor in industrial and urban America. And the subtreasury plan did not anticipate or promote the creation of an independent artisan class.

None of the Southern Populists ever really understood this. In his conclusion Tracy finally moved to the rationale behind the subtreasury plan, the ultimate end the Populists intended it to serve. It meant prosperity for every "true merchant, manufacturer, farmer, and laborer. . . . Let us align ourselves on the side of right, and forever free our people from the power of money to oppress, and march forward to a new civilization . . . and make of our people a nation of patriots, full of strength and prosperity. In such a country, every laboring man will own his own home, free from execution, across the threshold of which no usurer or other tyrant dare pass."[90] Tracy revealed that while he understood the operation and social implications of the subtreasury plan far better than almost all of his reform brethren, he shared with them his ultimate reasons for demanding it. "The side of right" was God's side and the side of the just. The subtreasury would protect society from the extremes of socialism and anarchy and would bring the millennium—a secular one, to be sure—of a "new civilization" where the independent producer would prosper in the enjoyment of the wealth he produced, free from the oppression of the nonproducing money power and usurer but still within a traditional market, private ownership and enterprise economic system. The subtreasury promised a simple market society geared primarily to the needs of the independent, rural, agricultural producer.

CHAPTER 9

Antimonopoly, Reform, and the
Simple Market Society

While it may appear from their concern with the financial system that the Southern Populists considered money the most important part of the proper social order, they did not. The importance of money in their reform program merely reflected an America in which money had become more important than the people whom it was supposed to serve. While the southern reformers could disagree mightily on the specifics of reform, they agreed on the need for a society in which everyone had a chance to live a decent life. When dealing with this kind of human consideration the Southern Populists revealed the strength of their thought and analysis. These positive qualities were most apparent when the reformers turned from their discussion of particular reforms to explanations of how their demands related to each other and why they were necessary.

"Man Over Money"

All of the Southern Populists at one time or another used the phrase "man over money" or something similar, often as a metaphor for their entire reform effort. "The issue is," wrote the editor of the Gracewood, Georgia, *Wool Hat* in the depression year of 1893, "which is greater, the citizen or the dollar?"[1] "The chief aim of the People's party," stated an Alabama Populist, "is to regulate this matter so that the dollar shall not control the individual, but shall be made just what it was intended to be—a means of facilitating the business and fostering the prosperity of the people."[2] This had not happened,[3] and America was headed for trouble. "When money gets to be the all powerful influence among a people," maintained a North Carolina Populist, "that people is on the verge of revolution, anarchy, and civil perdition. The history of three thousand years teaches this."[4] When money became more valuable than labor, gold more esteemed than human beings, the society began to break down. While the dollar ruled and capital was placed above labor, noted W. S. Morgan, the country would continue to teeter on the brink of revolution.[5] Labor had priority over capital because of the importance of production to society. Common sense and human decency taught a Texas Populist, like his brethren, that money ultimately depended on labor. Labor produced food, clothing, shelter, and "all useful machinery." "All of these things could be without a cent of money. Blot them out and what life could subsist on money? Can you eat money? Can you wear money as clothes? We repeat, money is the mere convenient medium of effecting exchanges." The "mission of the People's Party" was to assure that labor did not remain at the mercy of the money of the few. "[I]s this not, in the sight of our common Heavenly Father," the writer asked, "right[,] necessary and full of benedictions to every man who will work?"[6]

The "man over money" image also reflected the hostility of the southern reformers to one of the most prominent social characteristics of America's new financial and industrial capitalism, the growing importance of the social as well as the economic function of money and its increasingly common use as a standard for measuring individuals and their social position and value. When used in this manner money often represented all the problems of the new cities and industrial development, problems foreign to an older rural ideal but also the source of much of the injustice and inhumanity in late nineteenth-century America. Watson, as he often did, served as an articulate spokesman for his Populist brethren.

> Every year this maddening rush for money; this insane "get there" push for success, regardless of methods; sees us drawing nearer to the fatal limits over which so many nations have gone down to ruin. Whenever we lose entirely the belief in human accountability to Eternal powers; whenever we are possessed utterly by the creed that life ends at the grave, and therefore we must "eat, drink and be merry;" then, indeed, are we doomed.
>
> Money will be the God we worship. The basest passions of our animal nature will assert supreme authority over thought and speech and act. From January to January there will be the rush, the roar, the march, the deadly combat, the shout of onset, the cry of the wounded, the cheers of these relentless civilized savages whose only care, purpose, effort, religion, is to get money. In this mad saturnalia, so very ruinous of the better attributes of manhood, the catchwords of the procession will be precisely the same as those

under which all the old Pagan nations went headlong to perdition, "money, wine and women."[7]

The reformers based their antagonism to the new order on a hostility to the new depersonalization of people, on the new importance of money and wealth in setting the tone and pace of society. The Southern Populists' notion of a simple market society, with all its rural overtones, combined with their religious antipathy to the sins of great wealth and their feeling that somehow individuals were no longer judged according to their moral and personal worth or the value of their contribution to society but according to how much money they could manage, by hook or crook, to accumulate, gave much passion to the Populists' demand to free people from subservience to money, the symbol of a new age of depersonalized social, political, and economic relations.

Besides, they argued, to make humanity's one aim to gather wealth meant condoning the special privileges of the few and the poverty of the many. Nor could the solution be private, personal withdrawal from the rat race. The cause of the poor condition of American society, wrote a Georgia Populist editor, "can be easily and logically traced to the wrong systems now in vogue, which place money above humanity and make the getting thereof paramount to everything else."[8] In order to protect their own, many took advantage of every law and condition "to wring from those who may chance to be in their power, or who are weaker mentally, physically or financially than themselves, all that is possible, regardless of the results. ... The conditions which cause many to do as outlined above, permeate to a greater or less extent down through all departments of life and compel many others to adopt the same methods and measures in pure self-defence, or to save themselves from ruin, thus placing extra burdens on those in still humbler walks of life, or those less strong than they."[9] Only the wealthy benefited from this struggle. Those who actually produced the wealth fought each other over the table scraps. Escape for them lay not in struggling harder but combining to overthrow the system which permitted such conditions. "Men can be taught," wrote a Georgia Populist, "that contentment, liberty and happiness are incompatible with greed or 'all of self and none of thee.' "[10]

The priorities of society needed reordering. The tools required for the creation and distribution of wealth—land, transportation, and especially money—had ceased to be means of increasing the prosperity and happiness of the producing many. They had taken on a false importance by being misused by the few for their own selfish ends. Land, transportation, and money were prominent among the Southern Populists' demands because in the existing order of society they had become too important. The reformers stressed these areas to reduce their influence and to reassert the importance of the people who actually constituted organized society. The metaphor of men over money was one of the most important ways the Southern Populists gave voice to this idea.

Antimonopoly

The stress on people which integrated the Southern Populists' entire reform effort on a very basic human level also had a more analytical counterpart. Some of the Southern Populists, usually but not always the greenbackers, viewed the specific issues of the Omaha platform as more than a collection of separate reforms in land, transportation, and finance. These reformers usually unified the three major demands under a single heading that was older than any one of them, antimonopoly.

Ironically, much of the Southern Populists' antimonopoly thought originated with Jacksonian Democracy's original urban left wing, the Locofocos. William Leggett's emphasis on the natural laws of supply and demand and of competition came a long way, as did his attack on monopoly as special privilege and the cause of the extremes of wealth in society.[11] On the other hand, the Southern Populists did not share the unqualified commitment of these urban middle-class egalitarians to a laissez-faire society. The later reformers, like the more radical Jacksonian labor leaders of the 1830s, appreciated the dangers of a wide-open market place when only a few people controlled most of the capital.[12] Moreover, for the Jacksonians antimonopoly usually meant an attack on a special kind of privilege, exclusive government charters to individuals or groups. To the southern reformers it meant much more; it bespoke an attack on the dominant forces in American society. In the 1830s special privilege hurt; by the 1890s special privilege ruled. To those Southern Populists who used it antimonopoly turned the entire Populist reform program into a single weapon designed to destroy nineteenth-century American industrial and financial capitalism as they perceived it.

The most comprehensive demands for the integration of all the major Southern Populist reforms rested on an antimonopoly position and inevitably appeared when Southern Populists opposed committing the People's party to a single issue only.[13] J. A. Transom of Pfafftown, North Carolina, presented a detailed explanation in the *Caucasian* in July 1896 in order to explain why the Omaha platform ought not to be trimmed in preparation for the coming national campaign. Everyone's life depended on "the sustenance drawn from the bosom of mother earth." If a few were allowed to "own more land than they need or can cultivate, while others find it impossible even to own a home, we reduce the landless to the alternative of starving or selling themselves into slavery." God gave land, air, and water as free gifts to "all who wish to use them." Without land no one could be secure against want. Populists could never drop the land plank.

If all people had "free access to the land," a "division of labor" would quickly develop, since "the different sections of our vast country can each produce some of the things of common use better than any other section." This, however, made transportation necessary for the exchange of products which this "convenient and economical" division of labor demanded. Without it, even with free access to the land, production would not prosper. So the railroad monopoly had to be destroyed.

Nor would the free silver plank effect the radical change society needed. "It would, of course, under existing conditions, give temporary relief. . . . [But] the vast monopolies would soon swallow up silver as they have gold. . . . To increase our supply of money without, at the same time, destroying all monopolies would be as useless as to try to fill a tub with water while there was a big hole in the bottom." If the platform needed shortening, he stated, "'Tis easily done. The one word 'antimonopoly' expresses every demand in, and outside the Omaha platform necessary to establish justice among us."[14] To eliminate only one of the three major monopolies made no sense because the other two would quickly take up the slack in its robbery of the people.

Apparently few Southern Populists, however, visualized the organization of society as a complex combination of production, exchange, and distribution of commodities. Those who did were always greenbackers. They also, as we shall see, tended to be mid-road Populists in 1896, the most favorable to a more active central government and the least worried about accusations of socialism. His antimonopoly views led the North Carolina Populist quoted above to counsel ignoring the conservatives' cries of socialism, commenting that all "honest government is socialistic. . . . It cannot be wrong to follow where Justice leads the way, and if it leads to socialism, who can help it?" The editor of the *Arkansaw Kicker*, on the same day he called for the maintenance of all the planks of the Omaha platform, remarked that "there is not a good principle advocated by any party that is not socialistic."[15]

Among the Texas Populists, with their high concentration of greenbackers, a sophisticated antimonopoly theory appeared far more often than elsewhere. Although reformers in other southern states discussed the problem of monopoly often enough, only the party in Texas grounded itself specifically in the antimonopoly camp. In their 1894 state platform the Texans declared that the People's party was "an antimonopoly party."[16] Throughout the entire period, but especially in 1895 and 1896, the *Southern Mercury* prescribed the entire Omaha platform as an anti-monopoly physic for all the country's ills.[17] The Greenback party had demonstrated, wrote Judge Nugent in early 1895, the fallacy of intrinsic value by proving that law alone created money. Had the movement succeeded in gaining political power, however, "it is doubtful whether it would have brought more than temporary relief to the people, under the conditions which then prevailed." It would have done nothing about land speculation, private ownership of the railroads, or bank control of the circulating currency. After a short respite conditions would have grown worse, "for these are the factors in our industrial system which produce the undue concentration of wealth; and so long as they are left to operate, any sudden stimulation of productive forces, whether brought about by a redundant circulation, or otherwise, must, after a brief period, only aggravate social inequalities, by bringing more wealth within the power and control of monopoly."[18]

Nugent reminded the state Farmers' Alliance eight months later that monetary reform alone "may lead to increased production of wealth, but it will not afford the economic conditions necessary to an equitable distribution of wealth." By improving prices for farm products monetary reform would greatly increase the value of the land. Population growth would only make things worse. Tenancy and "enforced idleness" would increase, reducing the mass of people to worse poverty and diminishing seriously the production of wealth. Land, "enough and to spare," existed, but the wealthy few controlled nearly all of it. Reform of the financial system alone could not be sustained without a just and equitable distribution of the wealth created. The answer to that question lay partly in the end to speculative landholding.[19] The other part could be found in a proper solution to the transportation problem. Financial reform, argued another Texas Populist, was fine as far as it went. What, however, would be done "with transportation companies charging us so high for hauling our corn, cotton and wheat to market?"[20] If the producers could not get their products to market, what good did cheap land and plenty of money do them? Unable to sell their produce at a profit, they had no reason to produce anything they could not consume themselves.

To the antimonopoly greenback Populists the major planks of the Omaha platform constituted an inseparable whole. While the reformers who understood the reform program this way might admit, as the editor of the *Mercury* did in early 1895, that the repeal of the silver purchase clause and President Cleveland's issuing of gold bonds had forced the financial question to the front, they would never ignore the other anti-monopoly measures.[21] In March 1896 a radical Texan quite nicely summarized the whole argument.

[G]ive us our financial system with its $50 per capita in the pockets of the people, and watch the result. To the present high rate of taxation add the high salaries often paid to municipal, county, state and national officials, the high salaries of corporation lawyers and officials and the taxation through freight rates, express charges, land rentals, etc., [sic] How long would it require for these to absorb all the millions you have put into circulation? Not long.

Again, give every man a home in this broad land, and watch the results. Tens of thousands are too poor to reach the devoted spot; others are too poor to utilize them [sic] if placed on their farm; many are able to accept and utilize the home thus given. Withal, there are none who realize profit, for the contraction of the currency has destroyed the close-by markets, while transportation charges cut off the distant market, and all the while there is no reduction of the high salaries, taxation and debts.

If the government owned all transportation lines and offered a free exchange of products, what benefit to the millions who, from lack of land to till, have nothing to ship? Or to other millions who, out of employment, have not money to purchase the products that might be shipped by the few who now own the earth?

What a farce, then, to advocate either one of the three great questions without boldly upholding the other two?[22]

The greenback Populists held a far more integrated conception of social reform than the other Southern Populists, and it sprang from the most clearly articulated antimonopoly stance. The antimonopoly green-backers clung to the subtreasury longest and they were the most hostile to Bryan and free silver in 1896. Their more complete understanding of the whole range of reform generated their continued advocacy of the subtreasury, the single most promising reform for realizing the ideal society desired by many Southern Populists.

Overproduction

The strength of the integrated antimonopoly greenback position was readily apparent when the Southern Populists turned it, and the whole complex of their thought, on the notion of "overproduction," an explanation the Democrats and conservative opponents of the Southern Populists offered for low prices of farm commodities. The farmers, these people charged, grew too much cotton, wheat, and corn. The demand for these products had not risen as fast as production of them.[23] This, in basic human terms, made no sense to the southern reformers. "Such

doctrine is contrary to the laws of God and the necessities of man,"
announced a Georgia Populist.[24] How could there be too much corn or
cotton when people starved and had too few clothes to keep them warm?
Most Southern Populists were no more willing to acknowledge the overproduction argument than the Texas editor who found it "queer" that
"the people make so much cotton they have no clothes and so much
'grub' they can't get enough to eat."[25]

Although in a few cases they advanced such ideas,[26] the Southern
Populists did not accept the solution to overproduction offered by some
of their opponents, namely, diversification of crops to include more home
consumables and a corresponding reduction of acreage planted in cotton.
Years of the lien system and failure of the cooperative movement taught
them different lessons. Such notions had little reality, argued a Georgia
Populist, since in practice the furnishing merchant, not the farmer, controlled the amount of land planted in cotton.[27] Besides, the argument was
faulty in human terms. If the poor already had too little clothing, raising
the price of cotton by reducing its acreage would only make their precari-
ous position worse.[28] Nor did it make much more sense economically. As
Harry Tracy pointed out, "the most constant consumers of cotton" were
Western wheat, corn, and hog producers, who had nothing but their
produce to exchange for it. Worse, diversification, by reducing "the volume of commerce," threatened to drive the country back into barbarism.
"[C]ivilization begins with commerce, grows with it, prospers with it,
suffers with it, and finally disappears when commerce expires."[29] Cutting
back production of cotton solved nothing.

When a badly needed product went unpurchased the problem could
not be overproduction. Obviously, consumers lacked access to what they
needed. Although almost none of their contemporaries would have agreed,
the Southern Populists analyzed the problem as underconsumption. A
little-known British economist, John A. Hobson, was one of the few who
might have shared their opinion. During the last decade of the nineteenth
century he began asking questions similar to those of the Populists: What
accounts for the maldistribution of wealth and what is its engine? Although he took a dim view of possible solutions, Hobson located the
problem in the same place, underconsumption. A more "official" British
economist, Alfred Marshall, a bit earlier had talked about the importance
of demand in setting prices and allocating goods. It was left to John
Maynard Keynes, however, to turn these insights into a model for economic equilibrium in a capitalist economy by calling on the government
to keep demand up and provide consumption power to the general population in order to increase investment and expand production.[30] So while
the Southern Populists had neither the sophistication of analysis or solution, as in the case of the essential nature of the currency they perceived

the problem with a greater degree of clarity than their more orthodox American contemporaries.

A few Southern Populists argued that inadequate distribution caused underconsumption[31] but most of them probably lacked the analytical tools needed for this argument. They generally preferred a solution to underconsumption which more directly connected the producer and the consumer and concerned primarily a reform of the financial system. These reformers based their discussion of underconsumption on an observation about the relation of production to commodity prices, reasoning that if people had money to spend they would buy the products they needed. The problems of underconsumption, low farm prices, and currency reform all dovetailed neatly. Increase the supply of money available to people making purchases and farm prices would rise while underconsumption and poverty disappeared.[32]

Nor was this argument entirely self-serving. The Southern Populists, although their analysis might reflect their own problems, class position, and intellectual heritage, spoke as social reformers. An Alabama Populist noted that with thousands of Americans going poorly clothed "a ten million bale crop at 5 cents does the country more good than a five million bale crop at 10 cents." A larger crop, by requiring more working people to harvest it and produce the clothing, put more money into circulation. Besides, to urge the farmer to cut costs by employing less labor was the counsel not only of selfishness but danger. "[T]hese working people are here and they have got to live by either fair or by foul means. . . . [W]hen you decrease the wages of the working man, let him be farmer, mechanic, railroader, printer or tinner, you cut the throat of all business and all enterprise." The ideal solution was neither to cut prices to farmers nor raise prices paid by consumers, but to increase the supply of currency available, allowing a ten million bale crop at eight to ten cents a pound while, with decent wages, making the money available to working people to purchase it.[33]

The editor of the Nashville *Weekly Toiler* wanted a "stimulant" to increase people's ability to purchase produced wealth.[34] This sort of crude but obvious solution to the problems of underconsumption by using demand stimulus appeared all over the South among Populists. "Suppose that all the people in the country had enough money to buy everything that they actually need," posited a Georgia Populist. "What would be the results?" In a few weeks storehouses and warehouses would be empty and "idle mills" would resume production and employ idle workers. Increased demand for their products would bring farmers better prices and enable them to enlarge their acreage, thus employing more laborers. Their increased business would force the merchants to hire more clerks. With a greater demand for their goods, manufacturers would need more working people, and the demand for labor would raise wages. Talk of overproduction would become a thing of the past.[35]

The dominant political and economic opinion in late nineteenth-century America would solve the depression by encouraging businessmen and manufacturers to produce once again. The Southern Populists responded that production depended upon consumer demand, which in turn depended on how much money the people had. The confidence that businessmen and manufacturers really wanted was a confidence in continued profits from increased production, and this depended on a demand to fill.[36] "Good times and a revival of trade can only come by the capacity of consumers generally to buy goods and consume them," wrote the editor of the *Southern Mercury*. The wealthy few did not make business profitable; "the masses" did. "There is no profit in manufacture because the masses of people are too poor to consume the goods." The same held true for the merchants. And without an increase in the currency supply the cycle of depression fed upon itself. The farmers, unable to get good prices, reduced their consumption. The manufacturers, without a demand for their goods, did not increase the wages of their laborers.[37] The problem was not production; it was consumption.[38]

Americans could not produce too much tangible wealth, although a faulty system of government could create the appearance of overproduction by pauperizing the many for the enrichment of the few and hindering consumption by cutting demand for produced wealth. The editor of the *Texas Advance* distinguished between what he called overproduction—"that amount of any commodity remaining after every use to which it can be applied has been fully satisfied"—and a surplus—"that amount which remains unused from any cause whatsoever." Underconsumption, "want of ability to purchase," could produce a surplus but never overproduction. Until every American was "comfortably fed, housed and clothed there neither could nor would be an overproduction." Such patently was not the case in the 1890s. The solution was to provide the people with access to the money they needed. "The demand is there as well as the supply, but the medium of transfer is wanting."[39]

While only a few Southern Populists could articulate this argument as well as those we have discussed at length, almost all of them shared the belief that no overproduction of tangible wealth existed. Rather, most people consumed less than they needed because of a widespread lack of money to buy. The southern reformers did not demand outright redistribution of wealth; but they did want a reform of the system. If everyone had equal access to the potential wealth of nature in America, those who worked would enjoy prosperity and happiness. The improper ordering of American society prevented that, to which an ill-fed, ill-clothed, and ill-

housed population testified. To their credit the southern reformers refused to put system above obvious human need. They intended their
reforms to give everyone equal access to the means of producing, exchanging, and enjoying America's wealth. Reform in land, transportation, and finance would result in the proper social order, where those
who worked and produced a tangible product enjoyed the fruits of their
toil. The very rich and the very poor, unemployment, an idle moneyed
aristocracy, poverty-stricken wealth producers, overproduction and underconsumption would all disappear. The new social order would bring
decency, justice, prosperity, and happiness to a relatively homogeneous
society centered around people, not around money, banks, railroads, or
corporations.[40]

The Assumptions of Antimonopoly

Limits to the antimonopoly argument existed, of course, limits which the
reformers recognized when they spoke of socialism and the proper economic system and which arose from the historical situation in which they
found themselves. Because of their intellectual heritage, contemporary
experience, and class position, the Southern Populists believed they could
create a just, decent, and humane industrial America while retaining a
market society. Their solution was a two-tier economic structure[41] which
combined essentially a simple market society for the large number of
independent producers with democratic government ownership and operation of those elements of industrial society which for one reason or
another could not be controlled by individuals. This vision of society lay
behind the Omaha platform and its antimonopoly greenback analysis.

In a speech given in the early fall of 1894, Texas Populist Judge
Thomas Nugent provided perhaps the fullest and clearest exposition of
the antimonopoly greenback position made by any Southern Populist,
and in doing so revealed nearly all the elements which made the Southern
Populist analysis of and dream for their country radical, humanly perceptive and persuasive, and peculiarly American.[42] Nugent did not shy away
from the harsh realities of a United States which had just experienced the
Pullman strike and industrial armies. He opened his speech by telling his
audience that times were "ominous and threatening," with "capital—
organized, arrogant, intrenched [sic] in special privileges, and inspired by
confidence born of recent victories ... confronted by labor, smarting
under defeat, alert, resentful, holding its lines till the fateful hours shall
come."

He defended the Pullman strike and the strikers with a vigor unusual even for the Southern Populists. Their grievances were legitimate and they had the right to strike. He also noted that politicians offered only surface palliatives to end the confrontation. Seeing the strike and "its attendant evils" of rioting, loss of life, and the paralyzing of commerce, the politicians reacted with regulation or repression—the military—or "some scheme of arbitration which no one is bound to obey, and with which, therefore, corporate wealth may soothe while it throttles and enslaves labor." Nugent clearly sided with the strikers against their employers. Nor did he fall into the analytical trap so often used against labor by employers in the nineteenth century, the wages fund theory. Labor knew, Nugent argued, "that it produces the fund from which is derived its own compensation—nay more, that it not only thus pays its own wages, but gives to capital a bonus for the privilege of doing so."[43]

When he turned from description to an analysis of the causes and solutions to labor's situation, however, Nugent, like the other Southern Populists, did not envision socialism but a simple market society. The reason for labor's justified discontent and resentment was its "agony to be free, to taste the sweets of independence, to find an open door to its lost opportunities." This desire led to strikes and industrial disorder. This aspiration drove the farmer, artisan, and wage worker, black and white, and the clerk, lawyer, and doctor—"in fine all who work with brain or brawn in dependence upon those who hold the world's purse strings"— together to oppose monopoly. Committed and knowledgeable antimonopoly greenbackers like Nugent differed with the rest of the Southern Populists not in their vision but in its breadth and articulation. Although most of the southern reformers supported the Omaha platform, many did not completely understand the scope of change it implied. As we will see later, the more limited experience and grasp of the issues which many Southern Populists had eventually resulted in their breaking with the Omaha platform. But the dream of all the reformers remained the same, and in the years from 1891 through 1894 most of them shared with Nugent and the antimonopoly greenbackers not a sectional analysis of America's ills but the crude class analysis of men against money, the masses against monopoly, the producers against the exploiting capitalists.

Like almost all Southern Populists, for Nugent the "ascendency" of capital derived from legislation which gave it "unjust advantages and enabled it to monopolize both natural resources and public functions and utilities." The problem lay not with the operation of the market system but with its perversion by special legislation. "Every person is entitled by the law of natural justice to possess and enjoy the fruits of his own skill and industry. Give to all equal opportunities and under the operation of this law each would get his just share of the world's wealth; but give to any man the right to take not only the produce of his own labor, but a portion of that which is derived from the labor of his neighbor and you unjustly increase his opportunities of gain. Give to a few individuals organized into a corporation the right to dispense for a price services of a necessary and public character—services essential to the existence and well being of organized society—and you arm them with the power to levy tribute upon the whole community and acquire wealth almost without limit. You, in other words, provide for those consummate products of economic conditions—the millionaire and the tramp." Monopoly, not the market place, caused America's ills.

That Nugent desired a simple market society of private property, profit, and small unit competition was quite apparent. Equally clearly, however, Nugent, along with the overwhelming majority of his southern brethren, did not want to turn back the clock to a simpler time. What most Southern Populists realized implicitly, the firmest of the antimonopoly greenbackers made explicit: America's problem was not industrial development but the destruction of equitable and decent economic and social relations between people brought by the particular organization of that development. It was, as Nugent said, "not the excessive production of wealth but its unequal distribution which constitutes the menacing evil of the times."[44] Under normal conditions, as "the population increases and society becomes more highly organized, so ought the means and facilities of civilized life to be more and more within reach of the great body of people, and the comforts and conveniences of life to more and more abound. The point ought to be thus reached at which poverty would disappear." But it had not because the great mass of people had been denied "fair opportunities for the exertion of their faculties." Monopoly dominated the means of distribution—transportation and money—and robbed the producers of the rewards of their labor. The solution was obvious. Let the people on a cooperative basis, through the government, own, control, and operate these monopolies, and the simple market society would once again become a reality. Doing this would allow "free play to competition within the proper sphere of individual effort and investment," without the need to resort to "extreme socialistic schemes."

The analysis, of course, made a great deal of sense to anyone who considered production primarily in terms of agriculture, where individuals working alone or in small groups produced the great bulk of goods. Neither Nugent nor any of the other Southern Populists wanted to give up the benefits of industrial society. They did not realize, however, that in the shops and factories of urban industrial America not only had a quantitative change been made in production but a qualitative change in the organization of production had also occurred. They could understand the importance of access to the means and tools of production. Their demand that idle land be opened to settlers who would use it and that cheap credit be provided to those needing it made this clear. But they did not understand that industrial expansion had put these means and tools forever beyond the reach of individual working people, thus denying them access to individual economic independence. No single worker could hope to own a steel mill, much less operate it with the help of a few hired hands who themselves one day would own a steel mill if they worked hard enough and saved.

This inability to understand the extent to which industrial development had changed the nature of American society gave the antimonopoly greenback analysis in particular and Southern Populism in general a peculiar tone. On the one hand it harked back to an earlier, almost Jeffersonian ideal, a simple market society. On the other it accepted and desired a modern industrial society. The southern reformers understood as well as anyone in America the suffering and injustice which the organization of an industrial society on a capitalistic basis brought; they failed to appreciate the fundamental economic and social changes on which this organization was based. This failure, which must be attributed in great part to the Southern Populists' lack of experience with America's urban and industrial society and the general incapacity of the American intellectual heritage to compensate for this deficiency, meant that they saw little problem in proposing as sufficient reform the combination of a simple market society of producers on the one level with government ownership and operation of the means of distribution on another. The productive and distributive levels of society would be integrated through the democratic government ownership and operation of the means of distribution, particularly transportation and money, allowing the cooperative control of these things by all the people in the equal interest of each.

The antimonopoly greenbacker position and the Omaha platform were premised on the practicability of this two-tiered economic system. Most of the Southern Populists operated on this assumption in the years from 1891 to 1894, albeit implicitly. This implicitness, however, as we shall see later, helped cover up implications which not all Southern Populists were willing to accept. The antimonopoly greenback analysis raised issues which treatened not only industrial and financial capitalism but also the market system itself, acceptance of which the southern reformers shared with their opponents. The emergence of these implications into political dialogue by 1894 led directly to free silver and the debacle of 1896 for all but the most thorough and explicit of the antimonopoly greenbackers, and even for these few they remained a source of confusion. Before we examine this development, however, we need to take a look at the terms in which the southern reformers presented their analysis, because these metaphors and images, too, had an important effect on the eventual breakdown of the antimonopoly greenback position, implicit and explicit, by 1896.

CHAPTER 10

The Logic of a Metaphor

"The golden era is ahead of us and not behind us."

In December of 1891 Watson wrote a long piece for his paper entitled "A Dream of To-day and To-morrow." In his dream of today Watson found murder condemned but war praised; churches, schools, and charities flourishing alongside crime, ignorance, and beggars. Why? "Those who made the laws had so cunningly made them that the strong man was master of the weak. . . . [T]he unnatural was the rule. . . . [A] feverish haste had taken possession of mankind and . . . the race was madly run for things he [sic] did not really want. . . . [O]ne man pushed, because another pushed, cheated because others cheated, hoarded because others hoarded. Was cruel because he thought the same measure would be meted out to him were situations reversed."

The dream of tomorrow followed quickly, with no interlude. Looking out over the same world Watson now found it filled with "light" and "harmony." "The great rush and hurry" had disappeared. The earth had room and food enough for all and once again became the "home for God's children." "The Rulers of the People no longer scorned them nor defrauded them with Cunning Laws and sharp practices. The People themselves now ruled and the Laborer was no longer a serf." Beggars disappeared for all had homes, work, and fair wages. The source of their "rivalry and hatred" removed, people treated one another as human beings and crime disappeared, along with murder and war. The people were contented and prosperous.

Why did tomorrow shine so much brighter than today? "[T]he mistake of yesterday was found and corrected." A "few brave men all over the world" abolished "the old false order of things" and accorded "fair treatment" to the laborer. But his dream did not reveal to Watson how harmony and justice in a producer society came. He did not know how often the reformers had failed, how cruelly they had been tortured, or how much "battle and bloodshed" had preceded their victory.[1]

In September of the same year a North Carolina Allianceman, soon to become a Populist, voiced similar hopes in a letter to the *Progressive Farmer*. He felt that the "dark and foreboding" times through which America was passing presaged a new world. The great material gains of the last sixty years would be excelled by those of the next fifty and be accompanied by even greater "social, moral, intellectual and spiritual advancement. . . . The golden era is ahead of us and not behind us." "Universal material prosperity" approached. The United States was ready, he concluded, "to enter into the new dispensation where all shall know God inanimated [*sic*] in human flesh from the least to the greatest."[2] Once again nothing was said of the process which propelled contemporary American society into its glorious future.

The whole tone of these two rather long passages, both in avowedly political papers and from avowedly political writers, was almost completely apolitical, in the usual sense of political. Not only did these two men fail to connect the reforms they both advocated, sometimes at personal risk, with the future state of society, but they presented no details of the transformation and discussed little of the political, social, or economic organization of that future condition. The change had little content or process; it simply happened. Much of the reason was that both men, the second more apparently than the first, cast their ideas in terms and a framework borrowed from the religious idea of the millennium.

The analysis of contemporary society and its ideal replacement drawn from the Southern Populists' Jeffersonian and Jacksonian heritage had some serious drawbacks. It described a society without steam, electricity, telegraphs and telephones, railroads, Standard Oil, Carnegie Steel, or any of the physical and cultural accoutrements of the industrial and financial capitalist society which accompanied them. Having a less explicit content, the millenarian tradition, particularly lively in evangelical Protestantism, furnished the southern reformers with a more useful intellectual apparatus for dealing with the future state of society. Southern Populism was by no stretch of the imagination a millennial movement, but the millennial idea appealed to many Southern Populists as a familiar notion which they understood. Secularized, it helped them understand and believe in what they were trying to do. It also had the added advantage of being readily recognizable and understandable to most of the people to whom the Southern Populists addressed themselves.

Millennial eschatology, although now often divided by historians into pre- and postmillennial categories, appears to have been a much vaguer notion in much of nineteenth-century religion. Revivalism could include both. Finney was clearly a postmillennialist, while Moody, active after the Civil War, was a premillennialist.[3] In general, however, the major denominations in the late nineteenth century, because of their increasing concern with worldly improvement and reform, could be considered postmillennial.[4] Certainly this was true for the Social Gospelers, who shared a good deal with the Southern Populists in their criticism of the institutional church. In fact, Ahlstrom includes the Populists among the Social Gospelers, although unfortunately he uses William Jennings Bryan as his example.[5] Even the Southern Baptists and Methodists in the decades before 1900 grew increasingly involved in reform activity as opposed to concentrating solely on the salvation of individual souls.[6]

There was in the late nineteenth century, of course, a trend in American evangelical Protestantism toward a premillennial eschatology. Radical Adventism and dispensational premillennialism, the latter climaxing in the Scofield Bible and the Fundamentals in the early twentieth century, had roots in the nineteenth. The American Methodists also witnessed in the late nineteenth century a Holiness revival which eventually culminated in the Holiness and Pentecostal churches.[7] While Ahlstrom found most of the Holiness congregations located outside the rural South, Farish discovered disruption in the Southern Methodist church in the 1880s, brought by the appearance of the doctrine of "entire sanctification" and the associated Holiness movement, with its emphasis on "'otherworldliness'" and its premillennial tendencies.[8]

The Southern Populists undoubtedly would, if we could ask them, have considered themselves primarily postmillennial evangelical Protestants, although the concern among some of them with a possible bloody Armageddon around the corner[9] suggests perhaps some premillennial tendencies brought by fears of defeat. That no sharp delineation of pre- and postmillennial seems possible for large numbers of evangelical Protestants lying somewhere between the Social Gospelers and the Holiness or Pentecostal churches makes it difficult to say that *all* Southern Populists were postmillennialists, although logic suggests that they would be.

But probably the issue is not that important. Southern Populism was not a millennial movement; it did not exist to predict Christ's second coming. Southern Populists used the idea of the millennium as a descriptive and analytical tool, although at times, as discussed in the latter part of this chapter, the use of such images could have an impact on political analysis and action. When some Southern Populists began to sound like radical pre- or postmillennialists, it was more the result of the logic of the metaphors they used than because of a particular eschatological belief. The object or goal being described rather than the eschatological orientation determined how the Southern Populists used the metaphor.

Discussions of a Populist future, for instance, invariably had a postmillennial ring to them. The theme of chaos before order, an integral part of the religious millennium, enjoyed a prominent place in such discussions. Although very unhappy with the fraudulent election of 1892, one Georgia Populist did not think that "the nations" were "degenerating." God would guide the country to safety. "What now seems to be chaos and disorder is but the passing cloud heralding the coming of a new political era."[10] How would the new era come, how would spreading poverty and the increasingly bitter struggle for wealth end? "With a change," wrote a North Carolina editor in 1894, "so radical that no trace of the old disease will remain, so sudden that no black scoria of war, famine and crime will mark the transition. A change foreshadowed in the awakened conscience of the followers of the great teacher, and made actual by the sufferage, in the hands of a free, intelligent and determined people."[11] The suddenness of the change, its radical nature, the frequent absence of any discussion of process, and the allusion to Christ—a frequent occurrence in the reformers' references to the future state of society[12]—mark the presence of a millennial metaphor shaping Southern Populist thought about the ultimate goal of their reforms.

Obviously, however, in most cases the promise of future prosperity and happiness could not be construed as millennial. We saw earlier that as a legitimate political promise it often gave considerable substance to Southern Populist discussions of their specific plans for the reform of society.[13] This kind of rhetoric, however, lay on a continuum of such statements which moved from political promises and slight millenarian rhetoric to wider and more clearly millenarian promises, and beyond that to millenarian statements which remained little secularized by application to this world.

The explicit use of "millennium" was not unusual.[14] "I believe that the millennium is to take place on earth, and I don't believe that it is going to be forced on us," announced a Texas Populist. "I believe that Christ is now ready for His part and that man has got to do his before it comes."[15] A Populist victory would bear witness to humanity's readiness. Some, like one Alabama Populist in 1894, saw the millennium quite close. "The night of ignorance is far spent." God had heard "the prayers" of the masses of people. "We look in the near future for reformatory and saving influences which must at last banish crime, and which will hasten the rising of a glorious day, such as the prophets have foretold and earnest praying Christians have most sincerely desired. Yes, the light has come."[16] The gospel of Christ the Savior became that of Christ the Reformer. Heavenly paradise sometimes became "the grander civilization" of humanity's earthbound future and secular salvation rewarded the faithful. "Secular" is used advisedly, since in some cases the religious millennium of Christianity was not very distinct from that of the Southern Populists. This positive side of the millennial image served to justify the Southern Populists in their activities as reformers and helped explain what they were ultimately after by paralleling or equating it with a kingdom of God on earth.

The Southern Populists' use of the millennial metaphor could also have premillennial overtones, as when their use of the image intimated future disaster. That the bullet might replace the ballot remained a concern for many southern reformers from 1891 through 1896. "The money power on the one side and the producers and toilers on the other are marshalling their forces for the fight," wrote the editor of the Monroe, Georgia, *Populist* in 1893. "The grand battle of Armageddon is close at hand." The producers would resort to arms if conditions did not change.[17] With no reform along Populist lines, without elimination of the growing poverty of the "toiling masses," violent upheaval and chaos would destroy the American republic.[18] The images one Alabama Populist used provided a clue to the sources of these ideas. The concentration of wealth into a few hands, he maintained, created its own disaster.

> Next to capital, I know of no evil that so threatens the governmental structures as the mob—the people outraged. Capital makes the mob; the mob makes death thicker than the autumnal leaves of Vallambrosa. The mob is a wild beast that turns on its masters, and rends them to atoms. Capital can never learn that the people can suffer no more. It can never believe that the murmurings of the masses are deeper than superficial. The retributive angel may write upon the wall, but aristocratical knees no longer tremble. The hot blood of the libertine rushes on. Again the winecup is quaffed to the brim; again God and His people are blasphemed. Aristocractical contempt for the masses precludes belief in the omnipotence of the masses. Ere long the heavy tramp of Cyrus and his host (the people) will be heard in the Babylon of our aristocracy. There knees will smite together. Heads will roll, severed from the bodies they guided. Pillage, crime, rapine must inevitably follow. And will capital dare force us to the extremity?[19]

A mysterious, terrifying disaster loomed. Only the success of Populist reform, read the first address of the Populists to the people of Louisiana, could avoid "a revolution by violence . . . accompanied by horrors and injustices at which civilized humanity shudders."[20]

The violent revolution feared by many Southern Populists[21] was usually a blind striking out of the oppressed rather than a planned upheaval by them. The editor of the *Progressive Farmer* described it as a "convulsion" of the mass of people degraded and disgraced by poverty, shaking the ground under "the great and rich corporations and individuals," making them "hopeless targets before the stampede of the reckless, hunger-crazed millions."[22] At times the Lord's role was critical. The cry rising from the poverty-stricken masses surrounded by plenty, wrote W. S. Morgan, "will reach the ears of the 'Lord of Sabaoth,' and call down the wrathful vengeance of heaven. . . . It is the only intimation of the internal commotion that will sooner or later break with volcanic force the thin crust which surrounds it."[23] The revolution came not with the rising of the proletariat against its capitalist exploiters but with God's just anger at the oppression of the righteous; not the Internationale but "Mene, Mene, Tekel Upharsin" signaled its imminence. "His satanic majesty has come up, and, as in the days of Daniel, false prophets have hindered the messenger of peace, but the time is drawing near when the bonds will be broken, and it would be well for many to stand from under. The god [sic] of truth has waited long and patiently, but the groans of an oppressed people have reached His ears and He will come speedily to their rescue, and the overthrow of the powers that be will be like that of Babylon. The smoke of their torment will ascend and the merchants and midshipmen of plutocracy will wail and lament over the destruction of their greed."[24] From the Bible rather than Marx or Proudhon most Southern Populists formulated their ideas of revolution.[25] Although some carried this element of the metaphor farther than others, for almost all the Southern Populists the Biblical image of the millennium furnished the terms for their discussion of the process and the result of radical social change and upheaval in a secular world.

To a few Southern Populists, however, revolution had more immediately political overtones. "It is coming. Get down your rusty sword and revolver. We say ballots, but the capitalists say bullets."[26] In Texas this kind of talk was heard most often. The editor of the *Young County Call* wrote in March 1895 that if "the people" used the peaceful ballot to regain control of the government and broke "the power of organized capital . . . then the cry will go up from beneath the throne of mammon that the country is going into the hands of communists; the military arm of the government will be invoked for the protection of 'vested rights;' the representatives of the people will be arrested and imprisoned as conspirators and usurpers, and the country will stand face to face with a choice between meek submission and a forcible maintenance of the American Republic." Then, indeed, violence would break out and the revolution be at hand.[27]

The *Southern Mercury*, however, furnished the best example of a changing political attitude toward revolution. In December 1894 the editor wrote that times were so bad, so many Americans were being "pauperized" and destroyed "by the devils of greed," that "actual revolution" might be "the only means of deliverance."[28] By July 1895 he was warning that even if the Populists did elect a reform president in "a peaceful political revolution," the people would have to be ready for probable "war" with the money power to insure his inauguration.[29] The Baltimore plan of the national bankers, endorsed by Cleveland, moved the *Mercury*'s editor to state in November 1895 that "the fight will come, and let it come! In the meantime the masses should be making preparations for this irrepressible conflict."[30] Twice more in late 1895 and early 1896 he spoke of the probability of "revolution and chaos" being forced upon the country by the plutocracy.[31]

In the *Mercury*'s 4 June issue, the editor ceased to speak of revolution as a defensive response of the people. "The political conditions prevailing in this country," he stated, "are alarming!" Money had so corrupted legislatures that all the political power and most of the wealth lay in the hands of a tiny minority of people. "A proper distribution of wealth cannot again be secured without a revolution. . . . There is nothing more certain than that the time is coming when the masses of the people will demand the restoration of conditions upon which popular government can rest securely, and they will prosecute this demand to that end though it result in blood and revolution." Although millennial elements remained evident, in a two-year period the *Mercury* had moved from wondering about the necessity of revolution almost to the point of advocating it.[32]

A few of the most radical antimonopoly greenbackers began to deal with revolution not as a millennial Armageddon but as a legitimate, if undesirable, extension of the politics of social change. Most of the southern reformers, while they remained as committed as their antimonopoly greenback brethren to creating a better society in America, lacked a social analysis thoroughgoing enough to suggest that traditional electoral politics might not suffice. Seeing more clearly how extensively American society would have to be altered to achieve this ideal and understanding the degree to which such a change would be actively resisted, at least some of the antimonopoly greenbackers, like the editor of the *Southern Mercury*, began to consider the possibility of violence and move away from the millennial metaphor toward a more political analysis of the idea of revolution. The other southern reformers, not seeing the possible need of such radical change to achieve their ends and concerned about the impact of possible violence on the maintenance of a market system, private property, and profit, continued to regard revolution as the least desirable alternative, not as politics but as bloody anarchy, the destruction not only of the existing social order but the possibility of anything better. They never broke away from their religious heritage and experience in their analysis of political and social change. Revolution as Armageddon could not be considered a political activity. The radicals' handling of the idea of revolution only underscored the millennial nature of the other Southern Populists' use of it and its roots in their religious heritage.

"Where are the saints?"

The Southern Populists examined American society primarily by analogy, applying metaphors and images based on known and understood ways of thinking to the society they found around them, the outline of which, in turn, the metaphors and images frequently colored. They sought to create positive analogies for issues and ideas they favored and negative ones for those they did not. They drew on their evangelical Protestant background for metaphors to describe social change, condemn their opponents, define the "middle class," and give value to productive labor. A North Carolina Populist in August 1892 put his finger on what most if not all Southern Populists felt about the relationship between morals and social reform. "Men must in their political conduct be governed by the same moral laws, that control individual actions."[33] This association of political and social reform with moral and religious tenets allowed the reformers to attack the amoral and often inhuman effects of industrial and financial capitalism. By emphasizing personal and human qualities such as justice, equality, and decency, the moral and religious metaphors and imagery helped give the Southern Populists an eloquent and accurate insight into American society in the late nineteenth century that few of their more powerful or prosperous contemporaries had, caught up as they were in the promises and rewards of the American middle-class utopia.

The connection between religious and moral tenets and Populist reform thought had its drawbacks, however. When the Southerners extended it to explain what their party was doing and why it was doing it, they found themselves engaged in a religious and moral as much as a political and social battle. A delay or defeat in reform, asserted a North Carolina Populist, "is a victory for the money power and Satan."[34] A Georgia Populist was more optimistic. Satan, not God, created the order which permitted the idle few to possess all the wealth created by the producing many, and the Devil worked his way through "his earthly agents." But God was "with the people in this fight against Satan and his emissaries. Who can doubt the final result?"[35] In 1896 an Alabama editor asked his readers, "are you for God or Belial, for Christ or the Devil, for the right or the wrong? Your vote next Monday will show which you are for. You can't be for the truth and the right and vote against them."[36]

The employment of religious metaphors and imagery, of course, had a very practical purpose, as at least some of the Southern Populists realized. In an editorial written in September 1895 W. S. Morgan of Arkansas defended his use of a rhetorical device called "Letters from the Devil." He did not profane the words of God in his attacks on the false practices of lawyers, bankers, and preachers. He used allegory and parable to make a strong impression. "No book on earth," he argued, "presents subjects in a stronger light, or uses better methods for doing it, than the Bible. For this reason we resort to those methods to impress upon the people the importance of asserting the growing evils which are hurling this nation and its people toward the vortex of revolution."[37]

Sometimes, however, the use of the religious metaphor and imagery went beyond analogy to assume an identity with the particular issue in question, although the point at which this occurred was often hard to determine. When the Southern Populists, like one Texas editor, accused the Democrats of straying from "living issues" because of the "dishonest and corrupting influence begotten of worship of the golden calf, together with intense greed for the flesh pots of office,"[38] reform of the Democratic party remained remotely possible. He still used the metaphor to describe and evaluate. The distinction between the metaphor and what it was supposed to describe broke down, as it did when one North Carolina Populist announced that America's financial system, which redeemed one kind of money in another, "was concocted in Hades and transplanted to earth, and it has made a pandemonium of a garden of Eden. . . . [T]he father of lies, the incubator of all meanness, it has damned more souls, committed more perjury, it has made a hell of heaven, banished God from earth and set up the devil's kingdom, it has debauched our elections, established the reign of political thieves, it has brought the cause of Christ into disrepute and shut the minister's mouth, and it is the quintesence [sic] of all that is mean. It is upheld by knaves, endorsed by fools and it must be uprooted by patriots and sent to Hades to keep company with its author."[39] The metaphor lost its evaluative function; the existing financial system was not just bad but the engine of evil itself.

The fusion of the moral and religious metaphor with what it was intended to describe or explain brought a logic of its own to Populist thought, for it changed the terms of discussion. When Populism, for instance, became a religion, reform success became salvation and politics sometimes assumed a transcendent role in human society. "[I]f God be the author of all good, and all reform is good," reasoned a Louisiana Populist, "then God is the author of reform; hence, all godly people should be reformers."[40] He might well have added a last conclusion to his syllogism, that all reform must be of God. When it became "a man's religious duty to concern himself about his country's government," the state of his country's government became a religious and moral problem.

One of the clearest examples of this logic occurred in an extended discussion of poverty by the editor of the *Texas Advance*. He began by comparing "a condition of poverty among the peasantry and laboring people" to famine, war, and plague, and judged it worse; it was "a disease without a cure, an evil without a redemption." In the third paragraph the editor maintained that "no power on earth or known to man" could withstand "the blight and death-dealing effects of poverty." The tenuous distinction between poverty and its results broke down in the second sentence of the fourth paragraph. After writing that poverty "stalks abroad like an incarnate fiend," the editor gave up all pretence at analogy. Poverty "gulps down all grades of humanity, irrespective of sex or age. . . . It utterly blots out the home from the face of the earth, transforming its members into tramps and vagabonds, consigning them to a life of charity and crime." It filled the poor houses, fattened the jails, and filled "the dens of iniquity with victims."

In the last two paragraphs the logic of the metaphor became clear. Poverty had become evil incarnate, and what was the response? "Where are the saints?" asked the editor. "Where are the Christian people of which the country has boasted? There is a great need for your services in the public vineyards. Come to the rescue, you champions of the cause of the meek and lowly! If there ever was a time when you should gird on the armor of the savior of mankind it is now! Is there no Moses to go up on Mount Horeb and listen for the voice of Jehovah?"[41] While the use of the religious metaphor allowed this Texas editor to express in the most potent manner available to him his outrage at one of the most prominent fruits of American capitalism, its use also had another result. By the end of the discussion the metaphor no longer described the condition of poverty but had merged with its subject and transformed it. Poverty ceased to be an issue in and of itself and became evidence, even the vehicle, of the devil's presence in the world. As a result, the solution to poverty no longer lay primarily in the realm of social or political reform. The logic of the metaphor made its own demands.

When identified with the institutions and conditions of the wider public world, the use of the religious and moral metaphor and imagery often led to the personalization of these things. If we tend to objectify persons, the Southern Populists tended to personalize objects. When this happened in discussions of the gold standard, for instance, gold became a god, the financial system became the devil incarnate. "Gold," wrote a Virginia Populist, "is a tyrant. . . . It is an inherent coward, sniffs the battle from afar, and from danger hides, taking refuge in the bankers' vaults till the battle is over, and then it comes forth with the buzzard, the one to feast upon the slain, the other to prey upon the living." As "a labor robber" and "the world's panic breeder," this "Goliath" had to be "dethroned" and "its power to oppress" destroyed.[42] Gold took on a life of its own, with human qualities of consciousness, motivation, and a malevolent intelligence. The problems of gold's evil influence no longer remained confined to the realm of political policy but became a question of morality as well.

The same thing could occur in discussions of money and the financial system. A Texas editor addressed money in the second person singular in his indictment of the evils it brought. "Oh, thou ravisher of powerful nations, great cities and flourishing kingdoms!" he began. "Darker" and "more excrable [sic]" than the Bastile or Inquisition, "you have sealed the fountain of my country's prosperity, and henceforth pinching want, tattered garments, wasting hunger, fireless hearthstones, inhuman hovels, must be the heritage of millions. Each year will swell their number. . . . The motionless wheels, the silent mills, the closed mines, the hungry men and weeping women and children attest your power. The republic staggers beneath your blows."[43] Money became a raging, self-conscious, destructive entity with a personality of its own. Here was a second definition of money. The first defined money as a neutral object which had to be correctly understood and handled to bring a better social order. Under it the Populists took account of the various ways to define and use money, analyzed it as a tool for improving people's social and economic condition, and were aware of its many positive and negative facets. The second definition personalized it into "Money," shut out many questions about money's use, the need for it, or its particular abuses. It could exclude a definition of money based on its efficacy for improving humanity's economic and social lot.

We have seen a similar situation in our discussion of the millennial metaphor. Sometimes the reformers qualified the millennium by reference to social, political, and economic issues, but at other times they made almost no reference to existing social evils. When "the rich are weighed in the balances and found wanting," the "battle of Armageddon . . . God arrayed against Magog" represented the resolution of the conflict. The rich and "their unrighteous mammon" would "perish," and the poor, downtrodden, and righteous people of God would be saved in His triumph.[44] This kind of solution to society's problems rarely made direct reference to the particular grievances the Southern Populists enunciated in their platforms. When salvation or damnation were the choices the relative merits of a bimetallic or a greenback currency system sometimes became less important. When public issues turned into questions of personal morality the solutions to them tended to become those of personal and private morality, not those of social, economic, and political change. The agent of change often became God. The source of social and political change no longer rested exclusively with human beings. God's prior plan often played a crucial role. Reform could and sometimes did become a function of rallying the faithful without explaining why they should rally. Then failures of analysis like free silver and the advocacy of a redeemable currency system could stay hidden until no time remained to correct them.

That morality could not be divorced from social, political, and economic questions was a major strength of Southern Populist thought. Poverty and exploitation were not just economic problems. The danger lay not in the perception but in the use of the metaphors and images which conveyed it. When religious and moral metaphors and images fused with the specific issues they were intended to describe and evaluate, their use could lead to a double vision of the solution to America's problems. One solution depended on altering the structure of society through reform of its parts. The other, a logical one when the reformers created religious and moral metaphorical identities, had a religious and moral and consequently personalized destination which inclined toward salvation sometimes as often as social change. Particular problems of the social order became evidence of social decay rather than causes of it. Solutions might not require dealing with specific social, economic, and political grievances, but defeating Satan and his worldly minions. The reformers then sometimes measured the effectiveness of an issue not in terms of its social and economic value to human beings but in terms of driving evil from the world. The struggle between these two tendencies, indeed, is one way to look at what happened to the Southern Populists in 1896. As the moral and religious metaphors more and more often became identified with the issues and problems they were originally intended to define and evaluate, many Southern Populists might have found it progressively easier to seek the solution to America's crisis in the moral reorganization of society, in a millennium, than in the political and social analysis offered by the Omaha platform and antimonopoly greenbackism.

PART III

THE POLITICAL PRICE

INTRODUCTION

Historians have sometimes argued that ideas and beliefs, especially in politics, have little effect on behavior. "Watch what they do," the reader is cautioned, "not what they say. People act in their perceived self-interest and their explanations are very often unreliable justifications." Besides being rather cynical about human motivation, this argument also inclines toward simplicity in the explanation of behavior. On a day-to-day basis most people do not govern their behavior with reference to comprehensive philosophies. Like most other Americans the Southern Populists themselves rarely reflected on either the logic or the coherency of their economic and social beliefs. This argument, however, fails to explain why some Southerners risked social ostracism, physical violence, even death, to take a political position. It also fails to explain why a correspondence existed between what the Southern Populists thought and felt about the world around them and their political activity. No discussion that fails to consider these ideas can explain what happened to the Populist party in the southern states between 1891 and 1896 (see Appendix A).

A poor understanding of the antimonopoly greenback position among most North Carolina and Alabama Populists meant that the party in these states never really confronted the dilemma of reform. The party there quickly abandoned most of the Omaha platform and the rudimentary class politics of a poor black–poor white coalition and turned instead to an intense effort to carve political victory out of platforms limited primarily to free silver and fair elections and designed to attract old party free silver advocates. The plan succeeded admirably—for the Democrats, who by appropriating the free silver issue appropriated most of the Populists.

In Georgia the script read a bit differently. There a firm commitment to greenbackism combined with a weak understanding of the antimonopoly analysis led the Populists into an unsuccessful effort to divorce the rudimentary politics of class from the Omaha platform's antimonopoly basis. In Texas, however, where antimonopoly greenbackism had been preached for at least a decade, the Populists withstood pressures to exchange the Omaha platform and a coalition of poor blacks and whites for political victory under the guise of fusion and sectional politics. Interestingly, only in Texas did the Populist party continue through 1896 to increase its share of the vote.

The dilemma of reform, however, destroyed the party nationally. When forced to choose in 1896 most of the Southern Populists joined their western brethren and Bryan in a free silver crusade which united the South and West against the East rather than the exploited producers against their nonproducing enemies. With the national Populist party gone, the South's new middle class faced little opposition when after 1896 it tightened its grip on southern politics with disfranchisement and Jim Crow. By using this control to consolidate its economic position, the new middle class insured the South's continued subordination in the national economy.

CHAPTER 11

The Road to Fusion:
North Carolina and Alabama

"this broader class of business men"
William Jennings Bryan, 1896

North Carolina

In 1891, when North Carolina Alliancemen first debated the need for a third party, they based their discussion on the antimonopoly greenback St. Louis platform and considered the subtreasury plan their major issue.[1] In early July the editor of the *Progressive Farmer* denied that free silver and tariff reform were "the greatest issues before the people. It [the *Farmer*] stands to-day on the Sub-Treasury plan, where it has always stood, and where it will stand in the future."[2] Reports from county committees and letters from North Carolina reformers in the *Progressive Farmer* indicated that they shared the editor's sentiments, at least through the spring of 1892. Nor did the reformers in these years ignore other elements of the radical program. Government ownership of the railroads remained important[3] and legal tender fiat paper money continued to receive attention, sometimes aside from examinations of the subtreasury.[4] They also discussed in the 1892 elections the political alliance of black and white rural poor against the money power.[5]

By 1896, however, the People's party in North Carolina had moved far from these positions. Reference to and defense of the Omaha platform had disappeared almost entirely. Except for isolated individuals no reformer for a couple of years had mentioned government ownership of the railroads, a legal tender fiat currency, or the subtreasury.[6] Advocacy of a poor white–poor black political coalition had disappeared entirely. By the spring of 1896 most North Carolina Populists believed that the free silver would solve all of America's ills. This movement away from both an antimonopoly greenback analysis of American society and a liberal position on the race issue signaled a switch in political strategy and analysis by the North Carolina party and most of its members. They dropped their advocacy of a rudimentary class coalition of poor rural whites and blacks against an expanding industrial and financial capitalism which towns and cities represented, figuratively and in reality, in exchange for a sectional alliance based on free silver, the agricultural South and West versus the commercial and industrial North and East.

On the surface this change resulted from the conjunction of several interrelated political factors. The first although not necessarily most important was the political aspirations and judgments of the Populist leadership in North Carolina, particularly those of Marion Butler, the dominant figure in the state party after the death of L. L. Polk in June 1892. A second factor was the presence of a strong white Republican vote in the state. Last was the influx of free silver Democrats into the North Carolina party in late 1893 and 1894, usually to protest the Democratic party's role in the repeal of the Sherman Silver Purchase Act. These people, who had not been through the subtreasury campaigns of 1890, 1891, and 1892, brought into the Populist party a great number of bimetallic advocates who understood poorly, if at all, the radical position. None of these things, however, need have undermined the North Carolina party's adherence to the Omaha platform any more than they did in Texas. But the failure to understand adequately the technicalities and implications of antimonopoly greenbackism, including its crude class analysis, meant that the effort to substitute a free-silver, sectional politics for an economic and political coalition of poor whites and blacks enjoyed easy sailing. In addition, the increasing use of metaphorical identities as 1896 approached intensified the trend toward free silver politics, making it virtually impossible by that year for antimonopoly greenbackism to have significant impact in the state.

The move away from any form of racial liberalism started early in North Carolina. A few, like one Populist from Martin County, North Carolina, discounted the threat of "negro supremacy," pointing out that "the poor old negro is just like myself, they [sic] are never allowed to rule anything but hoe, axe and plow." Six-cent cotton did not discriminate. Reminding his white brethren that blacks wanted not social equality but "more meat and bread," he called for an interracial political alliance of the poor and dispossessed and implied that white reformers ought actively to recruit and work with blacks.[7] This latter notion was very unusual among North Carolina Populists. Those who argued for any sort of black and white alliance normally assumed that the reform party did not need to make "great professions of friendship" to gain black votes because, as a North Carolina Populist wrote in August 1892, the interests of white Populists were the same as the blacks.[8]

North Carolina Populists at best remained uneasy about their relationship to black voters in 1892. The *Progressive Farmer* defensively admitted that blacks had participated in the state convention but maintained that they came only from the black belt Republican counties where blacks were in a great majority. The Democrats would have done the same if they could.[9] The *Farmer*, unlike elements in both old parties, was not "negro-loving." The Southern Populists proposed only "to give the negroes justice and that is all any organization or party ought to offer."[10] Few if any North Carolina Populists ever came closer to the promise of legal and political equality so often made to blacks in Georgia and Texas. More frequently they said nothing or, like the Mount Olivet Alliance of Franklinton and Marion Butler, favored Jim Crow laws to separate further blacks and whites.[11] No evidence appeared of any effort by the Populists to organize blacks into the party on a local or state level, and more often the reformers made clear their allegiance to white supremacy.[12]

With few exceptions, after the elections of 1892 North Carolina Populists made no defense of black political rights. Usually they contented themselves with trying to balance a slender appeal to the self-interest of black voters with a defense of their party from the charge of advocating black supremacy and social equality.[13] This was particularly true after their fusion on the state level with the Republican party. They also constantly attacked the Democrats for race mixing,[14] using all the weapons available. They charged that Cleveland consciously promoted miscegenation with his New York City school ruling[15] and his 1886 invitation of Frederick Douglass to his White House wedding reception,[16] and that with their policy of appointing blacks to office the state and national Democratic parties intended to promote "social equality."[17] After the 1892 elections the North Carolina Populists never again even hinted at a special appeal to blacks based on the promise of equal civil and political rights. They had made their first and last attempt, minimal as it was, to create a biracial reform coalition within the People's party.

The most immediate effect of what effort the North Carolina Populists did make was a dismal showing among black voters in 1892.[18] Behind this performance and the subsequent abandonment of any effort to involve blacks directly in the Populist party lay a development which, on the surface, appeared unrelated to the race issue. By the summer of 1892 the North Carolina People's party was headed directly down the road to free silver and fusion in 1896. Although they defended the subtreasury a few times in the 1892 state campaign, the Populists no longer explained precisely how the plan would work. In June 1892 the editor of the *Progressive Farmer* asserted that essentially the subtreasury meant an increase in the money supply.[19] Except for a very few Populists, especially James Murdock, by the end of 1892 discussion in North Carolina of the subtreasury plan disappeared.[20] Letters from sub-Alliances and reports of county Populist and sub-Alliance meetings in the state after the summer of 1892 never mentioned the subtreasury plan, and from late 1892 without exception free silver and the perfidy of the old parties dominated the resolutions passed by these local groups.[21]

The closer the 1896 elections came the more completely free silver prevailed in North Carolina reform writing and speaking, although the weakness of the antimonopoly greenback analysis had become evident much earlier, even before the subtreasury dropped from view. In June 1891 Marion Butler blamed the decline of values on the demonetization of silver in 1873.[22] In January 1893 another North Carolina Populist maintained that with "a sufficiency of silver and a currency based thereon ... we can be a thriving, prosperous people without a dollar of gold."[23] The editor of the *Progressive Farmer* in February 1894 insisted that only free coinage of silver was necessary to put millions of unemployed men back to work and to feed and clothe them properly.[24]

Such statements were common by 1895, although some Populists attempted to widen the demand by calling "financial reform" the main issue. The state executive committee sent a delegation, headed by Butler, to the silver convention in Memphis in the summer of 1895, under the banner of "financial reform."[25] In the first half of 1896 Butler and the state executive committee, which he chaired, called "financial reform" the paramount issue in the coming campaign.[26] In most cases, however, "financial reform" proved to be almost exclusively "the free silver question."

More frequently free silver was not covered by a demand for financial reform but specifically named as the most important issue. As early as May 1895 the *Caucasian* called the struggle between gold and silver "the great contest of the century." This tendency became particularly widespread during 1896.[27] In March one North Carolina Populist specified that "any other issue" besides free silver was "a delusion and a snare. . . . The free coinage of silver is the last refuge of a people, whose government has made an assignment to the Morgan syndicate, the national banks and the money changers."[28] In mid-May a second was ready to drop the People's party name to win free silver.[29] "Free silver is the watchword here," wrote a Populist from Jackson County in June.[30] And so it went through the rest of the year.[31] The elaborate program for social and economic reform of 1891 and 1892, centering on the subtreasury and the Omaha platform, disappeared quickly in North Carolina. By 1895, certainly by 1896, most North Carolina Populists believed free silver the most important, if not the only issue involved in reform.

The weakness of the antimonopoly greenback analysis in North Carolina, however, did not alone account for the extreme fusionist position the North Carolina party reached by 1896. Marion Butler's own political diagnosis replaced it. The radical position, by 1895 at least, posed no serious threat to Butler's approach to national reform as sectional politics rather than the crude class politics implied in the Omaha platform.

The extent of Butler's adherence to the more radical elements of the Omaha platform had never been clear. He understood enough of the subtreasury plan, government ownership of the railroads, and legal tender fiat currency to support and explain them as president of the state Farmers' Alliance.[32] But only one month before his election to the presidency of the state Alliance in 1891 he had argued that financial reform was the most pressing issue and that the subtreasury was only a "means" to that end.[33] His new office led to a more forceful defense of that plan,[34] but after the early months of 1892 it quickly dropped from sight in the columns of the *Caucasian*. His advocacy of a legal tender fiat currency system and government ownership of the railroads tailed off sharply in 1893 and disappeared almost entirely after mid-1895.[35]

Butler also followed a curious political course as he moved in the spring and summer of 1892 from the Democratic to the Populist party. "Good politics," he wrote on 26 May 1892, required him to support Elias Carr and the state Democratic ticket, although the Democratic state platform said nothing about the subtreasury, legal tender fiat currency (at least directly), or the land and railroad planks of the February 1892 St. Louis platform.[36] A week later Butler questioned the Alliance's use of the St. Louis platform as a yardstick for measuring North Carolina Democracy's adherence to reform.[37] A week after that he sharply criticized the growing third party organization in the state and its formation in his own county, Sampson.[38] Through June he grew progressively warmer toward the Populists, however, and dropped the Democratic ticket from his editorial page in the second week in July. In the fourth week of that month, at the Democratic congressional district convention, he and another Democrat-soon-to-be-a-Populist, Dr. Cyrus Thompson, nominated an anti-Cleveland elector but supported the convention's congressional nominee, a man who openly opposed the subtreasury and government ownership of the railroads.[39]

The same issue of the *Caucasian* which reported the convention, however, also reported that Furnifold Simmons, the chairman of the Democratic state executive committee, had told Butler that the test of a Democrat in North Carolina in 1892 was a pledge to support Cleveland in the November election. Two weeks later the *Caucasian* reported a remarkable change in the politics of Marion Butler. An editorial charged that the Democrats had driven reluctant reformers out of the party. An article announced that a Sampson County Populist convention had met and nominated a full slate for county and state offices. Marion Butler was elected temporary, then permanent chairman of the county convention and nominated for state Senator.[40] A week later the paper reported that the state convention had made Butler its permanent chairman,[41] less than two weeks after he changed parties!

These events measured both Butler's political acumen and the leadership vacuum that existed in North Carolina with Polk's death. It also, however, measured the weakness of antimonopoly greenback sentiment in the state. When Leonidas Livingston, president of the Georgia Alliance, tried to convince that organization to repudiate the February 1892 St. Louis platform (adopted later with a few revisions at Omaha) and lead the organization back into the Democratic party, he faced the solid opposition of the vast majority of its membership.[42] Little or no such opposition greeted Alliance president Butler's course in North Carolina.[43] Butler maintained that the Democrats forced him into the Populist party by requiring him to vote for Cleveland. His comprehension of the antimonopoly greenback position never exceeded its technical aspects. If it had, he would have left the Democrats far earlier. To Butler reform meant basically free silver and currency expansion; the rest of the Alliance program was window dressing.

Free silver and Democratic perfidy dominated the columns of the *Caucasian* and the other North Carolina papers during 1893, although a few of the more radical North Carolina Populists like Harry Skinner and James Murdock continued to elaborate on the subtreasury plan and greenback monetary theory.[44] In early March of 1893 Butler made an important free silver speech to the third annual American Bimetallic Convention in Washington, D.C., and with the repeal of the Sherman Silver Purchase Act in late 1893 the free silver issue completely dominated the *Caucasian* and other North Carolina reform newspapers. Butler continued his climb in the party hierarchy. In early December 1893 he accepted the chairmanship of the state executive committee, a post he retained until the summer of 1896 when he became national executive committee chairman.[45]

While the rhetoric of North Carolina reform, Alliance and Populist, never had as sharp an edge of class conflict as it did in Georgia or Texas, in 1891 and 1892 some reformers talked of the struggle of the poor against the rich and the country against the towns.[46] The Homestead strikers elicited considerable sympathy from some North Carolina reformers.[47] Late 1893 and early 1894, however, saw increasing efforts to downplay this sort of rhetoric and emphasize the moderation of the

Populists. In February 1894 Butler assured North Carolinians of all political stripes that the Populists fought only "criminal capital," privileged
capital. They welcomed "such capital as is willing to stand on the same
footing as other citizens."[48] Butler also criticized Coxey severely for his
organization of a march on Washington, calling him in May a man
whose methods all "conservative reformers of the country" had to oppose.[49] Coxey incurred opposition among other Southern Populists, but
not like that which came from North Carolina's Populists, led by Marion
Butler's *Caucasian*.[50]

The political implications of a growing stress on free silver and financial reform appeared in a new emphasis on the sectional nature of reform
politics. As early as July 1893 the editor of the *Progressive Farmer* predicted a rebellion of the South and West against the Eastern "goldbugs"
over the financial issue. The "white men" of the South and West, unlike
"the politicians and the negroes," would unite in the Populist party to
defeat "Wall Street slavery."[51] The free silver revolt against the goldbugs
was a sectional fight, pitting the capitalistic, exploiting East against the
exploited, producing South and West. Within the South political appeals
were directed to unity on the free silver issue, not to conflict over government ownership, greenbacks, the subtreasury, or the Omaha platform. What had begun as a crude perception of class politics which
retained some sectional overtones became a proper political battle. The
emphasis on intrasectional class divisions disappeared or was stretched
beyond real meaning within a sectional analysis of reform politics.

The movement toward moderation and conservatism continued as attention to the Omaha platform receded. In June 1894 the state executive committee decided that anyone could participate in the Populist
primaries who favored on the national level free coinage of gold and
silver at a ratio of sixteen to one, an increase in "our legal tender currency without the intervention of banking corporations," a graduated
income tax, and a more economical government administration.[52] The
state platform advocated roughly the same national issues.[53] This was
a far cry from the Alliance "yardstick" of 1890 or even the issues of
1892. Free silver dominated reform politics and little remained of antimonopoly greenbackism in North Carolina.

With the abandonment of the Omaha platform and its crude class
analysis, most of the impetus for challenging white supremacy also disappeared. In states like Georgia and Alabama, with weak Republican
parties, the Populists abandoned a poor white–poor black political coalition primarily in order to attract support from the new middle class
elements of the towns and cities, people who were in the Democratic
party. In North Carolina, where the white as well as the black Republican vote had remained large, the effort also included trying to attract the

Republicans into a fusion agreement. It succeeded in 1894, especially in the face of continued Democratic unwillingness to combine with the Populists on any reform issue.[54]

Not every Populist in North Carolina, to be sure, agreed with Republican fusion, despite its local success. George Boggs, an old Allianceman and Populist from the ninth congressional district, maintained that such a course had hurt the third party cause badly. Since the Populists' demands were "mainly national" (an antimonopoly greenback sentiment), the North Carolina reformers should have put up their own candidate to defend the radical demands and continue to educate the people. This way, he felt, local cooperation on state issues would have been possible without loss of principle and the accompanying demoralization among reformers. Peace at the expense of principle, or victory at the same price, represented no gain at all.[55]

Most North Carolina Populists, however, favored the free silver-fusion course.[56] The influx of free silver Democrats into the party after the repeal of the Sherman Silver Purchase Act in the fall of 1893 undoubtedly caused some of this emphasis.[57] One such convert, W. C. Kitchin, came to the Populists explicitly on the tariff and free silver issues.[58] His subsequent speeches dealt solely with free silver and financial reform, making no mention of fiat legal tender paper money.[59]

The influx of free silver advocates, added to the early weakness of antimonopoly greenbackism in North Carolina, supported Butler's next move toward a completely free silver position. Butler, now United States senator as well as the chairman of the North Carolina party, attended the Memphis free silver convention in June 1895 as part of a delegation of North Carolina Populists sent by the state executive committee. He was the most prominent Southern Populist at this "nonpartisan" convention, which even free silver Populists admitted the Democrats dominated.[60] The platform the convention produced used many of the same metaphors and images that the Southern Populists did and worried over many of the same social ills—declining commodity prices and the drop in agricultural profits; the falling quantity of money; the increasing disparity in wealth between the country and the city; the burdens placed on productive labor in the interest of idle wealth; and the lack of opportunity for the producers to work. But the platform considered legislation creating a strictly bimetallic, redeemable currency—free silver and gold—a sufficient cure for all these problems.[61]

Upon his return to North Carolina, Butler helped organize free silver supporters throughout the state into nonpartisan "Honest Money Free Silver clubs."[62] He and B. F. Keith, a North Carolina Democrat who had been vice-president of the Memphis convention, also issued a call for a "non-partisan State Free Silver Convention, inviting all persons of all political parties who favor the free, independent and unlimited coinage of silver and gold into full legal tender dollars at the ratio of 16 to 1, to meet in Raleigh on September 25th." Its object was "to get all true friends of silver together under one banner to fight the foreign gold trust and its American tory Allies."[63] The resulting convention passed, almost verbatim, the resolutions Butler introduced, calling only for free silver legislation.[64] By October 1895 Butler no longer even made gestures toward the greenback position. A couple of weeks after he published the results of the Memphis convention, Butler wrote a solid defense of the legal tender fiat theory of money.[65] Within two weeks of the October Raleigh free silver convention, however, he was talking about the need for a "redeemable paper money."[66]

For any greenbackers left in North Carolina it was all over but the shouting.[67] In early February 1896 Butler wrote an address to the People's party of North Carolina which made it clear that he felt the reform fight would be over free silver in 1896, and that the party had to set its policy accordingly.[68] The next week the state executive committee endorsed the letter.[69] At the state convention in May a few Populists opposed Butler's course, including the onetime radical subtreasury advocate, Harry Skinner. That they did so in the name of free silver attested to the complete disappearance of the Omaha platform in North Carolina.[70] Without the antimonopoly greenback analysis to prevent it, the North Carolina Populists eventually fused with the Republicans on the state level[71] and with the Democrats on the national ticket.[72] By late 1895, perhaps even earlier, North Carolina Populists had followed the road to free silver and fusion almost to its end. All that remained was to realize its culmination in the 1896 campaign.

One last factor played an important role in preventing opposition among North Carolina Populists to free silver and fusion. A considerable increase in the identity of the religious and moral metaphors and imagery with free silver occurred in 1895 and 1896, accompanied by a significant decline in substantive discussions of any reform demand, even free silver. In March 1896 one North Carolina Populist predicted that the country's unrest would soon pass. "God will raise up a Moses to lead us out" under a free silver banner. "Free silver will save us."[73] Mammon could not stand against Christ, wrote another North Carolinian in May 1896. In the name of Christ, country, and humanity he called on all voters to join "the silver forces . . . against the idolatrous gold worshippers, and help restore the white metal of peace, prosperity, liberty, and happiness."[74] A monetary theory which focused on the quantity of money in circulation but dealt poorly with the fiat nature of money, the difficulties of resolving the Jeffersonian heritage with government ownership of the railroads, and an analysis of reform politics as a sectional rather than a crude class conflict, all made it much easier for most North Carolina Populists to view free silver as the solution to the many problems in American society of which they complained, especially when free silver became widely popular in the South among non-Populists. The urgency of obtaining free silver increasingly excluded any discussion of the rest of the Omaha platform. This was even more true when moral and religious metaphors became identified with Populist reform in general and free silver in particular. Then party victory became the key to salvation and failure assurance of imminent calamity.

Butler himself, in his last address to the people of the country before the 1896 election, envisioned a choice between free silver and disaster. Remember, he urged the Populists, the millions who were "the victims of greed . . . the unemployed, the poverty-striken [sic], the disappointed, the degraded, the hungry—'the line stretches out to the crack of doom.'" Why had this slaughter and suffering been inflicted on "the human family"? So the few could "possess more of the property of others than they could use . . . have more food than they could eat and more clothes than they could wear . . . indulge in an apelike emulation of display and vanity." This sort of outrage had made the Alliance and Populist crusade so powerful in 1890 and 1892. But Butler provided no further analysis. The terrible conditions in America proceeded directly from the demonetization of silver in 1873, caused by "the gigantic greed of the money power." Was man, Butler asked, "to be trampled into the mud of poverty or the darkness of the grave by the lineal successors of those whom Christ scourged out of the temple of the most high God?" No. The Populists demanded that "insofar as the precious metals are to be used as the basis of our exchange . . . both metals shall be used." "Splendid prosperity" would follow free silver; worldwide slavery would follow the gold standard. "This is man's one last, great opportunity. Forget everything else and do your whole duty."[75]

With the exception of one phrase in which he implied that money might be made of a material other than silver or gold, Butler considered the 1896 election a choice between victory or total, everlasting defeat at the hands of the same men who crucified Christ. Given a choice of millennial chaos or free silver, who would argue that the Omaha platform was more important than free silver? Very few, unless their original vision of reform was different, their conception of the original reform platform different. But 1896 found few antimonopoly greenbackers among the North Carolina Populists.

The fight for free silver, as Bryan made so clear in his Cross of Gold speech at the Democratic national convention in 1896, was a sectional political contest—the West and the South united against the goldbug East. Bryan would lead an intrasectional coalition of that "broader class of business men," in which he included wage earners, employers, farmers, lawyers, and merchants of the South and West against the speculators, merchant kings, and corporations and their counsels, of the East.[76] The Omaha platform, on the other hand, emphasized the conflict between "a plundered people" and the "capitalists, corporations, national banks, rings [and] trusts."[77] It contained no hint of sectionalism except to denounce it, and no hint of harmony between merchants and farmers, the exploited and their exploiters, whether southern, western, eastern, or northern, whether from the local crossroads, the county seat, or New York City. The perception of reform as a political struggle between the producers and the nonproducers was, to be sure, only a very crude kind of class orientation, and within its context the dichotomy of East versus South and West often played a part. But when the reformers considered free silver the sole object of reform, the sectional analysis controlled. The free silver coalition pitted all Southerners—bankers, merchants, the new town and city middle class, and the rural white (and sometimes black) farmers and tenants—against the East. When free silver and fusion held sway, the conflict of country against city, of lien-harassed farmer against local merchant and banker, disappeared. This was the function of the free silver, bimetallic rhetoric and analysis, as the southern Democrats realized full well. The weakness of the antimonopoly greenback position in North Carolina made the Populists vulnerable to this analysis and to the sectional politics accompanying it.

Finally, the Populist adherence to a sectional alliance lost them any black support. Such support had been poor in 1892, and only fusion with the Republicans made 1894 look better. W. A. Guthrie, running against both a Republican and a Democrat, did nearly as badly among black voters as W. P. Exum had in 1892.[78] The North Carolina Populists after 1892 dropped any thought of a biracial coalition, replacing it with an increasingly moderate, free silver approach designed to attract a white majority. The need to unify the southern white community behind free silver resulted in the acquiescence by North Carolina Populists to the politics of race. Helen Edmonds's description of the North Carolina People's party as "avowedly anti-Negro" was accurate,[79] although perhaps more so for the years after 1892 when they found fusion an ideal solution to the conflict between race and political success.

The heavy influx of free silver Democrats after mid-1893 into the People's party, the availability of a successful state-level fusion with the Republican party to solve the problem of getting black votes for Populist candidates, and the political aspirations of the Populist leadership, especially Marion Butler, all combined to make the North Carolina People's party free silver and fusionist by 1896. The weakness of the antimonopoly greenback position which underlay the Omaha platform meant few reformers resisted these influences, and the North Carolina Populists, after their opponents had used race to split the Republican-Populist coalition, either disappeared or returned to a Democratic party now led by the new southern middle class.

Alabama

Alabama Populists followed a more complicated path to 1896 than the reformers in any other state. In the late 1880s the Farmers' Alliance grew as rapidly in Alabama as it did elsewhere in the South. Likewise, in the election of 1890 the Alabama Alliance attempted to capture the Democratic party. Unlike the Alliance in other southern states, however, the reformers failed almost entirely to influence the Democratic leadership; conservatives firmly opposed to the Alliance and its program retained complete control of the state party. As a result, by September of 1892 two reform parties existed in Alabama, the People's party and the Jeffersonian Democratic party. This peculiar development explains much of the complexity of Alabama reform politics and its ultimate degeneration into an apparently inexplicable jumble of fusion, and confusion, by 1896.

The other major cause of the strange course of Alabama reform politics was Reuben F. Kolb. A prosperous farmer and aspiring Democratic politician by the mid-1880s, Kolb in 1887 became state commissioner of agriculture. By 1888 he had discovered the potential political power of the Farmers' Alliance in Alabama and used his position as commissioner to build up his political following among the newly radicalized Alabama farmers. By the time that Kolb announced for the Democratic gubernatorial nomination in December 1889, he had already become the popular, if not officially endorsed, candidate of Alabama's Farmers' Alliance.[80]

As with Marion Butler in North Carolina, however, the extent of Kolb's commitment to Alliance principles was never very clear. At the St. Louis meeting in December 1889 he spoke out against some of the resolutions, especially that one requiring disobeying the party caucus when a candidate did not stand on the entire St. Louis platform, and he voted against the St. Louis demands in their final form.[81] By mid-1891 Kolb was willing to support the Ocala demands, but only if they meant, in his words, "Democracy."[82] The American Bimetallic League elected Kolb a vice-president at the same 1893 convention in which Marion Butler gave the main address.[83] If Kolb was ever an antimonopoly greenbacker, his record did not show it. Issues of personal ambition apparently affected his political stances,[84] although as we shall see, Kolb, like Butler, obviously understood the technical aspects of greenbackism if not the antimonopoly position.

The movement toward third party politics developed in Alabama much as it did elsewhere in the South. Ben Terrell, the Alliance's national lecturer, launched the Alabama subtreasury campaign in January 1891, and the National Farmers' Alliance began the organizing effort which Texas Alliance radicals hoped would split the Farmers' Alliance in the South from the Democratic party.[85] Moving well away from the conservative position he shared with Kolb in early 1890, Alabama Alliance president Sam Adams in February 1891 made the Ocala demands, including the subtreasury plan, binding on Alliance members. His action stirred up a good deal of controversy because of opposition to the subtreasury plan, which indicated an early weakness in Alabama of the antimonopoly greenback position.[86] But Alliance speakers, including Kolb, supported both Ocala and the subtreasury,[87] as did the more radical Alliance press. All during 1891 letters and editorials in the Geneva *Record* explained and defended the subtreasury.[88] The editor of the paper, Daniel Swanner, and some of his supporters hovered around the third party the first half of the year,[89] and in July the Geneva County Alliance became the first in the state to go over to the Populist party on the basis of the Ocala platform[90]—legal tender fiat greenbacks, the subtreasury, and the abolition of the national banking system. The state Alliance journal, Frank Baltzell's *Alliance Herald*, in 1891 also supported the subtreasury plan and a legal tender fiat paper money system, analyzing the currency issue with a clearly explained quantity theory of money.[91] In addition, the *Herald* included an antimonopoly emphasis, Baltzell advocating firm national oversight of the railroads and defending government "paternalism" as beneficial to society.[92]

Other Alliance papers in the South, however, took the same stands and made the same analyses. Alabama's peculiarity did not lie there but in another species of reform that grew up around Kolb and the left wing of the Democratic party after the state Democratic convention of 1890. Not only the Farmers' Alliance but also a considerable element of the regular Democratic party supported Kolb in 1890. Henry D. Clayton, J. M. White, and John D. Roquemore, all well-known regular Democrats and none of them Alliancemen or particularly involved with Alliance issues, led Kolb's unsuccessful floor fight in the 1890 convention. Despite Alliance unhappiness with Jones, Kolb himself campaigned actively for the state ticket, sharing speech-making duties with E. T. Taliaferro, a Birmingham lawyer who became one of his leading lieutenants in the 1892 primary campaign.[93]

Although some of these men fell away when Kolb left the Democratic party in 1892 for the Jeffersonian Democrats,[94] he picked up a new group of supporters from the new middle class, men who played dominant roles in the subsequent activities of the Jeffersonian Democratic party. Zell Gaston and O. R. Hundley were Butler and Madison County lawyers who became prominent in the campaigns following 1892, Gaston first in the Jeffersonian and later in the Democratic party.[95] P. G. Bowman, elected chairman of the Jeffersonian Democratic state executive committee in 1892, was an attorney from Birmingham. Farley Maxwell, who also served on the state executive commitee, was a businessman in Tuscaloosa, Alabama, and a farmer, cotton buyer and speculator, land developer, and small but enterprising manufacturer as well.[96] O. D. Street of Guntersville, a well-known Jeffersonian in the state and his congressional district, was the lawyer son of a lawyer father, Judge Thomas A. Street, who had long been active in Democratic state politics.[97] These men were generally more representative of the South's new middle class than the ordinary Alliance or People's party member, or even of the Populist (not Jeffersonian) leadership in the state.[98]

The tentativeness which marked any moves toward independent political activity by those who considered themselves Jeffersonian appeared in journals like the Oxford Voice. This pro-Kolb paper did not match the swift conversion of the Geneva Record. The Voice began as a Democratic, pro-Alliance paper. At the end of January 1891 its editor, J. M. K. Guinn, argued that the farmers wanted the subtreasury system in order to get the free coinage of silver.[99] His understanding of what the Ocala demands meant and implied was even further in doubt when the Voice came out in February 1891 for Grover Cleveland.[100] This endorsement, however, marked the low point of the Voice's reform career. In May and June 1891 the new third party received some favorable, if wary attention,[101] and in the middle of July Guinn wrote a good substantive editorial on the need for a legal tender fiat currency system.[102] But his confusion did not end. On 9 April 1892 Guinn wrote that "we are for David B. Hill for President, Reuben F. Kolb for governor, tariff reform and free silver, this week."[103]

The Voice went with Kolb into the Jeffersonian Democratic party in the summer of 1892,[104] but stayed completely away from national issues. Only the state election in August forced Guinn's hand. Although unhappy about it, in early September he supported A. P. Longshore, the Populist candidate for Congress in his district, because the Jeffersonians had nominated no one.[105] In late September the Voice reluctantly broke with Senator Morgan over free silver and honest elections.[106] Nor was the Voice ever happy about supporting the national People's party ticket, doing so only because many of the state's Jeffersonians endorsed Weaver and Field.[107] After the summer of 1891 the Voice never mentioned the subtreasury or legal tender fiat currency. It never endorsed the Omaha platform. Free silver was the only national issue involved in the break with Senator Morgan and the national Democratic nominees. The *Voice*'s hesitancy toward reform and adherence to the Jeffersonian Democrats rather than the Populists revealed its weak understanding of the meaning of antimonopoly greenbackism.

Although historians of the reform movement in Alabama have not considered it so, in 1892 the People's party in Alabama differed considerably from the Jeffersonian Democrats, the distance being measured by that between the Oxford *Voice* and the Geneva *Record* and marked by the phrase used by Guinn to break with Morgan and the national Democratic nominees—"free silver and fair elections."[108] The two reform parties differed most importantly, at least in 1892, on their perception of reform. With only free silver and fair elections at stake, Alabama would have seen but one reform party, the Jeffersonian Democrats. If the Alabama Democratic party in 1892 had pledged for free silver, supported it by opposing Cleveland as the presidential nominee, and promised fair elections, only a People's party would have emerged. By 1892 in Alabama, however, unlike in the other southern states, the Alliance had already been counted out once, at the Democratic convention of 1890.[109] The Democratic county conventions and primaries for the 1892 gubernatorial convention, in which Kolb participated, once again appeared to Kolb partisans, especially the Alliance, as rigged against more often than for them.[110] The lesson the reformers in other southern states learned in the 1892 elections the Alabama reformers learned before that election.

Moreover, unlike most other southern states, in Alabama the conservative, gold-standard Democrats maintained a tight control over the Democratic party until the state convention of 1896. The combination of conservative control of the Democratic party and the early emergence of honest elections and free silver split the Alabama Democratic party three ways by the fall of 1892. The Populists occupied the left with an antimonopoly greenback program, the Omaha platform. The conservative regular Democrats, committed to white supremacy as their major issue and controlled by gold standard advocates, held the right. In the middle stood the free silver, fair election Jeffersonian Democrats. The free silver reformers, who in other southern states constituted the left wing of the regular Democratic party and the right wing of the Populists, in Alabama joined together in the Jeffersonian Democratic party.

The extensive movement of free silver Democrats into the People's party which occurred in 1893 and 1894 in the other southern states never happened in Alabama because of the Jeffersonians. Most of the free silver Democrats and free silver Populists belonged to the Jeffersonian party by 1892, to be joined by only a few others in 1893 and

1894. Because of this the reformers' most successful election in Alabama came in 1892. In Georgia and North Carolina the most successful Populist campaign was 1894, after the influx of free silver Democrats into the Populist party. The widening of the reform appeal to the new middle-class groups in towns and cities which occurred in Georgia, North Carolina, and Texas in 1893 and 1894 took place two years earlier in Alabama because of the Jeffersonian Democrats. The controversy of 1893 and 1894 between the financial reformers and the antimonopoly greenbackers within the North Carolina People's party occurred in Alabama as a struggle between two reform parties, the Populists and the Jeffersonians.

The platforms of the Jeffersonian Democrats demonstrated the limited focus of the party. Their 1892 platform did not endorse Omaha and mentioned as national issues only a general opposition to trusts, a graduated income tax, abolition of the national banking system, an expanded currency, and the free and unlimited coinage of silver.[111] On national issues their 1894 platform repeated, with the exception of a few details, that of 1892.[112] The Alabama People's party did not have a platform in 1892, but their platform in 1894 contrasted markedly to that of the Jeffersonians. They endorsed the Omaha platform in full and opposed any repeal of the federal tax on state bank notes.[113] The difference was not one between a state-oriented reform party and a nationally oriented one. Both platforms contained specifically national demands. The Populists' support of the Omaha platform, however, indicated an implicit endorsement of the antimonopoly position which the Jeffersonians purposely avoided.

The Jeffersonians knew a difference existed. Kolb was unhappy in 1892 with several aspects of the cooperation between Jeffersonians and Populists. The September 1892 Birmingham reform convention, involving Populists, Jeffersonians, Alliance representatives, and some Republicans, nominated congressional candidates. The Populists at the meeting also named an electoral ticket for Weaver and Field.[114] Kolb opposed the congressional nominations, wanting the convention instead to put out an electoral ticket for Cleveland. He felt "honor bound" to support the ticket, however, and explained later that he did so "without mentioning the names of Weaver or Cleveland."[115]

Kolb recognized a distinct difference between the two parties. Several times between 1892 and 1894 Kolb argued that the Populists could not, like the Jeffersonians, carry Alabama by attracting dissatisfied Democrats. He also made clear that Populist support did not make him or the Jeffersonians Populists.[116] The Jeffersonians, a free silver, fair elections party, already in 1892 provided a home for many of the free silver Democrats who in other southern states would not come into the Populist party until late 1893 and 1894. In 1892 the vote for Kolb in August, 115,524, and that for Weaver and Field in November, 85,128,[117] roughly measured the ratio of Populist strength to Jeffersonian and bore out Kolb's contention.

The movement of the Troy *Jeffersonian* from Jeffersonian to Populist emphasized the content of the continuing differences between the two. When the paper began publication in mid-November 1893 it stood on the Ocala platform and its title indicated its political position.[118] Although in early 1894 it opposed any single issue, free silver national party,[119] the *Jeffersonian* maintained a mild and moderate tone, talking only about free silver and honest elections, sticking almost entirely to state politics. In March 1894, however, an exchange introduced government ownership of the railroads to the *Jeffersonian*'s readers for the first time, and three weeks later the editor advocated government ownership of all "public utilities."[120] Meanwhile, the editor began to insist that free silver was not "the main issue" of reform but merely one part of the Omaha platform, beneficial only insofar as it increased the currency in circulation.[121] Still identifying himself as a Jeffersonian, in June the editor for the first time presented the greenback analysis in a couple of short editorials explaining the need for a legal tender fiat currency system,[122] and the end of the month saw publication of a letter defending the subtreasury plan.[123] In mid-August a new heading appeared on the *Jeffersonian*'s editorial page—"Money . . . Land . . . Transportation"— signaling the end of the *Jeffersonian*'s journey from free silver to the antimonopoly greenbackism of the Omaha platform.[124] The editor took the final step a week later. He publicly switched to the Populist party, berating those Jeffersonian Democrats who did not follow him for their failure to do so.[125] By shifting to an antimonopoly greenback position, the *Jeffersonian* moved itself out of the Jeffersonian Democratic party. The paper gave quite favorable coverage to the Pullman strikers in August and September, unusual even among Populist papers in Alabama, and by the first week in September argued that when human rights clashed with property rights, the former should always be considered paramount. Only an antimonopoly greenback analysis led to such radical sentiments among southern reformers.

Other Alabama reform papers identifying themselves as Populist rather than Jeffersonian tended to stick longer to the more radical issues.[126] The *Choctaw Alliance* identified itself as an antimonopoly paper late in 1892[127] and three weeks later called for government ownership of the railroad, telephone, and telegraph systems, asserting that vested rights ought never take precedence over human welfare.[128] As late as July 1893 the paper still mentioned the subtreasury plan, although the *Alliance* may not have understood completely the position it took. In the same editorial the editor called for a currency system in which all coinage would be of "equal intrinsic value."[129] Exchanges from out-of-state Southern Populist newspapers periodically explained a legal tender fiat currency system,[130] but the editorials and letters to the paper usually spoke only of free silver, showing little comprehension of a greenback analysis.[131] Still, the *Choctaw Alliance* continued to consider itself a Populist as opposed to a Jeffersonian paper.[132] The effort the paper made to advocate issues beyond free silver, no matter how well it understood them, indicated that the distinction was an accurate one.

The Ozark *Banner*, initiated in late May 1892, also identified itself with the Populist party, and again the treatment of reform issues demonstrated why. From the first the Ozark paper emphasized reform as a contest between town and country or producers and nonproducers.[133] In early August 1892 the paper endorsed Weaver and Field and government ownership of the railroads all on the same day.[134] The paper continued occasionally to explain or advocate government ownership of the railroads[135] and had several good editorials and letters doing the same for a legal tender fiat currency.[136] But, as in the *Choctaw Alliance*, the understanding of what these meant was sometimes suspect. In early 1893 the free silver issue began to grow in prominence in the *Banner*'s columns. In February the editor claimed that free silver would solve the problem of farm credit.[137] Although an editorial in August mentioned the subtreasury plan and the fiat currency it would distribute,[138] a few letters began appearing which advocated free silver as the road to prosperity.[139]

The weakness of the radical position in Alabama also appeared in the Populists' appeal to the blacks. The platform on which Kolb ran in 1892, with Populist support, represented their best effort: "We favor the protection of the colored race in their political rights, and should afford them encouragement and aid in the attainment of higher civilization and citizenship, so that through the means of kindness, a better understanding and more satisfactory condition may exist between the races."[140] Not all the reformers were as patronizing. A Blount County Allianceman wanted federal control of elections in the black belt, a force bill, "'so that the negro could get a fair vote.'"[141] Jeffersonian Democrat P. G. Bowman appears to have been the most outspoken advocate of black rights in Alabama in this election, hinting that he, too, would prefer a force bill to seeing blacks "'deprived of the privilege of voting for whom you please.'"[142] Most other Alabama reformers remained not nearly so positive. The Douglass-Cleveland affair turned up in most of the state's reform newspapers at the same time it did in North Carolina.[143] They also attacked Cleveland's appointment policy.[144] Jeffersonian and Populist papers in 1892 said little for or against black voting.

This soon changed. While Kolb in 1892 won a majority in the white counties, the Democrats used black votes from the black belt counties to count him out in the name of white supremacy.[145] The Jeffersonian state executive committee responded in early May 1893. It offered the Democrats a white primary to elect a Democratic state executive committee and select Democratic nominees for state office in 1894.[146] When the Democratic state executive committee turned the offer down, the Jeffersonians made a second, modified proposal which the Democrats again rejected.[147] Some Jeffersonians defended their offers by arguing that they had intended to expose Democratic hypocrisy on the race issue by offering that party a practical way to maintain the white supremacy about which they claimed to be so concerned. Other Jeffersonians made clear their goal was black exclusion.[148]

Although it met at the same time and in the same city as the Jeffersonian committee which made the first offer, the Populist state executive committee endorsed neither one. Historians have differed on whether or not the Populists supported these offers.[149] The Ozark *Banner*, a Populist paper, made no mention at all of the first offer and remarked on the second only to note that the Democrats had rejected it.[150] The *Choctaw Alliance* stated that Gaither and other members of the Populist state executive committee had been at the meeting of the Jeffersonian executive committee which decided to extend the first offer[151] and had agreed to the plan.[152] Apparently the Jeffersonians' first white primary offer caused consternation among Alabama Populists, although initially at least some of them supported it.

The Populists evidently almost unanimously disapproved of the second offer.[153] In June, after the Democrats rejected the first offer, the editor of the *Choctaw Alliance* hoped that the Jeffersonians had learned their lesson and would come over to the Populists.[154] The *Alliance* was glad to see the Democrats reject the second offer; if they had accepted, the *Alliance* thought that the Populists would not have joined in the white primary.[155] J. M. Whitehead, Populist editor of the Greenville *Living Truth* and an old greenbacker,[156] also hoped the compromise efforts were over and that the Jeffersonians would disband and come into the People's party.[157] That most Alabama Populists had opposed the white primary out of concern for black political rights, however, was doubtful, although by 1894 the only evidence of any continued appeal to blacks came from an avowedly antimonopoly greenback paper. In the Populist mass meeting in Choctaw County in May 1894 eight or ten "colored friends" participated and voted with about seventy whites,[158] and three weeks later the editor of the *Choctaw Alliance* felt sure that the blacks would vote with the Populists in the coming election.[159]

The race issue, however, did increase friction between Populists and

Jeffersonians; differences which had remained implicit came to the surface over the Jeffersonians' white primary offers.[160] By November of 1893 some Populist papers, including Whitehead's *Living Truth*, the black belt *Alabama Pioneer*, and the *Choctaw Alliance* were pushing the Jeffersonians to join the Populists.[161] Nevertheless, the Populist state executive committee in late 1893 reluctantly agreed to support Kolb in 1894, but with the proviso that they be able to name local and county Populist tickets wherever they thought they could win.[162] Despite his moderation, the Populists still considered Kolb the only candidate who could defeat the Democrats.

The Populist gamble did not work. The Democrats again used black belt votes to count Kolb out in August[163] and all but one reformer, Milford W. Howard, in the November elections.[164] The reformers responded to the fraud by calling a meeting in Montgomery for 12 November 1894, one day before the new state legislature convened. Populists and Jeffersonians both attended and two major resolutions passed. The first opposed setting up a rival state government. The second united both reform parties under the People's party label.[165] At first glance this action appeared to mean a radicalization of the reform movement in Alabama. A closer look, however, reveals the opposite. The combination of the two parties did not result in the Jeffersonians becoming Populists, but the Populists becoming Jeffersonians in all but name.

The combination had a background of several steps. One was the late 1893 decision by the Populist state executive committee, despite lack of enthusiasm on the part of many Alabama Populists, to support Kolb in the 1894 election. Kolb attributed the decision to the Populists' realization that they could not elect Populist state officials and preferred the Jeffersonian Democrats to the regular Democrats.[166] In addition, William C. Oates, a long-time gold monometallist and vigorous opponent of the Farmers' Alliance and the reform movement,[167] won the gubernatorial election, again the margin of victory being the immense black belt Democratic majorities.[168] Unable, without risking the loss of their white support, to prevent the Democrats from voting blacks in the black belt any way they chose, the Populists and especially the Jeffersonians generally neglected the blacks after 1892. Making almost no effort to appeal to black voters in 1894, the reformers worked to expand their coalition of the disadvantaged in a new direction.[169] The increase in labor demands in their 1894 platform evinced a Jeffersonian effort to recruit working people.[170] Evidence uncovered by Sheldon Hackney in Governor Jones's official correspondence indicates that the reformers not only supported the 1894 miners' strike in north and central Alabama but worked actively to keep the strike going at least through the state elections.[171]

With the failure to attract much labor support[172] the Alabama Populists, like their North Carolina brethren, began to shift their attention to a third group, the new middle class of Alabama's towns and cities. In that sense, Populist fusion with the Jeffersonians, who captured much of that middle-class free silver vote in 1892 and 1894, represented the same move to free silver and fusion that the North Carolina Populists accomplished by the state elections of 1894. The apparent source of the Populists' inability to win without support from the new middle class was Democratic fraud in the black belt.[173] If the Jeffersonians were counted out there, how well could the Populists do? More basically, however, the Populists had to turn to the Jeffersonians because they failed to reach blacks and working people with an appeal adequate to defeat or at least mitigate the efforts of the Democrats. That this appeal could have been made more effectively can be seen in Georgia, although it ultimately failed there also, and in Texas.

Underlying the failure to make a direct appeal to blacks and working people was a total absence of the antimonopoly greenback analysis among the Jeffersonians and its growing weakness among the Populists. The stress on a crude class coalition which this position demanded had never been a part of Jeffersonian politics. By 1894 it had also given way among the Populists to an increasing emphasis on free silver and the consequent transfer of southern internal political and economic antagonisms onto a sectional plane. The failure to understand the implications of the radical position led Alabama Populists toward the merger with the Jeffersonians by undermining any reason they might have once had for overcoming their historical racism in order to build a biracial reform coalition.

By November 1894 not much prevented the merger. All but a few, Populist and Jeffersonian, agreed on the primacy of the free silver issue. The Choctaw County Populists in January 1894 resolved that "currency reform" was "the paramount issue in our national politics," and mentioned only free silver.[174] The editor of the *Alliance* five months later wrote that some Choctaw Populists had become "a little sick on Kolb" and that if Johnston had been nominated by the Democrats on a free silver-fair elections platform, some Populists would have voted for him.[175] The remark highlighted the extent to which free silver already dominated not only the thinking of the Alabama Jeffersonians, but even the Populists.

After the merger of the Jeffersonians and the Populists the primacy of the free silver issue, for obvious reasons, continued to grow. The Ozark *Banner-Advertiser* was nearly all free silver by the fall of 1895.[176] By mid-1896 the editor of the *Choctaw Alliance* called for the casting aside of "all party fealty" for unity on a strictly bimetallic platform.[177] Here was the switch to free silver presaged in his earlier demand for money of "equal intrinsic value." The Alabama state executive committee, when it issued its call for the 1896 state convention, invited all voters who favored free silver, an increase in the volume of money issued by the national government, the abolition of national banks and interest-bearing government bonds, and "a free ballot and a fair count."[178] Except for the last, it was virtually identical to the 1896 national Democratic platform.

The belief in free silver as the be-all and end-all of reform arose from an understanding of what free silver meant for reform similar to that in North Carolina. In the early months of 1896 Alabama Populists several times called for an expansion of the money supply to raise prices, stimulate production, and expand trade, each time arguing that free silver alone would accomplish these things.[179] As we saw in the case of the *Choctaw Alliance*, these ideas dated from an earlier time. The Populist editor of the *Banner*, in February 1893, maintained that free silver alone would not only rescue the farmers from the lien system, but also save "the entire industrial and commercial classes of the country. . . . Remonetize silver, and the very overproduction of farm products, and the numberless incidental evils which now afflict the laboring people, will disappear."[180] The very problem which had given rise to an antimonopoly greenback analysis in Texas became, through a misunderstanding of it, the basis for a free silver position.[181]

This kind of reasoning was not unusual when reformers understood greenback theory poorly. Another Alabama Populist in December 1895 pointed out that the prices for products were down because "our already too small supply of money has to be drawn out into new channels with no increase of the currency to meet those increased demands. For that reason we advocate the free coinage of silver because it will broaden the base on which a redeemable currency sufficient in volume can be issued to meet those constantly increasing demands for money." It would raise prices and stimulate investment and production, ending unemployment and the farmers' plight. Free silver, in short, would "place our country immediately on the road to prosperity and greatness."[182] This Alabama reformer's combination of a good, substantive argument for expansion of the money supply with a demand for free silver alone would have horrified a greenbacker. Free silver, instead of the whole Omaha platform, became the key to prosperity and happiness and the salvation of the republic.

As in North Carolina, the religious and moral metaphor, and the development of rhetorical logic involved, played its part in this movement away from the radical position toward a concentration on free silver. The metaphor's increasing use paralleled a decline in substantive treatment of all reform issues and, as in North Carolina, was most popular in 1896. One Alabama Populist in March spoke of free silver as "the salvation" of the country.[183] In April a Populist told his brethren that 1896 was "the most important year of your life" because the free silver question would be decided. "Bimetallism" would bring back "good times." The single gold standard, on the other hand, meant "no more nor no less than the stagnation of all industry, the fall of civilization, the creation of thousands of paupers and tramps, the abolition of morality."[184] On the first of October, the day he chose to support the Democratic free silver congressional nominee, the editor of the Ozark Banner-Advertiser argued that the failure to achieve free silver legislation would mean a headlong plunge "into an absys [sic] from which it will take centuries to extricate the country."[185] The importance of free silver in their analysis and the increasing identity of religious and moral metaphors and imagery with that issue reinforced the decision of most Alabama reformers, former Populists and Jeffersonians alike, to support sectional unity in the name of a free silver crusade preached by Bryan Democrats, a crusade that would have been impossible among the Populists in 1892.[186]

Although the Populist papers before 1894 were much less likely to make blatant appeals to white racism,[187] neither reform party ever made very enthusiastic appeals for black support, and the blacks responded in a like manner. Kolb's 1894 showing in Alabama's black belt counties barely equaled that of the Populist national ticket in 1892 and fell way behind his showing in the gubernatorial elections of the same year.[188] Nor did the results improve. After the 1894 merger the reformers ceased completely making an effort to construct a black and white coalition of the disadvantaged. According to the author of a letter published in the 28 May 1896 People's Weekly Tribune, the Populists were "friends" to the blacks "not from choice but necessity;" they could not prevent the blacks from enjoying the benefits of prosperity equally with the whites.[189]

Indeed, intimations of the 1901 disfranchising convention began to appear. When the Democrats in 1896 urged black Republican voters to oppose cooperation with the Populists, the editor of the Banner-Advertiser warned the black voter that if he supported a gold monometallist "against the common masses of people [white, implicitly] who are struggling to reinstate silver to its rightful place, it will be the worst move he ever made." The blacks would suffer along with the whites if the single standard advocates won.[190] With disfranchisement in the air, however, the blacks might pay a greater penalty than common suffering.[191] Later in 1896, when defending the Populist party against accusations of being the "negro party," the Banner-Advertiser's editor pointed out that unlike the

Populists, "white supremacy" Democrats had allowed black voters in some of their 1896 county primaries. The Populist party had never gone that far![192] In June, Kolb, still leader of the party in Alabama, denied that any black had ever been promised "any political position by the Populists. . . . No negro ever held a seat in any Populist convention in Alabama."[193] Finally, when the Populists lost the gubernatorial election in August, Kolb's *Tribune* announced that the defeat proved that in "the last analysis of Alabama politics, the negro is in control."[194] Goodwyn, candidate of the Republicans as well as the Populists, carried only one black belt county.[195] Alabama blacks, with the aid of the Democratic party, answered the reformers in kind. A month and a half later Kolb became a Democrat once again, urging Alabama Populists to vote for free silver Democrats against Populist candidates in the November elections.[196]

The pre-1895 Populists never went as far as this on the issue of black voters in Alabama politics and on occasion could still defend the right of blacks to vote.[197] The old Jeffersonians, who had less distance to move to outright racism, often covered the ground quickly. Be they old Populists or Jeffersonians, however, the reformers in 1896 agreed, with some debate, to combine with the Republicans on their state ticket[198] and let them handle the recruiting of black voters while the reformers defended themselves as the real party of white supremacy in Alabama. With the disappearance of any antimonopoly sentiment among the Alabama reformers went the decline of whatever commitment they ever had to a political coalition of black and white poor in the state.

The same movement away from the Omaha platform also, as in North Carolina, accompanied and underwrote the change in the terms with which the Alabama Populists understood and analyzed the reform conflict. In 1891 and 1892 the subtreasury Alliancemen and the Populists (not the Jeffersonians) defended the Ocala and Omaha platforms most often in terms of idler against producer, rich against poor, and corporations and banks against the people.[199] They subordinated the theme of sectional struggle to that of the masses against the classes. In 1894 the Troy *Jeffersonian*, bucking the trend toward free silver and moderation in Alabama, also countered the trend toward seeing the reform struggle increasingly in sectional terms. In his first issue the editor used this particular theme, although he also described the struggle as one of capital against labor.[200] In late March 1894 he cautioned against making free silver "the main issue" and warned of revolution if prosperity did not return.[201] In May he saw Coxey's army as revolution's forerunner.[202] In September he spoke of the need to place human rights above property rights to avoid war between rich and poor.[203]

Few others, Populist or Jeffersonian, moved in this direction. The crude class analysis of the Omaha platform had rarely, if ever, appeared in the Jeffersonian papers,[204] and disappeared from the Populist papers by 1895 at the latest. The *Choctaw Alliance* occasionally in 1892 and 1893 spoke of the struggle of human rights against property rights,[205] but not in 1896. The early talk of town and country conflict in the Ozark *Banner*[206] disappeared in 1895 and 1896. If once the town merchants had wronged the farmers, by 1895 the *Banner-Advertiser* advised both to cooperate; they needed each other.[207]

Fusion and confusion resulted.[208] By late 1894 a combination of Democratic electoral fraud and the problems of creating in the South a political movement of the dispossessed, black and white, had overwhelmed the Alabama Populists. Underneath their inability to deal with these conditions and in addition to their historical white supremacy and Jeffersonian political stance, however, lay their inadequate understanding of antimonopoly greenbackism. Failing to create a successful coalition of the black and white poor, farmers and working people, they, like the North Carolina Populists, moved to widen their appeal to the new middle classes and solve the problem of race at the same time by joining the Jeffersonians. Like the North Carolina Populists in 1894, they only retained their name. No distinction remained between Populist and Jeffersonian.

The Democratic party in the state and nation confused the situation in Alabama even further by appropriating in 1896 the very issues that the Populists had merged with the Jeffersonians to win. With everyone to the left of the Republican party and gold monometallism fighting for the same thing, political decisions became contingent upon winning, not principle. The Jeffersonians had won their fight in Alabama by 1896. Kolb merely led the Jeffersonian return to an apparently free silver Democracy. With the loss of a radical analysis, the old Populists had only personal reasons for supporting or opposing fusion, state or national, with Democrats or Republicans, and Alabama reform politics in 1896 became chaos.[209] In the sense that Alabama Populists had also become Jeffersonians, 1895 and 1896 became a struggle for honest elections and free silver. Fusion and free silver won because the old Populists had moved themselves right so much that in 1896 all the Democrats had to do was move left a bit to remove any difference between the two parties; they agreed on the currency system and national banks on a national level, and on white supremacy locally.

A good indication of what happened to the Populists by 1896 was the presence of John DuBose in the same party as Joseph Manning and George Gaither, the two Alliancemen most responsible for creating the Alabama Populist party in 1892.[210] In late 1890 DuBose described the Farmers' Alliance as a "consolidation, trust, [a] scheme a whole flight of stairs in advance of the Republican party. As [Senator John] Morgan says, a Congressman must leave his official oath behind to live up to the demands of that organization."[211] In 1895 and 1896 DuBose helped edit Kolb's *People's Weekly Tribune* and was an important figure in the Alabama Populist party.[212] DuBose marked the distance between the Populists of 1892 and of 1896, the movement from one to the other being measured by the decreasing importance of the Omaha platform and antimonopoly greenbackism. DuBose returned to the Democratic party after 1896, while the defeat of the Populists paved the way in Alabama, as it had in North Carolina, for the accession to power of the new middle class. Accepting the South's semicolonial status, this group completed the process of welding industrial and financial capitalism on city and country in Alabama.[213]

CHAPTER 12

The Mid-Road Journey:
Georgia and Texas

*"The spirit of plutocratic
capitalism is the dominating force in our organized
social and industrial life."*
Judge Thomas A. Nugent, 1894

Georgia

The Populist party in North Carolina and Alabama opted for free silver and fusion by 1896. In Texas the party stayed with the Omaha platform. In Georgia the Populists tried to steer a middle path between the financial reformers, who by 1895 advocated fusion with free silver Democrats or Republicans on a bimetallic platform, and the antimonopoly greenbackers, whose radicalism many of the Georgians felt threatened the realization of the goals both groups shared. But the Georgia Populists learned in 1894 that they could not combine financial reform politics with antimonopoly greenbackism, and in 1896 that they could not successfully divorce antimonopoly from the Omaha platform.

In 1892, however, most Georgia Populists supported the subtreasury plan as the linchpin of reform.[1] They defended the Omaha platform in campaign speeches, letters, and county meetings.[2] Nor did the political implications of this position go unrecognized. The Georgians made considerable efforts to create a biracial reform coalition in the state without fusing with the Republican party. County Alliances and Populist conventions invited black participation[3] and reported black response.[4] Black meetings moved to join the Populists[5] and blacks wrote letters supporting them.[6] Populist speakers, editors, and letter writers called for black support and promised blacks equal political and economic rights.[7] Even when the black vote went against the Populists in many black belt counties, their leadership showed little hostility or dismay. The reformers' state chairman, M. W. Irwin, and their gubernatorial candidate, W. L. Peek, publicly stated that the blacks would have voted Populist if the Democrats had permitted them to do so.[8] Reports came from several counties of the intimidation of black Populists and of white Populists protecting them.[9] As in Alabama and North Carolina, blacks responded to the reformers in kind; the Georgia Populists appear to have received far greater support from them than their reform brethren in the other two states.[10]

Populist politics in Georgia in the summer and fall of 1892 were the rudimentary class politics of the Omaha platform. The Georgia reformers worked to unite the black and white poor of the state against the merchants, bankers, and politicians whom they blamed for their plight. In Richmond County, seat of Augusta, Populists also tried to include laboring people from the city's mills in the politics of class.[11] In both cases the producers opposed the idlers; labor battled capital. The Populists entered, in the words of the *Wool Hat*'s editor, "the mighty struggle . . . now in progress between the oppressed and their oppressors, between the working masses who produce and the favored parasites who prey and fatten upon the toil of others."[12] Watson caught the tone when he subtitled his campaign handbook "Not a Revolt; It is a Revolution." The violence and open fraud used in the campaign and election suggested that the Democrats understood the issues.[13]

The reformers lost, badly. Their gubernatorial candidate received only a third of the total vote and Watson failed in his bid to return to Congress. By the summer of 1893 the scope and nature of this loss began to suggest to some Georgia Populists, as similar events had to Populists in Alabama and North Carolina, that they might need to alter their tactics in 1894.[14] In mid-1893 Watson was already suggesting that Populist stump speakers woo Democratic votes with a sectional rather than a class appeal, stressing "the identity of interests between the South and West; and the antagonism of interest between the South and the East and North."[15] In his speech at Gracewood, Georgia, in July 1893 he described Populist politics as a struggle between the "agricultural" South and West and the "commercial, manufacturing, financial" North and East. "Their interests are diametrically opposite." He emphasized his desire to avoid the bitterness and conflict of 1892, denying that he wanted "to array one class against another, or country against city." The southern farmer, merchant, and "artisan" shared the same interests.[16]

Watson continued this approach into 1894, supported by other Georgia Populists.[17] In an editorial which followed by two months his election as chairman of the state executive committee in February 1894,[18] Watson called attention to the recent conversion to Populism of Judge James K.

Hines,[19] a prominent Georgia lawyer who had been state solicitor general, a Superior Court judge, and in 1890 a candidate for the United States Senate on the Ocala platform.[20] "Possessing as he does the confidence and esteem of so many professional and businessmen in the towns and cities, and having at the same time the confidence and esteem of the country people," Watson predicted that "his speeches in the campaign . . . will carry immense weight and do immense good."[21] Although it also marked how worried the Augusta *Chronicle* had become, this bitter opponent of Watson could find in his early April speech in the city nothing but government ownership of the railroads which a Democrat might not have supported.[22] The exception, however, indicated what Watson would successfully attempt to get the Georgia party to try in the coming election. The Populists, he argued, could not recover from a repeat of 1892. In order to pick up the growing number of "disaffected Democrats," the Populists would have to widen their appeal to the new middle class of Georgia's towns and cities. Unlike Marion Butler in North Carolina, however, Watson advocated no retreat from the Omaha platform. The Populists would have to attract a "following among the business and professional men" while standing squarely on the antimonopoly greenback principles of 1890 and 1892.[23]

The state convention, held near the end of May, and the campaign that followed it, reflected the effort of the Georgia Populists to follow this course. Elected temporary chairman of the state convention, Watson began his keynote address by stressing the representativeness of the convention—farmers, mechanics, professionals, and blacks all attending—and introduced what would be a common theme throughout the 1894 campaign. He told a cheering audience that "we oppose the man who grows unjustly rich by reason of special privilege; and we likewise oppose the man who hates every citizen whose honest toil has been rewarded by a legitimate accumulation of property. (Cheers.) We are not enemies to society nor to private property; nor are we reckless radicals whose only aim is to tear down and destroy. No! We simply favor moderate, reasonable, necessary and legitimate reforms; and by the blessings of God we are in this fight till we get them. (Cheers.)" Attacking the wealthy was an old theme; qualifying the attack was newer. In 1894 Watson no longer led a revolution; he concluded his speech with reference to the Georgia state motto, "Wisdom, Justice, and Moderation."[24]

The afternoon session of the convention revealed that Watson did not intend to abandon entirely, as the North Carolina and Alabama reformers did, the rudimentary class politics of the Omaha platform. Following the 1892 campaign Watson continued to speak out on the need for equal political and legal rights for blacks and on the necessity for black and white political cooperation,[25] although 1893 also saw him turn to attacking the Democrats for breaking down the color line.[26] This latter theme remained a minor one, however, and in their 1894 convention Georgia Populists continued to stress the need to create an economic and political alliance of black and white poor. They affirmed and defended black attendance at the state convention. They elected two blacks to the state executive committee, and Watson took the convention floor to make a spirited defense of black citizenship rights, including a free ballot and a fair count. "These colored people," he maintained at the end of his speech, "were our friends in the times when we needed friends two years ago. They stood by us through thick and thin. They stood by us when they knew their pockets could be lined with money by going with the Democratic party." This was not the time to abandon them.[27]

The peculiarly divided tone of the convention, a simultaneous commitment to moderation and a radical racial alliance, continued throughout the months that followed. Watson opened the campaign with a major speech in opposition territory at DiGive's Opera House in Atlanta. Saluting his audience of Atlanta business and professional people as "the best blood, the best brain, the best character the State of Georgia affords," Watson asked his listeners to see that the Populists did not oppose "prosperity," "private property," and "vested rights." He did not neglect the Omaha platform; he talked about the evils of concentrated wealth and the need for a legal tender fiat currency system, a graduated income tax, and government ownership of the railroads.[28] Neither did he relax his position on protection for black civil rights and the need for black and white political cooperation.[29] Watson made clear that none of this, however, should be construed as an attack on the rich. "In the race of life you have the right to accumulate property if you can. It is not only your right but your duty to do it." He avoided the rudimentary class appeals of 1892. Seeking to widen the appeal of Populism to the new middle class, Watson again emphasized a sectional politics which he hoped would unite the southern merchant and debtor. As "manufacturing," "commercial," "capitalistic" sections, the interests of the North and East stood with the gold standard, banker control of the currency, and falling prices. In the South and West, agricultural sections where countryside and town depended on each other, the prosperity of urban commercial and professional classes required the prosperity of the farmer.[30]

While Watson did not back down on the substance of the Populist reform program, at least in 1894, he changed the temper. The Georgia Populists muted their outrage at the injustice of rural poverty and conducted a careful, moderate, even defensive campaign.[31] Watson several times joined Democratic promotions of local and regional fairs which promised to advance the prosperity of all Georgians.[32] Hines's speeches throughout the campaign narrowly stressed free silver and broken Democratic campaign promises, although he did talk at times about the need for government ownership of the railroads. "We are not anarchists," he told a crowd at Macon. "We are not communists as you hear it charged. We represent the simon pure democracy of this country."[33] Populist letter writers and editors elsewhere echoed the sentiment.[34] Watson's use of the sectional metaphor to describe the reform struggle spread, as did his emphasis on the interdependence of merchants, farmers, and businessmen.[35] No one talked of revolution. Populists took care to make clear that they meant no harm to urban classes, either to the sources of their economic power or to their enjoyment of success.

The effort was doomed to disappointment. The new middle classes in Georgia already knew their real interest lay with the final expansion of industrial and financial capitalism into the southern countryside.[36] The Georgia Populists' failure to perceive that the new southern middle class had already made its choice permitted them to abandon many of the radical overtones of their rhetoric while retaining the most radical implication of antimonopoly greenbackism, a biracial political coalition.[37] They had not yet learned that a political position based on a crude but perceptive notion of class conflict would not support a reform politics based on the sectional coalition of classes. As a result, Watson spent much of his time on the race issue, continuing his unqualified advocacy of black legal and political rights.[38] So did other Georgia Populists. In fact, the effort to reach black voters in the 1894 election might have exceeded that of 1892. All sections of the state reported black participation in Populist mass meetings, on Populist nominating committees, and in Populist congressional district conventions,[39] despite evidence of the pressures on blacks not to do so—the "job lash,"[40] bulldozing,[41] and foreclosure.[42] As in 1892 some white Populists apparently helped black ones.[43]

A new element, however, did enter into the reformers' handling of the race issue. More than before they appealed to the racial antipathies of whites. Ironically, the first appearance in the *People's Party Paper* of Cleveland's New York City school decree—"Cleveland's Mixed Schools"—came on the same day in 1892 that it reported the Doyle incident.[44] The 1894 campaign saw a new and vigorous attack by Watson and other Georgia Populists on what they called "negro democrats," or in less formal terms, "nigger democrats."[45] During most of the campaign, especially in August and September, the *People's Party Paper* displayed Cleveland's "race-mixing decree" prominently.[46] As the stress on moderation in Populist politics increased, moderation on the race issue often decreased. Despite this, the appeal to the blacks seems to have had greater success in 1894 than in 1892. The party received partial or full support from black newspapers like the Macon *Vindicator*[47] and the

Georgia Baptist.[48] The *People's Party Paper* printed many letters from blacks explaining why black voters should support the Populist ticket.[49] The reformers added ten black belt counties to the six they had won in the 1892 gubernatorial election and doubled their share of the black vote.[50]

Causes other than the 1892 election loss, however, helped account for the changes apparent in the Populists' 1894 campaign. As in most other southern states, late 1893 and 1894 brought a great influx of Democrats like Judge Hines into the Georgia People's party, primarily because of Democratic participation in the repeal of the Sherman Silver Purchase Act in late 1893.[51] Claiborne Snead came over in November 1893.[52] In June, Bion Williams, editor of the Woodbury, Georgia, *Messenger*, joined the Populists.[53] John S. Perry, editor of the Irwinton, Georgia, *World*, switched parties in August.[54] Letters from new recruits suggest that this group brought in a number of free silver advocates who understood the Omaha platform poorly. To explain his action, Claiborne Snead wrote the Populist state chairman that "the people want the free coinage of silver in order to stop that continual decrease in values of labor, or land, and all the productions thereof, which has been steadily in motion since its demonetization in 1873 until now. . . . The people cry out for relief by this additional currency, which cannot be controlled by the pluto-cratic gamblers of Wall Street, New York, and of Lombard Street, in London."[55] Another convert wrote to the Dallas *Herald* in December 1893 that the Democratic "bosses" had made him a Populist by repealing the Sherman Act, thus demonetizing silver and allowing "the money lords" to get more easily "all of our labor and property."[56] Neither of these men showed much grasp of the legal tender fiat nature of money, to say nothing of the antimonopoly basis of the Omaha platform.

Despite his commitment to a new moderation and his appeal to sectional politics, Watson himself continued through 1894 to advocate and explain a legal tender fiat money system.[57] He even defended the subtreasury plan during the campaign, although not vigorously.[58] From June to August Watson discussed in a series of articles the need for government ownership of the railroads, printing them as a pamphlet in September.[59] After the election he continued to warn against platform trimming, resisting attacks on the radical elements of the Omaha platform coming from the *National Watchman*.[60] Watson also opposed the St. Louis conference of the national executive committee called to consider rewriting the platform for 1896.[61]

Letters indicated other reformers in the state seconded Watson's stand against trimming the Omaha platform.[62] Support also came from the Dallas *Herald*, the *Glascock Banner*, and the *Banner Watchman*. The Glascock paper ran W. S. Morgan's analysis of the St. Louis conference, a report praising the Chicago socialists for the firm stand they took on the Omaha platform.[63] The greenback analysis and opposition to a single issue party remained stronger in Georgia than in North Carolina or Alabama[64] and the *Herald* exhibited its continued adherence to anti-monopoly politics in its warm praise of local and state activity by black Populists.[65]

On the other hand, the great influx of free silver Democrats and the tendency of some Georgia Populists to identify reform with free silver made the meaning of Watson's success difficult to determine. While the Georgia reformers generally stated their intention to remain solidly behind the Omaha platform,[66] by the fall of 1894 free silver had become a primary concern for many of them.[67] Some signs of weakness had appeared earlier. In late 1893 and early 1894 a Populist from Lincolnton several times argued that "Tariff Reform, Free Coinage of Silver, Income Tax, and Financial Reform, constitute three-fourths or more of the fundamental principles of the People's Party."[68] In September of 1892 the editor of the *Wool Hat* seemed to say the same thing, although he was conversant with greenback theory.[69] J. B. Gregory, a Populist from Burke County, maintained in the fall of 1894 that "underconsumption" had been caused by "an insufficient currency to do the business of the country. The closing of the mints against silver is the seat of the whole trouble."[70] Judged by the space devoted to their discussion, the Georgia Populist papers made free silver and Democratic perfidy the main issues of the 1894 campaign. Aside from the few times Hines spoke of it[71] or the *Wool Hat* mentioned it,[72] only Watson discussed government ownership of the railroads, although he covered it often and thoroughly. The only comment on the land plank came on 2 June in the *Wool Hat*. Neither Watson nor Hines mentioned it, nor did the Dallas *Herald* or the Dahlonega *Signal*.

By 1895 concern with free silver among Georgia Populists had grown even more extensive. Although some editors and letter writers continued to oppose any fusion on the free silver issue[73] and Watson made it clear that Populist attendance at the Georgia Bimetallic Conference held at Griffin, Georgia, in late June meant no abandonment of the Omaha platform,[74] free silver dominated more and more the columns of the *People's Party Paper* and the letters from Georgia Populists. It even began affecting party statements. When the tenth congressional district People's party convention renominated Watson for the third time in March 1895, they pledged support for the Omaha platform but resolved that since increasing the volume of currency, "the money question," was uppermost in the public's mind, they would concentrate on free silver and the direct issue of all currency to the people by the government.[75] They mentioned none of the other Omaha platform issues and did not discuss fiat legal tender notes, formerly an explicit part of the money question in Georgia.

This action cast some doubt on precisely what the state executive committee had meant a month earlier when it voted unanimously against a free silver national platform and in favor of the Omaha demands.[76] So did the fact that by 1895 a few of the Georgia reformers no longer even spoke of the Omaha platform. In June of that year one Georgia Populist called "the financial question . . . by far the most important question that we have ever had to deal with in our entire history." The financial question consisted of "more money. . . . [T]he free and unlimited coinage of silver is what we need."[77] This reformer obviously could not distinguish between free silver and a legal tender fiat currency. Other Populists rooted their rejection in doubts about antimonopoly. H. P. Beck of Bowdan, Georgia, wanted to widen the appeal of the party by dropping the subtreasury and the railroad planks from the Omaha platform.[78]

In early August, Watson launched his first attack on socialism.[79] Politically, his opposition rested on his belief that the Georgia Populist party would not even have "a corporal's guard left, if it were generally understood among Populists that the Platform opposed individual ownership of homes and money."[80] Watson remained a firm disciple of Locke. Socialism could not succeed because average human beings were too selfish to work if others, lazier than they, could share the fruits with them. Besides, civilization and progress required a surplus of money accumulated by some who could spend it on art, education, etc.[81] Like Nugent, Watson defended essentially a simple market society, although he would have called it a middle-class producer society. "Let every man own his own home and his own pocketbook," he wrote in December 1895, "and pass your laws so as to allow to every man, able and willing to work, a fair chance to have both home and pocket book. Tampering with Socialism is tampering with revolution:—for it can only come by a total subversion of our present government. And this means war."[82] The Tom Watson from whose tongue the word "revolution" rolled rather easily in 1890 and 1892 had disappeared.

His attack on socialism measured the considerable distance Watson had moved since 1892 or 1893 from the antimonopoly greenbackism of the Omaha platform. The losses of 1894, his own and the state party's, and the growing free silver sentiment in the Southern Democratic party[83] appear to have convinced Watson by the late summer of 1895 that the tactics of 1894, the effort to combine a coalition of exploited black and white poor with a sectional appeal attractive to the new town and city middle classes, would not work in 1896. He decided to move further to the right. Watson agreed with Mr. Beck; the Omaha platform needed substantial changes.[84] On 30 August Watson ended his second attack on socialism by calling for the reformers to stand on the Ocala rather than the Omaha platform.[85] The Ocala platform demanded government ownership of the railroad, telephone, and telegraph systems, but only if government "control and supervision does not remove the abuses now existing." Nor did the earlier document make any condemnation of land "monopolized for speculative purposes," as the Omaha platform did.[86] A return to the Ocala demands would, Watson maintained, "deliver our land plank from the suspicion of Socialism" by eliminating any reference to speculation.[87] Watson realized as well as Mr. Barefield of Alabama what defining ownership by use could mean.

Watson also wanted to drop the subtreasury plan. Only "a detail of distribution," the essential principle was a legal tender fiat currency issued directly to the people. The plan never deserved the ridicule it received, he remarked, but the subtreasury had been a political failure.[88] He did not provide an alternative solution for the problems of distribution, currency flexibility, or the lien system, and, ironically, forgot that in 1890, the year he pointed to as the largest reform success in the South, the reformers had used the subtreasury as the yardstick for measuring candidates. By late 1895 Watson insisted that "Georgia is Populistic for *Reform*, not for *Revolution*."[89]

Watson did not move as far to the right as he might have, however. He never joined the bimetallic, financial reform Populists, despite their common attacks on radicalism in the party, partly because of a different definition of radicalism. The free silver Populists attacked the greenbackers, the Western and Southern editors whom Dunning labeled socialist, because they supported the entire Omaha platform and opposed a single plank, free silver party.[90] Watson felt that the danger to Populism lay in the Omaha platform's antimonopoly element; he continued to defend its greenback aspect. He approved of what he described as a cool reception given Coxey by the Georgia state Populist convention in December 1895, not because of Coxey's stand on greenbacks but because of his "radicalism" and his socialist proclivities.[91] In 1895 and 1896 Watson staunchly opposed any single-plank platform and attacked the bimetallic position inside[92] and outside the party.[93] "All there is to the free silver question," he wrote in the spring of 1896, "is this: Free coinage will give us an increase in the currency. That's all. For our part we had rather see this increase come in the shape of Greenbacks than in the shape of silver."[94] Free silver was fine as far as it went, but adequate financial reform required more.[95]

Watson continued in 1896 to try steering what he saw as a middle course. In an editorial written in May 1896 he attacked the efforts of Taubeneck, the national party chairman, to reduce the Omaha platform to its financial sections alone. The Populists could afford, Watson felt, to drop the subtreasury plan. "In fact," he argued, "the problem of distribution is easy of solution, and by leaving out that *detail* we concentrate the minds of the people on the *principle* of increased currency." But the Populists could relinquish no more. They needed all three planks—land, transportation, and finance—albeit modified. "Let us keep to the middle of the road," Watson wrote, "avoiding the Socialist fanatic on the one hand, and the old-party templers on the other." Watson preferred "honorable defeat" to success built on "the ruins of our platform."[96]

Tom Watson shared the dream of his southern reform brethren for a better society. Unlike the bimetallic, financial reform Populists, however, he knew it would take more than free silver to win it. As a greenbacker he understood the need for a new and expanded role for government. But he backed away from the antimonopoly elements in the Omaha platform, fearing that ultimately they would lead to a rejection of that simple market society which he and so many other Southern Populists envisioned when they sought a more just, decent, and human social order. He did not share Nugent's optimism about the possibilities of antimonopoly.

Watson and the antimonopoly radicals wound up in the same camp in 1896 when the bimetallic, financial reform wing of the national party won control. Although he argued with them in late 1895 and 1896 over socialism,[97] Watson chose to go with the radicals into "the middle of the road." Despite his fear of the implications of their analysis, he could not abandon his greenbackism. Free silver had always seemed to him dangerously simple. When tarred with the brush of fusion in 1896, it appeared not only inadequate but a threat to the very dream of the Populists for a better society. Whatever its errors, the politics of the antimonopoly greenbackers never threatened to betray that dream.

The actions of the Georgia party in 1895 and 1896 reflected Watson's influence and leadership. In late October 1895 the state executive committee unanimously recommended dropping the subtreasury plan from the national platform and freeing the land plank from the "taint of socialism."[98] The state convention in December accepted those recommendations[99] and county mass meetings[100] and letter writers[101] approved them. The state executive committee sent them as instructions with the Georgia delegation to the national convention in St. Louis, along with a demand for the free coinage of both gold and silver and a circulation of at least $50 per capita. The instructions did not mention legal tender fiat money. (Watson and any other greenbacker knew the demand for $50 per capita necessitated fiat legal tender paper money, but the new free silver Democrats in the party would not.) The instructions did not refer to the speculative use of land and made government ownership of the railroad, telephone, and telegraph systems contingent on a popular referendum.[102]

The Georgia Populists capped this move to the right with the nomination of Seaborn Wright for governor. Watson glowingly described Wright, an 1896 convert to Populism, as a "gentleman of wealth and refinement, an able and successful lawyer, and an orator of the very first class."[103] Watson did not add that Wright had twice, in 1892 and 1894, refused a Populist nomination for Congress "simply because I could not endorse their demands."[104] Presumably the Georgia Populists had moderated their position sufficiently to accomodate him. Wright presented quite a contrast to W. L. Peek, and they ran on platforms no more comparable. The differences between 1892 and 1896 spoke volumes for the success of Watson's efforts to change the course of Georgia Populism.

Other evidence indicated, however, that Georgia Populists, like Watson, remained committed to a greenback stance even while they moved to the right. Others during the 1896 campaign often echoed Watson's opposition to a single issue national party. The free silver question, wrote the editor of the Irwinton *Reform World*, "is the smallest one in the Populist platform."[105] In May 1896 a Georgia Populist insisted that all the noise about socialists in the People's party and the scare tactics designed to brand the Omaha platform as the product of "cranks and visionaries" represented a plot by the silver mine owners and office seekers in the West and South to sidetrack the People's party. All "honest and intelligent reformers" knew that to expand the currency by opening the mints to silver would only increase the power of the monied few to rob the people.[106]

As this letter suggested, not all Georgia Populists supported the retreat of the Georgia party from an antimonopoly position.[107] On four different occasions in 1895 either a letter writer or the editor of the *Glascock Banner* defended the subtreasury plan and opposed dropping it.[108] If the plan was not socialistic in 1892, how could it be in 1896?[109] In the fall of 1895 the editor of the Dallas *Herald* supported Watson's "timely . . . warning" against socialists, but only because they were generally from the city and politically unreliable. He had no quarrel with their doctrine,[110] which of course constituted the basis of Watson's objection to them. Nor did the editor share Watson's hostility to Coxey. He praised Coxey's speech to the Populist state convention in December[111] and supported Peek, the old Allianceman, farmer, and Populist, instead of Wright for the 1896 gubernatorial nomination.[112] The stronger the antimonopoly streak, the more likely the resistance to the Georgia party's move to the right.

Most Georgia Populists, however, went as Watson did, and the move included a decline of attention to blacks. Watson did warn in October 1895 of the danger of disfranchisement laws, pointing out that what disfranchised poor blacks also disfranchised poor whites.[113] A few black

The Political Price

Populist mass meetings were announced early in 1896, but calls for black attendance in Populist county meetings declined steeply.[114] Only a few letters written by blacks appeared in the *People's Party Paper*.[115] The speeches, editorials, and letters of the 1896 campaign said little to or about blacks, except to denounce the Democratic use of black votes.[116] One of the few exceptions to this trend came from the firmly antimonopoly greenback Dallas *Herald*. A fascinating editorial on 2 April 1896 asked the blacks what they thought of the Cleveland administration's calling Maceo, the black Cuban revolutionary general, a "nigger."

The progressive abandoning of a rudimentary politics of class for a sectional politicial analysis,[117] part of the trend to moderation and the appeal to the new middle class, appeared again in Watson's speeches and editorials on the race issue. The attention he gave to a biracial political and economic coalition in the years from 1890 to 1894 disappeared in 1895 and 1896, almost in direct proportion to his efforts to dissociate the Populist party in Georgia from the antimonopoly implications of the Omaha platform. What happened in North Carolina and Alabama happened in Georgia. The Georgia Populists lost a lot of ground in the black belt in the 1896 state elections, even though the Republicans did not nominate candidates for state office. We have no reason to suspect that Democratic fraud and coercion increased significantly over 1894; no evidence of it appeared in the Georgia Populist press. The new election laws[118] might have had an impact, but the party took eleven black belt counties, more than they should have if the Democrats carefully enforced the new laws but considerably less than they won in 1894.[119] While the move to the right may have represented as much a loss to poor white farmers and tenants in Georgia as to their black neighbors, the blacks had less reason to stay with the reformers. The Populists' attempt to moderate the more radical implications of the Omaha platform in order to defend interest, profit, and private property meant the disappearance of their advocacy of political and legal rights for blacks, who once again responded in kind.

Probably because of the path they took, Watson and most of the Georgia Populists did not tend to identify religious and moral metaphors with free silver. The necessity for careful distinctions in the effort to separate the antimonopoly from the greenback elements of the Omaha platform produced less evidence than in North Carolina and Alabama of a decline in the substantive treatment of reform issues.[120] Even so, the attempt was in vain. Greenbackism could not be split from antimonopoly; the two went hand in hand in the Omaha platform. Had the Georgia Populists accomplished this impossible task, however, the effort would still have been for naught. The moderation of 1894 failed to bring enough urban middle-class support to the reformers. The decision of the Georgia Populists to go farther to the right in 1896, undercutting the Omaha platform even more, did worse. Giving up black support in an attempt to rid themselves of the antimonopoly implications of the radical position won no more middle-class votes.

Neither Watson nor most of his Georgia followers understood clearly enough the indivisibility of the major elements of the Omaha platform. But only the analysis failed. Watson wrote tellingly in December 1896 about the dream he and the other Populists from free silver fusionists to antimonopoly greenbackers still shared.

> [W]e cannot let the people forget the mission of Populism.
>
> It is to evolve a better governmental administration than that which crushes the life out of so many helpless thousands. Humanity is moving onward and, we believe, upward.
>
> The laws under which we now fight each other to the death (and call it competition) have been stretched too far and the carnage is too horrible to be endured. . . .
>
> It is the glory of the People's Party that we seek a higher civilization—that wider acceptance of the brotherhood of man which our fathers intended when they issued the Declaration of Independence and framed the Constitution.[121]

This bears comparison, ironically, to the defenses of socialism offered by S. C. McCandless, against whom Watson reacted so vigorously in the fall of 1895. "Competition," McCandless wrote,

> is the law of the jungle, of the forest, of brute life, and should not be the life motive of man made in the image of God. . . . Cooperation is the making, the practice of Christianity, the vital offshoot of its profession, recognizing therefore in these two words competition and cooperation the cause of his failure and the hope of his success, the one the curse of the past, the other the inspiration of the future.[122]

They shared the goal if not the way. For Tom Watson an essentially simple market society represented humanity's hope. For McCandless only the change of environment that socialism would bring promised human salvation.

The difference meant little by November 1896. The Populists lost their dream in the collapse of the reform movement, which in Georgia, as elsewhere in the South, led eventually to Progressivism and disfranchisement. The new middle classes moved into control of Georgia politics, and although Hoke Smith, Evan Howell, and Joe Brown, Jr., would disagree among themselves[123] they and their class would dominate the political and economic life of the state. The Georgia Populists never really understood that the sources of their opponents' support were those new town and city middle classes. These people accepted American industrial and financial capitalism and set about maximizing the economic position of the South, and especially their own class, within the system. Failure to understand this fact grew not only from the Georgia Populists' own past and experience but also from the weakness of the antimonopoly greenback analysis in the state. The culmination was a futile attempt to attract this new urban group to Populism by abandoning the embryonic class analysis implicit in the Omaha platform. Although Watson and the Georgia Populists in general arrived at a mid-road position in 1896, the logic of the radical analysis did not lead them there. Only in Texas would McCandless have aroused little comment among Populists.

Texas

The Populist party in Texas clung longest and most tenaciously to antimonopoly greenbackism. Few signs of the free silver panacea appeared in the state; Texas Populists defended the subtreasury in 1891 and in 1896. In 1894 they declared themselves officially to be "an anti-monopoly party."[124] They never replaced a rudimentary politics of class with a sectional analysis which used similar metaphors and imagery, nor did they abandon their goal of a political coalition of the poor and exploited, black and white, farmer and laborer. Finally, and most interestingly, only in Texas did the People's party continue to grow from 1892 through 1896.

Many of the reasons for the difference between Texas and the rest of the South lay in the history of reform in the state. The Greenback party did well in Texas, particularly when it had Republican support,[125] and the greenback vote seems to have carried over to the Populists. Of eleven counties voting for the Greenback gubernatorial candidate in 1878, all but two went Populist at least once in the state gubernatorial elections of 1892, 1894, or 1896.[126] Of the fifty counties that voted in 1882 for G. W. Jones, a greenbacker running as an Independent with Republican support, twenty-eight voted Populist at least once between 1892 and 1896.[127]

Comparison of their economic and political analysis makes the continuity between the Greenbackers and Populists in Texas even clearer. The demand for gold, silver, and legal tender fiat paper money appeared first in Texas in the Greenback platforms of March and August 1878, along with calls for the abolition of the national banking system and a graduated income tax, planks designed to appeal to working people, and in the March platform a statement that "the object of our republican government is to protect alike the rights of every individual in the Union, irrespective of section, State, riches, poverty, race, color, or creed."[128] In 1880 and 1882 the state Greenback conventions endorsed the Greenback national platform which included the greenback financial demands; enforcement of the federal eight-hour law; a bureau of labor statistics; an end to employment of children under fourteen years of age; a graduated income tax; the recovery, for nonfulfillment of contracts, of the lands granted to the railroads; federal regulation of transportation and communications; and a denunciation of monopoly.[129] The Texas Farmers' Alliance at Cleburne in 1886, Waco and Fort Worth and Dallas in 1890, and the Texas Populists in 1891, 1892, 1894, and 1896 augmented and refined this radical program, particularly by adding the subtreasury plan, the Omaha land plank, and government ownership of the railroad, telegraph, and telephone systems. But they all built on the greenback foundation first presented to Texas voters in 1878.[130]

By 1890 some Texans had heard antimonopoly greenbackism expounded and explained for twelve years, and the intensity of this instruction increased following the 1886 Cleburne convention of the Texas Farmers' Alliance. In no other state was the scope of this kind of education even approached. The Omaha platform was forged within the Texas Alliance, honed by years of open debate, and driven home for good in the years of the subtreasury campaigns, 1890 and 1891.[131] This experience meant that the Populists in Texas understood the radical position better than Populists in any other southern state, and it showed. From the time the Texans officially organized the state People's party in August 1891, through the state campaigns of 1896, support for the antimonopoly greenback analysis slipped very little among Texas Populists.[132]

The Texas reformers demonstrated their commitment many ways. They continued to emphasize much more than "the financial issue" in their state platforms. The one adopted in May 1892 endorsed the entire St. Louis platform of February 1892 and appended to it thirteen state demands. They aimed at least four, including one demanding an eight-hour law covering all workers, at creating a farmer-laborer reform coalition. Several called for restrictions on the power and influence of corporations, including a constitutional amendment to prohibit national bankers and members of railroad, telegraph, and telephone companies, their attorneys, or anyone holding such positions within two years prior to an election, from holding any legislative or judicial office in the state. This was a class orientation with a vengeance.[133]

The 1894 state convention, after endorsing the Omaha platform, declared that the People's party was "an anti-monopoly party" and reiterated the reformers' "opposition to the monopolization of natural resources and public utilities by individuals or corporations for speculative purposes." The implications of this last statement spread well beyond even the Omaha platform. The Texans made absolutely clear their commitment to full legal tender fiat paper money supplemented by free coinage of gold and silver at a ratio of sixteen to one. They continued their appeals to working people, including a demand for an amendment to the vagrancy laws protecting laborers who could find no work. On the other hand, they also added a proviso to their eight-hour demand exempting domestic and agricultural labor, again reflecting the fundamental weakness of even the most radical of the Southern Populists. Their lack of experience with and comprehension of industrial capitalism often allowed their class position to restrict their analysis more than it otherwise might have done. The other implications of the radical position received recognition, however. For the first time the Texas Populists added a couple of planks designed to attract black voters, demanding that each race be given its own trustees and the control of its own schools, and that the state "provide sufficient accommodation for all its insane without discrimination in color."[134]

In 1896 the Texas Populists contented themselves with endorsing the 1896 national platform and, as in 1894, generally repeating with some changes the demands from previous state platforms. In addition to advocating black and white control of their own schools, they specified that school funds should be allocated between the races on a pro rata basis, giving the blacks the same per capita school money as whites. They repeated their labor demands, although for the second time they reduced the number of workers covered by the eight-hour law, this time to include only those working for "contractors and corporations." A new, more moderate tone also appeared in their reassurance to the voters that the Populists were not "enemies of railroads" and that until the federal government owned them, the property of the railroad corporations deserved the same "fair and impartial treatment" and protection accorded private property. Finally they added a new demand favoring "equal justice and protection under the law to all citizens, without reference to race, color, or nationality."[135] Despite some variation—in some ways the 1894 platform marked a peak for radicalism in the state—none of the Populist platforms in the other southern states, including Georgia, ever approached even the most moderate of the Texans' platforms. The Texas Populists never shied away from an antimonopoly greenback stance and never backed down on their efforts to create a political coalition of the disadvantaged.

The Texans also continued to stress all the elements of the Omaha platform. During 1891 and 1892 the subtreasury stayed a major issue.

The plan focused particular attention on the importance of a legal tender fiat currency system, without which it could not work.[136] Free silver, when mentioned, the Texas Populists described as a minor reform,[137] and government ownership of the railroads received analysis.[138] The concomitants of this radicalism also appeared. Some Texas Populists used a sectional analysis of reform politics in the election of 1892,[139] but most of them stressed overwhelmingly the conflict of capital and labor, rich and poor, idler and producer.[140]

In the years 1893 and 1894 discussions of the subtreasury plan decreased but did not disappear entirely[141] and did not correspond to any weakening of the commitment to or the understanding of a legal tender fiat currency system. On the contrary, the Texans increased their criticism of free silver,[142] particularly when they heard any rumor of a change in the Omaha platform or any advocacy of a single issue national Populist campaign for 1896.[143] In some papers, such as the *People's Advocate* and the *Argus*, the antimonopoly emphasis tended to be stronger. Others such as the *Texas Advance* and the *Southern Mercury* more often emphasized the greenback financial analysis. Neither, however, neglected either element entirely. Nor, with a few exceptions,[144] did the sectional analysis of politics increase.[145] The Texas reformers remained sensitive to the issue. Despite the lack of evidence for use of a sectional reform metaphor, one Texas Populist felt it necessary to warn some of the reform papers and speakers that they had fallen into "what may be termed a popular error, by setting forth that the interest of the north and east are opposed to that of the west and south." These reformers should have been stressing the unity of the people in the different sections. "[T]he man who labors for the support of himself and family is menaced by the same influence north, south, east and west, and . . . it will require the united effort of the laboring element of every section to bring about better conditions."[146]

Although in light of what happened elsewhere in the South this advice was well taken, the letter writer need not have worried about his home state. The Texas Populists did not drop their appeal to the working people in their newspapers, letters, or speeches any more than in their platforms. While their discussion of the problems of unions, strikes, and the issues facing working people tended to peak in 1894 because of the Pullman strike (for the same reason their discussion of free silver peaked in 1896 because of the national political situation), it continued in 1895 and 1896, at least until the summer, when the issue of free silver became so important.[147]

Nor did the effort to expand the economic and political coalition of black and white poor drop off. The Texas reformers, in fact, tended to increase their efforts among blacks. The first Populist convention, after a short debate and a reminder by a black member of the importance of black votes,[148] elected two to the state executive committee. In 1892 blacks played important roles in the party in several counties. Six of the nineteen delegates the Gonzales People's party sent to the June 1892 state convention and half of its county executive committee were black men. Half of the Colorado County People's party was reported to be black, as were two of the three county chairmen.[149] The *People's Paper* of Paris, Texas, reported in October 1892 that blacks in that area were "exceedingly numerous" in the People's party.[150] Reports of black participation in the party came from ten or fifteen different counties, many of them in the black belt.[151] After the election the state party chairman, H. S. P. Ashby, while acknowledging that the party had been "almost entirely" supported by whites, gave "full recognition of the fidelity and devotion of that comparatively small number of colored men, who with rare courage stood with us in the fight for principle," some of them "even at the risk of their lives."[152]

Ashby's praise augured well for the future. The Populists' efforts to reach black voters increased in 1893 and 1894. They added several planks to their 1894 platform designed to facilitate this.[153] In the fall of 1893 the *Texas Advance* several times condemned whitecapping in the strongest of terms.[154] Nine months later the editor of the *Advance*, Harry Tracy, provided perhaps the clearest statement in Southern Populism on the necessity of a political coalition of all black and white poor. The People's party, he wrote, was "the only great political organization that does not draw the color line in political work." It could not do so because of its principle of equal rights to all. More importantly, since black labor had been used again and again to lower wages for whites, "to emancipate white labor, black labor must also be freed." So the People's party "must do as much for the negro in this regard as it would do for the whites." The Democrats did not want blacks, Tracy continued, because in the first place they believed that the last person to buy the vote of a black received it, and in the second place they feared that a black face in their convention would drive "thousands of the best men in the country" out of the Democratic party. "These old party bosses," Tracy concluded, "esteem poor blacks and whites alike; they have driven them into the same slave pen and if the whites get out they must turn the negroes out also! Hence it is very natural for the populists to accept the negro's aid in the emancipating process, and it is equally as natural for the negro to join and vote the populist ticket." To emancipate white labor from "organized capital," black labor must also be freed. And without " 'financial freedom' . . . all other so-called freedom is a delusion, a snare and a fraud."[155] At least some Texas Populists understood the need for black support in any thorough antimonopoly greenback campaign.

Blacks participated again in the Texas Populists' 1896 convention.[156] And in October 1896, in the middle of the national campaign, the *Southern Mercury* again addressed the issue of what kind of political coalition the radical position required. Did the "poor 'white trash and niggers'" realize, the editor wanted to know, that if they did not join the Populists, the first time they refused to vote to suit the "corrupt gang of political bosses" every southern state that had not already done so would call a constitutional convention to disfranchise both groups. Unlike most Populists elsewhere in the South, the Texans understood that to cease appealing to the blacks and fail to attract them into the party, or to join the Democrats in an effort to protect white supremacy, would result not just in the disfranchisement of blacks but of whites as well. Only a political coalition of both in the reform party could avoid it.[157] The Texas Populists failed, but the next ten years in the South proved the accuracy of their analysis.[158]

When they spoke of it the Texas Populists supported white supremacy the same as Populists elsewhere in the South,[159] but the race issue took up much less of their time and energy. The disclaimers that no white or black Populist ever advocated social equality did not often appear in the strongest statements of Texas Populists on the need for a political and economic coalition of black and white poor. As a result, the Populist party in Texas attracted more black support than the reformers in the rest of the South outside states such as Virginia and North Carolina when the Populists and Republicans resorted to outright fusion. In 1892, with the conservative Democrats and Republicans fielding a ticket in the state elections, the Populists did poorly in black belt and nearly black belt counties. They considerably improved their vote in both these areas in 1894, and in 1896, when the Republicans nominated no state ticket, did even better. Unlike the Populists elsewhere in the South, the Texans continued to increase their support in both kinds of county in every election.[160]

The silver issue did, however, have an impact in Texas by 1895. The Austin *People's Advocate* published the Declaration and Resolutions of the November 1894 conference of the American Bimetallic League, titling the article "The One Great Issue."[161] Although during these years the *Southern Mercury* continued to hammer hard at the limitations of free silver, and most of the letters and speeches printed in the paper did the same,[162] a few Texas Populists, especially in 1896, wanted a single plank party focusing on free silver and "financial reform"—most often meaning free coinage of silver, the abolition of national banks, and an expanded currency.[163]

To counter the spread of such ideas some Texas Populists opposed a late national convention in 1896. They wanted an early convention in order to make the campaign an educational one.[164] The editor of the *Mercury* believed that because it looked forward to fusion with silverites, a late convention would drive out five veteran reformers for every new recruit.[165] He was right, of course. The national executive committee decided on a late convention to facilitate the Populist party's entry into the 1896 campaign either as the only free silver party or in cooperation with any other party supporting free silver.[166] And especially in Texas the results of the late convention fulfilled the prediction.

One reason that bimetallic sentiment increased among the Texans was that the Texas party apparently experienced the same influx of free silver Democrats in 1893 and 1894 that the party elsewhere in the South did.[167] Their party's role in repealing the Sherman Act undoubtedly influenced these Democrats, but the efforts of the Texas Populists during 1894 to moderate the radical tone of their rhetoric may also have attracted them. No more than in Georgia did this change affect the state platform, but as other Southern Populists did, the Texans began to stress the less radical aspects of Populism. In a letter to the *Texas Advance* in mid-1894 Populist gubernatorial candidate Judge Thomas Nugent made it clear that he did not advocate socialism. He looked for "a political state or condition in which strictly public or social functions shall be turned over to the government, and the private citizen left in undisturbed freedom to achieve his own destiny in his own way by the exercise of his own individual skill and industry, and the legitimate investment of his own capital."[168] Three months later in a campaign speech published in full in the Austin *Argus*, Nugent relinquished nothing of his antimonopoly greenback stance, but again found it necessary to emphasize that the Populists did not favor any "extreme socialistic schemes" to end the problems of strikes and unemployed marches in America, but wanted solutions designed to "give free play to competition within the proper sphere of individual effort and investment."[169] Nugent had not before taken such pains to make absolutely clear his opposition to any fiddling with the fundamentals of America's economic institutions as he understood them. Not that Nugent had changed; he had not. But as in Georgia, Alabama, and North Carolina, the need to widen Populism's appeal to include some of the new town and city middle class demanded a more precise affirmation of the Populists' commitment to maintaining the sources of the success of that class.

The Texans in 1896 nominated for governor Jerome Kearby, an old independent and greenbacker.[170] Like Nugent, and unlike Hines, Goodwyn, or Seaborn Wright, he never ceased advocating and explaining the entire Omaha platform. He talked about the subtreasury before and during his campaign[171] and continued to insist upon government ownership of the railroad, telephone, and telegraph systems and a legal tender fiat currency system.[172] But, like Nugent in 1894, he always carefully explained exactly where he stood. The Populists wanted justice and an end to starvation, strikes, and poverty, but they wanted it in a society where government protected each individual's property and guaranteed everyone "equal opportunities before the law in the achievement of the greatest success."[173] Defending government ownership of the railroads in June 1896 at Greenville, Texas, he told his audience that "I hold property to be as sacred and inviolable when owned by a corporation as when owned by an individual." Until the government could purchase the railroads at a fair price the Populists would protect their property just as any other person's.[174] The *Southern Mercury* felt much the same pressure. In early 1895, responding to a request from a reader, the *Mercury* explained that selling land did not make someone a speculator. The person must deal in land "for speculative purposes," holding a large quantity of usable land out of production, presumably hoping to profit without work on the increase of its value.[175] This was no Barefield. The *Mercury*'s answer penalized neither landlords nor land developers.

Its defense of private property, however, did not reflect any change in 1895 or 1896 of the *Mercury*'s attachment to an explicitly antimonopoly stance.[176] The paper's fidelity in this matter, in fact, exposed it to charges by the financial reform-free silver Populists that the *Mercury* advocated socialism. In 1895 and 1896 the paper's editor, Milton Park, faced the same issue that Watson had, but Park looked for a different way out of the dilemma. He ridiculed the charges of the free silver Populists, pointing out that Herman Taubeneck, the Populists' national executive committee chairman, James H. Turner, the secretary of the committee, and Nelson A. Dunning, editor of the Washington, D.C., *National Watchman*, had not discovered "this bugaboo of socialism" until after their conversion to a "one-plank silver party." Only then had they seen "this socialistic ghost walk."[177]

The continued attack on the Omaha platform by the financial reform Populists, however, made it necessary for the *Mercury* to take a more explicit stand on the socialist issue. Park understood better than Watson the importance to the Omaha platform of an antimonopoly analysis. He made clear that Populism was not socialism[178] and that demands like public ownership of all the means of communication and transportation were not socialism in disguise. Of course, he was right. But that he realized the import and reason for his decision became clear when he chided Watson in the summer of 1896 for his concern over "the socialistic ghost." Park asked Watson to "explain how a government of the people can be formed without the socialistic ingredient."[179] While Park's commitment to antimonopoly greenbackism meant that he had only the greatest scorn for Butler and the other financial reform Populists, it also meant that he saw the weakness implicit in Watson's effort to separate antimonopoly from greenbackism in Georgia.[180]

The *Mercury* provided other evidence that it understood the importance of retaining the entire Omaha platform. In 1895, when talk developed in the party of dropping the subtreasury plan, Park emphatically demurred. Without some expression of the subtreasury idea, the farmers would withdraw and the Populist party collapse. "The sub-treasury principle is the basic rock upon which the people's party rests."[181] The *Mercury* rebuked Watson for advocating dropping the subtreasury plan from the Omaha platform[182] and continued to defend it as the basic plank in the Populist program for change.[183] In these years the leaders and many of the rank and file of the Texas party in speeches, articles, resolutions, and letters also revived their discussion and defense of the subtreasury plan.[184]

By 1895 the Texans were also saying, however, that the financial issue was the most important one. Because of the actions of President Cleveland and his Wall Street allies, wrote Park in February 1895, the "financial question . . . has been forced to the front as the dominant issue." That did not mean, however, that "other issues of eqally [sic] as great moment in the Omaha platform, should be subordinated." Financial reform could not crush completely "the hydraheaded monster of monopoly." For those able to escape "land monopoly" and secure a home, the transportation monopoly would absorb the gains produced by financial reform. "Money, land, transportation, and antimonopoly must go hand in hand." "Force of circumstance" made the "money question" dominant. "But if these other reforms demanded by the populists are cut off," Park concluded, "the people's party will soon be a rudderless ship in a storm, and the masses will remain hewers of wood and drawers of water."[185] Its antimonopoly basis made the Omaha platform indivisible.

Most of the Texas reformers did the same thing Park did in 1895 and 1896. They continued to stress all three planks of the Omaha platform, including government ownership of the railroad, telephone, and telegraph,[186] and integrate them in a clearly articulated antimonopoly stance.[187] Under pressure to moderate their reforms, the Texas Populists did the opposite. In response to the increasing support among Southern Populists for modification of the Omaha platform to expand its appeal to free silver financial reformers, the Texas Populists strengthened their antimonopoly analysis and explored more fully its implications for reform politics. They generally opposed the arrangements made by the national executive committee in January 1896 for a late national convention and close cooperation with the new silver party.[188] Very few of them responded positively to Bryan's nomination. Most criticized him for his advocacy of a redemption money.

On the other hand, while continuing to emphasize and explain the need for a legal tender fiat paper currency system,[189] they allowed for free silver's current importance, making qualified demands for free silver legislation. In early 1895 a Texas Populist argued that "it may be the better part of wisdom" to make free silver "the leading issue in the next campaign," because it was important and the people understood it best. That did not mean, however, it should be the only issue in the campaign, since in addition to an adequate currency the people had to have access to land and cheap transportation in order to create wealth.[190] Free silver would not solve all America's "monetary ills" wrote the editor of the *Mercury* in early 1896, but "at this time [it] would prove a great blessing to the country." It would help the important silver industry, and until "the people" learned that all money was legal tender fiat only, silver coinage would provide a little flexibility and expansion in the currency and the Wall Street speculators and bankers would find it harder to corner a money supply augmented by silver.[191]

Most Texas reformers had a better sense of the need for an integrated program of reform, a greater ease with the implications of increasing the government's involvement in the economic and social life of the country and less fear of socialism, and a more adequate understanding of precisely what kind of financial reform the country needed and exactly what free silver would do to advance the financial and social reform they wanted. This meant that the free silver panacea fared far worse among Texas Populists than among those in North Carolina, Alabama, and even Georgia. The Texas Populists understood quite well what the editor of the *Southern Mercury*, Milton Park, meant when he told them in August 1895 that the time had come for the Populists to "throw conservatism to the dogs . . . and to get down to a radical basis."[192] Unlike their brethren elsewhere, most Texas Populists did just that.

At least one sign of a weakness in this solidarity, however, appeared among the Texas Populists, and it came from James H. "Cyclone" Davis.[193] In a letter to the Dallas *News* in the fall of 1895, Davis suggested that the free silver Populists and Democrats get together, appoint Nugent and Culberson, the Democratic governor, to high court positions, nominate Democrat John Reagan for governor, and designate a national ticket of free silver Democrats.[194] Neither Reagan nor any of the national nominees favored much more than "financial reform." None of them stood anywhere near the antimonopoly greenback position on which the radical Alliancemen and Populists had built the Omaha platform.

The *Mercury* quickly attacked Davis's suggestion, pointing out, as it had done for years, that free silver would not solve the country's problems because it continued the redemption fallacy and because it ignored other, equally important monopolies in land and transportation.[195] In his reply to the *Mercury* Davis denied advocating fusion, although it would have been hard to call what he suggested anything else. More to the point, Davis argued that if the goldbugs won in 1896, they would immediately fund all greenbacks and outstanding state and federal bond issues in fifty-year gold bonds, and use all of these new gold bonds as a base for a modified and expanded national banking system. Only by uniting all who opposed this scheme into one grand party could the reformers avert the crisis.[196] The *Mercury* answered exactly as it had a month earlier.[197] The debate did not surface again, and the 1896 national convention found Davis apparently firmly in the middle of the road. He never broke rank with the 103 mid-road Texas delegates.[198]

The Populist nomination of Bryan at St. Louis, however, threw Texas Populists into confusion. In August, Davis again called for fusion with the Democrats on the basis of free silver[199] and he quickly became the leader of the minority faction of Texas Populists who also advocated that position.[200] While at first most Texas Populists were apparently willing to cooperate with the Democrats if they took Sewall down and Watson replaced him as the vice-presidential candidate,[201] others opposed Bryan altogether and wanted an independent Populist national ticket.[202] Following the Democratic convention the *Mercury* guessed that by nominating Bryan the Democrats hoped to trick the Populists back into the Democratic party. Despite the fact that his enemies called him a Populist, the *Mercury* insisted that Bryan was not one.[203] Two weeks later, after the Populist convention at St. Louis, the *Mercury* was willing to tolerate Bryan only if he ran on the Populist platform, since the Democratic platform advocated a redeemable currency.[204] Populists elsewhere in the South maintained that Bryan made the Democrats acceptable. Consistent with its antimonopoly stance, the *Mercury* argued the opposite, that the Democrats blackened Bryan.[205]

During August the Texas situation grew more confused. Other Texas Populists besides the *Mercury* began to find the same cloven hoof in the 1896 Democratic platform that had trapped the greenbackers almost twenty years earlier, redeemable money. On this ground one Texan saw little difference between McKinley and Bryan.[206] The same week another letter writer found the same similarity, and because of his hatred for the Democrats announced he intended to vote for McKinley unless the Populists put up an independent national ticket.[207] A week later the *Mercury* reported that many mid-road Texans preferred McKinley to Bryan and Sewall. Except for free silver, they found little to distinguish between the two old parties, and even on this issue slight difference existed.[208] The People's party of Upshur County demanded in September a straight Populist national ticket because Bryan stood on a Democratic platform of redeemable currency and bonds.[209] By late September and early October the *Mercury* argued that while swapping votes with the Republicans meant sacrificing principles, it preferred that to sacrificing "manhood" as well by voting for Democratic "tax-raisers and ballot-box stuffers."[210]

Ironically, in the fall of 1896 the Texas Populists found themselves in the same kind of confusion as the Alabama reformers, but for different reasons. The Texans, because of their commitment to and understanding of the radical position, faced a national election with no one to vote for. Some voted for Bryan and Watson; many others apparently chose McKinley. The vote for Kearby was about 10,000 votes, or 1.5 percent less than the combined vote for Bryan and Watson and McKinley. The vote for Culberson was only about 8,000 votes greater than that for Bryan and Sewall.[211]

The reduction of any distinction between Bryan and McKinley to a level of meaninglessness, however, involved more than an antimonopoly greenback analysis, although it ultimately rested on that basis. Few Texas Populists, unlike many of their brethren elsewhere in the South, predicted the arrival of Armageddon with the failure of free silver.[212] To the contrary, in October 1895 the editor of the *Southern Mercury* attacked free silver Populists, predicting that "the free silver party may or may not succeed, but in any event, it will soon be swallowed up by one or both of the old parties and the death of reform resulting from this free silver policy will eventually lead to the destruction of liberty and the overthrow of the American republic."[213] By destroying the Populist party, the editor wrote later, free silver would remove the last impediment to domination by the money power. As "one of the least of the reforms needed," free silver might delay but could never avert "the impending catastrophe."[214] Free silver was "a bait for suckers," argued another Texan in March 1896, designed to destroy Populist opposition to the money power. "The so-called specie basis" for currency was "a relic of barbarism, and the father of every bondocracy the world ever knew, and the enslaver of nearly all nations." The Populists could have nothing to do with this "hell-born thing."[215] For some Texas Populists the free silver panacea threatened to bring, not avoid, millennial disaster.

While the differing analysis of Populist reform ideas must be considered a more basic cause for the free silver panacea's move into Southern Populism than the logic of the religious and moral metaphor and imagery, this logic played an important part in fragmenting Southern Populism after 1894. If Southern Populists did not have a relatively firm grasp of the technicalities and implications of the antimonopoly greenback position, when the religious and moral metaphor or image became identified with social or financial reform it reinforced a tendency to accept free silver as the primary or sole solution to the ills of American society. If, however, the Populists based their original understanding firmly on the radical position, the process of rhetorical logic which moved the religious and moral metaphors to religious and moral identities tended to reinforce the idea of an integrated and wide-ranging reform program.

In both cases, however, such rhetorical logic generally narrowed the room for discussion. If free silver Populists felt that any path but theirs led to perdition, and the Omaha platform supporters felt the same, they had little common ground available for meeting. By November 1896 the Texans, who constituted the bulk of the mid-road faction in the South, were calling the free silver financial reformers the very names they had reserved for Cleveland two years earlier, and vice versa. The issues, of course, had not changed, but the relation of different Populists and different state parties to each other around these issues had differed as early as 1891 and 1892. The way Southern Populists thought and expressed themselves, and the logic of these ways of thinking and speaking, accentuated the differences as they grew greater after 1892 and helped break up the southern party. While the differences between antimonopoly greenback and financial reform Southern Populists (exemplified by but not confined to the Texas-Southeast split) remained mute, the reformers worked well together. Although almost all the Southern Populists continued to share a similar vision of a just, humane, and decent American society, from 1893 on the religious and moral metaphors and imagery, in addition to outside circumstances such as the increase of free silver sentiment among non-Populist Southerners, focused attention on the differences in the way various Populists and state parties approached and explained reform and helped lead to the subsequent collapse of the party.[216]

The debacle of 1896, to the extent that the Southern Populists were responsible for it, was due to the failure of most southern reformers to perceive the political implications of the Omaha platform. The Alliance did not succeed in the years following the St. Louis convention of 1889 in teaching enough Southerners that the reform platforms from that year through 1892 were documents not of separate demands but of an antimonopoly whole, that they required a rudimentary politics of class, not section, of the exploited against their exploiters, not the South and West against the East. To be sure, not even the strongest of the mid-roaders ever came to grips with the implications of their demand that no property right ever be placed above a human right and that all people had a right to the decent livelihood which the full value of their labor would afford them. Nevertheless, ultimately neither patterns of deference politics nor the aspirations of a few Southern Populist leaders caused free silver fusion with the Democrats. In Texas, where the Populists best and most widely understood greenback monetary theory and the antimonopoly basis for reform, the Populist leadership remained radical. In Alabama and North Carolina a poor understanding of legal tender fiat currency quickly undermined the radical Populists' constituency, paving the way for the practical politics of men like Marion Butler and Reuben Kolb.

Georgia fell in between. The Georgia reformers understood the implications of the Omaha platform well enough to reject Livingston's efforts to lead the Alliance back into the Democratic party at the expense of the radical program, but continued pressure to win an election exposed a weakness. The Georgians never sufficiently comprehended the integral relationship between greenbackism and antimonopoly and followed Watson in his attempt to divorce the latter from the Omaha platform. Except in Texas, the failure to grasp fully the meaning and implications of the radical position made the Populists vulnerable to the appeal of free silver and sectional politics. This in turn undermined their critique of American industrial and financial capitalism and their effort to create a political and economic alliance of the South's poor, neither of which could stand alone. The rudimentary class politics of antimonopoly greenbackism produced both. Abandoning the radical position meant that the Southern Populists no longer had reason to resist either their section's historical racism or its more recent commitment to American capitalism. As a result, the reformers accepted as an answer to the problems of poverty, exploitation, and injustice a solution which ultimately resulted in the South's integration into the national economic and political system on an antidemocratic, racist, and exploitative semicolonial basis.

The Populists, of course, may well not have won even had they remained committed to the Omaha platform. The Democrats' control of the election machinery and their access to money and political expertise permitted them to count the Populists out more than once. Historians have offered many explanations for the failure of the Southern Populists—lack of money, organizational weakness, lack of economic power and political control and expertise. Most recently J. Morgan Kousser has suggested that the disfranchisement statutes placed a serious additional barrier between the Southern Populists and success.[217] This rings truest for Florida, Tennessee, Mississippi, and Arkansas, where the Democrats won their legal victories before the Populist party ever fully organized, but, interestingly, it was not true in Georgia.

The Georgia case is an important one. It illustrates the difficulties involved in equating legal structure with reality.[218] It also shows that ultimately political success or failure rested upon the ability of the Southern Populists to understand the nature of their situation adequately and act upon it. Alabama had no restrictive election laws in 1892, yet the reformers lost. The Jeffersonians' response to this loss and the Sayre election law, a white primary, suggests why. Their opposition to black disfranchisement, and consequently their own, was to say the least un-inspired and suffered from a failure to attack their society at a point of fundamental weakness.

To say the Populists lost because they were counted out is not enough. How they thought affected how they reacted, and how they reacted in part determined the success of their enemies. The Southern Populists were not able, in general, to mount an effective enough attack on the society which, among other things, defrauded and disfranchised them. Whether unwilling to do so or unable, they never questioned thoroughly enough the fundamental premises of that society, premises which in-cluded white supremacy, private property, profit, and the market system. The Southern Populists' most sincere effort to build a rudimentary bi-racial class coalition in a heavily black state, Georgia, fell short, but the effort made a difference, even with Georgia's poll tax. The Populists came close there, despite fraud and the legal disfranchisement used by the Democrats, because they offered a more basic challenge to the prevailing social order than did the Populists in North Carolina or Alabama. The same was true of Texas on a wider scale. Where their analysis remained most radical, where it questioned most fundamentally the whole social order which the Populists' opponents defended with all the legal and extralegal means at their command, the Southern Populists succeeded best.

The loss of the Populists meant the accession to regional social, eco-nomic, and political dominance of a new southern middle class, men such as those in North Carolina whom Helen Edmonds described as the "lawyers, textile mill owners, and railroad magnates," the "industrial or capitalistic element."[219] In the struggles of the 1890s, the Redeemers, aided and abetted by those who would soon rule in their places, tried to save their regimes by counting out white votes. By using the tactics of Redemption in the name of white supremacy, however, they more than used up the moral capital they had earned as the saviors of the South in the 1870s.[220] The South's new middle class quickly filled the vacuum. While it meant the destruction of the Populist party, free silver provided the opportunity for the South's new leaders to assume the Redeemers' mantle of sectional leadership. Free silver and sectional politics made them, not the Redeemers, the spokesmen for the South within the Demo-cratic party. This advantage gave them, in the absence of any important opposition, a political dominance in the South which they quickly took care to protect. The disfranchisement of almost all black and many white voters shored up their vulnerable political base. After the first decade of the twentieth century they had a lot fewer voters to cope with than the Redeemers did.[221] The elaboration of Jim Crow helped them solidify their hold on what remained of the white electorate by freezing white supremacy not only into the politics of the South but into its culture as well.

This new middle class, although they frequently fought among themselves, essentially accepted the South's semicolonial position in the national economy and sought to work out their salvation and the South's within it. Some of them, like Simmons in North Carolina, Martin in Virginia, Brown in Georgia, and Sayers and Colquitt in Texas, fell on the conservative side of the political spectrum. Others, like Montague of Virginia, Aycock and Daniels of North Carolina, Smith of Georgia, Comer of Alabama, and Hogg of Texas, regarded some adjustment within the national system with a bit more equanimity. The impulse to reform for these Southern Progressives looked to developing what local and regional markets the southern middle class found available.[222] Southern conservatives, members of the same middle class, might fight with the reformers over the extent to which change ought to occur, over the relative advantages to be gained by working with northern capitalists as opposed to trying to increase southern control of local markets and production, but like Brown in Georgia, they never wanted to abolish Progressive reforms.[223] Not that the reformers were that radical. Even while they promoted their railroad commission fight as a struggle of Alabamians in the name of southern prosperity and independence against the domination of J. P. Morgan and northern capitalists,[224] Comer and his conservative opponents both welcomed U.S. Steel's purchase of Tennessee Coal and Iron in 1907.[225]

Whether Progressive or conservative, the members of this new middle class—the lawyers, politicians, wholesalers, promoters, manufacturers, real estate developers, bankers, corporation managers, even successful farmers and landlords—led the final, unchallenged expansion of American industrial and financial capitalism into the South, country as well as town. They made their place as the conduits by which American capitalism and its business culture funneled much of the South's wealth out of the section.[226] Embittered, frustrated by defeat, and retreating into an agrarianism Woodward describes as marked by "militant sectionalism, fear of majority rule, racial domination, and perceptible overtones of a landed aristocracy,"[227] in the early twentieth century Tom Watson still retained enough of his old radicalism to understand not only what had happened in the South with the defeat of the Populists, but generally how it was accomplished. "Just as the English maintain their conquest of India by taking into copartnership with themselves a certain percentage of Hindus, so the North holds the South in subjection by enlisting Southern capitalists and politicians."[228] Northern capitalists controlled southern railroads,[229] furnished the capital for southern mills and street railways, and supplied southern banks, "always taking Southern men in with them to a certain extent, and they appoint some of our politicians to good positions. United themselves, the Northern capitalists divide the Southerners, and thus rule and despoil the South." The proof lay in the pudding. What constituted the progress of which this new middle class boasted and which they used to justify their leadership? The Southerners built the railroads, grew the cotton, and manufactured the cloth, but "who got the increased wealth?" "*Have* the people got more *general* prosperity?" The towns and cities and their new middle class generally prospered, but the mill hands and sharecroppers and tenants, an ever-increasing proportion of the southern population, black and white, saw little or nothing of it.[230]

The collapse of Southern Populism witnessed the defeat of the last mainstream effort by Southerners to overcome their sectional history and habits and join other American reformers in the creation of a truly national identity. Ironically, this very collapse permitted the new southern middle class to integrate the South, as a distinct section, more thoroughly than ever before into the national economic system, albeit as a semi-colonial junior partner. To this end, then, the sectional politics of free silver led. Large numbers of Southern Populists, lacking an adequate comprehension of the intimate relationship between the better society they dreamed of and the antimonopoly greenback Omaha platform, unwittingly joined the Democrats in what appeared to them to be a crusade for reform but in reality proved to be the opening shot in a campaign that led to the triumph of conservatism in the South. It was not what the Populists had wanted. Not at all.

CONCLUSION

A Critique for Industrial Capitalism

For all the Southern Populists, financial reformers and antimonopoly greenbackers alike, the proper society bore a great resemblance to the rural, agricultural communities in which most of them lived or had grown up. Farmers, or at least producers, formed its center, and nearly all its members earned their living by producing or facilitating the production and distribution of some form of tangible wealth. While individual economic competition and the market system for the most part went unchallenged, personal relationships and moral and religious precept more importantly than Adam Smith's invisible hand and the local police force appeared to delineate and guide the social and economic life of the community. The Southerners distrusted institutions and persons who dealt with intangible things such as credit, interest, and some kinds of written law, and suspected those with whom they had impersonal relationships.[1]

The Southern Populists' ways of thinking and writing about the world they found around them, and its ideal alternative, were not only the heritage of the community in which they lived or had been raised but also reflected it. The Jeffersonian-Jacksonian metaphors dealt with and described a relatively homogeneous and harmonious rural society which knew little of railroad corporations, Andrew Carnegie, Standard Oil, or an industrial proletariat. Their religious and moral metaphors and imagery were premised on and reflected the assumption that society was best organized and governed on a personal and moral basis. The producite metaphor, harder to pin down than these two and partaking of both of them, described a society whose most important function was the production of tangible wealth and in which the physical labor involved in producing that wealth was the most valuable and virtuous activity one could undertake. The Southern Populists used these metaphors and images which so well described their experience in a southern, rural, evangelical Protestant community to criticize another world they found developing around them—an impersonal, amoral, urban-centered, non-

Conclusion

southern, industrial society—and to project their reform plans for a new social order.

The particulars of the Southern Populists' reform plans and the differences among them were discussed first. While these differences had a considerable impact on the Populists' political behavior, for the most part the differences did not affect the reformers' vision of the proper social order, because they all shared the critique of financial and industrial capitalist society which provided the impetus for their varying reform demands. All the Southern Populists, for instance, frequently and vigorously attacked cities, the home of this new society. Bringing to bear on the city the Jeffersonian, the producerite, and the religious and moral metaphors and imagery, the reformers found a number of discrepancies between it and the society they wanted. Kid-gloved, silk-hatted men lived in the city and ran politics. They did no hard work, produced no wealth, yet controlled the country.[2] The town's dominance of the countryside, like the nonproducer's dominance of the producer, stood the proper order of society on its head because the town ultimately depended on the countryside for survival.[3] Some Southern Populists held the failure of existing society to reflect this truth responsible for many of America's problems. An Alabama Populist pointed out that the huge land holdings of aliens and American corporations, having "driven thousands of people out of the country into towns and cities to compete with skilled labor and caused strikes, lock outs, riots, and bloodshed, and caused our nation to be filled with tramps and paupers," brought not only the decline of the countryside but unrest in the cities.[4]

While they muted the sharp accents of class conflict in their rhetoric and analysis as 1896 approached and most of the southern state parties moderated their reform programs to appeal to the new southern town and city middle class, moral condemnation of city life remained a constant theme. Conditions unique to urban areas prevented the development of good citizens. Like Jefferson,[5] the editor of the *Progressive Farmer* felt something in the relationship of people to each other in cities destroyed character. Their dependence on their employers for a livelihood made clerks and tradesmen slaves to their master's politics. "Stay in the country," the editor advised his readers; "be free to think and act."[6]

Other Populists, like W. J. Peele of North Carolina, expanded on the tone if not the substance of Jefferson's indictment. "Cancers upon the body politic," in them originated the "schemes of plunder" which destroyed the moral fiber and virtue necessary to hold America together.[7] A Texas Populist in 1894 warned that it was "from the cities, with their brothels, their low-down grogeries, their sweatshops, from districts where dirt, and disease, and rats, and hunger, and despair blot out all that is god-like in man and makes him a ravening beast, that the red hand of anarchy is raised, and it is from the cities that the hosts of old partyism are brought forth."[8] Only the country, most Southern Populists felt, produced the character and morality necessary to save the nation and run it properly. Speaking for most of his brethren, a North Carolina reformer in late 1891 admonished farmers who did not know the cities' sorrows and vices to "feel proud of your mission; honor your calling; for from behind many a plow there has [sic] gone forth the leaders of nations. . . . The plow is the power behind the throne in this land."[9]

In combination with their almost complete lack of immediate experience with it, the lack of an analytical framework which dealt with urbanization made the Southern Populists' rejection of the city nearly complete. But their critique of industrial capitalist society usually was not so parochially hostile, although it grew from the same roots from which the attack on the cities sprouted. Many reformers, for instance, noted angrily that money spoke louder than personal virtue and morality, and the many without it went unconsidered, regardless of their worth or ability. Especially in towns and cities, stated one North Carolina Populist, with a few thousand dollars "the moral prostitute or the polished ignoramus" could win all the social recognition desired.[10] This idea usually accompanied the Southern Populists' concern with the decline within the new industrial, urban society of older personal relationships and moral codes of behavior. Watson deplored the trend in some large urban churches toward celebrating communion from individual cups rather than a common one. It seemed to him "that religion in the great cities is trying . . . to abolish the simple ways and brotherly teachings of Christ."[11]

The whole tone of modern life bothered Watson even more. "Move on" had become the watchword of civilization. The policeman said it to the tramp, the law to the vagrant, society "to the soldier in the battle of life. . . . [T]o stop is to be run over."[12] Under much of the new haste and impersonality Watson saw an accelerating race for wealth that seemed to dominate all social life, with no respect for human beings or their needs. He continually objected to opening the Chicago World's Fair on Sunday, not for religious reasons but because a country "threatened with a heartless, tireless, pitiless race for wealth such as the world never saw before" needed a day of rest. The whole year witnessed "this maddening rush for money, this insane 'get there' push for success, regardless of methods," moving the country closer to ruin. "In this mad saturnalia, so very ruinous of the better attributes of manhood," America was becoming a state of constant personal warfare for a larger share of the spoils.[13] Others felt the same way.[14] The incessant drive for the dollar was destroying the good in the rural society that the Southern Populists found around them, the values of which they wished to recreate at a national level. At least some saw these traits for what they were, products of the business culture created by American capitalism. "It is an age of greed. Don't forget that fact," a North Carolina editor reminded his readers. "There are men who would coin the bones of their dead mothers into gold, if they could, and they form the most aggressive business class."[15]

Part of this hostility toward a new urban society obviously reflected the attitude of a farming population which accurately perceived a relative, and often absolute, decline of its wealth and social status. Some of their disapproval did spring from the new middle-class morality of which we spoke earlier. But the growing tempo of life in an increasingly impersonal and amoral industrial society was no fiction. In fact, for the Southern Populists the most serious consequence of this was not the decline of rural society but the human toll it took. The exploitation involved in nineteenth-century industrial capitalism appalled them. "A low estimate," wrote the editor of the *Texas Advance* in 1894, "places the enforced paupers of the country at one million." The system that caused this created "thousands of women surrendering their lives to greed, stitch by stitch, fifteen hours a day." It set thousands of unemployed laboring men to tramping the country in search of work, "depending for life on the charity of the people," "all of their pride and manhood" slowly being ground to dust in "this plutocratic mill." Few remained who said with the Redeemer, "'Inasmuch as ye did it unto the least of them, ye did it to me.'"[16]

Measured in terms of human destruction, many Southern Populists, radical and moderate, questioned whether the existing social order had any claim to civilization. A North Carolina reformer found it strange that a Brazilian man who ate human flesh shocked the "civilized world." Where, he asked, lay the difference between "this ignorant depraved man, who ate human beings because he had no other way of satisfying his hunger," and "the thousands of educated, wealthy, and in many cases personally refined employers in this country who willfully and intentionally take advantage of the necessities of their employees to grind their wages down to the lowest possible point that will keep soul and body together? Both the cannibal and the grinding employer are living on human flesh, the ignorant one devouring it outright and the intelligent one wearing it out for his benefit, and of the two which is the greatest sinner? Can there be a doubt? We think not."[17]

Charity offered no solution to the suffering; the problem lay with the system. "When plutocracy defrauds the people of this nation out of a billion dollars of value a year through the law, it is business," observed a North Carolinian. When they established soup kitchens, "it is charity."[18] The idea of charity outraged the editor of the *Southern Mercury*. Charity, he wrote in 1895, was "the crust the robber gives back to the man he has robbed. Charity is an apology for justice, and apology will not pay the wages of the toiler, nor feed the hungry in comfort."[19] "If the enriching of the few, through the conscienceless robbing of the people under form of law was put to a stop," remarked the editor of Georgia's *Wool Hat*, "there would be no need of calling on the wealthy for the exercise of wholesale charity to relieve the suffering of those who are plundered. . . . To relieve suffering among the people we ask not charity, we demand justice."[20] The Southern Populists often felt, in fact, that American industrial society depended on the destruction, or at least the complete degradation, of the large mass of people. It had to be reorganized and governed so that it served not just a few but the many. "If civilization is worth anything to humanity," maintained another Georgia editor, "its blessings should be extended to all . . . in proportion to their honest, earnest efforts to attain them. This is not so now."[21] The Southern Populists could not accept industrial development at the cost of millions of poor.

The rule of thumb for correcting these abuses cut straight to the heart of the problem. As an Alabama editor wrote, "any nation that holds property rights above human rights is barbarian."[22] A society in which the rush for gain and property exceeded acceptable limits and included the destruction of human rights the Southern Populists felt was neither proper nor decent. "Our people should be greater than our money, our commerce, or anything else in our America."[23] So not only the limitations of their analysis but also the power of their critique flowed from the Southern Populists' evangelical Protestant past, their Jeffersonian and Jacksonian heritage, and their rural experience. Through these things they articulated and reinforced their belief in a personal, moral standard of human responsibility which society had to meet, criticized the inhumanity of industrial and financial capitalism, and mounted their demands for new ends, human ends, for American society to serve. "Life," wrote the radical antimonopoly greenbacker W. S. Morgan, "is more sacred than property always and everywhere if the two are in peril, life should be saved if property perish. Capitalism places property above life, thereby declaring war upon humanity. This war must not cease until capitalism is vanquished and property becomes the servant, not the master of man."[24]

The Southern Populists also revealed their recognition of the enemy in their demand that society protect the weak from the strong. It provided a focus for both their critique and their desire for a new social order. Human history, a Texas editor noted, told the story of how the strong crushed the weak "in the mad race for place and power and pelf. Over the bodies of its victims have been built the great and mighty wonders of the world."[25] The right to life, liberty, and happiness, "inherent in every human being," implied to a North Carolina Populist that every person had "a right to the means of comfortable existence, the right to the condition that produce [*sic*] happiness. . . . Society commits a grave fault when it honors the strong and intelligent who have grown rich by robbing the weak and ignorant."[26] "Man generally knows," maintained a Georgia Populist in mid-1894, "that we are bound together in families, communities, states and nations for mutual protection and material happiness and not for self-aggrandizement or the survival of the fittest."[27] That "survival of the fittest" should in the late nineteenth century continue to dictate society's organization and operation repelled the Southern Populists. "Survival of the fittest," wrote James Murdock, made America into "one vast battlefield where daily warfare is being waged for the necessities of life and for supremacy." Not only an inhuman way to organize society, this method also worked badly. "Hundreds of millions of misguided energies are wasted each year. The energies of the people are not half utilized."[28] The social order needed a fundamental change.

When they limited themselves to a discussion of the ideal system of production and exchange between individuals, the Southern Populists often lamented the decline of competition. Almost all of them, however, opposed using competition as a guide for humanity's wider social life and development. "Under a system where every man is for himself," wrote an Arkansas Populist, "the devil will get most of them."[29] Few could choose consciously to accept competition if it meant that the struggle to survive destroyed most people. "Free competition," argued a Virginia Alliance editor, "is the great principle of Anglo-Saxon development, and we have all been nurtured on that principle since infancy, and yet it is clearly responsible for the present distressing inequalities of society. Under its operation the strong become stronger at the expense of the weak, and the power of money to oppress is supreme." The principle "guarantees to every citizen an equal right to compete for the possession of wealth, but it is powerless to prevent the strong from taking the share of the weak." In the name of "free competition, a fair field and no favor," American society had become "every man for himself, and the devil take the hindmost," and, as such, was unacceptable.[30] The southern reformers agreed with the Texas Populist who wrote that the "Darwinian theory of the survival of the strongest" could no longer coexist with "the Christian theory of the survival of all," especially since the new industrial developments of the generation following the Civil War had made the effects of competition on society worse.[31]

Obviously human need demanded a change in the system, but what would replace it? For the answer the Southern Populists drew on their Alliance heritage and expanded it to include the whole of society.[32] "Competition forces the employer to cut down wages; he must do so or go under," reasoned an Alabama editor. "Those employers who are guided by feelings of humanity are forced out of business by competition. The system is rotten, and we toss our hat and exclaim, all hail the co-operative commonwealth!"[33] Cooperation would once again value decency above destruction, human beings above money or property. "Each for All and All for Each" ran the motto of the *Virginia Sun*.[34] Cooperation would end strikes, the "war between capital and labor," wrote a Georgia Populist, because "the motive and cause for them would be removed. Co-operative industry means that all wealth will belong to him who creates it."[35] Under this rule people could work together to advance their interests instead of destroying each other in the name of a competition speciously defended as promoting development and expansion. The competitive system had outlived its usefulness, both as a device for increasing production and economic growth and as a means of improving the lot of all. The future would see no slowdown in economic and social development as a result of the cooperative system, but the human wastage caused by competition would disappear.[36]

Focusing on the human wreckage it strewed behind it, the Southern Populists grounded their criticism of the competitive order on a personal, moral analysis of society. They did not, however, question the fundamental tenets of the American economic system as they understood them—the market, supply and demand, private ownership and profit, and the beneficence of economic competition between small economic units. The only exceptions to this, the editors of the *People's Advocate* and the *Argus*, both of Austin, Texas, provided once again a striking example of the grip these ideas had on the southern reformers. These editors and their southern brethren saw the same wrongs and attributed them to the same cause, the malfunctioning of the social system. The old ideas of competition had not worked. Obviously something had to change. People had to work with and for each other.[37] But of all the Southern Populists, only these editors accepted the logic of this position. Real cooperation, they argued, meant at least the nationalization of all monopolies and the end that this implied to the market system, private profit, and economic competition. "Socialism will set the wheels of industry in motion to satisfy the wants of every human being," insisted the editor of the *Advocate*. "It alone will give us the key to prosperity, a higher civilization."[38] Almost all other Southern Populists rejected such a radical demand for change, although in practice they sometimes criticized the existing system more harshly that these editors. They did not follow through on the implications of their demand that American society replace economic competition with cooperation, the "cooperative commonwealth." They identified themselves as independent producers, or aspiring independent producers, within a simple market society, where economically independent individuals competed with each other while everyone, through a democratic government, owned cooperatively the major elements of distribution.

Part of the reason the Southern Populists stopped short of an attack on the market system lay in the sources to which they turned for a justification of this cooperative order. They measured the existing social order by its human refuse; they measured their cooperative society by its promise of brotherhood. An emphasis on the rights of man marked one important element in the thinking behind this metaphor, an objection to the movement away from the homogeneous, harmonious Jeffersonian ideal entailed in the growth of rigid class lines and an end to economic and social mobility.[39] This change also involved the drift away from the concern of every person for every other, the brotherhood of men, one of the best faces of the Southern Populists' producer-centered community. The Populist party had a duty, wrote an Alabama editor, "to show to the world by its actions that there is a reality in the just and equitable relationship which, according to natures [sic] laws, each and every man sustains to every other man and to his Creator."[40]

The main roots of the metaphor lay in the evangelical Protestant experience of the Southern Populists. In the idea of cooperative effort, wrote the editor of the *Virginia Sun* in early 1892, "is contained the secret to all true life and progress—the grand emancipating principle of brotherhood. A man, living to himself alone, can achieve but little. But once let him free himself from his narrow selfishness, and boldly throw himself into work for the good of all, and his share of the good of all shall be returned to him—a hundredfold more than his puny effort could ever have yielded. Thus does the spiritual law find its economic counterpart— if a man would save his life, he must first lose it."[41] Until people realized the responsibility of each for the other, nothing would change. The editor of the *Texas Advance* maintained that the Brotherhood of Locomotive Firemen, by defining their own self-interest so narrowly that they failed to strike in support of the American Railway Union and the Pullman workers, had made a serious mistake. Such limited principles of immediate self-interest allowed the wealthy few to keep "those who produce all, and handle all, the wealth in separate, unsympathetic camps." To defeat their opponents, the producers and laboring people "must make up their minds to enter an organization whose fundamental principles are the universal fatherhood of God and the brotherhood of man and recognize the great truth that the interest of one is the interest of all—and walk to the ballot box in a solid phalanx and there redress every wrong."[42] Reform ultimately rested on the brotherhood of all producers, employed laborers or independent farmers.

Many Southern Populists shared this attitude. How could there be peace on earth, asked a North Carolina Populist at Easter 1894, "while men are struggling, one against another, to the injury of the many and the benefit of the few. There is no peace. Our everyday existence is a constant warfare—a struggle for life." Goodwill toward men could not survive when a million starved, another million had no work, and a few had uncountable wealth. "Let this year usher in the good time when men shall realize the grand truth that all men are brothers. The fatherhood of God and the brotherhood of men."[43] Humanity and justice demanded a new social order where brotherhood was a reality.

> After nineteen centuries, during this first forced pause in the storm of dog-eat-dog policy that has swept the world's surface throughout the cycles of iniquity [sic], they [the producers] are catching a glimpse of the golden light of hope that is breaking through the veil above them, and are pausing to find their latitude, and to learn, if possible, how far they have been driven from the course marked out by their God, in which all men could reap the first fruits of honest toil. Beware! The lion is awakening in its lair. . . . The combined power of the world's brawn and muscle is being united to grapple with caste and cunning in one grand effort to restore the long-lost diadem, the equality and brotherhood of man.[44]

The Southern Populists' hostility to a social system justifying itself in terms of the "survival of the fittest," a competitive system of dog-eat-dog which, as it was, was as good as it could ever be, required basic changes. "The arrogance of wealth and place," wrote W. S. Morgan, "must be resolved into feelings of responsibility to humanity. . . . Institutions must be made servants of the people instead of masters. The spirit of destructive anarchy is a merciless red-handed menace, and should be suppressed. But we are all responsible for it to some extent. With just and equitable laws and a governing principle of brotherly love, neither rich nor poor, anarchist or criminal, could long exist."[45]

American society's inhumanity to most of its members seemed to the Southern Populists the most compelling reason for a change toward a new society regulated by the principle of cooperative brotherhood, where every person would be responsible for every other. The responsibility was personal, the compulsion to it moral. It was a responsibility which the Southern Populists accused the new urban industrial America of ignoring and destroying. Their Jeffersonian and Jacksonian heritage stressed the equality of all people in a relatively homogeneous, producer-oriented society; their rural experience emphasized the personal, moral connections of each person to every other; their religious background insisted on the essential equality of all people before God. All of these underlined the need for personal responsibility. On this ideal of brotherhood they built their critique of the new industrial capitalist society in America and then constructed their ideal alternative to it. It was not to be everyone for themselves but all for each other.

The irony was, of course, that they saw no particular conflict between this and the retention of a market society based on private ownership and profit, the same base on which rested the industrial and financial capitalist society they opposed. None of their sources for the ideal of brotherhood and responsibility in a cooperative society suggested any problem. And when their experience did, the Southern Populists proposed as a solution a simple market society within a cooperative national economy. This resolution became untenable only when they turned to dealing with the benefits of America's existing industrial structure, benefits they wished to retain.

By no means did the Southern Populists reject industrial society. Their exposure to some aspects of it in America, particularly the social suffering it caused, resulted in only an apparent repudiation; they actually responded far differently. They disliked not industrial development but its impact on American society. The New South and railroads attracted them precisely because they promised economic improvement and even industrial expansion. The editor of the *Progressive Farmer* in August 1893 criticized the gold standard because by reducing the money supply, it would stop all trains, shut every factory in the land, and put three-quarters of the merchants and bankers in the country out of business. Few newspapers could be published, and telegraph and communcations would remain only between large cities. "In short, the progress we have made in the past hundred years will be forgotten as we get poorer and progress backward."[46] This reformer and others conceived of Populist reform as a way to save America's complex industrial society before the social effects attending its organization destroyed it.

For this task, however, what had worked in the past would not necessarily work in the future. Times had changed. The Populists of Bibb County, Alabama, felt in 1892 that old principles needed only slight alteration. The tenets of the People's party were "identical with the true teachings of Jefferson modernized and made applicable to the changed condition of this country."[47] Others felt more change might be necessary. "This government was good when it was formed," wrote the editor of the *Wool Hat* in early 1894. "But the conservative control which bars all changes and insists that garments fit which were long ago outgrown, which tries to press a nineteenth-century civilization into an eighteenth-century mould [sic]" prevented the "gradual evolution and natural growth" of a more perfect system of government.[48] "Is it reasonable," asked a North Carolina editor, "to say that our forefathers who lived a century ago, could have enacted perfect laws to suit this age and generation?" They had known nothing of the "gigantic trusts, greedy monopolists and soulless corporations" that the masses had to contend with in the 1890s. Populist reform had to be new to deal with these new conditions.[49] The people had new enemies from whom to protect themselves, and they had to tailor their defense to the attack. The people's response had to be as radical and as new as the conditions which threatened them.

While the Southern Populists, both financial reformers and antimonopoly greenbackers, often called for a restoration of Jeffersonian and Jacksonian politics,[50] they consciously designed their specific reforms to meet the needs of a new society. The allusions to older forms most often referred only to general principles of government. America needed to return to earlier forms, maintained a North Carolina Allianceman, to regain a government which protected all Americans rather than a special few, a government "founded upon the principle of justice and equality to the whole people," a government "restored to its primitive parity."[51] Neither Jeffersonian nor Jacksonian politics produced specific demands for a subtreasury, for legal tender irredeemable fiat paper money, for government ownership of the railroads, for an increase in the effort of the national government to guarantee the well-being of all the members of society. Only their standards did the Southern Populists discover in the past. Like any thoughtful and creative reform group, they tried to make use of their heritage without allowing themselves to be limited by it, to recreate with new policies a society of equal rights for all and special privileges to none.

But what of the times southern reformers seemed to be calling for a return not just to the principles but the reality of a pre-Civil War America? In most of these cases the reformers did not specifically reject post-Civil War American society, although they appeared at times to imply it.[52] In part these implications disclosed again the Southern Populists' failure to realize what their reform vision might mean for the continued economic development they wanted to retain. The harmonious, homogeneous, producer-oriented society—Jeffersonian America—had little to do with the reality of industrial America. The Southern Populists who made these apparent rejections of late nineteenth-century America, however, did not consciously reject industrial society. In only one instance, that of a Georgia Populist in December 1893, was there an explicit call for a return to the economic organization of an earlier time. If the "agricultural people" wanted to become "independent," he wrote, they would have to "retrace their steps from the culture of cotton to raising their own hog and hominy, and women must do the same, until they get back from the organ, piano, etc., and let the spinning wheel, cards and loom make their music as did their grandmothers." When the farmer realized his own economic independence and won "wholesome laws to protect his interest," lost confidence would be restored and religion again have the influence it ought.[53] As we have already seen, almost all Southern Populists explicitly rejected such ideas.

Further evidence of the specific meaning with which nearly all Southern Populists invested their calls for "return" lay in their interpretation of their own reform demands. They intended the specific planks in their platforms, among other things, to further industrial development. "The sub-treasury," a North Carolina Populist contended, "will bring Manchester to the South."[54] "[R]ailroads are a public necessity," wrote a Texas Populist, "and ought to be more and more perfected and extended. ... [H]e is a fool who expects that the third part of the stars in the firmament of science and civilization should be blotted out by crippling and killing railroads. They are intended by divine providence to be, and can be made, grand, solid blessings."[55] The Southern Populists proposed their reforms not to end industrial development but to stimulate it while making its benefits available to a much greater number. They wanted to alter the system in which this change had occurred in order to make it more responsive to human needs, to reduce the suffering it had so far produced. They did not consider such reforms incompatible with the continued, even increased, tempo of industrial expansion as they variously understood it.

Not all the ideas the Southern Populists held about American industrial society derived from older notions. Continued exposure to it made them, like many other Americans of their generation, more aware of and attuned to its realities. Their acceptance of the fruits of the new order and its physical manifestations—railroads, factories, steam and electric power—testified to the effect of contemporary experience. So did their attitude toward self-sufficient farming, which directly contradicted important elements in their Jeffersonian heritage.

Their opponents constantly told the Southern Populists that they could solve all their economic problems by diversifying their agriculture and raising on the farm all of what they needed. Some Southern Populists did admit that until social and economic conditions improved a degree of self-sufficiency might be warranted. But self-sufficiency as an ideal they rejected almost completely.[56] In an editorial entitled "Progressing Backwards," the editor of the Gracewood, Georgia, *Wool Hat* maintained that while excessive railroad rates might force farmers to diversify their crops, as a rule of thumb such a policy was "a wrong system. ... It will result in a farmer living more at home, that acme of rural independence which the aforesaid asses [the Democratic press] prate so much about, but it will also result in less trade, less transportation, less business and less progress."[57] Two months earlier Marion Butler's paper advised farmers, given hard times, to try to raise more of their own food "not because it is right that they should live this way, but because it is necessary." To accept it as right and proper "requires the farmer to step out of the line of progress, to refuse to avail themselves [sic] of the industrial improvements of the nineteenth century, turn back the wheels of civilization three thousand years, become a hermit and have nothing to do with the outside world." With the proper reforms "the farmers can make that which he [sic] can produce best, turn it into money and buy the products of another man's labor, who can produce another article better than he can."[58] The problem of the farmer, and society, lay not with regional agricultural specialization but with distribution, a social, not a natural problem.

A few blamed the failure of regional specialization on the railroad system. Only government ownership of the railroads could ensure an exchange of goods at cost.[59] More Southern Populists felt that the financial system prevented successful regional specialization. The nineteenth century, contended a North Carolina Populist, was an age of economic development. "True wisdom does not sanction a retrograde movement . . . [to] 'hog and hominy.'" Progress demanded regional specialization, but the existing financial conditions made prices so low that people could not exchange goods. A faulty monetary system brought prices so poor that farmers had to burn corn for fuel while people starved and sell cotton below production cost while people froze.[60]

A system of regional interchange also complemented the Southern Populists' ideas for a simple market society within a cooperative rather than a competitive national social and economic system. When each section, because of transportation at cost, could produce what its soil grew best and exchange it for things other sections could produce more cheaply, posited James Murdock, the whole nation would become "like one vast community making their exchanges to an advantage." No panics could occur and no one suffer biting poverty.[61] With people freezing and starving, a policy of economic self-sufficiency for the farmer made no sense. Besides being against all notions of economic and social progress, a policy of "hog and hominy" also would reduce the quality of life for the farmers and all those whom their products benefited. This perception took into account changes from an earlier society and economy and accepted their significance and value while rejecting the use to which they had so far been put.

The new industrial America also affected the Southern Populists at a deeper level. As the country moved from a primarily agricultural society to an industrial one, the meaning of words common to both often altered significantly. The Southern Populists' use of words like "industry," "manufacturing," and "capital" demonstrated their halfway position between two worlds and illustrated their efforts, conscious and unconscious, to come to terms with a new and strange form of social organization without rejecting the whole of it.

The southern reformers' use of the word "industry" generally reflected an older definition of the word, referring primarily to diligent physical labor which resulted in a tangible product. The editor of the *Progressive Farmer* meant this when in 1895 he urged that every boy and girl be provided with a garden of his or her own in order to "teach them that faithful labor has its reward, and . . . prompt them forever to ways of industry."[62] The word also retained older moral loadings of the virtue of physical labor as opposed to the evils of sloth and laziness. The great evils of existing society, stated a North Carolina Allianceman, all sprang from the privileged aristocracy's ability to live high off the products of the "industrial classes," those people who worked for a living by producing tangible goods.[63]

This particular use of the word also revealed the Southern Populists' peculiar class position, the source of many of the inconsistencies in their approach to industrial America, especially their effort to combine a simple market society for small independent producers with the nationalization of distribution facilities. Being landowners or aspiring landowners and having little experience or knowledge of urban industrial America, the Southern Populists overlooked the growth of huge manufacturing complexes like Standard Oil and Carnegie Steel as well as the new classes created by them. For the reformers the most significant alignments in society did not parallel the division between employer and employee or wage laborer and owner, but ran along lines demarked by the kind of work people did, between those who by their physical effort produced tangible goods and those who did not. That put farmers and laborers together in what the Southern Populists considered the most important "class" in society, the "industrial" class.[64] The Southern Populists intended to reform society in their interest. A Virginia Populist joined a Texan in arguing that "the farmers' interests are identical with the laborer and mechanic," the Texan adding that "any man who attempts to make them believe otherwise is an enemy to justice and right."[65] L. L. Polk described the St. Louis convention of February 1892 as a meeting of all the states, sections, and "all the great industries of the country. . . . They are here from the farm, the factory, the workshop and all the departments of industry throughout this broad land." The efforts of these "wealth producers" made "industrial progress" possible.[66]

Some things, however, suggested the massive changes in American society had begun to affect the Southern Populists. Their use of the word "industry" did not always reflect clearly either the past or the future. It did not when an Alabama editor referred to the last thirty years of

American history as "a period of productive energy and industrial development without a parallel."[67] He could have been speaking as easily of an increase in the ability of the individual producer to create tangible wealth with the aid of new machinery as to the development of industrial capitalism in this country after the Civil War.

Occasionally the Southern Populists even used the word in its more modern sense. A frequent August contributor to the *Wool Hat*, J. L. Cartledge, normally distinguished between the farmers and what he called the "industrial classes," the urban wage earners.[68] References to "manufacturing industries" also signified the switch to a new definition of the word,[69] a use which combined the older way of referring to the organization of production of goods by hand or machine—manufacturing—with a newer term. The actual process of making an article was becoming less important than the organization of the manufacture and sale of that article. The replacement in some Southern Populists' vocabulary of "manufacturer," one who makes, with "industrialist," one who organizes making, reflected that change.[70]

One Georgia Populist in 1893 actually defined the change in the meaning of the term while discussing the "industrial revolution" of the past one hundred years. "From a period of hand looms and home manufactories in the literal meaning of the word," he wrote, "we have passed to that of engines and immense industrial establishments, where loads of workers are assembled in close quarters and under one management."[71] That the changes he described had imparted a new meaning to the word "industry" this Populist realized consciously. But while most of his brethren remained little aware of it, the emerging industrial society to which they also reacted affected their reactions to it. Not all of their tools for dealing with the existing social order did they acquire solely from their past. According to one Alabama editor, the questions worth studying in early 1896 were not the Venezuelan crisis, or the situation in Armenia or Cuba, but "how shall we start new and successful industries which will build up our country and give steady and profitable employment to our wage workers?"[72] Along with the use of the word "industry" which reflected an ideal social order of the past—a personal, rural, producer-oriented society—went a new use of the word which indicated that some of the Southern Populists some of the time tried to take account of a new America, a more recent development, and to fit it into their conception of the proper social order.

The use of the word "capital," and its other forms, "capitalist" and "capitalism," showed the same double meaning that "industry" did. For some of the Southern Populists "capital" and "capitalist" remained synonomous with access to and possession of large amounts of money. Capitalists put their money to use through a financial system which they controlled and which allowed them to rob the producer. By contracting the money supply the capitalists exploited the producer by assuring the dominance of money over humanity.[73]

But however unnecessary capitalists and their immense monetary wealth might be in a simple market society of independent producers, of American industrial society they constituted a very necessary part, and a few Southern Populists realized it. Some argued, for instance, that capital needed labor and labor needed capital. "It is not the object of the People's party," wrote a Georgia Populist, "to array labor against capital, as has been charged, but to secure by legislation such harmony that will do away with that friction."[74] At least part of this idea of interdependence grew from the reformers' greenback inheritance[75]—their desire for a harmonious, cooperative society—and their experience as farmers needing credit. Acceptance of the idea, however, showed other sources, for it often forced the Populists to choose between their contention that "wealth belongs to him who creates it"[76] and their commitment to private property, profit, and the market system. The two might coexist in a simple market society where no market in labor occurred,[77] but in an industrial capitalist America the two were mutually exclusive. If the laborers had a right to all the wealth they created, none would be left over for the investor, the capitalist. Averse to tinkering with what they perceived to be the basic foundations of America's economic system and eager for the benefits the new industrial order promised, the more perceptive Southern Populists sometimes had to acknowledge the importance of capital, and in doing so tended to change their definition of the term.

Out of this concept of interdependence grew a recognition of the importance of capital to economic progress. In a speech given in 1891 Watson denounced only "that capital which is used tyrannically." Without some "surplus" (capital) accumulated beyond labor's consumption of wealth, "there could be no manufactories, no railroads, no steamboats, no foundries, no merchants and no bankers," not to speak of education, science, and the arts. In the "healthy, happy, prosperous community" capitalists and laborers worked together.[78] The Populists may have been exploited farmers, but even the most radical of them still had entrepreneurial ambitions. In the partnership of capital and labor, wrote the editor of the antimonopoly greenback *Southern Mercury*, capital supplied the money, labor the muscle. That being the case, however, "the profits should be equally divided. But they are not so divided, as capital wants to gobble up all the profits. Labor objects to this, and insists on a fair division of the profits of the business."[79] Regarded this way, capital became an important aid to labor in the production of tangible wealth.

The notion that capital equaled money accumulated in the hands of one person, the capitalist as moneylender or usurer, remained strong, but alongside it appeared the more modern notion that expanded production required capital, the concept of capitalist as investor and aid to the producer. In support of capital investment in agriculture a Georgia Populist maintained that it increased production more per dollar invested than capital invested in "manufactories."[80] Others were not so partial to the farmers. A Virginia Populist arguing for an increase in the circulating currency claimed that "it requires capital to develop production and maintain the commerce and industries of a country, as well as for financial purposes."[81] The editor of the *Texas Advance* opposed a suggested tax on the net income of corporations because it "would tend to deter men of moderate means from taking stock, thus hampering every industry requiring a combination of capital, while the millionaires would go free." The tax should fall on the millionaires who produced nothing, built up no industry, provided no one with employment.[82] However accurate his notion of how the millionaires acquired or spent their wealth, this Populist distinguished between invested and idle capital, the former being necessary to economic development. An idea of the importance of investment capital, while not common, appeared often enough among Southern Populists to demonstrate their effort to deal—consciously sometimes, but often unconsciously—with American industrial capitalism in terms of that society's needs and their own aspirations within it.

Perhaps more than anything else, however, the noticeable occurrence of a machine image in their language illustrated the impact of industrial America on the Southern Populists. A North Carolina editor defended the farmers' lack of starched collars with the assertion that despite the fact, the farmers were "the driving wheel of the nation."[83] Other Southern Populists agreed.[84] Some uses of the wheel image apparently came from the Bible. The notion of wheels within wheels may have originated there.[85] On the other hand, frequent references to driving wheels indicated a different source, most likely railroad locomotives. Without power-driven engines, the idea of driving wheels would make little sense.

One of the most startling examples of this image is found in an extremely rare instance of an undeniable advocacy of return to an earlier America. This Populist, discussed earlier in the chapter, finished with a final reference to the farmers as "the foundation and driving wheel of this once grand and prosperous nation."[86] The very world he wanted to escape appeared in his demand for its rejection. By increasing the currency, argued a Texan, the Populists would start up and "grease" the "machinery," returning the social and economic system to proper operation.[87] The great majority of the American people could never enjoy prosperity, insisted the editor of the *Southern Mercury*, without monetary reform. "Our whole financial system is out of gear, and the machine will not run smoothly until it is geared aright, no matter how much oil is poured on it."[88] Both these uses of the metaphor also underlined the Southern Populists' particular class position. The reformers might make basic readjustments in the machine that was American society, but they never considered dismantling it and building anew.

In only one instance did a Southern Populist use the machine image to criticize American industrial capitalism. The editor of the *Southern Mercury* in the fall of 1895 attacked capital's effort "to force labor to be a machine in the business. Labor . . . rebels against being unhumanized, and demands recognition, as muscle and brains, and refuses to be considered as the mere gear to the machinery. Capital then calls on the courts to declare labor in contempt, and if labor does not freely consent to be a machine, capital asks the government to call out the standing army and shoot labor down." Since capital had the government "by the throat," holding over its head the threat of bankrupting the treasury, government obeyed capital. "Then labor wakes up and finds that it is not really flesh and blood, but only a machine owned and run by capital."[89] Only this Populist came so close to understanding some of what an increasing mechanization in an industrial capitalist society might do to its labor force. He alone glimpsed some of the implications lying behind the machine image, implications hostile to the personal, moral, homogeneous, and harmonious America the Southern Populists wanted.

The machine image, and newly defined terms like "capital" and "industry," represented the entering wedge not only of a new understanding of American industrial society, but a new way of thinking. The earliest definition of industry referred to the individual activity necessary to produce some particular and tangible product. Capital as money, associated with those who did no work and lived by preying directly off those who did, the Southern Populists rejected as distinctly amoral. The newer use of the term "industry" no longer referred much to some particularly personal enterprise but to a whole complex of social and economic arrangements which had little immediate reference to any chiefly concrete or discreet human activity. Capital retained its impersonality and intangibility, its essential amorality, and the reformers accepted it as such as an aid to labor in a harmonious society where they could retain the market place along with industrial expansion.

Almost all of the southern reformers had enough experience with industrial society to realize the great potential of machines for improving human life. They turned to machine images and metaphors because those they had inherited—Jeffersonian, producerite, and religious and moral—proved inadequate for describing and interpreting a modern industrial society. They lacked enough experience, however, to realize the implications of what they did. Except for perhaps the editor of the *Southern*

Mercury, they had no idea of how the very impersonality, inhumanity, and amorality of the industrial and financial capitalism at which they aimed their severest criticisms could creep into their thinking anyway, a product of their increased experience with the manifestations of that society and their requirement that its material benefits be retained along with the essentials of the economic system in which it grew. Their class position made it impossible for them to understand that in the very process of accepting, either from ignorance or necessity, some of the adjuncts to industrial development in a market-oriented, private enterprise, capitalist economy, they paved the way for a vitiation of their criticism of that society, a criticism which they based on their personal and moral judgment of the needs of a decent and human America.

Once again, as in the case of how much equality ought to be granted the blacks, as in the case of how far reform of the economic structure of the country should go, as in the case of the degree to which the government should be involved in the social and economic life of the country, as in the case of how rigorously they should define landownership by use, the Southern Populists ran afoul of contradictions within their own beliefs and demands. They wanted black support without relinquishing white dominance. They wanted to prohibit really large-scale landholding and speculation without threatening their position as landlords or potential landlords. They wanted the subtreasury system and government ownership of the railroad, telegraph, and telephone systems while retaining a small economical government. They wanted to eliminate harmful competition and spread the benefits of industrialization more widely, but do it while preserving in the form of a simple market society the very competitive, private ownership, profit-oriented market economy and social order which they criticized for seriously breaking down. They wanted a personal, moral society while retaining the industrial system which bred an America characterized by the very opposite of these qualities. An inadequate understanding of the operation of an industrial capitalist society led to an ineffective effort to reform it.

That is not to say that at least some Southern Populists did not try to resolve a few of these ambiguities. Like most of their brethren, the antimonopoly greenbackers took from their past Locke's labor theory of value, added to it the Jeffersonian commitment to equality and the Jacksonian idea of antimonopoly, and combined these with perceptions from their own experience, reinforced by a long tradition of labor and greenback reform and certain elements in their evangelical Protestant tradition which stressed that all people had the right to a decent life and that human rights took precedence over property rights. As a result of their application of these to a society whose exploitation they understood because they had witnessed and experienced it, the Southern

Conclusion

Populists began to redefine their heritage in new terms applicable to industrial and financial capitalism. This effort led the radicals in particular toward a rudimentary class politics based on a critical questioning of that most basic commitment to a market system and private property and profit, even as it was cast within a simple market society of independent producers.

Nevertheless, among the Southern Populists, including the radical antimonopoly greenbackers, the commitment to private profit and property and some sort of competitive market economy remained quite strong, even in 1896. Their equivocating on the land issue, their ideas about the cooperation of capital and labor for industrial growth, and their advocacy of the simple market society of independent producers all suggested how far even the radical Populists had to go to reach a position from which to build a more viable alternative to American capitalism, one which avoided the problems of trying to alter the very nature of the system while retaining its most basic elements. But their ease with the idea of socialism, their advocacy of the precedence of human rights over those of property, and the *Mercury*'s realization that machinery when owned by a few could be used to exploit workers as well as increase the benefits of industrial society for farmers, indicated that the antimonopoly greenbackers were headed in the right direction.

But the radical Southern Populists did not move far enough fast enough. They had neither sufficient time nor analysis to build by 1896 a viable political movement outside the two major parties. By that year large numbers of Americans had already begun to make other arrangements for their future. The "full dinner pail" promised by William McKinley and his backers in 1896 proved more appealing, and more promising, than the hazy class politics of the radical Populists.

For financial reform Southern Populists the dream did not fail, but their analysis did, and they joined Bryan in what proved to be an empty crusade. But then the radicals could not yet offer a very clear alternative, much less explain it even to a majority of their own Populist brethren. The radicals had traveled only a bit further down the line than many of those Southern Populists who joined Bryan. They did not yet sufficiently comprehend the workings of American industrial and financial capitalism and could not prevent Bryan from speaking for many of those Americans yet unwilling to join their fellows in accepting the corporate state in exchange for the American Way of Life.

Ironically, even indications of a greater understanding of that society suggest that it, too, would not have sufficed. The Southern Populists' movements toward understanding that system well may have been at the expense of the very qualities upon which they based their demands for change. The inability to understand adequately the industrial system they sought to retain contributed considerably to their immediate failure in 1896. The long-range loss, however, may not have been the machine metaphor but older notions of a just and decent America. The Southern Populists lost in 1896 because they retained too much of what the rest of the nation lost in McKinley's victory. For these reasons 1896 marked the demise of the last large-scale threat to the values and ideals of our contemporary capitalist society.

How were we caught?

What, what is it has happened? What is it has been happening that we are living the way we are?

The children are not the way it seemed they might be:

She is no longer beautiful:

He no longer cares for me, he just takes me when he wants me:

There's so much work it seems like you never see the end of it:

I'm so hot when I get through cooking a meal it's more than I can do to sit down to it and eat it:

How was it we were caught?[90]

The Southern Populists did not generally come from nor speak much for the mudsill of their society, the tenant farmers black and white, although they obviously, and with good reason, feared their decline into it.[91] They did number, however, among those who suffered from and helped pay for, economically and socially, the expansion of American industrial capitalism in the thirty-five years following the Civil War. They were only the last in a line of rural movements protesting this situation.

Their ambiguous position in their own community, neither top nor bottom but losing ground rapidly, very probably had a great deal to do with the peculiar duality of much of their response to a new America. Their acceptance and rejection of the new order, their acceptance and rejection of their own experience and past, accounted for much of the complexity of their thought. On balance, however, the ideal social order which the Southern Populists wanted to create, and even more the critique they made of the existing order, came out of their experience living in a personal, intimate, relatively simple, tangible, homogeneous, and moral community. This world was supported and described by their inherited ways of interpreting and understanding the world around them—the producerite, Jeffersonian-Jacksonian, religious and moral metaphors and images. They found themselves in the 1880s and 1890s increasingly threatened by collapse into economic servitude and social dependency while a world of cities, vast industrial developments, a complicated and stratified social organization, a world of impersonality, important intangibles, complexity and distance, and amoral in the traditional, personal sense of morality, destroyed the community and values they knew and understood and in which they believed.

While they learned to understand the intimate connection between the destruction of their personal lives and communities and the growth of that new world, literally every Southern Populist wanted to retain the material benefits of industrial development. They rejected only the social consequences which followed in the wake of America's particular organization of that expansion. The acceptance of the new order involved in deliberately choosing the benefits of American industrial capitalism had begun already before 1896 to change their view of the ideal society in important ways, but not enough. They did not really comprehend the new order. They did not really know how it worked. Their background and experience did not equip them to understand industrial capitalist society and its manifestations—cities, proletariats, factories, concentrated wealth, and capital.

In response to the threat this new social and economic order posed to their personal lives and the community they knew, the Southern Populists set out to create a society which was both relatively homogeneous and simple yet enjoyed the benefits of the new industrial expansion, in which the relations of people to each other remained relatively personal and the laws of personal morality and responsibility guided a society which contained giant railroads and industry. But the Populists failed to convince enough Americans that the reforms they wanted would retain that new society's benefits. They lacked the analytical tools which experience might have given them and which they needed to construct such a program, although they were picking them up. Even if they had succeeded in acquiring this kind of analytical sophistication, however, their class position as landowners, or aspiring landowners, would have betrayed them. Although they questioned such things more thoroughly than most of their contemporaries, almost all the Southern Populists remained ultimately unwilling to surrender the fundamental premises of a capitalist society—the market system, competition, and private property and profit. A more adequate and complete understanding of American industrial and financial capitalism may well have come, as it had already started to do, only at the expense of the powerful and human critique they had forged from the best and most workable elements in their inheritance from Jeffersonian and Jacksonian thought and their experience as rural, evangelical Protestant southern farmers. They did not understand enough.

So the Southern Populist lost in 1896, but so did a whole range of values which produced a distinctive and valid criticism of American industrial and financial capitalism based on that society's inability to serve all the members of the community. For all their provincialism, narrow-mindedness, and confusion, the Southern Populists, at their best and from their own particular standpoint, realized that a social order which set every person against every other, each group or class in society against every other, the Devil taking the hindmost, represented only exploitation to most of its members and would very likely destroy itself eventually. They never denied the benefits of industrial development, but unless these could be attained within the context of a more decent, responsible, and human social order, in which all benefited according to their contribution, this development could not be considered progress, or even very worthwhile by most of the people it affected.

In 1896 Americans lost this critique and the still vital heritage which produced and supported it. Those who won have since governed most of our usable, and used, past. Southern Populism ought to show us that our history holds material that we can use, that we need not always learn our lessons as we are told, and that if we look closely enough at our past we can construct a more humane and decent America.

APPENDIXES

Appendix A: Method

This discussion involves two problems. One is the question of the presentation of the evidence. The other is a question of the validity of my assumption that inherited traditions of thought and belief plus contemporary experience do affect political behavior.

Parts I and II and to a certain extent the Conclusion generally do not involve a temporal sequence of events. The material presented usually relies on evidence selected from Alliance and Populist newspapers and letters written between January 1891 and December 1896. I started in 1891 because, except for Texas, the subtreasury campaign of the National Farmers' Alliance and Industrial Union started in the spring of that year in the southern states. This campaign, as Lawrence Goodwyn has demonstrated in *Democratic Promise* (chaps. 8, 9, especially pp. 248–59), began the splitting of the Alliance from the Democratic party. I concluded in late 1896 because the election of 1896 marked the demise of all hopes of the People's party to the national existence necessary for its reform program. The first two parts consider the underlying ideas and attitudes of Southern Populist thought. Where these ideas and attitudes changed significantly during the period, I began to indicate how. I reserved much of the discussion of change, however, until Part III, so that all the elements of change in Southern Populist thought could be considered in relation to each other.

I deliberately avoided use of the terms "ideology" and "worldview" in the text. Professor Woodward's earliest advice to me proved correct: both terms cover up more than they reveal. Sociologists and political scientists most often treat ideology as a given. Rarely do they examine the historical context from which the ideology emerged, and if they do they usually make their discussion cursory. They consider ideologies fixed, inviolable entities, not flexible, adjustable efforts by people to come to terms with their environment without completely cutting themselves off from their past. For overviews of sociological thinking on ideology, see John Wilson, *Introduction to Social Movements*, Basic Books: New York, 1973, especially chap. 3; and Anthony Oberschall,

Social Conflict and Social Movements, Prentice-Hall: Englewood Cliffs, New Jersey, 1973, particularly pp. 178–203. For one of the original uses of the idea of ideology, see Karl Marx, *The German Ideology* and his *Class Struggles in France: 1848–1850* and *The Eighteenth Brumaire of Louis Bonaparte*. Particularly germane to what I attempted in the text are Peter L. Berger and Thomas Luckmann, *The Social Construction of Reality: A Treatise in the Sociology of Knowledge*, Doubleday and Company: Garden City, New York, 1967; and Benjamin Lee Whorf, *Language, Thought, and Reality*, edited by John B. Carroll, Massachusetts Institute of Technology Press: Cambridge, 1964. Both stress the dialectic between human belief and experience and the shape of the world people perceive.

I do not want to get into the complicated philosophical debate on the relationship of thought and belief to human activity. I start from the assumption that a relation exists. History only makes sense if the past has some connection to the present. If this is the case, then inherited ideas and beliefs will play some role in a person's response to contemporary events. The question is not whether they play a role, but how much and in what manner. Bernard Bailyn's *The Ideological Origins of the American Revolution*, E. P. Thompson's *The Making of the English Working Class*, and Winthrop Jordan's *White Over Black* provide three outstanding examples among many of the historian's necessary assumption that a connection exists between inherited ideas and beliefs, as well as contemporary experience, and human activity.

Appendix B: Populist Newspapers as Source Material

With few exceptions, primarily in North Carolina, manuscript collections contain very little on Southern Populism. Because of this I used Populist newspapers very extensively. They provided coverage for the Populist movement in Texas, Georgia, Alabama, Arkansas, Tennessee, Louisiana, and Virginia, where little or no manuscript material existed. The newspapers served Southern Populism not only as mouthpieces for their editors but also as nerve centers for local, sometimes statewide, Populist party organizations. They contained policy debates, notices and reports of meetings, resolutions, speeches, and letters from the rank and file as well as the leadership. The Populists used them to organize and recruit new members.

While I realize that my heavy concentration on newspapers biases my findings toward the more literate and sophisticated southern reformers, especially editors and local and state leaders, the papers do contain many letters from less prominent Populists. Little else exists, moreover, for examining a wide range of Southern Populist thought and belief. The newspapers, especially the more local ones, allowed me to get as close as still possible to the grass roots of Southern Populism. With few exceptions I have distinguished in the text between citations from editors and those from other Populists, assuming that this might make a difference. The extensive material from reformers who did not edit newspapers should indicate the wide number, if not variety, of Southern Populists I drew on. Because of the haphazard layout of many of the papers, I often found distinguishing between letters and articles difficult, so I did not normally try. If no one signed the letter or article, I assumed the editor wrote it and credited him. I used very little plate material, distributed usually by the Reform Press Association, because frequently it came from journals and newspapers written and published outside the South. While I commented on occasion about the plate material's content, I did not use it as evidence of how Southern Populists thought because of its origin. Only when the material clearly came from a Southern source did I make an exception.

Most of the Populist papers in the South were small, both in size and circulation. They were almost exclusively weeklies, although I found a copy of one daily, the Birmingham, Alabama, *People's Daily Tribune*, and evidence for at least two other attempts, one by Watson in Atlanta and one in Dallas, Texas. Most of the Populist papers seem to have had circulations under 1000, contained largely within one or two counties. Most had four pages, although a few ran to eight, with five to seven columns per page. Except in cases where Alliance papers became Populist, the editors generally came very new to their trade, having purchased their plant from a local paper which had folded or having assumed charge of a paper purchased by a local Alliance. Publishing a local county paper in the South, Democratic or Populist, seems to have been a business with a great deal of turnover in the 1890s. For fascinating advice from an expert, W. S. Morgan of Arkansas, on how to start and run a Populist newspaper, including how much to charge for subscriptions and advertising, how much to plan on for operating expenses, and how much to spend for equipment, see Hardy (Ark.) *National Reformer*, Mar. 1895.

Appendix C: Alabama Black Belt Vote[1]

Alabama had 66 counties in 1890. In 20 (30.3%) the blacks made up 50.0% or more of the population. Of these black belt counties, 6 (30.0%) voted for the reform ticket in at least one of the following elections.

1. Population figures from the United States Bureau of the Census, *Negro Population in the United States, 1790–1915*, p. 776. Election results for the 1892 presidential campaign

	Governor 1892	Governor 1894	Governor 1896	President 1892
Autauga				x
Chambers	x	x		
Choctaw	x	x	x	x
Lee	x	x		
Macon	x			x
Pickens	x			

Appendix D: Georgia Black Belt Vote[2]

Georgia had 137 counties in 1890. In 60 (43.8%) blacks made up 50.0% or more of the population. Of these black belt counties, 17 (28.3%) voted for the Populist ticket in at least one of the following elections. (Counties marked with an "a" were in Watson's tenth congressional district.)

	Governor 1892	Governor 1894	Governor 1896	President 1892
Baldwin		x	x	
Chattahoochee		x		
Columbia[a]	x	x	x	x
Greene		x	x	
Harris		x		
Jefferson[a]		x	x	x
Liberty		x	x	
Lincoln[a]	x	x	x	x
Macon		x	x	
Meriwether		x		
Oconee	x	x		x
Pike		x		
Quitman			x	
Screven		x	x	x
Taliaferro[a]	x	x	x	x
Warren[a]	x	x	x	x
Washington[a]	x	x		x

from W. Dean Burnham, *Presidential Ballots, 1836–1892*, pp. 260–74. Election results for the gubernatorial campaigns in 1892, 1894, and 1896 from *The Tribune Almanac and Political Register*, 1893 p. 260, 1896 p. 227, and 1897 p. 228.

2. Population figures from the United States Bureau of the Census, *Negro Population*, pp. 778–80. Election results for the 1892 presidential campaign from Burnham, *Presidential Ballots*, pp. 332–62. Election results for the gubernatorial campaigns in 1892,

Appendix E: Mississippi Black Belt Vote[3]

Mississippi had 76 counties in 1890. In 37 (48.7%) blacks made up 50.0% or more of the population. Of these black belt counties, 2 (5.4%) voted Populist in at least one of the following elections.

	Congress 1892	Congress 1894	Congress 1896	President 1892
Amite		x		x
Chickasaw	x	x		x

Appendix F: North Carolina Black Belt Vote[4]

North Carolina had 96 counties in 1890. In 15 (15.6%) blacks made up 50.0% or more of the population. Of these black belt counties, 14 (93.3%) voted for the reform ticket at least once in the following elections. (Counties marked with an "a" voted the reform ticket *only* in the 1894 Republican-Populist fusion election.)

	Governor 1892	State Treasurer 1894	Governor 1896	President 1892
Caswell[a]		x		
Chowan[a]		x		
Craven[a]		x		
Edgecombe[a]		x		
Granville[a]		x		
Hertford[a]		x		
New Hanover[a]		x		
Northampton[a]		x		
Pasquotank[a]		x		
Pender[a]		x		
Richmond[a]		x		
Vance[a]		x		
Warren[a]		x		
Washington[a]		x		

1894, and 1896 from *Tribune Almanac*, 1893 pp. 268–69, 1895 pp. 281–82, and 1897 pp. 233–34.

3. Population figures from the United States Bureau of the Census, *Negro Population*, pp. 783–84. Election results for the 1892 presidential campaign from Burnham, *Presidential Ballots*, pp. 551–70. Election results for the congressional races in 1892, 1894, and 1896 from the Office of the Secretary of State for Mississippi, *Election Returns for the State of Mississippi*, Jackson, Mississippi.

4. Population figures from the United States Bureau of the Census, *Negro Population*,

Appendixes

Appendix G: Texas Black Belt Vote[5]

Texas had 196 counties in 1890. In 12 (6.1%) blacks made up 50.0% or more of the population. Of these black belt counties, 7 (58.3%) voted Populist at least once in the following elections. (Counties marked with an "a" voted Greenback at least once in the state gubernatorial elections of 1878 and 1880, or Independent in the election of 1882.)

	Governor 1892	Governor 1894	Governor 1896	President 1892
Brazoria[a]			x	
Gregg		x		
Grimes[a]			x	
Matagorda			x	
San Jacinto[a]		x	x	
Walker[a]	x	x	x	x
Washington[a]			x	

Appendix H: Virginia Black Belt Vote[6]

Virginia had 101 counties and cities in 1890. In 35 counties and 1 city (35.6%) blacks made up 50.0% or more of the population. Of these black belt counties and cities, none voted Populist in 1892 and 14 (38.9%) voted for the Republican-Populist fusion candidate for governor in 1893.

---

pp. 784–85. Election results for the 1892 presidential campaign from Burnham, *Presidential Ballots*, pp. 646–68. Election results for the gubernatorial campaigns of 1892 and 1896 from Helen Edmonds, *The Negro and Fusion Politics in North Carolina, 1894–1901*, pp. 230–32. Election results for the state treasurer's campaign in 1894 from *Tribune Almanac*, 1895 p. 304.

5. Population figures from the United States Bureau of the Census, *Negro Population*, pp. 789–92. Election results for the 1892 presidential campaign from Burnham, *Presidential Ballots*, pp. 764–812. Election results for the gubernatorial campaigns of 1892, 1894, and 1896 from *Tribune Almanac*, 1894 pp. 348–50, 1896 pp. 259–60, and 1898 pp. 261–62.

6. Population figures from the United States Bureau of the Census, *Negro Population*, pp. 792–93. Election results for the 1892 presidential campaign from Burnham, *Presidential Ballots*, pp. 816–42. Election results for the gubernatorial campaign of 1893 from *Tribune Almanac*, 1894 pp. 351–52.

NOTES

Introduction to Part One

1. On the difficulties with urban labor, see Chester McArthur Destler, *American Radicalism, 1865–1901*, pp. 28–30, chaps. 9, 11; Gerald N. Grob, *Workers and Utopia*, pp. 90–98, 167–71; Lawrence Goodwyn, *Democratic Promise*, pp. 307–11; Norman Pollack, *The Populist Response to Industrial America*, chap. 3.

2. Don F. Hadwiger has argued that this peripheral position is a critical factor in explaining why farmers, despite their majority position in nineteenth-century America, so often turned to third party politics. "Farmers in Politics," pp. 156–70.

3. Hunter Dickinson Farish, *The Circuit Rider Dismounts*, pp. 75–76; C. Vann Woodward, *Origins of the New South, 1877–1913*, p. 170.

4. Most furnishing merchants were evidently not all that wealthy, although their opportunities were great. When they did succeed, they left for town and other investments. For the best recent examinations of the furnishing merchant, see Roger L. Ransom and Richard Sutch, *One Kind of Freedom*, pp. 122, 137–40; Harold D. Woodman, *King Cotton and His Retainers*, chap. 24.

5. For an interesting example, see Theodore Rosengarten, ed., *All God's Dangers*. Nate Shaw's world changed little in essence despite his automobiles and improved farm equipment. He and the rest of his rural community, black and white, changed little between the 1890s and the 1930s.

6. For examples of a positive response to the "New South" and general economic growth, see Atlanta *People's Party Paper*, 17 Mar. 1892; Raleigh *Progressive Farmer*, 29 Sept. 1891 and 22 Sept. 1896; Ozark (Ala.) *Banner*, 2 and 9 June 1892; C. Vann Woodward, *Tom Watson, Agrarian Rebel*, pp. 118–19.

7. Goodwyn, *Democratic Promise*, p. 169; Robert C. McMath, Jr., *Populist Vanguard*, p. 91. Michael Schwartz, in *Radical Protest and Social Structure*, completely misses the importance of the subtreasury plan.

8. Among others, Leo Marx, *The Machine in the Garden*, pp. 122–31.

9. Irwin Unger, *The Greenback Era*, p. 30.

Chapter 1

1. Raleigh *Progressive Farmer*, 21 Apr. 1891; also Nashville *Weekly Toiler*, 3 June 1891.

2. See John Locke, *Two Treatises of Government*, "Second Treatise," §§26–29; C. B. MacPherson, *The Political Theory of Possessive Individualism*, pp. 232–36.

3. Tarboro (N.C.) *Farmers' Advocate*, 3 June 1891; also Dallas (Ga.) *Herald*, 19 Oct. 1893; Hardy (Ark.) *Morgan's Buzz Saw*, June 1896; Dallas (Tex.) *Southern Mercury*, 7 Nov. 1895; Atlanta *People's Party Paper*, 16 Dec. 1892; James H. Davis, *A Political Revelation*, p. 242; M. W. Howard, *The American Plutocracy*, chaps. 1, 4.

4. This argument may appear to give too much credit to Southern Populist reasoning. I

do not think so, for two reasons. First, as we will see later in chap. 3, the Southern Populists understood the connection between material incentives and a market society. Secondly, a person does not have to reason out all responses step-by-step to make them rational and consistent in a given social environment. Some social premises are so basic that this need not be done, unless one is challenging those premises. Certainly, most people today who believe in a "free enterprise" system would understand that it is necessary for them to oppose eliminating private ownership, although for any number of reasons, including the vagueness of the terms themselves, the same people might find the logical relationship between the two somewhat difficult to articulate.

5. Stephenville (Tex.) *Empire*, 28 May 1892; also Harry Tracy, Appendix, in Davis, *A Political Revelation*, p. i; Raleigh *Progressive Farmer*, 10 Oct. 1893; Austin (Tex.) *Argus*, 31 July 1894; Atlanta *Sunny South* in Atlanta *People's Party Paper*, 19 July 1895. An additional problem was that some people did not even perceive their own self-interest correctly. See Goldsboro (N.C.) *Caucasian*, 8 June 1893; Hickory (N.C.) *Mercury* in Raleigh *Progressive Farmer*, 14 Nov. 1893.

6. Austin (Tex.) *Statesman* in Beaver Dam (N.C.) *Our Home*, 26 May 1893; also Goldsboro (N.C.) *Caucasian*, 13 Sept. 1894; Dallas (Ga.) *Herald*, 30 May 1895. In the Atlanta *People's Party Paper*, 6 Mar. 1896, Tom Watson enumerated almost all of the particulars of this decent living. The speech had been given in mid-1891. Watson held that labor was entitled to: "A sufficiency of food, clothing and lodging for the needs of to-day; a sufficiency of leisure from daily toil to preserve the strength of body and to cultivate the capacity of the mind; the shortening of the hours of labor so that a citizen, who, like other citizens, has a portion of the day for recreation, for social intercourse and for self-improvement. But further still, I believe that he should have his fair proportion of the profits made by his labor to constitute a surplus for his time of sickness or old age and to transmit to his children, so that the condition of the producer may prosper in just proportion to the amount of his production."

7. Salisbury (N.C.) *Carolina Watchman*, 17 Nov. 1892; also Atlanta *People's Party Paper*, 14 Apr. 1893.

8. Dahlonega (Ga.) *Signal*, 13 May 1892; also Atlanta *People's Party Paper*, 14 Dec. 1894; Salisbury (N.C.) *Carolina Watchman*, 12 May 1892; Ozark (Ala.) *Banner*, 12 Oct. 1893; Anniston *Alabama Leader*, 10 Oct. 1895; W. Scott Morgan, *History of the Wheel and Alliance, and the Impending Revolution*, p. 397; Davis, *A Political Revelation*, p. 5.

9. Austin (Tex.) *Argus*, 2 Oct. 1894.

10. Morgan, *History of the Wheel and Alliance*, p. 677; also pp. 20–21; Atlanta *People's Party Paper*, 14 Apr. 1892; Stephenville (Tex.) *Empire*, 28 Oct. 1892; Raleigh *Progressive Farmer*, 13 Oct. 1891.

11. Atlanta *People's Party Paper*, 6 Mar. 1896; Raleigh *Progressive Farmer*, 13 Oct. 1891; Dallas (Ga.) *Herald*, 6 July 1893.

12. Raleigh *Progressive Farmer*, 13 Oct. 1891; also Atlanta *People's Party Paper*, 31 Mar. 1893; Tarboro (N.C.) *Farmers' Advocate*, 14 Sept. 1892; Beaver Dam (N.C.) *Our Home*, 21 June 1893; Dallas (Tex.) *Southern Mercury*, 8 Jan. 1891; Dallas *Texas Advance*, 28 Apr. and 2 June 1894; Hardy (Ark.) *Morgan's Buzz Saw*, Oct. 1894; Richmond *Virginia Sun*, 27 Apr. 1892; Thomas E. Watson, *People's Party Campaign Handbook, 1892*, p. 222.

13. Raleigh *Progressive Farmer*, 13 Oct. 1891 and 6 Feb. 1894; Oxford (Ala.) *Voice*, 18 July 1891; Gracewood (Ga.) *Wool Hat*, 1 July 1893; Atlanta *People's Party Paper*, 17 Mar. 1892; Dallas (Ga.) *Herald*, 6 July and 28 Sept. 1893; Dallas *Texas Advance*, 25 Aug. 1894; Dallas (Tex.) *Southern Mercury*, 3 Nov. 1892 and 21 May 1896; Richmond *Virginia Sun*, 18 May 1892; Hardy (Ark.) *National Reformer*, Oct. 1894 and Mar. 1895; Warren Plains (N.C.) *People's Paper*, 20 Dec. 1895.

14. See Atlanta *People's Party Paper*, 18 May 1894; Goldsboro (N.C.) *Caucasian*, 13

Sept. 1894; Dallas (Ga.) *Herald*, 6 July 1893; Gracewood (Ga.) *Wool Hat*, 1 Apr. and 15 July 1893; Morgan, *History of the Wheel and Alliance*, p. 22.

15. Gracewood (Ga.) *Wool Hat*, 20 May 1893; also 29 Apr. 1893.

16. Dallas (Tex.) *Southern Mercury*, 2 Apr. 1896.

17. Atlanta *People's Party Paper*, 6 Mar. 1896; also Dallas (Tex.) *Southern Mercury*, 19 Sept. 1895; Austin (Tex.) *Argus*, 31 July and 4 Sept. 1894. There should be no clash between "labor" and "capital," wrote the editor of the Tarboro (N.C.) *Farmers' Advocate*. "They are both interdependent" (20 July 1892).

18. Raleigh *Progressive Farmer*, 10 Nov. 1891; Austin (Tex.) *Argus*, 10 July 1894; Atlanta *Living Issues* in Gracewood (Ga.) *Wool Hat*, 4 Feb. 1893; Morgan, *History of the Wheel and Alliance*, pp. 21–22.

19. Locke, *Two Treatises*, "Second Treatise," §§39–40.

20. Richmond *Virginia Sun*, 1 Feb. 1893. Kellogg's influence also appeared at times in the idea that the proper rate of interest should not exceed the annual increase in the nation's produced wealth, or about 3 percent. See Richmond *Virginia Sun*, 27 Apr. 1892; Little Rock (Ark.) *Dollar*, 13 Dec. 1895.

21. For how this worked, see chap. 8, below, on the subtreasury plan. For Kellogg, see Chester McArthur Destler, *American Radicalism, 1865–1901*, pp. 50–55; Robert P. Sharkey, *Money, Class, and Party*, pp. 187–91; Irwin Unger, *The Greenback Era*, pp. 94–100. For Campbell, see David Montgomery, *Beyond Equality*, pp. 426–33; Sharkey, *Money, Class, and Party*, pp. 191–92; Unger, *The Greenback Era*, pp. 97–100.

22. Tarboro (N.C.) *Farmers' Advocate*, 24 Aug. 1892.

23. Gracewood (Ga.) *Wool Hat*, 22 July 1893; also 27 July 1892. The editor also added "artisans" and "wage-workers," "men who own homes."

24. MacPherson, *Possessive Individualism*, pp. 51–53.

25. See Edward Pessen, *Most Uncommon Jacksonians*, chaps. 7, 11; Eric Foner, *Free Soil, Free Labor, Free Men*, chap. 1; and Montgomery, *Beyond Equality*, chaps. 10, 11.

26. See chap. 6, Land and Transportation.

27. I do not mean to suggest that this same moral rhetoric did not appear everywhere in American political life and thought. It did, and in some cases it dominated thinking quite a bit more than it did with the Southern Populists. Nor do I wish to suggest that the moral outrage expressed in many of the statements of the southern reformers was *mere* rhetoric. It was not. Neither of these qualifications, however, means that the moral element in Southern Populist thought did not affect their ideas and analysis and should not be considered. These qualifications merely underscore the need for care in such an examination.

28. Norman Pollack, ed., *The Populist Mind*, p. 60; also Salisbury (N.C.) *Carolina Watchman*, 19 May 1892; Austin (Tex.) *People's Advocate*, 30 Aug. 1894; Dallas (Ga.) *Herald*, 27 June 1895.

29. Atlanta *People's Party Paper*, 20 Nov. 1896.

30. Dallas *Texas Advance* in Anniston *Alabama Leader*, 27 June 1895.

31. Raleigh *Caucasian*, 7 Nov. 1895.

32. Ibid., 6 June 1895; also Dallas (Tex.) *Southern Mercury*, 27 Aug. 1891 and 7 Nov. 1895; Washington, D.C., *National Economist* in Dahlonega (Ga.) *Signal*, 17 Apr. 1891.

33. The 1880s and the 1890s in the South were years of fervent religious concern. The period witnessed a great increase in intense religious revivals. (See C. Vann Woodward, *Origins of the New South, 1877–1913*, pp. 169–70.) At the same time a crisis swept through the Methodist church in the South, focusing on what religious Southerners felt to be the increasing moral decay of society. Some of them found the solution to this problem in the doctrine of "entire sanctification," which enabled the believer to enter a state of Christian perfection on this earth. Hunter Dickinson Farish, an historian of the post-Civil War Southern Methodist church, considered the "holiness" movement the "natural recoil of

the religious mind from the rampant worldliness of the time." (*The Circuit Rider Dismounts*, pp. 71–75.) This religious radicalism might have had its counterpart in the 1880s and 1890s in the Southern Farmers' Alliance and the Southern Populist party. That there should be some interchange of fervency would be quite understandable. At the least, this religious ferment might well have given further impetus to many Southern Populists to explain and justify their ideas in a moral or religious framework.

34. Leo Marx, *The Machine in the Garden*, pp. 126–27; also W. R. Brock, *The Character of American History*, p. 20.

35. Unger, *The Greenback Era*, p. 30.

36. Ozark (Ala.) *Banner*, 19 July 1894.

37. Stephenville (Tex.) *Empire*, 28 Oct. 1892; also Atlanta *Freedom* in Dallas (Ga.) *Herald*, 31 Aug. 1893; Dallas (Tex.) *Southern Mercury* in Wedowee (Ala.) *Randolph Toiler*, 19 June 1896.

38. This view of the importance of the farmers could and probably did spring more from the Southern Populists' background than from the logic of the producer idea, but the end result was the same—the Southern Populists felt that the farmers were the most important group in society because they were the basic producers.

39. Tarboro (N.C.) *Farmers' Advocate*, 15 Apr. 1891; also 2 Sept. 1891.

40. See Richmond *Virginia Sun*, 6 July 1892; Raleigh *Progressive Farmer*, 3 Jan. 1893 and 17 July 1894; Gadsden (Ala.) *Alliance Advocate*, 17 Nov. 1892; L. L. Polk's Ocala speech, Dec. 1890, box 12, vol. 64, L. L. Polk Papers; Tracy, Appendix, in Davis, *A Political Revelation*, pp. 381, 395–96.

41. Troy (Ala.) *Jeffersonian*, 4 May 1894; also L. L. Polk's Ocala speech, Dec. 1890, box 12, vol. 64, L. L. Polk Papers.

42. See Atlanta *People's Party Paper*, 21 Jan. 1892 and 5 Oct. 1894; Hardy (Ark.) *National Reformer*, Apr. 1895.

43. Richmond *Virginia Sun*, 6 July 1892.

44. I found only two examples of a classification of merchants as "laboring people" (Tarboro, N.C., *Farmer's Advocate*, 13 July 1892) or as "producers" (Raleigh *Progressive Farmer*, 10 Nov. 1891), and in neither case did the author explain the reference. Southern Populists, so far as I can tell, never classified merchants as producers, and only once did I find them classified as laboring people. A conservative North Carolina Populist did accord them a role as "relative wealth producers," along with lawyers, doctors, and manufacturers. But this distinction was not as important as it seems, for the speaker took pains to point out that easily the most important class in society was the "absolute wealth producers," the farmers (Raleigh *Progressive Farmer*, 5 Apr. 1892).

45. See Atlanta *People's Party Paper*, 12 Aug. 1892; Troy (Ala.) *Jeffersonian*, 6 July 1894.

46. See Atlanta *People's Party Paper*, 23 Dec. 1892 and 25 Aug. 1893; *Tennessee Currant* in Raleigh *Progressive Farmer*, 12 June 1894; Wadesboro (N.C.) *Plow Boy*, 16 Oct. 1895; Natchitoches *Louisiana Populist*, 12 Oct. 1894.

47. See Lawrence Goodwyn, *Democratic Promise*, pp. 26–31; Fred A. Shannon, *The Farmer's Last Frontier*, chap. 4, especially pp. 89–95; Harold D. Woodman, *King Cotton and His Retainers*, chap. 24; Woodward, *Origins*, pp. 180–85. The most thorough recent examination of the post-Civil War southern economy, Roger L. Ransom and Richard Sutch's *One Kind of Freedom*, has an extensive analysis of the exploitative role of the furnishing merchant on pp. 117–40, 146–48, 159–64, 168–70, 186–87. On the growth and dynamics of the tenancy system, see chaps. 4–9. For some questioning of the view that the merchants exploited the farmers, see William Brown and Morgan Reynolds, "Debt Peonage Re-examined," pp. 865–67; Joseph D. Reid, "Sharecropping as an Understand-

able Market Response—the Post-Bellum South," p. 107; Robert Higgs, *Competition and Coercion*, pp. 56–57, 71–75.

48. Dallas (Ga.) *Herald*, 20 Sept. 1894; Atlanta *People's Party Paper*, 28 Apr. and 12 Aug. 1892; *Faulkner County Wheel* (Ark.), 1 July 1891; Gracewood (Ga.) *Wool Hat*, 22 Apr. 1893.

49. For exceptions, see Raleigh *Progressive Farmer*, 11 Aug. and 27 Oct. 1891, 23 May and 24 Oct. 1893, and 12 Mar. 1895.

50. Goldsboro (N.C.) *Caucasian*, 16 Nov. 1893.

51. Goodwyn, *Democratic Promise*, pp. 117–31; Michael Schwartz, *Radical Protest and Social Structure*, chap. 14.

52. Although a much more complicated problem than this, there obviously was truth in what the Southern Populists felt. Bankers did control the flow of credit to the credit-starved South, and they doled it out sparingly, to say the least. The banking community also had, since the depression of 1873 particularly, solidly supported gold monometallism and currency deflation, and had on this issue enjoyed the support of increasingly influential elements within both major parties. Lastly, the currency imbalance between the Northeast and the West and the South grew greater and greater in the 1880s and 1890s, and the plethora of currency-issuing national banks in the Northeast did nothing to rectify this problem, since they often stopped using the privilege. See John D. Hicks, *The Populist Revolt*, pp. 39–40; Theodore Saloutos, *Farmer Movements in the South, 1865–1933*, p. 13; Woodman, *King Cotton*, pp. 346–57; Woodward, *Origins*, p. 183.

53. Dallas (Tex.) *Southern Mercury*, 28 Nov. 1895; also 11 July 1895 and 23 Apr. 1896; Dallas (Ga.) *Herald*, 30 May 1895; Anniston *Alabama Leader*, 8 Aug. 1895; Hickory (N.C.) *Mercury*, 29 June 1892; Atlanta *People's Party Paper*, 20 Jan. 1893; Austin (Tex.) *Argus*, 7 Aug. 1894.

54. Exceptions were the Atlanta *People's Party Paper*, some of the Texas papers at times, the Ozark (Ala.) *Banner* during 1894, and the New Orleans *Issue*.

55. Raleigh *Progressive Farmer*, 1 Dec. 1896. For the importance of the working people, see Raleigh *Progressive Farmer*, 1 Sept. 1896; Atlanta *People's Party Paper*, 6 Mar. 1896; Dallas *Texas Advance*, 14 July 1894; Hardy (Ark.) *Morgan's Buzz Saw*, Oct. 1894.

56. For exceptions, see Dallas *Texas Advance*, 10 Mar. 1894; Gracewood (Ga.) *Wool Hat*, 15 July 1893; Atlanta *People's Party Paper*, 10 May 1895; Ozark (Ala.) *Banner*, 18 Jan. 1894; Dallas (Tex.) *Southern Mercury* in Tarboro (N.C.) *Farmers' Advocate*, 18 Nov. 1891; Tracy, Appendix, in Davis, *A Political Revelation*, p. 357.

57. Dallas (Tex.) *Southern Mercury* in Tarboro (N.C.) *Farmers' Advocate*, 18 Nov. 1891; Goldsboro (N.C.) *Caucasian*, 25 Aug. 1892; Atlanta *People's Party Paper*, 21 Jan. 1892 and 22 Mar. 1895; Raleigh *Progressive Farmer*, 29 Mar. 1892 and 23 May 1893; Ozark (Ala.) *Banner*, 14 June 1894; Dallas *Texas Advance*, 10 and 17 Mar. 1894; Dallas (Tex.) *Southern Mercury*, 11 July 1895; Tracy, Appendix, in Davis, *A Political Revelation*, p. 398.

58. Austin (Tex.) *Argus*, 4 Sept. 1894; Lampasas (Tex.) *People's Journal*, 9 Dec. 1892; Dallas (Tex.) *Southern Mercury*, 11 July 1895; Atlanta *People's Party Paper*, 10 May 1895; Tracy, Appendix, in Davis, *A Political Revelation*, pp. 357, 393.

59. Goodwyn, *Democratic Promise*, pp. 51–65; Sheldon Hackney, *Populism to Progressivism in Alabama*, pp. 60–62.

60. Ozark (Ala.) *Banner*, 12 July 1894.

61. The Gracewood, Ga., *Wool Hat*, located in the same county as Augusta, provided an interesting exception to this. The *Wool Hat*, especially in 1892 and 1893, showed considerable sympathy for working people. (See 13 July, 20 Aug., and 1 Oct. 1892; 11 Feb., 1 Apr., and 12 Aug. 1893; and 24 Feb. and 10 Mar. 1894.) Two frequent corrrespondents of the *Wool Hat*, "Diogenes" and J. L. Cartledge, often treated working people's issues with

a sympathy and insight unusual in Southern Populist papers. (For Cartledge, see 3 June 1893 and 10 and 24 Mar. 1894. For "Diogenes," see 4 and 18 Aug. 1894.) The *Wool Hat* took the workers' side completely in the Homestead strike (see 13 July 1892 and 22 July 1893), and despite considerable advice about striking at the ballot box instead, favored the workers' side in the Pullman strike (see 14 and 21 July 1894). The editor of and the letter writers to the *Wool Hat* also shared a great deal more sophistication about who the working people were than any of the smaller Southern Populist papers (and all of the major ones except for the *Texas Advance*, the *Southern Mercury*, the *People's Advocate*, and perhaps the *People's Party Paper*). Although they often used "artisan," "mechanic," and "laboringman," sometimes they used the term "operatives," reflecting contact with the mill workers, who were known by that term, as opposed to the laborers, hourly unskilled workers outside the mills, and mechanics, skilled workers, or craftsmen. (For "operatives," see 11 Aug. 1894. For the distinctions among "operative," "mechanic," and "laborer," see 15 July 1893.) "Wage worker" was another name used which rarely appeared elsewhere in Southern Populist papers. (See 13 Aug. and 17 Sept. 1892 and 22 July 1893.) For the use of "operative" elsewhere among Southern Populists, see Atlanta *People's Party Paper*, 8 Mar. 1895. For "wage earner" or "wage worker," see Raleigh *Caucasian*, 7 Nov. 1895; Dallas (Ga.) *Herald*, 21 Dec. 1893; Austin (Tex.) *People's Advocate*, 23 Aug. 1894; Dallas *Texas Advance*, 6 Jan., 14 and 21 July, and 4 Aug. 1894.

62. For an exception, see Ozark (Ala.) *Banner*, 5 Oct. 1893.

63. See Atlanta *People's Party Paper*, 21 Jan. 1892 and 4 Oct. 1895; *Faulkner County Wheel* (Ark.), 1 July 1891; Nashville *Weekly Toiler*, 21 Oct. 1891.

64. Atlanta *People's Party Paper*, 6 Mar. 1896.

65. See Raleigh *Progressive Farmer*, 10 Nov. 1891; Richmond *Virginia Sun*, 1 Feb. 1893.

66. See Dallas *Texas Advance*, 14 Apr. and 7 July 1894; Austin (Tex.) *Argus*, 31 Aug. 1894.

67. Salisbury (N.C.) *Carolina Watchman*, 13 Aug. 1891; also Raleigh *Progressive Farmer* in Atlanta *People's Party Paper*, 14 Dec. 1894. Davis, in *A Political Revelation*, showed a similar confusion. What he described as the proper Populist society on pp. 14–15, 100, and 130–31, was one in which, because of the elimination of monopoly in land, transportation, and finance, "each industrious individual would have the privilege of a home where he could produce and enjoy the comforts of life" (p. 14)—a simple market society. Yet elsewhere he recognized the existence of "factories," "furnaces and mills" (p. 183), and of "operatives" (p. 127) and "factory hands" (p. 246).

68. Tarboro (N.C.) *Farmers' Advocate*, 8 Apr. 1891; also Raleigh *Progressive Farmer*, 5 Mar. 1895; Clinton (N.C.) *Caucasian*, 31 Dec. 1891.

Chapter 2

1. Tarboro (N.C.) *Farmers' Advocate*, 1 July 1891; also Dallas *Texas Advance*, 2 Dec. 1893; Austin (Tex.) *Argus*, 4 Sept. 1894; Atlanta *People's Party Paper*, 12 Apr. 1895 and 6 Mar. 1896. For some earlier uses of this idea, see Walter T. K. Nugent, *Money and American Society*, pp. 25–26.

2. Lampasas (Tex.) *People's Journal*, 9 Dec. 1892 and Raleigh *Progressive Farmer*, 5 Apr. 1892.

3. L. L. Polk's Ocala speech, Dec. 1890, box 12, vol. 64, L. L. Polk Papers; also Raleigh *Progressive Farmer*, 6 Sept. 1892; Troy (Ala.) *Jeffersonian*, 4 May 1894.

4. Atlanta *People's Party Paper*, 31 Mar. 1892; also Clinton (N.C.) *Caucasian*, 14 Jan. 1892.

5. Atlanta *People's Party Paper*, 28 Oct. 1892; also 13 July 1894; Gracewood (Ga.) *Wool*

Hat, 29 Apr. 1893 and 24 Mar. 1894; Austin (Tex.) *People's Advocate*, 30 Aug. 1894. The idea of the "middle class" here is not that used by Robert Wiebe in *The Search for Order, 1877–1920*, chap. 5, or by contemporary sociologists. It is the Populists' definition, drawn from a considerable intellectual heritage, and referring to those producing people whose social position lay between the rich and the poor, who won a solid competency from their labor. For some of the history of the idea, usually associated with the producer ideology, see Edward Pessen, *Most Uncommon Jacksonians*, pp. 174–75, 182–83; Marvin Meyers, *The Jacksonian Persuasian*, chap. 2, especially pp. 12–17; Eric Foner, *Free Soil, Free Labor, Free Men*, chap. 1, especially pp. 15–18.

6. Gracewood (Ga.) *Wool Hat*, 10 Feb. 1894 and Atlanta *People's Party Paper*, 26 Apr. 1895.

7. Gracewood (Ga.) *Wool Hat*, 22 July 1893.

8. Atlanta *People's Party Paper*, 13 Jan. 1893; also Tarboro (N.C.) *Farmers' Advocate*, 19 Aug. 1891; Watson speech, 10 Sept. 1889, box 1, folder 1, Thomas E. Watson Papers.

9. Dallas *Texas Advance*, 4 Aug. 1894; also Atlanta *People's Party Paper*, 14 Jan. 1892; Butler (Ala.) *Choctaw Alliance*, 2 Nov. 1892; Richmond *Virginia Sun*, 25 May 1892; Gracewood (Ga.) *Wool Hat*, 27 July 1892.

10. Tarboro (N.C.) *Southerner* in Tarboro (N.C.) *Farmers' Advocate*, 26 Oct. 1892; also *Nebraska Independent* in Atlanta *People's Party Paper*, 9 Oct. 1896.

11. Dallas (Ga.) *Herald*, 4 May 1893; also Hardy (Ark.) *National Reformer*, Oct. 1894; Nashville *Weekly Toiler*, 21 Oct. 1891; Goldsboro (N.C.) *Caucasian*, 2 June 1892; Austin (Tex.) *Argus*, 4 Sept. 1894; Dallas (Tex.) *Southern Mercury*, 2 Apr. 1896; Dallas *Texas Advance* 28 Apr. 1894; Richmond *Exchange Reporter*, 18 Aug. 1891; N. A. Dunning, ed., *The Farmers' Alliance History and Agricultural Digest*, p. 185.

12. Hardy (Ark.) *National Reformer*, Oct. 1894; also Ozark (Ala.) *Banner*, 22 June 1893; Raleigh *Progressive Farmer*, 29 Oct. 1895; Hardy (Ark.) *Morgan's Buzz Saw*, Feb. 1896; Raleigh *Caucasian*, 23 May 1895.

13. Gonzales (Tex.) *Signal* in Lampasas (Tex.) *People's Journal*, 19 Aug. 1892; also Hardy (Ark.) *Morgan's Buzz Saw*, July 1896.

14. Atlanta *People's Party Paper*, 14 Jan. 1892; also 19 and 26 Jan. 1894; Ozark (Ala.) *Banner-Advertiser*, 11 June 1896; Dunning, *The Farmers' Alliance History*, p. 185; Thomas E. Watson, *The People's Party Campaign Handbook, 1892*, pp. 218–20.

15. Watson, *People's Party Campaign Handbook*, p. 216; also Dallas *Texas Advance*, 16 Sept. 1893.

16. Lawrence Goodwyn, *Democratic Promise*, pp. 6–11; C. Vann Woodward, *Origins of the New South, 1877–1913*, p. 249.

17. See Raleigh *Progressive Farmer*, 19 June 1894; Tarboro (N.C.) *Farmers' Advocate*, 28 Oct. 1891; Hardy (Ark.) *National Reformer*, Apr. 1895; Hardy (Ark.) *Morgan's Buzz Saw*, Jan. 1895; Washington, D.C., *National Watchman* in Dallas (Ga.) *Herald*, 7 Feb. 1895; Atlanta *People's Party Paper*, 7 Apr. 1893; Dallas *Texas Advance*, 30 Sept. 1893 and 10 Mar. 1894; Gracewood (Ga.) *Wool Hat*, 24 June 1893; *Texas Labor Journal* in Runge (Tex.) *Karnes County News*, 1 May 1891; Watson, *People's Party Campaign Handbook*, p. 221; Harry Tracy, Appendix, in James H. Davis, *A Political Revelation*, p. 295.

18. See Dallas (Tex.) *Southern Mercury*, 9 May 1895; Dallas *Texas Advance*, 4 Aug. 1894; Tarboro (N.C.) *Farmers' Advocate*, 19 Aug. 1891; Raleigh *Progressive Farmer*, 17 Mar. 1891; Gracewood (Ga.) *Wool Hat*, 27 July 1892 and 29 Apr. and 22 July 1893.

19. Tarboro (N.C.) *Farmers' Advocate*, 6 Jan. 1892. The importance of equal rights can be seen in Raleigh *Progressive Farmer*, 17 July 1894; Richmond *Virginia Sun*, 17 May 1893; Goldsboro (N.C.) *Caucasian*, 5 Jan. 1893.

20. Atlanta *People's Party Paper*, 4 Oct. 1895; also 31 Dec. 1891 and 3 June and 25 Nov. 1892; Tarboro (N.C.) *Farmers' Advocate*, 22 July and 2 Sept. 1891; Raleigh *Progressive*

Farmer, 21 Apr. and 21 July 1891; Nashville *Weekly Toiler*, 13 May 1891.

21. Goldsboro (N.C.) *Caucasian*, 23 Feb. 1893.

22. See ibid., 13 Sept. 1894.

23. Ozark (Ala.) *Banner*, 23 June 1892.

24. Atlanta *People's Party Paper*, 6 Jan. 1893; also Hickory (N.C.) *Mercury*, 9 Mar. 1892; Ozark (Ala.) *Banner*, 21 Sept. 1893; Butler (Ala.) *Choctaw Alliance*, 2 Aug. 1892; Raleigh *Progressive Farmer*, 24 Apr. 1894; A. D. K. Wallace to Thompson, 11 May 1894, box 1, vol. 5, Dr. Cyrus Thompson Papers; W. J. Brooks to J. W. Denmark of the *Progressive Farmer*, 13 June 1892, box 7, vol. 105, L. L. Polk Papers; Tracy, Appendix, in Davis, *A Political Revelation*, p. 389. An excellent discussion of the religious function of the Alliance and the People's party in Kansas is Peter Argersinger's "Pentacostal Politics in Kansas," pp. 24–35. The Gospel of Populism was quite similar among the Southern Populists, and probably for many of the same reasons, although the "frontier adjustment" idea might have to be modified for much of the South.

25. Austin (Tex.) *People's Advocate*, 22 Mar. 1894; also Salisbury (N.C.) *Carolina Watchman*, 1 Dec. 1892; Atlanta *People's Party Paper*, 16 Mar. 1894; Dallas (Ga.) *Herald*, 28 Dec. 1893; Gibson (Ga.) *Glascock Banner*, 31 Jan. 1895.

26. Atlanta *People's Party Paper*, 7 Sept. 1894; also Wadesboro (N.C.) *Plow Boy*, 13 Feb. 1895; Richmond *Virginia Sun*, 20 July 1892; Hardy (Ark.) *Arkansaw Kicker*, 14 Mar. 1896; Gracewood (Ga.) *Wool Hat*, 23 Sept. 1893; Tracy, Appendix, in Davis, *A Political Revelation*, p. ii.

27. See Atlanta *People's Party Paper*, 31 Mar. 1892; Clinton (N.C.) *Caucasian*, 31 Dec. 1891; Wadesboro (N.C.) *Plow Boy*, 16 Oct. 1895.

28. Tarboro (N.C.) *Farmers' Advocate*, 9 Nov. 1892; also Austin (Tex.) *People's Advocate*, 22 Mar. 1894; Butler (Ala.) *Choctaw Alliance*, 19 July 1893.

29. It is outlined in Frederick A. Bode, *Protestantism and the New South*, chap. 3.

30. Raleigh *Caucasian*, 12 Dec. 1895.

31. Ibid., 2 Jan. 1896.

32. Ibid., 19 Sept. 1895.

33. For the dominance of the "scripturalist" mission of the church which defined the church's role as strictly separate from the secular world, over the "humanitarian" mission of the church which involved relating the church to the secular world by allowing it to attack sin there, see Hunter Dickinson Farish, *The Circuit Rider Dismounts*, pp. 3, 16, 54–61. For some discussion of it in the southern Churches of Christ, see David Edwin Harrell, "The Sectional Origins of the Churches of Christ," pp. 261–77. For the southern Baptist church after the Civil War, see Rufus B. Spain, *At Ease in Zion*, pp. 209–13. For an interesting statement of the same idea, see Robert Moats Miller, "Southern White Protestantism and the Negro, 1865–1965," pp. 244–45.

34. Dallas (Tex.) *Southern Mercury*, 4 July 1895; also Houston (Tex.) *National Alliance* in Tarboro (N.C.) *Farmers' Advocate*, 24 June 1891.

35. See Hardy (Ark.) *Morgan's Buzz Saw*, Mar. 1896; Wadesboro (N.C.) *Plow Boy*, 16 Oct. 1895. The Populists' belief that theirs was a righteous cause, of course, accounted for some of the opposition to a southern church which, unless it said nothing, supported the Democrats. The church's opposition might have increased the amount of criticism, or the publicity given to it, since the Southern Populists may have felt that they had nothing to lose. That did not mean, however, that the reformers did not believe what they said. The contrast they perceived between what the church professed—to love the poor and alleviate their suffering—and what it practiced—opposition to most measures of social reform aimed at doing just that—seemed remarkable and repellent. See, for instance, Butler (Ala.) *Choctaw Alliance*, 25 Apr. 1894.

36. Troy (Ala.) *Jeffersonian*, 15 June 1894; also Atlanta *People's Party Paper*, 8 May

1896; Raleigh *Progressive Farmer*, 2 June 1896; Raleigh *Caucasian*, 21 Nov. 1895; Gracewood (Ga.) *Wool Hat*, 15 July 1893; Bode, *Protestantism and the New South*, pp. 49–52.

37. Raleigh *Caucasian*, 6 June 1895; also Hardy (Ark.) *Morgan's Buzz Saw*, Jan. 1895 and Mar. 1896; Wadesboro (N.C.) *Plow Boy*, 23 Oct. 1895; Butler (Ala.) *Choctaw Alliance*, 24 Oct. 1894; Tuscaloosa (Ala.) *Journal*, 10 Oct. 1894; Atlanta *People's Party Paper*, 22 Dec. 1893; Salisbury (N.C.) *Carolina Watchman*, 19 May 1892; Charlotte (N.C.) *People's Paper* in Atlanta *People's Party Paper*, 28 June 1895; Isom P. Langley, "Religion in the Alliance," in Dunning, *The Farmers' Alliance History*, pp. 314–16. The Socialists later also emphasized a Christian radicalism to attract rural Southwesterners. James R. Green, *Grass-Roots Socialism*, pp. 143–45, 168–75. They made the same distinctions between "'Christianity'" and "'churchianity'" (Green, *Socialism*, p. 168).

38. Dallas (Tex.) *Southern Mercury*, 19 Mar. 1896. W. S. Morgan, a radical antimonopoly greenbacker from Arkansas, went a little further. "It has been well said that 'Populism is religion in motion'" (Hardy, Ark., *National Reformer*, Mar. 1895). Morgan later became an active member of the Socialist party (Green, *Socialism*, pp. 17, 136).

39. Cullman (Ala.) *People's Protest* in Wedowee (Ala.) *Randolph Toiler*, 28 Nov. 1895; also Ozark (Ala.) *Banner*, 21 Sept. 1893; Hardy (Ark.) *National Reformer*, Mar. 1895.

40. Goldsboro (N.C.) *Caucasian*, 22 Nov. 1894; also Dallas (Ga.) *Herald*, 21 June 1894.

41. Goldsboro (N.C.) *Caucasian*, 13 Apr. 1893; also Atlanta *People's Party Paper*, 17 Mar. and 14 Apr. 1893 and 23 Feb. 1894.

42. Dallas *Texas Advance*, 30 Sept. 1893.

Chapter 3

1. Paul M. Gaston, *The New South Creed*, p. 7; C. Vann Woodward, *Origins of the New South, 1877–1913*, pp. 142–55.

2. This middle class—urban, commercial, professional, landholding—is not that to which the Southern Populists referred when they used the same terms. It is the southern component of that class which Robert Wiebe calls the "new middle class," a creation of American industrial capitalism. Robert Wiebe, *The Search for Order, 1877–1920*, pp. 111–13, 176–81.

3. C. Vann Woodward, *The Strange Career of Jim Crow*, pp. 74–81.

4. Thomas D. Clark, "The Country Newspaper," pp. 3–33.

5. Those Democrats who became reformers and progressives after 1896 almost all sided with the Redeemers against the Populists. For North Carolina, see Helen Edmonds, *The Negro and Fusion Politics in North Carolina, 1894–1901*, pp. 8–14. For Georgia, see Dewey Grantham, Jr., *Hoke Smith and the Politics of the New South*, chaps. 4, 7. For Alabama, see Sheldon Hackney, *Populism to Progressivism in Alabama*, chap. 7. For Mississippi, see Albert D. Kirwan, *Revolt of the Rednecks*, chaps. 9–14. For Texas, see Alwyn Barr, *Reconstruction to Reform*, chaps. 9, 10, 14, 15.

6. Woodward, *Origins*, pp. 175–81; and C. Vann Woodward, *Tom Watson, Agrarian Rebel*, pp. 126–29.

7. Philip Roy Muller, in chap. 1 of his "New South Populism," argues that the leaders of the Alliance and the Populist party in North Carolina considered them vehicles for achieving the "New South" of Grady and Page.

8. Raleigh *Progressive Farmer*, 29 Sept. 1891. Also for North Carolina, see Muller, "New South Populism," chap. 1.

9. Gibson (Ga.) *Glascock Banner*, 31 Oct. 1895; Richmond *Virginia Sun*, 20 Feb. 1892; Wadesboro (N.C.) *Plow Boy*, 18 Sept. 1895; Raleigh *Progressive Farmer*, 29 Oct. 1895;

Tarboro (N.C.) *Farmers' Advocate*, 29 July 1891. For an exception, see the end of the 1894 Georgia Populist convention in Atlanta *People's Party Paper*, 25 May 1894. The Texans said little one way or the other about fairs. This may have been due to the newness of much of Texas settlement, or it may have been related to the large proportion of antimonopoly greenbackers among the Texas Populists. On the other hand, Watson and the editor of the Dallas, Ga., *Herald*, both committed greenbackers, were affected by this form of New South boosterism.

10. Raleigh *Progressive Farmer*, 7 June 1892.

11. Ibid., 22 Sept. 1896; also 25 Feb. 1896; Richmond *Virginia Sun*, 6 July 1892; Tarboro (N.C.) *Farmers' Advocate*, 20 May 1891.

12. See Gadsden (Ala.) *Alliance Advocate*, 1 Dec. 1892; Atlanta *People's Party Paper*, 1 Mar. 1895.

13. See, for instance, Dallas *Texas Advance*, 30 Sept. 1893; Thomas E. Watson, *People's Party Campaign Handbook, 1892*, p. 219; Woodward, *Origins*, pp. 250–51.

14. Atlanta *People's Party Paper*, 17 Mar. 1892. For the advertisement, Atlanta *People's Party Paper*, 10 Mar. 1892.

15. Ibid., 19 Apr. 1895. Four years earlier the editor of the Tarboro (N.C.) *Farmers' Advocate* eagerly awaited the real estate boom he felt Tarboro was on the brink of (22 Apr. 1891).

16. Dallas (Ga.) *Herald*, 5 Apr. 1894.

17. See Salisbury (N.C.) *Carolina Watchman*, 16 July 1891 and 3 Mar. 1892; Lampasas (Tex.) *People's Journal*, 27 Jan. 1893. Much less evidence existed of a positive response to the New South from the Texas Populists. I lacked, however, enough copies of small town newspapers from Texas. Significantly, the *People's Journal*, an exception to this general deficiency, provided an example of such a response.

18. Ozark (Ala.) *Banner-Advertiser*, 7 Feb., 7 Mar., 4 Apr., and 30 May 1895; and 9 Jan. and 5 Mar. 1896.

19. See Hardy (Ark.) *National Reformer*, Nov. 1894 and Mar. 1895; Hardy (Ark.) *Morgan's Buzz Saw*, July and Aug. 1895 and Apr. 1896. The editor of the Nashville *Weekly Toiler*, 28 Oct. 1891, urged making Savannah a deep water port so it could compete with New York and "add greatly to Southern enterprise by unfettering our commerce." See also Tarboro (N.C.) *Farmers' Advocate*, 8 Apr. 1891.

20. For the exceptions, see Woodward, *Origins*, pp. 173–74; Gaston, *New South Creed*, pp. 154–58.

21. Wedowee (Ala.) *Randolph Toiler*, 13 Feb. 1896. The Dallas (Ga.) *Herald*, on the same day that it praised the Southern Railway for promising to develop Paulding County, Georgia, and the South, displayed its ambiguity about such development in a long editorial on Macon, Georgia. Macon had been built "before the city lot fiend had got in his work." "Broad-minded, generous builders," not "speculative genius," had raised it. Built when the "producing interests" controlled the wealth of the community, beauty and fitness had played a part in the design. The business houses were constructed not "to entrap the dollars," but to afford "convenience and comfort" to those trading in them. Wide sidewalks allowed space "for leisurely promenade of rich shoppers rather than the rush and scramble of the multitude in quest of the present day 'cheap counter' or 'bargain day.' . . . The residences were built for homes, not tenements." The editor wondered about the value of hustle, efficiency, progress, and their inevitable concomitants—the "city lot fiend," crowded tenements, the "cheap counter" and the "bargain day" (11 July 1895). The irony of an antimonopoly greenback Southern Populist having to choose between a society dominated by aristocratic slaveholders and one dominated by middle-class commission merchants is striking. That he favored the former despite Southern Populist hostility to slavery, slaveowners, and slave society testifies eloquently to how the Southern Populists responded

to America's new business culture, not to speak of its economic effects on them. For the Southern Populist hostility to the antebellum economic and social system, see Bruce Palmer, "The Southern Populists Remember," pp. 133–35.

22. Raleigh *Progressive Farmer*, 14 Mar. 1893.

23. Richmond *Virginia Sun*, 17 May 1893.

24. See Atlanta *People's Party Paper*, 25 May 1894; Gracewood (Ga.) *Wool Hat*, 14 Apr. 1894; Stephenville (Tex.) *Empire*, 28 May 1892; Austin (Tex.) *Argus*, 4 Sept. 1894. On this basis James A. "Cyclone" Davis of Texas distinguished between "Democracy," which he favored, and "socialism." Democracy recognized "private property"; socialism did not (*A Political Revelation*, p. 95).

25. For the Southern Populist critique of competition as a guide for social development, see the Conclusion, pp.204–5 below.

26. Atlanta *People's Party Paper*, 16 Nov. 1894.

27. See ibid., 23 Nov. 1894; Raleigh *Progressive Farmer*, 28 June 1892; Tarboro (N.C.) *Farmers' Advocate*, 2 Sept. 1891; Troy (Ala.) *Jeffersonian*, 19 Jan. 1894; Watson, *People's Party Campaign Handbook*, p. 207; "Don't Throw Your Vote Away," Populist campaign pamphlet, 38–360, William DuBose Sheldon Papers.

28. Raleigh *Caucasian*, 30 May 1895.

29. Dallas *Texas Advance*, 2 June 1894; also Austin (Tex.) *Argus*, 31 July 1894; Davis, *A Political Revelation*, pp. 93, 130.

30. See Austin (Tex.) *Argus*, 4 Sept. 1894.

31. For the debate between the Populist left and right wing, see Lawrence Goodwyn, *Democratic Promise*, chap. 14, and Chester McArthur Destler, *American Radicalism, 1865–1901*, pp. 226–31.

32. Atlanta *People's Party Paper*, 27 Dec. 1895; also 20 Dec. 1895.

33. Ozark (Ala.) *Banner*, 26 Oct. 1893; also Anniston *Alabama Leader*, 3 Oct. 1895; Atlanta *People's Party Paper*, 2 Aug. and 1 Nov. 1895.

34. Austin (Tex.) *Argus*, 4 Sept. 1894.

35. Anniston *Alabama Leader*, 3 Oct. 1895; also Gracewood (Ga.) *Wool Hat*, 20 May 1893; Hardy (Ark.) *National Reformer*, Feb. 1895; Dallas (Tex.) *Southern Mercury*, 31 Jan. 1895; Dallas *Texas Advance*, 16 Sept. 1893.

36. See Raleigh *Progressive Farmer*, 25 June 1895; Gibson (Ga.) *Glascock Banner*, 31 Jan. 1895; Raleigh *Caucasian*, 6 June 1895.

37. Dallas (Tex.) *Southern Mercury*, 23 May 1895; also 9 July 1896; Austin (Tex.) *Argus*, 14 Aug. 1894; Hardy (Ark.) *National Reformer*, Apr. 1894; Hardy (Ark.) *Morgan's Buzz Saw*, Aug. 1896; Davis, *A Political Revelation*, pp. 95–96, 130.

38. Hardy (Ark.) *Arkansaw Kicker*, 14 Mar. 1896.

39. Austin (Tex.) *People's Advocate*, 26 Apr. 1894.

40. Ibid., 22 Feb. and 5 Apr. 1894.

41. Austin (Tex.) *Argus*, 28 Aug. 1894.

42. After 1896 antimonopoly greenbackism exerted a considerable influence on the development of southwestern socialism. Although the Socialist party in Texas and Oklahoma had to outgrow its Populist roots, a close programmatic tie existed at least until 1908 or 1910, and Populist ideas remained evident until the Socialist party's demise. See James R. Green, *Grass-Roots Socialism*, chap. 1 and pp. 53, 80–83, 383–84, 388, 391.

43. Atlanta *People's Party Paper*, 16 Aug. 1895.

44. Hardy (Ark.) *National Reformer*, Apr. 1895; also June 1895; Hardy (Ark.) *Morgan's Buzz Saw*, July 1895.

45. It would be a mistake to overemphasize the political elements in the decision to avoid socialism. The Southern Populists risked quite a bit as it was for their political stands. There is no reason to suspect that at least a few of the more radical of them in the South would not

have been willing to move into socialism. Very few of them did, at least until after 1896, although the antimonopoly greenbackers were always willing to work with socialists.

46. See Ozark (Ala.) *Banner*, 19 June 1894; Dahlonega (Ga.) *Signal*, 29 June 1894; Dallas *Texas Advance*, 25 Aug. 1894; Gracewood (Ga.) *Wool Hat*, 14 July 1894; Austin (Tex.) *Argus*, 10 July 1894; Atlanta *People's Party Paper*, 23 Feb. 1894.

47. Goldsboro (N.C.) *Caucasian*, 3 Nov. 1892; also Richmond *Virginia Sun*, 5 Oct. 1892; Hardy (Ark.) *Morgan's Buzz Saw*, Oct. 1894.

48. "Don't Throw Your Vote Away," Populist campaign pamphlet, 38–360, William DuBose Sheldon Papers; also Atlanta *People's Party Paper*, 25 May and 13 July 1894; Gracewood (Ga.) *Wool Hat*, 8 Apr. 1893 and 28 Apr. and 14 July 1894.

49. Goldsboro (N.C.) *Caucasian*, 2 Aug. 1894. This attitude was not universal. The editor of the Raleigh *Progressive Farmer* on 12 July 1892 supported the Homestead strikers' defense against the Pinkerton agents. The most antimonopoly greenback paper in the state, the Tarboro *Farmers' Advocate*, was quite supportive of the Homestead strikers, although it, too, counseled voting right instead of striking (13 and 20 July 1892). Some of the same kind of hostility to strikes existed in Virginia. An Allianceman writing in the spring of 1892 called strikes and boycotts "illegal" (Richmond *Virginia Sun*, 27 Apr. 1892).

50. Melton Alonza McLaurin, *Paternalism and Protest*, pp. 77–85.

51. See Atlanta *People's Party Paper*, 19 Aug. 1892; Gadsden (Ala.) *Alliance Advocate*, 15 Dec. 1892; Austin (Tex.) *Argus*, 4 Sept. 1894; Gracewood (Ga.) *Wool Hat*, 14 and 21 July 1894. This was not always true, however. See Ozark (Ala.) *Banner*, 22 Dec. 1892.

52. See Goldsboro (N.C.) *Caucasian*, 4 May 1893; Hardy (Ark.) *National Reformer*, Oct. 1894 and Apr. and May 1895; Gracewood (Ga.) *Wool Hat*, 5 Aug. 1893 and 21 Apr., 14 and 21 July 1894; Austin (Tex.) *Argus*, 31 July and 30 Oct. 1894; Dallas *Texas Advance*, 21 July 1894; Dallas (Tex.) *Southern Mercury*, 14 Nov. 1895; Jacksonville (Ala.?) *Advocate* in Gadsden (Ala.) *Alliance Advocate*, 15 Dec. 1892; Wedowee (Ala.) *Randolph Toiler*, 2 Jan. 1896; Beaver Dam (N.C.) *Our Home*, 26 May 1893; Tarboro (N.C.) *Farmers' Advocate*, 20 July 1892.

53. Hackney, *Populism to Progressivism*, pp. 60–62.

54. Lawrence Goodwyn, *Democratic Promise*, pp. 51–77.

55. The Gracewood (Ga.) *Wool Hat*, located in the same county as Augusta, was a good example also. See chap. 1, n. 58, above, for a longer discussion of the *Wool Hat*.

56. Austin (Tex.) *Argus*, 31 July 1894.

57. Almont Lindsey, *The Pullman Strike*, chap. 5; Stanley Buder, *Pullman*, chaps. 11, 12.

58. See, for instance, Irving G. Wyllie, *The Self-Made Man in America*, chap. 1.

59. Wyllie, *The Self-Made Man*, chap. 3 and pp. 60–64.

60. See, for Alabama, Hackney, *Populism to Progressivism*, pp. 81–87, 328.

61. Milford Howard in Raleigh *Progressive Farmer*, 16 Apr. 1895; also Dallas (Tex.) *Southern Mercury*, 11 June 1896; Atlanta *People's Party Paper*, 3 Mar. 1892.

62. Some of the Texas Populists had played important roles in the temperance campaigns of the 1880s. See Barr, *Reconstruction to Reform*, pp. 149, 151, 152. The editor of the Gracewood (Ga.) *Wool Hat* was a prohibitionist, and prohibition appeared every once in a while in the *Wool Hat*'s columns (see 22 June and 6 July 1892; 25 Mar., 17 June, and 23 Sept. 1893). Even he, however, in the first issue of the *Wool Hat*, wrote that he would leave prohibition to the Prohibitionists, for "the special mission of the WOOL-HAT [is] to strike at a greater evil"—special privilege (1 June 1892).

63. Raleigh *Progressive Farmer*, 9 Apr. 1895 and 25 Aug. 1896; also Atlanta *People's Party Paper*, 25 Nov. 1892, 3 Mar. 1893, and 16 Mar. 1894; Tuscaloosa (Ala.) *Journal*, 10 Oct. 1894.

64. Dallas (Tex.) *Southern Mercury*, 1 Jan. 1891; also Dallas *Texas Advance*, 5 May

1894; Tarboro (N.C.) *Farmers' Advocate*, 20 Jan. 1892; Raleigh *Progressive Farmer*, 27 June 1893.

65. Raleigh *Progressive Farmer*, 23 Jan. 1894; also 27 June 1893.

66. Dallas (Tex.) *Southern Mercury*, 15 Nov. 1894; also Raleigh *Progressive Farmer*, 23 May 1893; Ozark (Ala.) *Banner*, 22 Dec. 1892.

67. Hackney, *Populism to Progressivism*, pp. 77–78.

68. Atlanta *People's Party Paper*, 21 Apr. 1892; also Wedowee (Ala.) *Randolph Toiler*, 23 Jan. 1896; Salisbury (N.C.) *Carolina Watchman*, 14 Jan. 1892; Butler (Ala.) *Choctaw Alliance*, 21 Dec. 1892; Dallas (Tex.) *Southern Mercury*, 3 Nov. 1892.

69. John G. Cawelti, *Apostles of the Self-Made Man*, pp. 43–44; Stephen Thernstrom, *Poverty and Progress*, pp. 57–59; Eric Foner, *Free Soil, Free Labor, Free Men*, pp. 23–26.

70. Unlike their middle-class contemporaries, part of the Populists' emphasis on work came from the much older notion of the value of the producer in society. Perhaps the main difference between the two groups, however, was that for the reformers, the success myth meant an opportunity to earn wealth by productive labor, production of tangible goods. To their contemporaries this was no longer the sole, or even the most important emphasis. On the absence of the producer idea in the success myth, see Wyllie, *The Self-Made Man*, chaps. 1, 2.

Chapter 4

1. For Locke, see Peter Laslett's introduction in his edition of John Locke, *Two Treatises of Government*, pp. 93–97. For the Jeffersonians and the American Enlightenment in general, see Charles M. Wiltse, *The Jeffersonian Tradition in American Democracy*, pp. 157–61, 175–77; Merle Curti, *The Growth of American Thought*, pp. 98–99; Adrienne Koch, *The Philosophy of Thomas Jefferson*, pp. 144–48. For Revolutionary America and law, see Paul K. Conkin, *Self-Evident Truths*, chaps. 5, 6.

2. "But it is to Locke, whose 'little book on government is perfect as far as it goes,' that we must turn for the ultimate source of the ideas which most influenced Jefferson during his formative years" (Wiltse, *The Jeffersonian Tradition*, p. 47). Wiltse also points out that by the mid-eighteenth century Locke's ideas on government were "axiomatic" with most political writers in the American colonies (p. 48). Even a cursory reading of Benjamin Fletcher Wright, Jr., *American Interpretations of Natural Law*, reveals the extensive influence of Locke in the eighteenth and early nineteenth centuries. In Wright, see especially pp. 67–116. Bailyn, however, takes some exception to the absolute importance of Locke for the Revolutionary generation. Bernard Bailyn, *The Ideological Origins of the American Revolution*, chap. 2. See also Conkin, *Self-Evident Truths*, p. 103.

3. Locke, in the "Second Treatise," of *Two Treatises*, §195, argued that the "Laws of God and Nature" were "so great, and so strong . . . that Omnipotency it self can be tyed by them."

4. Tarboro (N.C.) *Southerner* in Tarboro (N.C.) *Farmers' Advocate*, 26 Oct. 1892; Atlanta *People's Party Paper*, 8 June 1894; Dallas *Texas Advance*, 10 Mar. 1894; Gracewood (Ga.) *Wool Hat*, 24 Dec. 1892 and 2 June 1894; Little Rock (Ark.) *Dollar*, 13 Dec. 1895.

5. See Dallas (Ga.) *Herald*, 6 July 1893; W. Scott Morgan, *History of the Wheel and Alliance, and the Impending Revolution*, pp. 13, 21–24, 677.

6. Hardy (Ark.) *Morgan's Buzz Saw*, July 1896; also Troy (Ala.) *Jeffersonian*, 9 Mar. 1894; Atlanta *People's Party Paper*, 8 Feb. 1895; Raleigh *Progressive Farmer*, 9 May 1893;

Goldsboro (N.C.) *Caucasian*, 10 Dec. 1892 and 30 Mar. 1893; Dallas *Texas Advance*, 28 Apr. 1894; Gracewood (Ga.) *Wool Hat*, 24 Feb. 1894; James H. Davis, *A Political Revelation*, p. 102. Natural law as the manifestation of divine law was a major premise of the American, and European, Enlightenment. For the equation of natural and divine law in Locke, see, among other instances, *Two Treatises*, "Second Treatise," §135. See, for the Enlightenment, Carl Becker, *The Heavenly City of the Eighteenth-Century Philosophers*, pp. 47–53. For the Jeffersonians, see Daniel Boorstin, *The Lost World of Thomas Jefferson*, pp. 41–44. For Revolutionary American thinkers, see Conkin, *Self-Evident Truths*, pp. 104–5, 120–21.

7. See Raleigh *Progressive Farmer*, 21 Mar. 1893; Dallas (Tex.) *Southern Mercury*, 24 Jan. 1895.

8. See Dallas *Texas Advance*, 3 Feb. and 28 Apr. 1894; Atlanta *People's Party Paper*, 4 Jan. 1892, 25 Aug. 1893, and 22 Mar. 1895.

9. Ozark (Ala.) *Banner-Advertiser*, 7 May 1896; also Austin (Tex.) *People's Advocate*, 18 Jan. 1894; Stephenville (Tex.) *Empire*, 28 Oct. 1892; Dallas (Tex.) *Southern Mercury*, 25 July 1895; Dallas *Texas Advance*, 25 Nov. 1893; Morgan, *History of the Wheel and Alliance*, p. 511. Their opposition, of course, believed the same, although they also believed, unlike the Southern Populists, that this law had not been violated. See Edward Chase Kirkland, *Dream and Thought in the Business Community, 1860–1900*, pp. 11–14, 18–28; Sidney Fine, *Laissez-Faire and the General Welfare State*, pp. 104–17.

10. Nashville *Weekly Toiler*, 13 May 1891.

11. Locke was very specific on this: "Thus the Law of Nature stands as an Eternal Rule to all Men, *Legislators* as well as others. The *Rules* that they make for other Mens Actions, must, as well as their own and other Mens Actions, be conformable to the Law of Nature, *i.e.*, to the Will of God, of which that is a Declaration." (*Two Treatises*, "Second Treatise," §135.) See, for the Enlightenment attitude, which was almost identical to Locke's, Becker, *The Heavenly City*, pp. 51–53. See also Boorstin, *The Lost World of Thomas Jefferson*, pp. 171–73, 194; Conkin, *Self-Evident Truths*, pp. 104–5.

12. Atlanta *People's Party Paper*, 31 Dec. 1891; also Salisbury (N.C.) *Carolina Watchman*, 3 Mar. 1892; Dallas (Ga.) *Herald*, 8 Mar. 1894; Ozark (Ala.) *Banner-Advertiser*, 17 Oct. 1895; Ozark (Ala.) *Banner*, 20 Oct. 1892.

13. Dallas (Tex.) *Southern Mercury*, 2 Apr. 1896; also 26 Apr. and 15 Nov. 1894; Goldsboro (N.C.) *Caucasian*, 10 Dec. 1892; Dallas *Texas Advance*, 18 Nov. 1893 and 24 Feb., 28 Apr. and 2 June 1894; Atlanta *People's Party Paper*, 17 Dec. 1891, 7 Jan. 1892, and 14 Dec. 1894; Wadesboro (N.C.) *Plow Boy*, 13 Feb. 1895; Troy (Ala.) *Jeffersonian*, 26 Jan. 1894; Gracewood (Ga.) *Wool Hat*, 24 Feb. 1894; Raleigh *Progressive Farmer*, 9 Apr. 1895; Anniston *Alabama Leader*, 14 Nov. 1895; Tarboro (N.C.) *Farmers' Advocate*, 30 Mar. 1892.

14. Wiltse argues that Jefferson perceived the law and its function this way. See *The Jeffersonian Tradition*, pp. 157–61.

15. Goldsboro (N.C.) *Caucasian*, 5 Jan. 1893; also 23 Feb. 1893 and 22 Nov. 1894; Atlanta *People's Party Paper*, 31 Dec. 1891 and 4 Oct. 1895; Hardy (Ark.) *National Reformer*, Apr. 1895.

16. Beaver Dam (N.C.) *Our Home*, 2 Aug. 1893; also Goldsboro (N.C.) *Caucasian*, 12 July 1894; Ozark (Ala.) *Banner*, 20 Oct. 1892; Montgomery (Ala.) *Alliance Herald*, 4 May 1893.

17. See Atlanta *People's Party Paper*, 10 Nov. 1893; Goldsboro (N.C.) *Caucasian*, 9 Mar. 1893 and 22 Nov. 1894; Ozark (Ala.) *Banner*, 21 Sept. 1893; Austin (Tex.) *Argus*, 25 Sept. 1894; Tarboro (N.C.) *Farmers' Advocate*, 6 Jan. 1892.

18. Hardy (Ark.) *National Reformer*, Oct. 1894; also Dallas (Tex.) *Southern Mercury*, 26 Sept. 1895; Dallas *Texas Advance*, 17 Mar. 1894; Atlanta *People's Party Paper*, 8 June

1894 and 29 Mar. 1895; Raleigh *Progressive Farmer*, 21 June 1892; Richmond *Virginia Sun*, 27 Apr. 1892; "Don't Throw Your Vote Away," Populist campaign pamphlet, 38–360, William DuBose Sheldon Papers; Gracewood (Ga.) *Wool Hat*, 29 Oct. 1892; Oxford (N.C.) *Granville County Reformer*, 21 June 1894; Lampasas (Tex.) *People's Journal*, 16 Sept. 1892; Harry Tracy, Appendix, in Davis, *A Political Revelation*, p. 365. The idea that government should attempt to bring the greatest good to the greatest number provided a popular alternative way of putting this. See Montgomery (Ala.) *Alliance Herald*, 19 Nov. 1891; Lampasas (Tex.) *People's Journal*, 7 Oct. 1892; Richmond *Virginia Sun*, 17 May 1893; Hardy (Ark.) *Morgan's Buzz Saw*, Oct. 1894. The slogan "vox Populi, vox dei," although not often used by the Southern Populists, brought the religious metaphor into discussions of government by providing an important justification of and an explanation for "the people governing themselves." If God instituted government, He made His will known through the vote of the people. See Oxford (Ala.) *Voice*, 12 Mar. 1892; Raleigh *Progressive Farmer*, 8 May 1894; Tarboro (N.C.) *Farmers' Advocate*, 30 Mar. 1892; Centreville (Ala.) *People's Reflector*, 13 Oct. 1892. The proper form of government would be realized by a government of, by, and for the people because God chose to state His rules for that government through the voice of the people, or, as the Southern Populists generally believed it to be, the voice of the producing middle class. The divine order God dictated was realized in human society through the medium of the ballot, which lent divine sanction to "the government of the people." See Birmingham *People's Weekly Tribune*, 24 Sept. 1896.

19. Atlanta *People's Party Paper*, 8 June 1894.

20. Dallas (Tex.) *Southern Mercury*, 30 Jan. 1896; also Gracewood (Ga.) *Wool Hat*, 25 Mar. 1893; Beaver Dam (N.C.) *Our Home*, 21 June 1893; Ozark (Ala.) *Banner*, 28 July 1892; Richmond *Exchange Reporter*, 23 Jan. 1892; Morgan, *History of the Wheel and Alliance*, p. 609; Davis, *A Political Revelation*, p. 97. Considering the importance of the people controlling the government, the lack of interest in direct democracy among the Southern Populists was surprising. Discussions of the initiative or referendum which exceeded more than a couple of sentences number about ten to a dozen, most of them coming from W. S. Morgan's papers, *Morgan's Buzz Saw* and the *National Reformer*. For other exceptions, see Atlanta *People's Party Paper*, 23 Sept. 1892; Davis, *A Political Revelation*, pp. 284–86; Raleigh *Caucasian*, 16 July 1896; Anniston *Alabama Leader*, 21 Nov. 1895. One or two sentence references, however, did occur in nearly every Populist newspaper in the South from time to time. Most of the extended discussions of these ideas outside Arkansas came from North Carolina reform journals. See, for instance, Wadesboro (N.C.) *Plow Boy*, 30 Oct. 1895, but also Dallas (Ga.) *Herald*, 2 May 1895, and New Orleans *Issue*, 31 Dec. 1892. Even the direct election of the president, vice-president, and United States senators received very little attention. By and large, the Southern Populists seem to have regarded the ballot, if properly used and free from fraud, adequate for realizing the reforms necessary for society. The Jeffersonian and Jacksonian tradition had little or nothing to say about direct democracy, and a lot to say about the republican ideal. The strength of the Southern Populists' adherence to the idea of the people ruling probably accounted for what little interest they showed in the processes of direct democracy rather than vice versa—that the effect of ideas of initiative and referendum built up the Southern reformers' adherence to the idea that government should be run for the people by the people. In the proper government, modeled on Jeffersonian ideas, the people would rule without the need for methods of direct democracy.

21. See Raleigh *Progressive Farmer*, 8 Mar. 1892; Salisbury (N.C.) *Carolina Watchman*, 5 Feb. 1891; Dahlonega (Ga.) *Signal*, 29 July 1892; Tracy, Appendix, in Davis, *A Political Revelation*, p. ii.

22. See Montgomery (Ala.) *Alliance Herald*, 17 May 1894. For a more general view from a similar standpoint, see Richmond *Exchange Reporter*, 18 Aug. 1891.

23. Montgomery (Ala.) *Alliance Herald*, 16 July 1891; also Nashville *Weekly Toiler*, 28 Oct. 1891; Richmond *Virginia Sun*, 17 May 1893; Hardy (Ark.) *National Reformer*, Aug. 1893 and Apr. 1895; Hardy (Ark.) *Morgan's Buzz Saw*, Nov. 1895; Davis, *A Political Revelation*, pp. 95–96.

24. Lampasas (Tex.) *People's Journal* in Troy (Ala.) *Jeffersonian*, 26 Jan. 1894.

25. Dallas (Tex.) *Southern Mercury*, 24 Dec. 1896.

26. See ibid., 17 Jan. and 26 Sept. 1895; Dallas *Texas Advance*, 17 Mar. 1894.

27. See Thomas E. Watson, *People's Party Campaign Handbook, 1892*, p. 7; Goldsboro (N.C.) *Caucasian*, 3 May 1894; Atlanta *People's Party Paper*, 14 Dec. 1894; Richmond *Virginia Sun*, 15 June 1892. References to the need for economy in government can be found in Raleigh *Progressive Farmer*, 10 Feb. and 17 Mar. 1891; Atlanta *People's Party Paper*, 31 Aug. 1894; Natchitoches *Louisiana Populist*, 24 Aug. 1894; Geneva (Ala.) *Record*, 3 June 1891; Wadesboro (N.C.) *Plow Boy*, 9 Jan. 1895.

28. Dallas (Tex.) *Southern Mercury*, 7 May 1896.

29. For the single exception I could find, see the report of a Marion Butler speech in the Tarboro (N.C.) *Farmers' Advocate*, 27 Apr. 1892.

30. See Atlanta *People's Party Paper*, 28 Jan. and 11 Feb. 1892 and 3 Aug. 1894; Austin (Tex.) *Argus*, 4 Sept. 1894.

31. See Austin (Tex.) *Argus*, 24 July 1894; Morgan, *History of the Wheel and Alliance*, p. 609; Richmond *Exchange Reporter*, 23 Jan. 1892.

32. Nashville *Weekly Toiler*, 4 May 1892; also Richmond *Virginia Sun*, 26 Mar. 1892.

33. Anniston *Alabama Leader*, 12 Sept. 1895; also Robeline (La.) *Battle Flag* in Gracewood (Ga.) *Wool Hat*, 25 Aug. 1894; Raleigh *Progressive Farmer*, 6 Sept. 1892; Lampasas (Tex.) *People's Journal*, 16 Sept. 1892; Atlanta *People's Party Paper*, 3 Aug. 1894; Dallas (Ga.) *Herald*, 18 May 1893; Richmond *Virginia Sun*, 20 Apr. 1892.

34. Washington, D.C., *National Economist* in Atlanta *People's Party Paper*, 10 Mar. 1892; also Dallas (Tex.) *Southern Mercury*, 5 Mar. 1896; Dallas *Texas Advance*, 2 June 1894; Hardy (Ark.) *Morgan's Buzz Saw*, Oct. 1894.

35. Atlanta *People's Party Paper*, 13 July 1894; also 3 Aug. 1894. "Cyclone" Davis argued that the Populists wanted the federal government to do only what the people could not do for themselves (*A Political Revelation*, pp. 96, 130).

36. Dallas (Tex.) *Southern Mercury*, 6 Feb. 1896.

37. Ibid., 19 Mar. 1896.

38. Salisbury (N.C.) *Carolina Watchman*, 14 Jan. 1892.

39. The preamble: "We the People of the United States, in Order to form a more perfect Union, establish Justice, insure domestic Tranquility, provide for the common defense, promote the general Welfare, and secure the Blessings of Liberty to ourselves and our Posterity, do ordain and establish this CONSTITUTION for the United States of America."

40. Davis, *A Political Revelation*, pp. 70–86.

41. Robert McCloskey, *American Conservatism in the Age of Enterprise, 1865–1910*, pp. 1–3, 111–23.

42. Atlanta *People's Party Paper*, 10 June 1892.

43. Dallas (Ga.) *Herald*, 6 July 1893; also Ozark (Ala.) *Banner*, 14 June 1894.

44. Ozark (Ala.) *Banner*, 20 Oct. 1892.

45. Atlanta *People's Party Paper*, 14 Dec. 1894.

46. Ibid., 29 July 1892. The religious metaphor, when applied to elected leaders of the Southern Populist party, tended to push the qualities of righteousness and virtue to the fore. As when the Populists applied this metaphor to the party itself, on a few occasions it became identified with the subject for which it was intended to serve as a vehicle for understanding. When God became the guide, the People's party the church, and the Omaha platform the creed, it was not uncommon to find appeals for a Populist messiah. The Populist movement,

wrote an Alabama Populist in 1896, could not fail to succeed unless the Populists attempted "to substitute the Divine plan with one of our own devising." God's plan included providing the Populists a "Moses" whom He had chosen, for unless "our David" had "the annointing oil poured upon him by divine command . . . all our labors and cunningly devised plans will come to naught." (Article from Greenville, Ala., *Living Truth*, 1896, in box 25, vol. 5, item 551, Thomas E. Watson Papers; also Atlanta *People's Party Paper*, 17 June 1892; Raleigh *Caucasian*, 12 Mar. 1896.) Moses was a common figure. "The situation at present looks dark, and the future looks darker still," wrote an Alabama Populist editor in 1894. "If there ever was a time that the people needed a Moses to guide them out of a terrible wilderness of danger and destruction, that time is now. Will he appear in time? God in His infinite wisdom only knows." (Troy, Ala., *Jeffersonian*, 13 Apr. 1894; also Raleigh *Progressive Farmer*, 18 Aug. 1891.) Interestingly, eight months earlier another Alabama reformer had already identified him. "A new Messiah is born who is to bring deliverance to the debt cursed children of toil—that Messiah is the people themselves. They are going to save themselves, their power is ubiquitous." (Butler, Ala., *Choctaw Alliance*, 16 Aug. 1893.) Here was the best Southern Populist messiah of all, come to return the government, the laws, and society to the paths of justice and righteousness.

47. Atlanta *People's Party Paper*, 21 Dec. 1894; also 24 June 1892 and 20 Oct. 1893; Raleigh *Progressive Farmer*, 8 May 1894; Tarboro (N.C.) *Farmers' Advocate*, 9 Mar. 1892. In the following discussion I do not intend to imply that other political parties, to a greater or lesser extent, did not stress the personal, moral abilities of their candidates. The Southern Populists were certainly not unique in this respect. That does not invalidate the point made in the section. The southern reformers shared more than one of their ideas with their Democratic and Republican opponents.

48. Atlanta *People's Party Paper*, 29 Dec. 1893.

49. Austin (Tex.) *People's Advocate*, 12 Oct. 1893.

50. Warren Plains (N.C.) *People's Paper*, 20 Dec. 1895.

51. William L. Riordan, ed., *Plunkitt of Tammany Hall*, p. 19.

52. Hickory (N.C.) *Mercury*, 31 Aug. 1892; also Anniston *Alabama Leader*, 29 Aug. 1895.

Chapter 5

1. J. Morgan Kousser, *The Shaping of Southern Politics*, chap. 1; C. Vann Woodward, *Origins of the New South, 1877–1913*, pp. 80–84, 98–106.

2. See Atlanta *People's Party Paper*, 26 Aug. 1892 and 20 July 1894; Raleigh *Caucasian*, 14 Mar. 1895.

3. Atlanta *People's Party Paper*, 28 Apr. 1892.

4. Raleigh *Progressive Farmer*, 1 Nov. 1892; also 17 Mar. 1891; Raleigh *Caucasian*, 12 and 19 Mar. 1896.

5. Dallas (Ga.) *Herald*, 2 Aug. 1894; also Atlanta *People's Party Paper*, 25 May 1894; Dallas *Texas Advance*, 30 June 1894.

6. Atlanta *People's Party Paper*, 28 Apr. 1892; also 21 Apr. 1894; Gracewood (Ga.) *Wool Hat*, 13 Aug. and 3 Sept. 1892.

7. See Atlanta *People's Party Paper*, 17 Mar. 1892 and 25 May and 13 July 1894; Gracewood (Ga.) *Wool Hat*, 29 July 1893 and 28 July 1894. Other Georgia Populists agreed. See Dallas (Ga.) *Herald*, 21 Mar. 1895.

8. See Raleigh *Progressive Farmer*, 19 Apr. and 26 July 1892; Goldsboro (N.C.) *Caucasian*, 3 Nov. 1892; Burgaw (N.C.) *Sun* in Goldsboro (N.C.) *Caucasian*, 30 Mar. 1893; Austin (Tex.) *Argus*, 4 Sept. 1894; Richmond *Virginia Sun*, 27 July 1892.

9. Dallas (Ga.) *Herald*, 28 June 1894; also Gracewood (Ga.) *Wool Hat*, 12 Aug. 1893; Raleigh *Caucasian*, 10 Jan. 1895 and 14 May 1896; Richmond *Virginia Sun*, 27 July 1892 and 20 Dec. 1894; Nashville *Weekly Toiler*, 26 Oct. 1892. The same sentiments emerged in Alabama in the 1896 debate over Populist gubernatorial candidate A. T. Goodwyn's decision, as a congressman, to vote for the black rather than the white man in a congressional seating challenge. See Ozark (Ala.) *Banner-Advertiser*, 25 June 1896.

10. Dallas *Texas Advance*, 30 June 1894. For a short statement on other kinds of priorities southern blacks had, see Gerald Gaither, *Blacks and the Populist Revolt*, pp. 61–62.

11. Atlanta *People's Party Paper*, 29 July 1892.

12. Ibid., 27 Dec. 1895.

13. Ibid., 29 July 1892, 7 Feb. 1896, and other campaign issues in 1892, 1894, and 1896; Gracewood (Ga.) *Wool Hat*, 3 and 10 Sept. 1892; 12 Aug. 1893; and 19 May, 1 and 15 Sept. 1894.

14. Woodward, *Origins*, p. 256. Lawrence C. Goodwyn, "Populist Dreams and Negro Rights," pp. 1435–56, indicates that there may have been much more local cooperation than has heretofore been thought, and which went unreported.

15. Lawrence D. Rice, *The Negro in Texas, 1874–1900*, pp. 69–72, 78.

16. Ibid., pp. 82–84.

17. Raleigh *Progressive Farmer*, 30 Aug. 1892.

18. Populist poster with a call for the 1892 Virginia Populist convention, 38–360, William DuBose Sheldon Papers.

19. Richmond *Virginia Sun*, 6 and 20 July 1892.

20. Ibid., 27 July and 14 Sept. 1892.

21. Ibid., 5 Oct. 1892.

22. See Appendix H; William DuBose Sheldon, *Populism in the Old Dominion*, pp. 90–92.

23. Richmond *Virginia Sun*, 16 Nov. 1892 and 1 Feb. 1893. See also, for Virginia, Georgia, Texas, Alabama, and Mississippi, Robert Saunders, "Southern Populists and the Negro, 1893–1895," pp. 240–61; and by the same author, "The Ideology of Southern Populists, 1892–1895," chaps. 3, 5; also Gaither, *Blacks and the Populist Revolt*, pp. 83–84.

24. Butler (Ala.) *Choctaw Alliance*, 19 Oct. 1892 and 2 May 1894.

25. Natchitoches *Louisiana Populist*, 5 July 1895.

26. See Raleigh *Caucasian*, 16 May 1895; Dallas (Ga.) *Herald*, 18 Oct. 1894; Hardy (Ark.) *Morgan's Buzz Saw*, Oct. 1894. The Gracewood (Ga.) *Wool Hat* capitalized the word "Negro" twice in 1893—3 June and 8 July. Both were in editorials, however, not particularly flattering to blacks, suggesting that the capitalizations might have been typographical errors.

27. Gracewood (Ga.) *Wool Hat*, 23 Dec. 1893.

28. Dahlonega (Ga.) *Signal*, 9 Sept. 1892.

29. Raleigh *Progressive Farmer*, 15 Aug. 1893; also Birmingham *People's Weekly Tribune*, 20 Aug. 1896; Lafayette (Ala.) *People's Advocate* in Gracewood (Ga.) *Wool Hat*, 20 Jan. 1894.

30. Ozark (Ala.) *Banner-Advertiser*, 24 Oct. 1895.

31. Birmingham *People's Weekly Tribune*, 4 June 1896; also Troy (Ala.) *Jeffersonian*, 26 Jan. and 2 Feb. 1894; Sheffield (Ala.) *Reaper* in Wedowee (Ala.) *Randolph Toiler*, 7 Nov. 1895.

32. In Alabama, until November 1894 when they merged with the People's party to form the People's party of Alabama, two different third party organizations existed in the state, the Jeffersonian Democratic party and the Alabama People's party. Although we will

discuss the differences between the two in greater detail in chap. 11, below, the Jeffersonian Democrats were generally less radical on race and reform than the Populists.

33. *Alliance News* (Ala.) in Butler (Ala.) *Choctaw Alliance*, 4 Oct. 1893.

34. Natchitoches *Louisiana Populist*, 31 Aug. 1894.

35. See ibid., 7 Sept. 1894, 21 June 1895, and 28 Feb. 1896.

36. Ibid., 15 Nov. 1895; also 24 Aug. 1894, 1 and 22 Nov. 1895, and 10 Apr. 1896.

37. In *Bourbonism and Agrarian Protest*, pp. 240–41, William Ivy Hair argues that the Louisiana Populists were forced into their white primary offer by the Democrats. Hardy Brian's attack on the DeSoto parish Democrats cited above in note 36, and the same editor's censure of the Grant parish Populists for allowing black Populists into their candidate selection process in 1892 indicate that such a move did not run entirely against their grain. For the latter, see Natchitoches *Louisiana Populist*, 5 July 1895.

38. Atlanta *People's Party Paper*, 17 May 1895.

39. Raleigh *Progressive Farmer*, 13 June 1893; also Bowersville (Ga.) *Free Press* in Gracewood (Ga.) *Wool Hat*, 3 June 1893; Buford (Ga.) *Alliance Plow Boy* in Gracewood (Ga.) *Wool Hat*, 7 Oct. 1893.

40. Dallas *Texas Advance*, 11 Aug. 1894; also Hardy (Ark.) *National Reformer*, Nov. and Dec. 1893 and Apr. 1895.

41. Atlanta *People's Party Paper*, 28 Oct. 1892; also 7 and 28 Sept. 1894. For use of the "mixed schools" charge elsewhere, see Raleigh *Progressive Farmer*, 1 Nov. 1892 and 18 Sept. 1894; Goldsboro (N.C.) *Caucasian*, 27 Oct. 1892; Natchitoches *Louisiana Populist*, 21 Sept. and 2 Nov. 1894; Buford (Ga.) *Alliance Plow Boy* in Gracewood (Ga.) *Wool Hat*, 7 Oct. 1893.

42. Atlanta *People's Party Paper*, 28 Oct. 1892 and 24 Aug. 1894; Gracewood (Ga.) *Wool Hat*, 23 Sept. and 14 Oct. 1893; Raleigh *Caucasian*, 16 May 1895.

43. See Atlanta *People's Party Paper*, 27 Oct. 1893 and 12 Apr. 1895; Raleigh *Progressive Farmer*, 12 Mar. 1895.

44. Hickory (N.C.) *Mercury*, 31 Aug. and 14 and 21 Sept. 1892.

45. Richmond *Virginia Sun*, 12 Oct. 1892; Ozark (Ala.) *Banner*, 20 Oct. 1892; Dallas (Tex.) *Southern Mercury* in Centreville (Ala.) *People's Reflector*, 13 Oct. 1892.

46. Atlanta *People's Party Paper*, 28 Oct. 1892.

47. Ibid., 22 Mar. 1895; Gibson (Ga.) *Glascock Banner*, 28 Mar. 1895.

48. Raleigh *Progressive Farmer*, 26 Mar. 1895; also 2 Apr. 1895; Raleigh *Caucasian*, 28 Mar. 1895.

49. Raleigh *Progressive Farmer*, 1 Mar. 1892; also Goldsboro (N.C.) *Caucasian*, 2 June 1892.

50. Atlanta *People's Party Paper*, 28 Sept. 1894. Gaither, *Blacks and the Populist Revolt*, pp. 70–72, has other examples of Southern Populist support for Jim Crow laws.

51. Atlanta *People's Party Paper*, 22 June 1894; also 21 and 28 Apr. and 22 July 1892; Dallas (Ga.) *Herald*, 28 June 1894; Gracewood (Ga.) *Wool Hat*, 12 Aug. 1893.

52. See Richmond *Virginia Sun*, 26 Oct. 1892, 15 Feb. 1893, and 20 Dec. 1894; Raleigh *Progressive Farmer*, 26 July 1892 and 26 Mar. 1895; Gaither, *Blacks and the Populist Revolt*, pp. 119–20.

53. Birmingham *People's Weekly Tribune*, 28 May 1896. A similar comment came from an Augusta, Georgia, Populist writing to the Gracewood (Ga.) *Wool Hat*, 9 Sept. 1893.

54. I have not discussed this point further, for while it and attitudes toward the family eventually must be examined to understand the racial attitudes of the Southern Populists and the context in which they appeared, neither can be included in this short a treatment. Problems of evidence, framework, and conception and extent of the treatment make it impossible. I mention it only because of its obvious importance, and because it needs considerable work.

55. Atlanta *People's Party Paper*, 25 May 1894; also 14 Oct. 1892 and 24 Aug. 1894; Gracewood (Ga.) *Wool Hat*, 29 July and 23 Sept. 1893, 28 Apr. and 28 July 1894.

56. Atlanta *People's Party Paper*, 21 Apr. 1892; also 22 July 1892 and 13 Apr. 1894; Richmond *Virginia Sun*, 27 July 1892.

57. Goldsboro (N.C.) *Caucasian*, 26 Oct. 1893; also Richmond *Virginia Sun*, 15 Feb. 1893.

58. Atlanta *People's Party Paper*, 7 July 1893; also 3 Nov. 1893.

59. See ibid., 31 Mar. and 12 May 1893. Whitecapping was a Reconstruction practice which reemerged during the Independent and Populist campaigns of the 1880s and 1890s, especially the early ones, and involved a return to white sheets, hoods, and extralegal violence and terror to intimidate blacks. See William F. Holmes, "Whitecapping," pp. 166–67, and Saunders, "The Ideology of Southern Populists," pp. 72–74, for accounts of it in Mississippi in the early 1890s.

60. See Atlanta *People's Party Paper*, 19 Oct. 1894.

61. Ibid., 25 May 1894.

62. Dahlonega (Ga.) *Signal*, 13 Mar. 1891.

63. See ibid., 19 May, 2 June, and all of July 1893, and summer and fall 1894.

64. See also Nashville *Weekly Toiler*, 4 May 1892; Gracewood (Ga.) *Wool Hat*, 22 Apr., 6 May, and 30 Sept. 1893; Clinton (N.C.) *Caucasian*, 10 Sept. 1891. The *Caucasian*, while it was still in Clinton and for part of the early 1892 period when it was in Goldsboro—still an Alliance but also a Democratic paper—had as its motto "Pure Democracy and White Supremacy." Of course, the paper's title was a constant reminder of its publisher's attitudes toward blacks. Butler edited and published the *Caucasian* for most of its career.

65. Raleigh *Progressive Farmer*, 26 July 1892.

66. Austin (Tex.) *Argus*, 4 Sept. 1894.

67. Gracewood (Ga.) *Wool Hat*, 28 Oct. 1893.

68. Atlanta *People's Party Paper*, 12 Aug. 1892; also 24 May 1895. For other examples of the paternalist tone, see Raleigh *Progressive Farmer*, 15 Sept. 1891, 26 July 1892, and 7 July 1896; Raleigh *Caucasian*, 19 Mar. 1896; J. H. Turner, "The Race Problem," in N. A. Dunning, ed., *The Farmers' Alliance History and Agricultural Digest*, pp. 278–79.

69. C. Vann Woodward, *The Strange Career of Jim Crow*, pp. 47–59.

70. Atlanta *People's Party Paper*, 13 Jan. 1893.

71. Ibid., 30 Sept. 1892. The titles of the contestants gave away their racial identity. The Populist was Glenn Harper, the "darkey." The Democratic lawyer was Colonel Watterson, of Jonesboro. That small town Georgia in 1892 had no black lawyer colonels should be a relatively safe assumption.

72. Dallas (Ga.) *Herald*, 2 Apr. 1896.

73. Atlanta *People's Party Paper*, 25 May 1894. Robert Saunders, in "The Ideology of Southern Populists," chaps. 3, 5, and 7, shows the increasing disaffection of the Southern Populists with the blacks. He does the same for Watson in chap. 6, especially pp. 171–75, although I think he overestimates Watson's rejection of the appeal to blacks. On the one hand, Watson did use an appeal to racial hostility more often after 1894, but he had done so earlier as well. On the other hand, as we have seen, his appeal to blacks did not die entirely after 1894. For a closer examination of the changing appeal to blacks by Southern Populists, see chaps. 11 and 12, below.

74. Dallas (Ga.) *Herald*, 4 Oct. 1894.

75. Lampasas (Tex.) *People's Journal*, 9 Dec. 1892.

76. See Atlanta *People's Party Paper*, 17 June 1892; Goldsboro (N.C.) *Caucasian*, 22 Mar. 1894; Wedowee (Ala.) *Randolph Toiler*, 19 June 1896; Oxford (Ala.) *Voice*, 2 July 1892.

77. Dallas *Texas Advance*, 30 June 1894. For a similar argument, see Lamar (Mo.) *Political Review* in Gracewood (Ga.) *Wool Hat*, 5 Aug. 1893.

78. Atlanta *People's Party Paper*, 16 Sept. 1892.

79. In 1910, when he compared Bryan's political career with his own even less successful one, Watson found that the basic difference lay in the fact that "Bryan had *no everlasting and overshadowing Negro Question to hamper and handicap his progress*: I HAD." (Quoted in C. Vann Woodward, *Tom Watson, Agrarian Rebel*, p. 220, from Atlanta *Jeffersonian Weekly*, 20 Jan. 1910.) See *Tom Watson* for Watson's subsequent career.

80. Georgia and Texas were the more radical states. For some indication of their relative success, see chaps. 11 and 12, below; Appendixes D and G; and the tables in Kousser, *The Shaping of Southern Politics*: Alabama, p. 137; Louisiana, p. 163; Virginia, p. 174 (the 1893 gubernatorial election was a Republican-Populist fusion); North Carolina, p. 183; Texas, p. 199; and Georgia, p. 215.

81. See Clinton (N.C.) *Caucasian*, 17 Sept. 1891; Raleigh *Progressive Farmer*, 15 Sept. 1891. For the same assumption outside the context of the strike, see Raleigh *Caucasian*, 19 Mar. 1896.

82. Tarboro (N.C.) *Farmers' Advocate*, 23 Sept. 1891. For the strike, see William F. Holmes, "The Demise of the Colored Farmers' Alliance," pp. 196–200.

83. Winthrop D. Jordan, *White Over Black*, chap. 12; Thomas Jefferson, *Notes on the State of Virginia*, pp. 137–43.

84. Hunter Dickinson Farish, *The Circuit Rider Dismounts*, chap. 6; Rufus B. Spain, *At Ease In Zion*, chaps. 2, 3, 4; Robert Moats Miller, "Southern White Protestantism and the Negro, 1865–1965," pp. 231–47.

85. Atlanta *People's Party Paper*, 28 Oct. 1892.

86. For a considerably different view of Watson, see Charles Crowe, "Tom Watson, Blacks, and Populists Reconsidered," pp. 99–116; Lawrence J. Friedman, *The White Savage*, chap. 5. For a somewhat milder view than Crowe or Friedman, see Gaither, *Blacks and the Populist Revolt*, pp. 66, 70–71, 80–82, 95–96.

Chapter 6

1. Between 1870 and 1890 the population of Texas increased 173 percent. The conflict over land made concern with land monopoly central to Texas's rural reformers, from the Grange to the Populists. The first set of demands in the 1886 Cleburne demands of the Texas Farmers' Alliance (the first formulation and the essence of which would become the Omaha platform) concerned land monopoly. For the considerable importance of land in Texas politics and the reasons for it, see John S. Spratt, *The Road to Spindletop*, pp. 29–30, 119–26. The problem of land monopoly, however, was not unique to Texas. For the role played in the development of Louisiana Populism by the "Backbone Railroad" land grant, involving over 2 million acres, see William Ivy Hair, *Bourbonism and Agrarian Protest*, pp. 49–51, 206.

2. See Raleigh *Progressive Farmer*, 19 May 1896; Salisbury (N.C.) *Carolina Watchman*, 30 Apr. 1891; Gracewood (Ga.) *Wool Hat*, 2 June 1894; Lampasas (Tex.) *People's Journal*, 28 Oct. 1892; James H. Davis, *A Political Revelation*, pp. 248–49. Their estimates of the amount of land held by the railroads appears to have been quite close, or sometimes even a little short. John F. Stover, in his *American Railroads*, pp. 87–89, estimates that 170 million acres were originally granted to the railroads, over 131 million of which they finally retained. To this figure Stover adds almost 49 million acres granted the railroads by individual states. See also Edward Kirkland, *Industry Comes of Age*, pp. 57–59.

3. Lampasas (Tex.) *People's Journal*, 28 Oct. 1892; also Little Rock (Ark.) *Dollar*, 13 Dec. 1895.

4. Gracewood (Ga.) *Wool Hat*, 2 June 1894.

5. Dallas (Tex.) *Southern Mercury*, 7 Feb. 1895; also Austin (Tex.) *Argus*, 4 Sept. 1894.

6. See Dallas *Texas Advance*, 16 Sept. 1893; Dallas (Tex.) *Southern Mercury*, 21 Mar. 1895.

7. See, for instance, Tuscaloosa (Ala.) *Journal*, 10 Oct. 1894; Gracewood (Ga.) *Wool Hat*, 2 June 1894; Hardy (Ark.) *Morgan's Buzz Saw*, Oct. 1894.

8. Ozark (Ala.) *Banner-Advertiser*, 23 Jan. and 20 Feb. 1896. In the spring of 1887 R. G. Malone became editor of the Isbell *Alabama State Wheel*, the Alabama order's official paper. A single-taxer, Malone advocated a "general confiscation and redistribution" of all land. Malone's ideas, Rogers reports, became known even in south Alabama, where Ozark is located (William Warren Rogers, *The One-Gallused Rebellion*, pp. 125–26). The author of a letter to the Gracewood (Ga.) *Wool Hat* on 2 June 1894 went almost as far as Barefield, denying that landlords had any right to the land they held beyond that which they worked. "So you [the landlord] can easily see that your title to it now, is not established in justice whatever it may have been at first because if you had not been trying all these years to make your neighbors pay you the additional value that they themselves were giving to your land by their presence, you would have let them have, ere this, all that you did not actually need yourself, but instead of doing so, you still claim some thousands of acres of unimproved land, land upon which you have never done a day's work, while many of your neighbors do not own a foot, and cannot, simply because you want to force them to give you, in addition to the three dollars you paid for it, seventeen dollars additional value which is their own, and not yours, so that according to your theory the man who gets there first has a perfect right to eclipse the sun and charge rent for sun shares. Spread canvas under the clouds and levy a rain tax, and fence in the ocean and establish toll-gates." There was hostility elsewhere in Georgia as well, although no solution. "We want more houses and fewer landlords," wrote the editor of the Dahlonega (Ga.) *Signal* on 2 Nov. 1894. "Who feeds the landlords?" he went on to ask. "Their poor and often defrauded tenants." This problem, and the class differences between landowning farmers and nonlandowning tenants it implied, was central to the Socialist party approach to rural voters in the Southwest after 1900. See James R. Green, *Grass-Roots Socialism*, especially pp. 79–86, 110–11, 145–51.

9. Ozark (Ala.) *Banner-Advertiser*, 30 Jan. 1896.

10. Atlanta *People's Party Paper*, 21 Sept. 1894.

11. Ibid., 17 Jan. 1896. For Watson's first reference to the need to drop the Omaha land plank, see ibid., 18 Oct. 1895.

12. Austin (Tex.) *Argus*, 14 Aug. 1894. James H. "Cyclone" Davis also maintained that landownership ought to be determined by use (*A Political Revelation*, pp. 3, 107–8). Like other Southern Populists, including antimonopoly greenbackers, he did not apply the idea to local landlords, although unlike Nugent and a few others, he did not explain why. See *A Political Revelation*, Part III, especially pp. 102–12, 124–31.

13. Dallas (Tex.) *Southern Mercury*, 26 Mar. 1896; also Austin (Tex.) *Argus*, 4 Sept. 1894; Evan Jones, "Annual Presidential Address," St. Louis convention, National Farmers' Alliance and Industrial Union, 4 Dec. 1889, in N. A. Dunning, ed., *The Farmers' Alliance History and Agricultural Digest*, p. 102.

14. Davis, *A Political Revelation*, pp. 99–100. Here is a good statement of the simple market society. For another, in some ways even clearer, see p. 14.

15. Jones, "Presidential Address," 4 Dec. 1889, in Dunning, *The Farmers Alliance History*, p. 103; also W. Scott Morgan, *History of the Wheel and Alliance, and the*

Impending Revolution, pp. 29, 567; Richmond *Exchange Reporter*, 17 Oct. 1891.

16. See Fred A. Shannon, *The Farmers' Last Frontier*, pp. 106–10, 295–303, chaps. 5, 13; also John D. Hicks, *The Populist Revolt*, pp. 60–74.

17. Dallas *Texas Advance*, 21 Apr. 1894; also Raleigh *Progressive Farmer*, 5 June 1894; Dallas (Ga.) *Herald*, 16 Nov. 1893.

18. Raleigh *Progressive Farmer*, 27 Aug. 1895; also Ozark (Ala.) *Banner-Advertiser*, 4 Apr. 1895; Atlanta *People's Party Paper*, 13 Oct. 1893.

19. See, for instance, Dallas *Texas Advance*, 17 Mar. 1894; Atlanta *People's Party Paper*, 25 May 1894; Thomas E. Watson, *People's Party Campaign Handbook, 1892*, p. 212. For something of an exception, see "Diogenes" in the Gracewood (Ga.) *Wool Hat*, 18 Aug. 1894. He maintained that the Populist party promised to workingmen the "nationalization" of the railroads, telegraph and telephone systems, as well as "the nationalization of every enterprise whenever private control endangers the happiness and contentment of the people who are directly or indirectly concerned." This promised much more than all but a few Arkansas and Texas antimonopoly greenbackers ventured, but it was directed at workingmen only. The demand for public ownership of all public utilities appeared every once in a while in other antimonopoly papers outside Texas. See Hardy (Ark.) *National Reformer*, Apr. 1894; Troy (Ala.) *Jeffersonian*, 6 Apr. 1894; Butler (Ala.) *Choctaw Alliance*, 18 Jan. 1893.

20. See Natchitoches *Louisiana Populist*, 24 Aug. 1894; Atlanta *People's Party Paper*, 20 July 1894; Gracewood (Ga.) *Wool Hat*, 14, 21, and 28 July 1894.

21. See Dallas *Texas Advance*, 28 July 1894; Gracewood (Ga.) *Wool Hat*, 21 July 1894.

22. Watson, *People's Party Campaign Handbook*, pp. 212–13.

23. Goldsboro (N.C.) *Caucasian*, 31 May 1894; also Stephenville (Tex.) *Empire*, 7 Oct. 1892; Raleigh *Caucasian*, 16 July 1896.

24. Raleigh *Caucasian*, 30 May 1895.

25. See Dallas *Texas Advance*, 28 July 1894; Gracewood (Ga.) *Wool Hat*, 10 Mar. 1894.

26. Southern reform papers and books before 1892 did not envisage government ownership as the solution to the problem of the railroads, although their lists of complaints were quite similar before and after, as were their promised results of reform—stimulation of production and protection for the producers, social harmony and balance with an end to strikes, etc. See, for instance, Clinton (N.C.) *Caucasian*, 15 Oct. 1891; Tarboro (N.C.) *Farmers' Advocate*, 9 Sept. 1891; Montgomery (Ala.) *Alliance Herald*, 16 July 1891. Interestingly, in all these early arguments for reforming the railroads appeared the notion that a commission which improved competition would go a long way toward ending the problems caused by the railroads. The adherence of the Southern Alliance to the existing economic system, as they understood it, may have been stronger than that of the Southern Populists. The two Alliance histories published in 1891 spoke for the commission plan with rhetoric that had not altered four years later following the Pullman strike, when the demand had changed to government ownership. See Jones, "Presidential Address," 4 Dec. 1889, in Dunning, *The Farmers' Alliance History*, p. 103; and Morgan, *History of the Wheel and Alliance*, pp. 29–30, 558–609. The partial loosening of the commitment to America's economic system favored a move toward government ownership. By early March 1892 Watson was telling Georgia Populists that the commission plan had failed to control the abuses of the roads and that the only way out was government ownership. See Atlanta *People's Party Paper*, 17 Mar. 1892. Others made the same point at various times, although all supported government ownership by mid-1892. See Tarboro (N.C.) *Farmers' Advocate*, 27 Apr. 1892; Dallas *Texas Advance*, 2 June 1894; Palo Pinto (Tex.) *Tribune*, 17 May 1895; Dallas (Tex.) *Southern Mercury*, 17 Oct. 1895 and 18 June 1896; Stephenville (Tex.) *Empire*, 28 May 1892; Lampasas (Tex.) *People's Journal*, 26 Aug. 1892. In general, during

these first months of 1892 most of the Southern Populists seem to have expressly rejected the idea of government regulation of the railroads as infeasible and moved to advocating government ownership.

27. See Raleigh *Progressive Farmer*, 5 June 1894; Butler (Ala.) *Choctaw Alliance*, 23 Nov. 1892.

28. Dallas (Tex.) *Southern Mercury* in Tarboro (N.C.) *Farmers' Advocate*, 2 Nov. 1892; also Dallas *Texas Advance*, 2 June 1894; Dallas (Tex.) *Southern Mercury*, 24 Oct. 1895; Austin (Tex.) *Argus*, 17 July and 28 Aug. 1894; Hardy (Ark.) *Morgan's Buzz Saw*, Oct. 1894; Butler (Ala.) *Choctaw Alliance*, 23 Nov. 1892.

29. Atlanta *People's Party Paper*, 14 Oct. 1892; also Dallas (Ga.) *Herald*, 28 June 1894.

30. See Atlanta *People's Party Paper*, 15 June 1894; Stephenville (Tex.) *Empire*, 28 May 1892; Richmond *Virginia Sun*, 26 Oct. 1892.

31. Dallas *Texas Advance*, 16 Sept. 1894; also Davis, *A Political Revelation*, p. 210; Watson *People's Party Campaign Handbook*, p. 211.

32. Dallas (Tex.) *Southern Mercury*, 17 Oct. 1895; also 18 June 1896.

33. Ironically, J. H. "Cyclone" Davis, whom some have called Southern Populism's high priest of Jeffersonianism (Merrill D. Peterson, *The Jefferson Image in the American Mind*, p. 257, and C. Vann Woodward, *Origins of the New South, 1877–1913*, pp. 249–50), made the most thorough use among the Southern Populists of the commerce clause, the general welfare clause, and a loose construction of the Constitution. See Davis, *A Political Revelation*, pp. 70–86 and Part IV, especially pp. 140–49.

Chapter 7

1. Atlanta *People's Party Paper*, 21 Apr. 1892; also Austin (Tex.) *People's Advocate*, 24 May 1894; Dallas (Tex.) *Southern Mercury*, 2 May and 25 July 1895 and 30 Jan. 1896; Raleigh *Progressive Farmer*, 27 Sept. 1892; Richmond *Virginia Sun*, 31 May 1893.

2. Natchitoches *Louisiana Populist*, 17 May 1895; also Richmond *Virginia Sun*, 27 July 1892; Atlanta *People's Party Paper*, 8 June 1894 and 6 Sept. 1895; Tarboro (N.C.) *Farmers' Advocate*, 2 Dec. 1891; Dallas *Texas Advance*, 28 Oct. 1893; Anniston *Alabama Leader*, 14 Nov. 1895; Harry Tracy, Appendix, in James H. Davis, *A Political Revelation*, p. 293.

3. See Birmingham *People's Weekly Tribune*, 28 May 1896; Goldsboro (N.C.) *Caucasian*, 12 Jan. 1893; Raleigh *Progressive Farmer*, 9 Feb. 1892; Gracewood (Ga.) *Wool Hat*, 17 Feb. 1894.

4. Dallas (Ga.) *Herald*, 9 Jan. 1896; also, for example, Natchitoches *Louisiana Populist*, 1 Feb. 1895; Atlanta *People's Party Paper*, 10 Apr. 1896; Richmond *Virginia Sun*, 4 May 1892; Little Rock (Ark.) *Dollar*, 13 Dec. 1895; Hardy (Ark.) *Morgan's Buzz Saw*, Oct. 1894; Greenville (Ala.) *Living Truth* in Ozark (Ala.) *Banner-Advertiser*, 6 June 1895.

5. See, for example, Ozark (Ala.) *Banner-Advertiser*, 17 Oct. 1895 and 16 Apr. 1896; Anniston *Alabama Leader*, 26 Sept. 1895; Gibson (Ga.) *Glascock Banner*, 14 Feb. 1895; Clinton (N.C.) *Caucasian*, 23 July 1891; Goldsboro (N.C.) *Caucasian*, 3 Aug. 1893; Raleigh *Caucasian*, 11 Apr. 1895; Raleigh *Progressive Farmer*, 14 May 1895; Stephenville (Tex.) *Empire*, 28 Oct. 1892; Richmond *Virginia Sun*, 9 Oct. 1892; Atlanta *People's Party Paper*, 24 Feb. 1893.

6. Dallas (Tex.) *Southern Mercury*, 21 May 1896; also Atlanta *People's Party Paper*, 25 Aug. 1893.

7. If, for instance, a year's loan of $1000 at ten percent interest was made when ten bales of cotton brought $1000, at the end of the year eleven bales would suffice to pay the principal and the interest for the year. If, however, during the year the supply of money declined fifty percent, the supply of and demand for cotton remaining the same, eleven bales

of cotton would bring only $550, and it would take twice as much work to pay off the loan as it would have when the money was borrowed. The creditor would receive back a dollar worth twice as much in product purchasable as the one loaned.

8. See Ozark (Ala.) *Banner*, 17 May 1894; Ozark (Ala.) *Banner-Advertiser*, 4 June 1896.

9. Wedowee (Ala.) *Randolph Toiler*, 10 Apr. 1896; also Ozark (Ala.) *Banner*, 8 Sept. 1892 and 1 June 1893; Richmond *Virginia Sun*, 5 Apr. 1893; Hardy (Ark.) *Morgan's Buzz Saw*, Oct. 1894. A few southern reformers, particularly the antimonopoly greenbackers, used this idea in a cogent critique of the reasons which their conservative opponents gave for the cause of the panic and depression of the 1890s. Evan Jones, a long-time Alliance leader and prominent Texas Populist, in 1893 pointed out that no one had lost confidence in the "usefulness or value of farm products," "the skill, industry or patriotism of the people," "the stability of the government," or "the productive power of labor and the effectiveness of machinery." These, "the wealth producing factors," remained intact. The people had lost confidence only in a financial system which reduced the "prices of products and the wages of labor" by contracting the money supply. The solution to hard times was not to restore confidence under the old system, but under a new one in which such a contraction and the consequent loss of confidence would be impossible (Dallas *Texas Advance*, 30 Sept. 1893; also Anniston *Alabama Leader*, 28 Nov. 1895; Hardy, Ark., *Morgan's Buzz Saw*, Oct. 1894; Hardy, Ark., *National Reformer*, Oct. 1895). For a more sophisticated form of this idea, one which reveals the accuracy of the Southern Populists' ordering of priorities, see below and chap. 9.

10. Catherine Nugent, ed., *Life Work of Thomas L. Nugent*, p. 223; also Austin (Tex.) *Argus*, 23 Oct. 1894; Hardy (Ark.) *National Reformer*, Apr. 1895.

11. Austin (Tex.) *Argus*, 17 July 1894; also Hardy (Ark.) *Morgan's Buzz Saw*, Oct. 1894. Their simple market society, an ideal which depended on the market exchanges between individual producers, made clear to the reformers the need for consumers in any economic system. Their opponents, more concerned with industrial expansion, tended to assume with the classical economists that consumption would take care of itself. The businessman's form of Social Darwinism helped to perpetuate this simplification by maintaining that the ability to earn great wealth or build an industrial or financial empire was the major determinant of social fitness. On businessmen and Social Darwinism, see Sidney Fine, *Laissez-Faire and the General Welfare State*, pp. 97–102; Richard Hofstadter, *Social Darwinism in American Thought*, pp. 44–46. On the classical economists' notion that there would be a demand for everything produced, see Robert L. Heilbroner, *The Worldly Philosophers*, pp. 91–93.

12. Dallas (Tex.) *Southern Mercury*, 6 Oct. 1892; also, Tracy, Appendix, in Davis, *A Political Revelation*, pp. 335–36.

13. See Dallas (Tex.) *Southern Mercury*, 28 Feb. 1895.

14. Dallas *Texas Advance*, 16 Sept. 1893; also Austin (Tex.) *Argus*, 10 July and 2 Oct. 1894; Ozark (Ala.) *Banner-Advertiser*, 17 Oct. 1895; Richmond *Virginia Sun*, 4 May 1892; Tracy, Appendix, in Davis, *A Political Revelation*, pp. 355–56.

15. Dallas *Texas Advance*, 16 Sept. 1893. This article made the only demand for an expansion of the money supply which might have implied a policy of continued expansion, and this advocacy occurred only once.

16. Raleigh *Caucasian*, 11 Apr. 1895; also 7 Mar. 1895; Goldsboro (N.C.) *Caucasian*, 4 Oct. 1894; Salisbury (N.C.) *Carolina Watchman*, 2 Apr. 1891; Tracy, Appendix, in Davis, *A Political Revelation*, pp. 376–77.

17. The Southern Populists used the immediate post-Civil War period to establish the ideal amount of currency in circulation. This period, the southern reformers felt, had been highly prosperous for farmers; prices had been good and the per capita circulation had been about fifty dollars. Generally, however, the Southern Populists were far less adamant about an ideal per capita circulation of fifty dollars than about an end to contraction and a

stabilizing of the currency in circulation at a much higher level than was current in the 1890s.

18. P = MV/Q. Then if the velocity of money (V) doubles while the quantity of money (M) and the number of transactions (Q) stay the same, the price level (P) doubles. For example: If Q = 10; M = 10; V = 10; then P = 10. If Q = 10; M = 10; V = 20; then P = 20. The same effect on prices could be obtained by doubling the supply of money or halving the number of transactions.

19. Edward Kirkland, *Industry Comes of Age*, pp. 31–33. A few of the antimonopoly greenbackers knew the importance of velocity. Macune did (see Tarboro, N.C., *Farmers' Advocate*, 15 Apr. 1891). So did Harry Tracy in his "The Sub-Treasury Plan," in N. A. Dunning, ed., *The Farmers' Alliance History and Agricultural Digest*, p. 341, although he did not mention it in his Appendix on the subtreasury written for Davis, *A Political Revelation*. Marion Butler, too, apparently also was familiar with the idea. (See Clinton, N.C., *Caucasian*, 2 Apr. 1891.)

20. Natchitoches *Louisiana Populist*, 1 Feb. 1895; also Ozark (Ala.) *Banner-Advertiser*, 9 Apr. 1896; Atlanta *People's Party Paper*, 26 Aug. 1892 and 17 Feb. 1893; Dallas (Ga.) *Herald*, 6 July 1893 and 15 May 1895; Gracewood (Ga.) *Wool Hat*, 17 June 1893 and 4 Aug. 1894; Rutledge (Ga.) *Gleaner* in Ozark (Ala.) *Banner-Advertiser*, 5 Dec. 1895; Wadesboro (N.C.) *Plow Boy*, 18 Mar. 1896; Raleigh *Progressive Farmer*, 31 May and 27 Sept. 1892, 11 and 25 Aug. 1896; Goldsboro (N.C.) *Caucasian*, 6 July and 21 Sept. 1893; Tarboro (N.C.) *Farmers' Advocate*, 6 Jan. 1892; Salisbury (N.C.) *Carolina Watchman*, 17 Dec. 1891; Anniston *Alabama Leader*, 3 Oct. 1895; Dallas (Tex.) *Southern Mercury*, 21 May 1896; Dallas *Texas Advance*, 28 Oct. 1893; Hardy (Ark.) *Morgan's Buzz Saw*, Aug. 1895; Hardy (Ark.) *National Reformer*, Jan. 1894; Richmond *Virginia Sun*, 31 May 1893; Davis, *A Political Revelation*, p. 221.

21. Ozark (Ala.) *Banner*, 22 June 1893; also 18 Aug. 1892; Austin (Tex.) *Argus*, 7 Aug. 1894; Hardy (Ark.) *National Reformer*, Mar. 1894; Ozark (Ala.) *Banner-Advertiser*, 6 June 1895; Natchitoches *Louisiana Populist*, 3 May 1895; Richmond *Virginia Sun*, 31 May 1893; Raleigh *Caucasian*, 4 July 1895; Raleigh *Progressive Farmer*, 2 June 1891 and 17 Apr. 1894; Beaver Dam (N.C.) *Our Home*, 21 June 1893; Salisbury (N.C.) *Carolina Watchman*, 3 Nov. 1892; Atlanta *People's Party Paper*, 14 Jan. 1892; Dallas (Ga.) *Herald*, 24 Aug. 1893; Gracewood (Ga.) *Wool Hat*, 4 Mar. 1893.

22. See Dallas (Tex.) *Southern Mercury*, 19 Apr. 1894, 3 Jan. 1895, and 18 June 1896; Raleigh *Progressive Farmer*, 31 Mar. 1896; Raleigh *Caucasian*, 27 Dec. 1894; Dallas *Texas Advance*, 23 Dec. 1893; Greenville (Ala.) *Living Truth* in Ozark (Ala.) *Banner-Advertiser*, 4 Apr. 1895; Hardy (Ark.) *Morgan's Buzz Saw*, Oct. 1895; Gracewood (Ga.) *Wool Hat*, 26 Aug. 1893; Ozark (Ala.) *Banner-Advertiser*, 9 Apr. 1896. Harry Tracy, the Texas antimonopoly greenbacker, made the same point using English metallic currency to show that even in England, on the gold standard, money was basically fiat (Tracy, Appendix, in Davis, *A Political Revelation*, pp. 339–40).

23. Dallas *Texas Advance*, 21 Apr. 1894; also 28 Apr. 1894; Dallas (Tex.) *Southern Mercury*, 3 Jan. and 19 Dec. 1895; Raleigh *Caucasian*, 21 Nov. 1895; Dallas (Ga.) *Herald*, 30 May 1895; Tracy, Appendix, in Davis, *A Political Revelation*, p. 338.

24. Dallas (Tex.) *Southern Mercury*, 29 Nov. 1894 and 2 May 1895.

25. Anniston *Alabama Leader*, 26 Sept. 1895. The Southern Populists' simple market society did not obviate the use of money but required that it serve solely to facilitate the exchange of goods between individual independent producers.

26. Dallas (Tex.) *Southern Mercury*, 3 Jan. 1895; also Raleigh *Progressive Farmer*, 27 Sept. 1892; Atlanta *People's Party Paper*, 21 and 28 Jan. 1892; Gracewood (Ga.) *Wool Hat*, 15 July 1893.

27. Gibson (Ga.) *Glascock Banner*, 14 Feb. 1895.

28. Warren Plains (N.C.) *People's Paper*, 16 Oct. 1896.

29. Dallas *Texas Advance*, 14 Oct. 1893; also Anniston *Alabama Leader*, 22 June 1894.

30. Goldsboro (N.C.) *Caucasian*, 6 July 1893; also 18 Feb. 1892; Raleigh *Progressive Farmer*, 27 Oct. and 15 Dec. 1891; Dallas (Tex.) *Southern Mercury*, 3 Nov. 1892 and 1 Aug. 1895; Hardy (Ark.) *National Reformer*, Mar. 1894; Richmond *Virginia Sun*, 25 May 1892; Austin (Tex.) *Argus*, 7 Aug. 1894; Dallas *Texas Advance*, 19 May 1894.

31. Stephenville (Tex.) *Empire*, 28 Oct. 1892.

32. Ibid.; also Dallas (Tex.) *Southern Mercury*, 28 Mar. 1895; Dahlonega (Ga.) *Signal*, 2 Nov. 1894.

33. Atlanta *People's Party Paper*, 29 July 1892; also 30 Sept. 1892.

34. Dallas (Tex.) *Southern Mercury*, 26 Apr. 1894.

35. Lawrence Goodwyn, *Democratic Promise*, pp. 152–53, 167–68.

36. Lampasas (Tex.) *People's Journal*, 28 Oct. 1892; also Dallas *Texas Advance*, 25 Nov. 1893. On the need for a flexible currency, see also *Florida Alliance* in Tarboro (N.C.) *Farmers' Advocate*, 5 Aug. 1891; Raleigh *Progressive Farmer*, 27 Oct. 1891; Clinton (N.C.) *Caucasian*, 23 July 1891; Montgomery (Ala.) *Alliance Herald*, 4 May 1893; Dallas (Tex.) *Southern Mercury*, 18 Jan. 1894 and 1 Aug. 1895; Beaver Dam (N.C.) *Our Home*, 26 May 1893; Davis, *A Political Revelation*, pp. 230–31; Tracy, Appendix, in Davis, *A Political Revelation*, pp. iii, 355–56.

37. Tarboro (N.C.) *Farmers' Advocate*, 15 Apr. 1891; also Richmond *Exchange Reporter*, 17 Oct. 1891; Dunning, *The Farmers' Alliance History*, pp. 341–42; Tracy, Appendix, in Davis, *A Political Revelation*, pp. iii, 353–54. The question of how such a seasonal fluctuation in the money supply—up to forty percent—affected other groups in society, notably the working people, usually went unconsidered. It was another mark on their thinking of the Southern Populists' largely rural orientation and experience. For an exception, see Tracy, Appendix, in Davis, *A Political Revelation*, pp. 316, 357–59, 367, 380–81; Tracy, "The Sub-Treasury Plan," in Dunning, *The Farmers' Alliance History*, p. 341.

38. C. W. Macune, L. L. Polk, L. F. Livingston, W. S. Morgan, H. S. P. Ashby, "Report of the Committee on the Monetary System," St. Louis convention, National Farmers' Alliance and Industrial Union, 7 Dec. 1889, in Dunning, *The Farmers' Alliance History*, p. 127; also Hardy (Ark.) *National Reformer*, Feb. 1895.

39. Montgomery (Ala.) *Alliance Herald*, 19 Nov. 1891; also 4 May 1893; Raleigh *Progressive Farmer*, 8 Jan. and 27 Aug. 1895; Atlanta *People's Party Paper*, 28 Apr. 1892 and 8 June 1894; Clinton (N.C.) *Caucasian*, 17 Sept. 1891; Dallas (Tex.) *Southern Mercury*, 1 Aug. 1895 and 16 Jan. 1896.

40. See Dallas *Texas Advance*, 28 Oct. 1893; Atlanta *People's Party Paper*, 14 Oct. 1892; Dallas (Ga.) *Herald*, 1 Feb. 1894; Butler (Ala.) *Choctaw Alliance*, 19 July 1893; Dallas (Tex.) *Southern Mercury*, 29 Apr. 1894.

41. For banker control, see Dallas *Texas Advance*, 16 Sept. 1893; Gracewood (Ga.) *Wool Hat*, 17 June 1893; Goldsboro (N.C.) *Caucasian*, 18 Feb. 1892; Montgomery (Ala.) *Alliance Herald*, 10 May 1894; C. W. Macune, et al., "Report of the Committee on the Monetary System," 7 Dec. 1889, in Dunning, *The Farmers' Alliance History*, pp. 125–26.

42. Although Kellogg, like the Southern Populists, did not have a clearly articulated labor theory of value (see David Montgomery, *Beyond Equality*, n. 7 p. 428), his linking of labor and the creation of wealth to a definition of money as a legal tender, whose only function was to represent wealth, was closer to the Southern Populists' ideas than Campbell's definition of value as usefulness. See Robert P. Sharkey, *Money, Class, and Party*, p. 188; Montgomery, *Beyond Equality*, p. 428.

43. Atlanta *People's Party Paper*, 18 Feb. 1892; also 28 Apr. 1892; Richmond *Virginia Sun*, 27 Apr. 1892; Gracewood (Ga.) *Wool Hat*, 7 Jan. 1893. This is another example of the influence of Kellogg referred to above and below.

44. Atlanta *People's Party Paper*, 14 Oct. 1892.

45. See Harold D. Woodman, *King Cotton and His Retainers*, pp. 347–48, on the difficulties of imposing a usury law where high credit costs were the life blood of the tenancy system.

46. Austin (Tex.) *Argus*, 14 Aug. 1894.

47. Chester McArthur Destler, *American Radicalism, 1865–1901*, pp. 51–55; Walter T. K. Nugent, *Money and American Society*, pp. 51–53; Sharkey, *Money, Class, and Party*, p. 189.

48. Montgomery (Ala.) *Alliance Herald*, 3 May 1894; also Ozark (Ala.) *Banner*, 2 June 1892; Dallas (Tex.) *Southern Mercury*, 19 Apr. 1894; Goldsboro (N.C.) *Caucasian*, 12 May 1892; Richmond *Virginia Sun*, 27 Apr. 1892; Little Rock (Ark.) *Dollar*, 13 Dec. 1895; J. F. Tillman, S. B. Erwin, W. H. Barton, B. J. Kendrick, "Report of the Commitee on Land," St. Louis convention, National Farmers' Alliance and Industrial Union, 7 Dec. 1889, in Dunning, *The Farmers' Alliance History*, pp. 131–32.

49. Ozark (Ala.) *Banner-Advertiser*, 7 May 1896.

50. For exceptions, see Anniston *Alabama Leader*, 26 Sept. 1895; Raleigh *Progressive Farmer*, 10 Nov. 1891; Mineola (Tex.) *Alliance Courier* in Gracewood (Ga.) *Wool Hat*, 21 Oct. 1893.

51. Raleigh *Progressive Farmer*, 23 June 1896; also Salisbury (N.C.) *Carolina Watchman*, 20 Aug. 1891; Anniston *Alabama Leader*, 24 Oct. and 14 Nov. 1895; Birmingham *People's Weekly Tribune*, 28 May 1896; Hardy (Ark.) *Morgan's Buzz Saw*, July 1895 and July 1896; Gracewood (Ga.) *Wool Hat*, 28 Jan. and 22 July 1893; Atlanta *Freedom* in Dallas (Ga.) *Herald*, 31 Aug. 1893; Atlanta *People's Party Paper*, 31 Mar. 1893.

52. *Farm Record* (Tex.) in Comanche (Tex.) *Pioneer Exponent*, 2 Jan. 1896; also Hardy (Ark.) *National Reformer*, Aug. 1893; Hardy (Ark.) *Morgan's Buzz Saw*, July 1895.

53. *Florida Alliance* in Atlanta *People's Party Paper*, 28 Apr. 1892; also Salisbury (N.C.) *Carolina Watchman*, 8 Oct. 1891; Goldsboro (N.C.) *Caucasian*, 31 Aug. 1893.

54. For the exceptions, see the antimonopoly greenbackers in Texas. For instance, Austin (Tex.) *Argus*, 14 Aug. 1894; Dallas *Texas Advance*, 31 Mar. 1894.

55. Atlanta *People's Party Paper*, 28 Sept. 1894.

56. Raleigh *Progressive Farmer*, 8 Oct. 1895; also Atlanta *People's Party Paper*, 29 Nov. 1895; Dallas (Ga.) *Herald*, 1 June 1893.

57. A few others, like the editor of the *Carolina Watchman*, had no such perceptual difficulty. The large number of transactions carried out on a credit basis indicated to him the lack of an adequate supply of currency to do the nation's business. The backing for this credit was only the "changing, unreliable forms of individual responsibility, fortified by only a fraction of a cent on the dollar." This kind of credit inflation, with its accompanying high interest rate, allowed Wall Street to rob the people of their hard-earned wealth. He wanted it ended by an expansion of the money supply and the direct issue of legal tender currency to the producers at a very low rate of interest (Salisbury, N.C., *Carolina Watchman*, 23 July 1891). While he obviously shared with the editor of the *Texas Advance* some understanding of the function of credit in an industrial capitalist society, this man also wanted to see it by and large eliminated.

58. See Ozark (Ala.) *Banner*, 20 Oct. 1892; Dallas (Tex.) *Southern Mercury*, 18 May 1893.

59. Raleigh *Progressive Farmer*, 8 Dec. 1891. For Murdock's whole argument, see 13 Oct., 10 Nov., and 15 Dec. 1891 and 12 Jan., 9 and 16 Feb. 1892.

60. Troy (Ala.) *Jeffersonian*, 19 Jan. 1894. For the demand for a cash basis, see also Atlanta *Living Issues* in Gracewood (Ga.) *Wool Hat*, 6 May 1893; Ozark (Ala.) *Banner*, 8 Sept. 1892.

61. For the demand for a cash-only financial system, see Hamilton (Tex.) *Progress*, 31 Mar. 1893; Dallas (Tex.) *Southern Mercury*, 23 May and 11 July 1895; Hardy (Ark.) *Morgan's Buzz Saw*, Oct. 1895; Tracy, Appendix, in Davis, *A Political Revelation*, p. 292.

62. Dallas *Texas Advance*, 31 Mar. 1894.

63. Ibid., 16 Sept. 1893.

64. Polk's Ocala speech, Dec. 1890, box 12, vol. 64, L. L. Polk Papers.

65. See Tarboro (N.C.) *Farmers' Advocate*, 2 Sept. 1891; Raleigh *Progressive Farmer*, 23 June and 21 July 1891.

66. Osborne to Butler, 19 Sept. 1896, box 3, folder 37, Marion Butler Papers; also Raleigh *Caucasian*, 7 Mar., 4 Apr., and 21 Nov. 1895 and 13 Feb. 1896; Raleigh *Progressive Farmer*, 8 Jan. 1895; Washington, D.C., *National Economist* in Atlanta *People's Party Paper*, 11 Feb. 1892; Atlanta *People's Party Paper*, 31 Mar. 1893 and 12 July 1895; Henderson (N.C.) *Vance Farmer*, 20 Sept. 1892; Butler (Ala.) *Choctaw Alliance*, 24 Jan. 1894; Natchitoches *Louisiana Populist*, 21 Sept. 1894; Dallas (Tex.) *Southern Mercury*, 26 Apr. 1894; Fountain to Butler, 13 Aug. 1895, box 1, folder 16, Marion Butler Papers.

Chapter 8

1. See, for instance, Goldsboro (N.C.) *Caucasian*, 15 June and 13 July 1893 and 15 Feb. 1894; Raleigh *Caucasian*, 21 Nov. 1895; Atlanta *People's Party Paper*, 14 Apr. 1892, 7 Dec. 1894, 1 Feb. and 18 Oct. 1895, and 10 July 1896; Wadesboro (N.C.) *Plow Boy*, 18 Mar. 1896; Raleigh *Progressive Farmer*, 17 Apr. 1894 and 13 Aug. 1895; Dahlonega (Ga.) *Signal*, 18 Nov. 1892 and 18 Aug. 1893; Dallas (Ga.) *Herald*, 15 June 1893 and 1 Feb. 1894; Gibson (Ga.) *Glascock Banner*, 21 Mar. 1895; Gracewood (Ga.) *Wool Hat*, 17 June 1893 and 28 July 1894; Anniston *Alabama Leader*, 19 Dec. 1895; Wedowee (Ala.) *Randolph Toiler*, 1 May 1896; Geneva (Ala.) *Record*, 3 June 1891; Natchitoches *Louisiana Populist*, 15 Mar. 1895; Ozark (Ala.) *Banner-Advertiser*, 9 Apr. 1896; Dallas (Tex.) *Southern Mercury*, 19 Apr. 1894, 24 Jan. and 26 Sept. 1895, and 2 Jan., 12 Mar. 1896; Dallas *Texas Advance*, 18 Nov. and 2 Dec. 1893 and 19 May, 30 June 1894; Richmond *Virginia Sun*, 18 May 1892, 28 June 1893, and 20 Dec. 1894; Hardy (Ark.) *National Reformer*, Mar. 1894; Little Rock (Ark.) *Dollar*, 13 Dec. 1895; Searcy (Ark.) *Southern Economist*, 23 May 1895.

2. See, for instance, Atlanta *People's Party Paper*, 19 Jan., 23 Nov., and 7 Dec. 1894; Comanche (Tex.) *Pioneer Exponent*, 2 Jan. 1896; Raleigh *Progressive Farmer*, 11 July 1893; Goldsboro (N.C.) *Caucasian*, 23 Nov. 1893 and 1 Feb. 1894; Dallas (Ga.) *Herald*, 2 Nov. 1893 and 10 Jan. 1895; Montgomery *Alabama Monitor*, 30 Oct. 1896; Dallas (Tex.) *Southern Mercury*, 19 Apr. 1894 and 1 Aug. 1895; Dallas *Texas Advance*, 24 Mar. 1894.

3. See Atlanta *People's Party Paper*, 8 Sept. 1893, 23 Nov. 1894, and 18 Oct. 1895; Raleigh *Progressive Farmer*, 11 July 1893; Dallas (Tex.) *Southern Mercury*, 29 Nov. 1894; Hardy (Ark.) *National Reformer*, Mar. 1894.

4. Dallas (Tex.) *Southern Mercury*, 2 May 1895; also Goldsboro (N.C.) *Caucasian*, 13 July 1893; Nashville *Weekly Toiler*, 28 Oct. 1891.

5. See Dallas (Ga.) *Herald*, 30 May 1895; Atlanta *People's Party Paper*, 23 Nov. 1894.

6. See Raleigh *Caucasian*, 21 May 1896; Hardy (Ark.) *National Reformer*, Jan. 1894.

7. See Raleigh *Caucasian*, 21 May 1896; Richmond *Virginia Sun*, 23 Aug. 1893 and 20 Dec. 1894; Hardy (Ark.) *Morgan's Buzz Saw*, July 1896; Gracewood (Ga.) *Wool Hat*, 25

Mar. 1893; Hardy (Ark.) *National Reformer*, Oct. 1893; Montgomery (Ala.) *Alliance Herald*, 19 Nov. 1891.

8. Dallas (Tex.) *Southern Mercury*, 11 July 1895; Dallas *Texas Advance*, 14 Apr. 1894; Atlanta *People's Party Paper*, 23 Nov. 1894; Hamilton (Tex.) *Progress*, 31 Mar. 1893; James H. Davis, *A Political Revelation*, pp. 230–31; Harry Tracy, Appendix, in Davis, *A Political Revelation*, pp. 313–14, 378.

9. These mentors included Radical Republicans such as Thaddeus Stevens, Ben Wade, and Ben Butler. For Butler, see Hans Trefousse, *Ben Butler*, pp. 193–94, 206, 218, 236–37. For William Kelley, see David Montgomery, *Beyond Equality*, pp. 344–45; Robert P. Sharkey, *Money, Class, and Party*, pp. 131, 279, 304. For Ignatius Donnelly, see Martin Ridge, *Ignatius Donnelly*, pp. 165–74. For Weaver, see Fred Emory Haynes, *James Baird Weaver*, pp. 94–95, chaps. 7–9. And the southern reformers acknowledged their debt. See, for instance, W. Scott Morgan, *History of the Wheel and Alliance, and the Impending Revolution*, pp. 529–41; Tuscaloosa (Ala.) *Journal*, 10 Oct. 1894; Thomas E. Watson, *People's Party Campaign Handbook, 1892*, p. 65; Hardy (Ark.) *Morgan's Buzz Saw*, July 1895. For some discussion of this Populist historical inheritance, see Bruce Palmer, "The Southern Populists Remember," pp. 131–49.

10. Watson, *People's Party Campaign Handbook*, pp. 14–15; also Dallas *Texas Advance*, 18 Nov. 1893.

11. See Butler (Ala.) *Choctaw Alliance*, 11 Feb. 1896; Natchitoches *Louisiana Populist*, 1 Feb. 1895; Dallas *Texas Advance*, 14 Oct. and 18 Nov. 1893; Dallas (Tex.) *Southern Mercury*, 18 Jan. 1894, 28 Nov. 1895, and 6 Feb. 1896; Hardy (Ark.) *Morgan's Buzz Saw*, Dec. 1895; Watson, *People's Party Campaign Handbook*, pp. 65–66. Insofar as this created extra demand for gold the Populist charge was true. Of course, the greenbacks did not lose value in comparison to the gold dollar but in comparison with the gold in the dollar. For information on the exception clauses, see Edward Kirkland, *Industry Comes of Age*, pp. 16–17; Wesley C. Mitchell, *A History of the Greenbacks with Special Reference to the Economic Consequences of their Issue*, pp. 76–79; Sharkey, *Money, Class, and Party*, pp. 42, 50.

12. Dallas (Tex.) *Southern Mercury*, 18 Jan. 1894; also Morgan, *History of the Wheel and Alliance*, pp. 524–32.

13. Dallas *Texas Advance*, 18 Nov. 1893; Austin (Tex.) *Argus*, 31 July 1894.

14. From their wartime peak in Jan. 1864 of $449 million, they were reduced to $356 million by the end of 1867. In 1873 and 1874 the amount was raised to $382 million but set at $347 million in May 1878 (Milton Friedman and Anna Jacobson Schwartz, *A Monetary History of the United States, 1867–1960*, p. 24).

15. Watson, *People's Party Campaign Handbook*, p. 68; also *Nebraska Independent* in Atlanta *People's Party Paper*, 9 Oct. 1896. Others sometimes talked of the postwar contraction. See Dahlonega (Ga.) *Signal*, 6 May 1892; Richmond *Virginia Sun*, 5 Apr. 1893; *Faulkner County Wheel* (Ark.), 1 July 1891; "Don't Throw Your Vote Away," Populist campaign pamphlet, 38–360, William DuBose Sheldon Papers; Dallas (Tex.) *Southern Mercury*, 6 Oct. 1892; Comanche (Tex.) *Pioneer Exponent*, 2 Jan. 1896; Stephenville (Tex.) *Empire*, 25 June 1892. It should be noted that the Southern Populists did not argue that all the greenbacks had been destroyed. They had little reason to do so, since in the 1890s greenbacks represented a large part of whatever currency they saw. The act of 31 May 1878 stabilized the U.S. notes in circulation at $347 million (Friedman and Schwartz, *A Monetary History*, p. 24).

16. Natchitoches *Louisiana Populist*, 31 Aug. 1894. However, this greenbacker's figures for the amount of greenbacks issued—$1,800,000,000—was vastly inflated. Perhaps it included some of the war bonds and treasury notes which often had, like the 5–20s (government bonds payable in five years and redeemable in twenty), quasi-monetary

qualities. For the 5–20s, see Irwin Unger, *The Greenback Era*, pp. 16–17. For the same story the Louisiana Populist told, see Dallas (Tex.) *Southern Mercury*, 6 Oct. 1892.

17. Stephenville (Tex.) *Empire*, 28 Oct. 1892; Richmond *Virginia Sun*, 28 June 1893.

18. Atlanta *People's Party Paper*, 16 Aug. 1895; Dallas *Texas Advance*, 25 Nov. 1893. This, of course, harks back to the Pendleton plan of 1868 and the earlier ultraradical demand that the 5–20s be redeemed in greenbacks. See Montgomery, *Beyond Equality*, pp. 344–51; Sharkey, *Money, Class, and Party*, pp. 99–101.

19. Stephenville (Tex.) *Empire*, 28 Oct. 1892; Dallas (Ga.) *Herald*, 11 May 1893.

20. Stephenville (Tex.) *Empire*, 28 Oct. 1892.

21. See ibid.; Hardy (Ark.) *Morgan's Buzz Saw*, Oct. 1894; Atlanta *People's Party Paper*, 27 Sept. 1895.

22. Dallas (Tex.) *Southern Mercury*, 25 Oct. 1894.

23. Stephenville (Tex.) *Empire*, 28 Oct. 1892; Hardy (Ark.) *Morgan's Buzz Saw*, Oct. 1894.

24. Dallas *Texas Advance*, 19 May 1894.

25. They correctly assumed that with an entirely greenback monetary system, a "fiduciary standard," the government alone controlled the supply of currency (Friedman and Schwartz, *A Monetary History*, p. 51).

26. Dallas (Ga.) *Herald*, 18 Apr. 1895. Although a couple of strong greenbackers wrote in the Gracewood (Ga.) *Wool Hat*, and the editor was conversant with greenback theory, little if any substantive discussion of greenbacks appeared in the *Wool Hat*'s pages. For exceptions, see J. L. Cartledge, 4 and 25 Mar. 1893.

27. Dallas (Ga.) *Herald*, 4 July 1895; also 6 July 1893.

28. See Raleigh *Progressive Farmer*, 31 Jan. 1893; Hardy (Ark.) *National Reformer*, Nov. 1893 and Mar. 1894; Montgomery *Alabama Monitor*, 30 Oct. 1896.

29. Dallas (Tex.) *Southern Mercury*, 11 Oct. 1894; also 29 Nov. 1894 and 2 May 1895.

30. Lampasas (Tex.) *People's Journal*, 20 Jan. 1893.

31. Dallas (Ga.) *Herald*, 3 Aug. 1893.

32. Atlanta *People's Party Paper*, 19 Jan. 1894; Dallas *Texas Advance*, 2 Dec. 1893. Of the fifty or so letters printed for the *Advance*'s contest, every one advocated the government issue of greenbacks as the proper solution to the deficit.

33. The Southern Populists rarely discussed the possibility that free coinage of silver would drive gold out of circulation. They rarely, if ever, saw any gold. Nor were they concerned, since silver was far more plentiful than gold. They felt little need to debate the issue, since free silver was primarily important for its promise to expand the money supply. See below.

34. Friedman and Schwartz, *A Monetary History*, n. 52 p. 134.

35. Ibid., p. 115.

36. See Atlanta *People's Party Paper*, 8 July 1892, 3 Nov. 1893, 22 Mar. 1895, and 24 July 1896; Dahlonega (Ga.) *Signal*, 1 Apr. 1892; Dallas (Ga.) *Herald*, 6 July 1893 and 23 May 1895; Ozark (Ala.) *Banner-Advertiser*, 17 Oct. 1895 and 7 May 1896; Austin (Tex.) *Argus*, 11 Sept. 1894; Hardy (Ark.) *Morgan's Buzz Saw*, Oct. 1895; Raleigh *Caucasian*, 6 Aug. 1896; Gracewood (Ga.) *Wool Hat*, 24 June 1893; Nashville *Weekly Toiler*, 2 Feb. 1892.

37. Dallas (Tex.) *Southern Mercury*, 3 Sept. 1896; also 4 July 1895; Austin (Tex.) *Argus*, 11 Sept. 1894; Greenville (Ala.) *Living Truth* in Ozark (Ala.) *Banner-Advertiser*, 6 June 1895.

38. Atlanta *People's Party Paper*, 29 July 1892 and 3 Nov. 1893; Dallas (Ga.) *Herald*, 23 May 1895.

39. Nashville *Weekly Toiler*, 25 Feb. 1891.

40. Salisbury (N.C.) *Carolina Watchman*, 21 Apr. 1892; also Tarboro (N.C.) *Farmers'*

Notes to Pages 101–4

Advocate, 23 Mar. 1892; Atlanta *People's Party Paper*, 28 July 1893; Richmond *Virginia Sun*, 4 May 1892; Hardy (Ark.) *National Reformer*, Apr. 1894; Natchitoches *Louisiana Populist*, 1 Mar. 1895; Wadesboro (N.C.) *Plow Boy*, 18 Mar. 1896 .

41. Ozark (Ala.) *Banner*, 9 Feb. 1893; also Butler (Ala.) *Choctaw Alliance*, 19 July 1893; Dallas (Ga.) *Herald*, 25 Oct. 1894; Gibson (Ga.) *Glascock Banner*, 18 July 1895; Gracewood (Ga.) *Wool Hat*, 27 Oct. 1894; Raleigh *Caucasian*, 30 Apr., 4 June, and 5 Nov. 1896; Wadesboro (N.C.) *Plow Boy*, 25 Sept. 1895; Raleigh *Progressive Farmer*, 19 May 1891 and 8 Jan., 14 May 1895; Ozark (Ala.) *Banner-Advertiser*, 19 Dec. 1895; Richmond *Virginia Sun*, 18 May 1892, 5 July and 3 Nov. 1893, and 13 Feb. 1896.

42. Raleigh *Progressive Farmer*, 3 Jan. and 21 Nov. 1893.

43. Raleigh *Caucasian*, 15 Oct. 1896.

44. J. B. Schulken to Butler, 2 Dec. 1896, box 4, folder 49, Marion Butler Papers.

45. Dallas (Tex.) *Southern Mercury*, 2 Mar. 1893.

46. Another notion contrary to the greenbackers' ideas about money was that the 1873 demonetization of silver had caused most, if not all, of the contraction from which Americans suffered. In Mar. 1894 the editor of the *Progressive Farmer* stated that "the shrinkage of values began in 1873, immediately after silver was demonetized" (20 Mar. 1894). It was not the first time he had said so (Raleigh *Progressive Farmer*, 14 Mar. 1893). An important North Carolina Populist, W. H. Kitchin, wrote in May 1895 that 1873 marked the beginning of the disastrous drop in farm prices, because of the demonetization of silver (Raleigh *Progressive Farmer*, 14 May 1895). Marion Butler's paper, the *Caucasian*, marked the contraction of the currency from the same year and the same act of infamy. (Raleigh *Caucasian*, 9 May 1895; also Salisbury, N.C., *Carolina Watchman*, 3 Nov. 1892.)

47. Raleigh *Progressive Farmer*, 25 Aug. 1896.

48. See chap. 11, below.

49. Gibson (Ga.) *Glascock Banner*, 18 July 1895.

50. Richmond *Virginia Sun*, 31 May 1893.

51. Wadesboro (N.C.) *Plow Boy*, 18 Mar. 1896.

52. Dallas (Tex.) *Southern Mercury*, 16 May 1895 and 5 Mar. 1896.

53. See Raleigh *Caucasian*, 18 June 1891 and 30 Apr. 1896; Atlanta *People's Party Paper*, 3 Nov. 1893; Oxford (Ala.) *Voice*, 23 Jan. 1891; Ozark (Ala.) *Banner-Advertiser*, 12 Mar. and 23 Apr. 1896; Butler (Ala.) *Choctaw Alliance*, 15 Feb. 1893; Gracewood (Ga.) *Wool Hat*, 27 Oct. 1894.

54. Atlanta *People's Party Paper*, 28 Sept. 1894.

55. See Raleigh *Caucasian*, 17 Oct. 1895 and 15 Oct. 1896; Raleigh *Progressive Farmer*, 23 May 1893; Ozark (Ala.) *Banner-Advertiser*, 23 Apr. 1896; Richmond *Virginia Sun*, 18 May 1892.

56. See Ozark (Ala.) *Banner*, 8 Sept. 1892; Montgomery (Ala.) *Alliance Herald*, 4 May 1893; Dallas (Tex.) *Southern Mercury*, 2 Mar. 1893; Richmond *Virginia Sun*, 6 July 1892 and 14 June 1893.

57. Dallas (Tex.) *Southern Mercury*, 17 Oct. 1895.

58. Ibid., 7 Nov. 1895.

59. Ibid., 20 Aug. and 15 Oct. 1896.

60. This, of course, was what happened to the Treasury's gold reserve in late 1894, 1895, and 1896 (Friedman and Schwartz, *A Monetary History*, pp. 111–13). And the continued sale of gold bonds by the Cleveland administration was what Nugent said it was, an effort to preserve the Treasury reserve and keep the United States on the gold standard (Friedman and Schwartz, *A Monetary History*, n. 35 p. 111 and pp. 111–12, 117, 128).

61. Catherine Nugent, ed., *Life Work of Thomas L. Nugent*, pp. 227–29; also Dallas (Tex.) *Southern Mercury*, 25 Dec. 1895 and 5 Mar., 6 and 20 Aug., 3 Sept., 1 Oct., and 26 Nov. 1896.

62. The only exception to this which I could find was George Boggs, an old Allianceman and Populist leader in North Carolina. For his recognition of the difference between the Populists and the Democrats on free silver in 1896, see n. 72, chap. 11, below.

63. C. W. Macune, L. L. Polk, L. F. Livingston, W. S. Morgan, H. S. P. Ashby, "Report of the Committee on the Monetary System," St. Louis convention, National Farmers' Alliance and Industrial Union, 7 Dec. 1889, in N. A. Dunning, ed., *The Farmers' Alliance History and Agricultural Digest*, pp. 124–30.

64. Ibid., pp. 127–28. Two outstanding discussions of the subtreasury plan, which contain most of the points I cover below, are Harry Tracy, Appendix, in Davis, *A Political Revelation*, pp. 292–399, and Harry Tracy, "The Sub-Treasury Plan," in Dunning, *The Farmers' Alliance History*, pp. 336–54.

65. Tarboro (N.C.) *Farmers' Advocate*, 2 Sept. 1891; also Raleigh *Progressive Farmer*, 5 May and 7 July 1891 and 19 Jan. 1892; Salisbury (N.C.) *Carolina Watchman*, 23 Apr. 1891 and 14 Jan. and 26 May 1892; Atlanta *People's Party Paper*, 31 Dec. 1891 and 21 Jan. 1892; Dallas (Tex.) *Southern Mercury*, 8 Jan. 1891.

66. See Atlanta *People's Party Paper*, 18 Feb. 1892. The plan Watson offered Congress in late 1891, in fact, had some important changes in detail from the St. Louis plan. See also Raleigh *Progressive Farmer*, 19 Jan. 1892; Salisbury (N.C.) *Carolina Watchman*, 2 Apr. and 1 Oct. 1891 and 18 Feb. 1892; Clinton (N.C.) *Caucasian*, 23 July, 22 Oct., and 31 Dec. 1891. For the Omaha platform, see Norman Pollack, ed., *The Populist Mind*, pp. 60–66.

67. See Tarboro (N.C.) *Farmers' Advocate*, 8 July 1891 and 13 Jan. 1892; Atlanta *People's Party Paper*, 30 Sept. 1892 and 31 July 1896; Salisbury (N.C.) *Carolina Watchman*, 29 Jan. and 16 July 1891; Raleigh *Progressive Farmer*, 14 July and 24 Nov. 1891; Gracewood (Ga.) *Wool Hat*, 8 Apr. 1893.

68. Concord (N.C.) *Standard* in Salisbury (N.C.) *Carolina Watchman*, 29 Oct. 1891.

69. Lampasas (Tex.) *People's Journal*, 19 Aug. 1892; also Salisbury (N.C.) *Carolina Watchman*, 15 Jan. and 16 July 1891; Raleigh *Progressive Farmer*, 3 Jan. 1893; Clinton (N.C.) *Caucasian*, 7 May 1891; Butler (Ala.) *Choctaw Alliance*, 26 July 1893; Atlanta *People's Party Paper*, 16 Sept. 1892; Dallas (Tex.) *Southern Mercury* in Butler (Ala.) *Choctaw Alliance*, 31 May 1893.

70. See Dallas (Tex.) *Southern Mercury*, 16 Jan. 1896. A North Carolina Alliance editor suggested that to guarantee that free silver coinage reached the people, "the principle involved in the sub-treasury" should regulate its distribution (Tarboro, N.C., *Farmers' Advocate*, 21 Oct. 1891). This application was rare, however. Unless they were committed greenbackers most southern reformers did not specify what kind of money the subtreasuries should distribute. Greenbackers did not care, since all money was fiat anyway.

71. Lawrence Goodwyn, *Democratic Promise*, pp. 150–53, 167–69, 566–67; C. Vann Woodward, *Origins of the New South, 1877–1913*, p. 199. John D. Hicks in *The Populist Revolt*, pp. 188–89, apparently erred in crediting Harry Skinner of North Carolina with the original idea.

72. Actually there were four steps. The farmer sold to a buyer or a broker, who in turn sold to a carrier. Fred A. Shannon, *The Farmer's Last Frontier*, p. 117.

73. Charles W. Macune in Tarboro (N.C.) *Farmers' Advocate*, 15 Apr. 1891; Salisbury (N.C.) *Carolina Watchman*, 16 July 1891.

74. Watson, *People's Party Campaign Handbook*, pp. 200–201; Atlanta *People's Party Paper*, 17 Mar. 1892.

75. Salisbury (N.C.) *Carolina Watchman*, 16 July 1891; Clinton (N.C.) *Caucasian*, 6 Aug. 1891; Goldsboro (N.C.) *Caucasian*, 13 July 1893; Montgomery (Ala.) *Alliance Herald*, 19 Nov. 1891; Richmond *Virginia Sun*, 8 June 1892; Nashville *Weekly Toiler*, 27 Jan. 1892; Notes from President Pierson's speech on the currency question in the minute

book of the Old Hickory Alliance, 5 Mar. 1890, file 38–139, Charles H. Pierson Papers.

76. Lampasas (Tex.) *People's Journal*, 19 Aug. and 28 Oct. 1892; Dallas (Tex.) *Southern Mercury*, 21 Nov. 1895 and 6 Feb. 1896; Dallas (Tex.) *Southern Mercury* in Butler (Ala.) *Choctaw Alliance*, 31 May 1893; Davis, *A Political Revelation*, pp. 230–33.

77. Goodwyn, *Democratic Promise*, pp. 152–53, 167–68. See also Atlanta *People's Party Paper*, 14 Jan. 1892; *Faulkner County Wheel* (Ark.), 1 July 1891; Gracewood (Ga.) *Wool Hat*, 24 Dec. 1892; Lampasas (Tex.) *People's Journal*, 19 Aug. 1892.

78. Raleigh *Progressive Farmer*, 7 June 1892.

79. Montgomery (Ala.) *Alliance Herald*, 19 Nov. 1891; also Raleigh *Progressive Farmer*, 7 June 1892 and 3 Jan. 1893; Salisbury (N.C.) *Carolina Watchman*, 16 July 1891; Lampasas (Tex.) *People's Journal*, 19 Aug. 1892; Dallas (Tex.) *Southern Mercury*, 27 Aug. 1891; Geneva (Ala.) *Record*, 28 Oct. 1891; Centreville (Ala.) *People's Reflector*, 20 Oct. and 10 Nov. 1892; Atlanta *People's Party Paper*, 17 Dec. 1891 and 16 Sept. 1892; Watson, *People's Party Campaign Handbook*, p. 200.

80. Dallas (Tex.) *Southern Mercury*, 21 Nov. 1895; also 19 Dec. 1895; Tarboro (N.C.) *Farmers' Advocate*, 8 Apr. 1891; Salisbury (N.C.) *Carolina Watchman*, 16 July 1891; Raleigh *Progressive Farmer*, 3 Jan. 1893.

81. Gibson (Ga.) *Glascock Banner*, 30 May 1895; also Concord (N.C.) *Standard* in Salisbury (N.C.) *Carolina Watchman*, 29 Oct. 1891; Atlanta *People's Party Paper*, 21 Jan. and 28 Apr. 1892; Tracy, Appendix, in Davis, *A Political Revelation*, pp. 316, 357–58, 367–68, 381–87.

82. Centreville (Ala.) *People's Reflector*, 10 Nov. 1892; also Raleigh *Progressive Farmer*, 23 Feb. 1892; Salisbury (N.C.) *Carolina Watchman*, 15 Jan. 1891.

83. Dallas (Tex.) *Southern Mercury*, 27 Aug. 1891.

84. Marion Butler was another exception. See the Clinton (N.C.) *Caucasian*, 2 Apr. 1891. Although he may have learned it from Macune, an editorial in this issue indicated that Butler could explain the effect of velocity on the currency supply. For Macune, see Tarboro (N.C.) *Farmers' Advocate*, 15 Apr. 1891.

85. Tracy, "The Sub-Treasury Plan," in Dunning, *The Farmers' Alliance History*, pp. 342–46 (Tracy's emphasis). For a later defense of a slightly but not essentially different version of the plan, as well as its land loan aspect, see Tracy, Appendix, in Davis, *A Political Revelation*, pp. 292–399.

86. Goodwyn, *Democratic Promise*, pp. 149–73.

87. Ironically, Macune hoped to use the subtreasury plan to keep the Southern Alliancemen out of third party politics, but the plan became the basis on which the Alliance radicals created the third party (Goodwyn, *Democratic Promise*, pp. 169–72).

88. Michael Schwartz, in *Radical Protest and Social Structure*, chaps. 13, 14, discusses cooperation as an effort of the farmers to build counterinstitutions to replace those which exploited them.

89. Goodwyn also talks about the failure of the southern radicals to reach urban workers with a program which fitted their needs (*Democratic Promise*, pp. 307–11).

90. Tracy, "The Sub-Treasury Plan," in Dunning, *The Farmers' Alliance History*, p. 354.

Chapter 9

1. Gracewood (Ga.) *Wool Hat*, 1 July 1893; also Hardy (Ark.) *National Reformer*, Dec. 1893 and Nov. 1894; Richmond *Virginia Sun*, 1 June and 27 July 1892; Atlanta *People's Party Paper*, 2 and 9 Dec. 1892 and 14 Sept. 1894; Oxford (Ala.) *Voice*, 19 Mar. 1892; Troy (Ala.) *Jeffersonian*, 24 Aug. 1894; Salisbury (N.C.) *Carolina Watchman*, 3 Mar. 1892; Raleigh *Progressive Farmer*, 27 Oct. 1896; Thomas E. Watson, *People's Party Campaign*

Handbook, 1892, p. 221; Polk's Ocala speech, Dec. 1890, box 12, vol. 64, L. L. Polk Papers.

2. Anniston *Alabama Leader*, 17 Oct. 1895; also Natchitoches *Louisiana Populist*, 10 May 1895; Austin (Tex.) *People's Advocate*, 7 Dec. 1893.

3. See Tarboro (N.C.) *Farmers' Advocate*, 6 May 1891.

4. Raleigh *Caucasian*, 25 Apr. 1895; also Atlanta *People's Party Paper*, 1 Mar. 1895; Gracewood (Ga.) *Wool Hat*, 21 Jan. 1893.

5. Hardy (Ark.) *National Reformer*, Oct. 1894.

6. Stephenville (Tex.) *Empire*, 28 Oct. 1892; also Tarboro (N.C.) *Farmers' Advocate*, 3 Aug. 1892; Gracewood (Ga.) *Wool Hat*, 29 Apr. and 13 and 20 May 1893.

7. Atlanta *People's Party Paper*, 16 Dec. 1892.

8. For a more extended discussion of this attitude, see Conclusion, below.

9. Carthage (Ga.) *Press* in Dallas (Ga.) *Herald*, 16 Nov. 1893.

10. Gracewood (Ga.) *Wool Hat*, 18 Aug. 1894.

11. Marvin Meyers, *The Jacksonian Persuasion*, chap. 9; Edward Pessen, *Jacksonian America*, pp. 293–97.

12. Edward Pessen, *Most Uncommon Jacksonians*, chaps. 8, 10.

13. See Dalton (Ga.) *Tribune* in Atlanta *People's Party Paper*, 5 Apr. 1895; Natchitoches *Louisiana Populist*, 8 Mar. 1895; Anniston *Alabama Leader*, 3 Oct. 1895; A. D. K. Wallace to Butler, 20 May 1896, box 2, folder 27, and M. I. Williams to Butler, 16 Nov. 1896, box 4, folder 47, Marion Butler Papers. For one of the exceptions to the connection between integration and the antimonopoly argument, Watson once integrated the railroad and subtreasury demands with no mention of antimonopoly. Atlanta *People's Party Paper*, 28 Apr. 1892.

14. Raleigh *Caucasian*, 16 July 1896; also Hardy (Ark.) *Morgan's Buzz Saw*, Oct. 1895.

15. Hardy *Arkansaw Kicker*, 14 Mar. 1896; also Hardy (Ark.) *National Reformer*, Apr. and June 1895; Hardy (Ark.) *Morgan's Buzz Saw*, July 1895 and Aug. 1896.

16. Dallas *Texas Advance*, 30 June 1894.

17. Dallas (Tex.) *Southern Mercury*, 11 July 1895; also 14 Feb., 13 June, 31 Oct. 1895 and 27 Feb., 5 Mar., 26 May, and 25 June 1896.

18. Ibid., 24 Jan. 1895.

19. Ibid., 29 Aug. 1895.

20. Ibid., 25 July 1895.

21. Ibid., 14 Feb. 1895.

22. Ibid., 19 Mar. 1896.

23. This is true of more modern day analysts as well. See Douglass C. North, *Growth and Welfare in the American Past*, pp. 142–44; Albert W. Niemi, Jr., *U.S. Economic History*, p. 237. For the more standard economic history textbooks, see Harold U. Faulkner, *American Economic History*, p. 378; Gilbert C. Fite and Jim E. Reese, *An Economic History of the United States*, p. 405; Ross M. Robertson, *History of the American Economy*, pp. 262–64. See also the recent econometric literature on the post-Civil War South, summarized in Harold D. Woodman, "The New History and the New South," pp. 523–54. What these authors fail to realize is that their analysis assumes a developed capitalist economy. The Southern Populists did not so assume. They saw people without food and clothing and farmers unable to sell large crops at decent prices. The problem to them was obvious; people lacked the means to purchase what they needed.

24. Wadesboro (N.C.) *Plow Boy*, 13 Feb. 1895; also Raleigh *Progressive Farmer*, 21 Mar. 1893; Ozark (Ala.) *Banner*, 10 Aug. 1893.

25. Mineola (Tex.) *Alliance Courier*, 6 Oct. 1892; also Geneva (Ala.) *Record*, 30 Dec. 1891; Ozark (Ala.) *Banner*, 4 Oct. 1894; Dallas (Tex.) *Southern Mercury*, 4 Apr. and 25 July 1895; Dallas *Texas Advance*, 30 June 1894; Gracewood (Ga.) *Wool Hat*, 1 Apr., 6

May, 5 Aug., and 14 Oct. 1893; Butler (Ala.) *Choctaw Alliance*, 26 Apr. 1893; Atlanta *People's Party Paper*, 18 May 1894 and 25 Jan. 1895; Troy (Ala.) *Jeffersonian*, 6 Apr. 1894; Henderson (N.C.) *Vance Farmer*, 20 Sept. 1892; Richmond *Virginia Sun*, 15 June 1892; Hardy (Ark.) *Morgan's Buzz Saw*, Oct. 1894; Nashville *Weekly Toiler*, 27 Jan. 1892; Tuscaloosa (Ala.) *Vindicator* in Butler (Ala.) *Choctaw Alliance*, 10 May 1893. A longer discussion of the overproduction fallacy can be found in W. Scott Morgan, *History of the Wheel and Alliance, and the Impending Revolution*, pp. 510–18.

26. For instance, Ozark (Ala.) *Banner-Advertiser*, 18 Apr. 1895; Tarboro (N.C.) *Farmers' Advocate*, 29 Apr. 1891. In most of these cases the reformers argued that until consumers had access to the means of consumption, the problem of cotton prices might have to be dealt with by cutting production. See also Nashville *Weekly Toiler*, 27 Jan. 1892. For the advice, see Harold D. Woodman, *King Cotton and His Retainers*, pp. 341–42.

27. Atlanta *People's Party Paper*, 1 Feb. 1895; also Nashville *Weekly Toiler*, 14 Oct. 1891; Montgomery (Ala.) *Alliance Herald*, 4 May 1893; W. L. Peek in Tarboro (N.C.) *Farmers' Advocate*, 13 Feb. 1895. See also Woodman, *King Cotton*, pp. 343–44.

28. See Tarboro (N.C.) *Farmers' Advocate*, 20 Jan. 1892.

29. Dallas (Tex.) *Southern Mercury*, 4 Apr. 1895.

30. This development is most easily accessible in Robert L. Heilbroner, *The Worldly Philosophers*, pp. 184–91, chap. 9. Most textbooks on the history of economic theory have material on Marshall. Few do much with Hobson. All the more recent ones consider Keynes.

31. See Morgan, *History of the Wheel and Alliance*, pp. 513–14.

32. See Atlanta *People's Party Paper*, 17 Mar. 1892 and 1 Feb. 1895; Raleigh *Progressive Farmer*, 17 Mar. 1891; Goldsboro (N.C.) *Caucasian*, 3 Aug. 1893; Salisbury (N.C.) *Carolina Watchman*, 14 Jan. 1892; W. L. Peek in Wadesboro (N.C.) *Plow Boy*, 13 Feb. 1895; Dallas (Ga.) *Herald*, 25 Oct. 1894; Gracewood (Ga.) *Wool Hat*, 1 Apr. 1893 and 15 Sept. 1894; Tallahassee (Fla.) *Alliance* in Tarboro (N.C.) *Farmers' Advocate*, 25 Nov. 1891; Harry Tracy, Appendix, in James H. Davis, *A Political Revelation*, pp. 380–82.

33. Ozark (Ala.) *Banner-Advertiser*, 7 Oct. 1895.

34. Nashville *Weekly Toiler*, 2 Dec. 1891.

35. Gibson (Ga.) *Glascock Banner*, 25 Apr. 1895; also 30 May 1895; Dallas *Texas Advance*, 18 Nov. 1893; Atlanta *People's Party Paper*, 21 Jan. 1892; Raleigh *Progressive Farmer*, 17 May 1892; Butler (Ala.) *Choctaw Alliance*, 24 Oct. 1894; Dallas (Tex.) *Southern Mercury*, 17 Sept. 1896; Troy (Ala.) *Jeffersonian*, 26 Jan. 1894; Tracy, Appendix, in Davis, *A Political Revelation*, pp. 316, 367, 380–82. As in their analysis of the proper monetary system, historical developments bore out the Southern Populists. Crude as the theory was, by the 1930s it had become clear that stimulating demand was far more important in ending depression than stimulating production. See Niemi, *U.S. Economic History*, chap. 18; North, *Growth and Welfare*, pp. 167–72; Robertson, *History of the American Economy*, pp. 634–43.

36. Again, the southern reformers usually understood better than their opponents that the driving force of a capitalist society was neither the gold standard nor business confidence in productive capacity, but profits. With profits assured, the gold standard mattered little.

37. Dallas (Tex.) *Southern Mercury*, 12 Nov. 1896; also 26 Nov. 1896; Gracewood (Ga.) *Wool Hat*, 22 Apr. 1893 and 25 Sept. 1894.

38. Dallas (Tex.) *Southern Mercury*, 7 Feb. 1895; Dallas *Texas Advance*, 14 July 1894.

39. Dallas *Texas Advance*, 30 June 1894.

40. This picture of America's economy was an entirely domestic one. Except for a few of the most sophisticated discussions of the financial issue, the reformers perceived little or no economic connection between the United States and the rest of the world, even though their

major crop found much of its market in Europe. This fact suggests that whatever the response to the Spanish-American war was among former Populists, it was probably not related to their perception of the need for overseas markets. Most likely this kind of support for American imperialism came from more established, wealthier farmers, those whose ties to the Democratic party remained firm, whose political voice remained powerful, and who were able to survive the 1880s and 1890s without falling into some sort of tenancy. For the overseas markets argument, see William A. Williams, *The Roots of the Modern American Empire*, pp. 338, 390–92, 400.

41. I would like to thank Bob Greenberg for first calling this to my attention. Although the idea of a "two-tier" economy might appear to resemble the notion of a "dual economy," frequently used in the analysis of the political economies of developing nations, it does not. A dual economy is one in which a traditional economy, functioning largely outside a market system, exists alongside a modernized, capitalistic sector. Although a case might be made for the early post-Civil War South being an example of such an economy, by the 1890s southern agriculture was fully integrated into the marketplace; self-sufficiency was a thing of the past for all but a very few farmers. Indeed, this penetration of the southern countryside by the financial apparatus of American capitalism gave rise to the Southern Populists' protest. Nor did the Southern Populists advocate returning to a dual economy, as their attitude toward industrialization and agricultural self-sufficiency indicate. (See Harry Tracy's comment on underconsumption earlier in this chapter and the Southern Populists' rejection of agricultural self-sufficiency in the Conclusion, below.) Agricultural self-sufficiency was not a goal of a simple market society. The Southern Populists did not reject industrialization, agricultural specialization, or the marketplace. They objected to the *organization* of American industrial society. For a discussion of the dual economy idea, see Gerald M. Meier, *Leading Issues in Economic Development*, chap. 3. For an interesting but tentative application of the same idea to the antebellum South, see Morton Rothstein, "The Ante-Bellum South as a Dual Economy," pp. 373–82.

42. The rest of this section, through p. 123, involves Nugent's speech, which can be found in the Austin (Tex.) *Argus*, 4 Sept. 1894, or in Catherine Nugent, ed., *Life Work of Thomas L. Nugent*, pp. 179–205.

43. Southern Populists rarely noted this. For an extended argument on this idea, see "Diogenes" letters, Gracewood (Ga.) *Wool Hat*, 20 and 27 May 1893 and especially 13 May 1893, where he maintained that labor advances capital to the capitalist, not vice versa.

44. Other Southern Populists, particularly antimonopoly greenbackers, made the same point. See W. S. Morgan in Hardy (Ark.) *Morgan's Buzz Saw*, Oct. 1894; also Nashville *Weekly Toiler*, 18 May 1892.

Chapter 10

1. Atlanta *People's Party Paper*, 17 Dec. 1891.

2. Raleigh *Progressive Farmer*, 1 Sept. 1891.

3. Martin E. Marty, *Righteous Empire*, pp. 93, 180; William G. McLoughlin, Jr., *Modern Revivalism*, pp. 256–59.

4. Sidney E. Ahlstrom, *A Religious History of the American People*, p. 811.

5. Ibid., pp. 786, 788; also Marty, *Righteous Empire*, pp. 181, 204.

6. Hunter Dickinson Farish, *The Circuit Rider Dismounts*, pp. 97–105, chaps. 9, 10; Rufus B. Spain, *At Ease in Zion*, chaps. 6, 7.

7. See Ahlstrom, *A Religious History*, chap. 48.

8. Farish, *The Circuit Rider Dismounts*, pp. 71–75; Ahlstrom, *A Religious History*, pp. 817–18.

9. See this chapter, below, p. 130.

10. Atlanta *People's Party Paper*, 9 Dec. 1892; also Gracewood (Ga.) *Wool Hat*, 27 Aug. 1892; W. L. Scott to Butler, 12 Jan. 1896, box 2, folder 19, Marion Butler Papers.

11. Raleigh *Progressive Farmer*, 3 July 1894. For a prediction of a similar change, with violence, see Gracewood (Ga.) *Wool Hat*, 11 Nov. 1893.

12. See Raleigh *Caucasian*, 23 Jan. 1896; Gracewood (Ga.) *Wool Hat*, 30 June 1894; Atlanta *People's Party Paper*, 15 July 1892; Dallas (Ga.) *Herald*, 4 Oct. 1894.

13. In the following discussion I want to establish the extent of the relationship between Southern Populist rhetoric and the religious millennium, and the consequences, which will be discussed later. The millennial element had a long history in American politics before the Populists and was practiced with vigor in the South of the 1890s by both Democrats and Republicans, although they might not have used it as extensively as the Populists.

14. See Atlanta *People's Party Paper*, 22 July 1892 and 14 Apr. 1893; Dahlonega (Ga.) *Signal*, 6 May 1892; Dallas (Ga.) *Herald*, 7 Feb. 1895; Butler (Ala.) *Choctaw Alliance*, 9 May 1894; Wadesboro (N.C.) *Plow Boy*, 16 Oct. 1895; Raleigh *Progressive Farmer*, 6 Jan. 1891; John A. Parker to Butler, 16 Dec. 1896, box 4, folder 50, Marion Butler Papers.

15. Dallas *Texas Advance*, 31 Mar. 1894. This, of course, is a specifically postmillennial statement. See also Hardy (Ark.) *National Reformer*, Feb. 1895; Ozark (Ala.) *Banner-Advertiser*, 17 Oct. 1895.

16. Troy (Ala.) *Jeffersonian*, 13 Apr. 1894; also Dallas (Tex.) *Southern Mercury*, 24 Jan. 1895.

17. Monroe (Ga.) *Populist* in Gracewood (Ga.) *Wool Hat*, 19 Aug. 1893.

18. See Atlanta *People's Party Paper*, 17 Dec. 1891 and 3 Mar. 1892; Gracewood (Ga.) *Wool Hat*, 21 July 1894; Salisbury (N.C.) *Carolina Watchman*, 21 July 1892.

19. Ozark (Ala.) *Banner*, 22 June 1893.

20. Address of the temporary state executive committee of the Louisiana People's party, Oct. 1891, H. L. Brian Papers.

21. See Raleigh *Caucasian*, 30 May 1895; Atlanta *People's Party Paper*, 24 Dec. 1891, 11 Feb. and 17 Mar. 1892, and 15 Mar. 1895; Ozark (Ala.) *Banner*, 19 July 1894; Dallas *Texas Advance*, 14 July 1894; Hardy (Ark.) *National Reformer*, July 1893 and Apr. 1894; Hardy (Ark.) *Morgan's Buzz Saw*, Feb. 1896.

22. Raleigh *Progressive Farmer*, 29 Oct. 1895; also Wedowee (Ala.) *Randolph Toiler*, 28 Nov. 1895.

23. Hardy (Ark.) *National Reformer*, Oct. 1893; also Oct. 1894.

24. Atlanta *People's Party Paper*, 26 May 1893; also 24 Mar. 1893.

25. A more minor source was the French revolution. The editor of the Gracewood (Ga.) *Wool Hat* liked to use the French example more than most of his Southern Populist colleagues. See, for instance, 26 Aug. 1893. For examples elsewhere, see Raleigh *Progressive Farmer*, 30 June 1891; Troy (Ala.) *Jeffersonian*, 26 Jan. 1894; Wedowee (Ala.) *Randolph Toiler*, 28 Nov. 1895.

26. Troy (Ala.) *Jeffersonian*, 29 June 1894; also Atlanta *People's Party Paper*, 10 May 1895; D. Schenk, Sr., to Butler, 10 or 15 Mar. 1896, box 2, folder 23, Marion Butler Papers.

27. Graham (Tex.) *Young County Call*, 22 Mar. 1895; also Dallas *Texas Advance*, 4 and 18 Aug. 1894.

28. Dallas (Tex.) *Southern Mercury*, 27 Dec. 1894.

29. Ibid., 4 July 1895.

30. Ibid., 7 Nov. 1895.

31. Ibid., 9 Apr. 1896; also 21 Nov. 1895.

32. "Diogenes" in the Gracewood (Ga.) *Wool Hat*, a radical on the subject of labor, also

was willing to have a revolution, "if it's necessary," to free labor from capital (27 May 1893).

33. Hickory (N.C.) *Mercury*, 31 Aug. 1892; also 14 Sept. 1892; Raleigh *Progressive Farmer*, 27 June 1893 and 2 July 1895; Dallas *Texas Advance* in Anniston *Alabama Leader*, 27 June 1895; Austin (Tex.) *People's Advocate*, 30 Aug. 1894; Dallas (Tex.) *Southern Mercury*, 7 Nov. 1895.

34. Raleigh *Progressive Farmer*, 19 June 1894.

35. Dallas (Ga.) *Herald*, 6 June 1895; also 6 July 1893; Birmingham *People's Weekly Tribune*, 30 July 1896.

36. Butler (Ala.) *Choctaw Alliance*, 28 July 1896.

37. Hardy (Ark.) *Morgan's Buzz Saw*, Sept. 1895.

38. Austin (Tex.) *Argus*, 23 Oct. 1894; also Dallas (Tex.) *Southern Mercury*, 26 Sept. 1895.

39. Raleigh *Progressive Farmer*, 22 Jan. 1895; also Birmingham *People's Weekly Tribune*, 25 June 1896; Hardy (Ark.) *Morgan's Buzz Saw*, Jan. 1895; Dallas (Tex.) *Southern Mercury*, 1 Oct. 1896; Atlanta *People's Party Paper*, 12 July 1895. Such language may strike a modern reader as a kind of overstatement endemic in politics and, as such, not to be taken seriously. I think this would be an error. In many revival tents and in many temperance meetings the same rhetoric has been taken seriously, and with good reason. The crisis atmosphere and attitude to which this language contributed was not limited to the Populists, as Stanley Jones and C. Vann Woodward have both pointed out. The whole period, especially the 1896 election, partook of this apocalyptic tone on the part of many of those involved (Stanley L. Jones, *The Presidential Election of 1896*, pp. 293, 305–6, 332–40; C. Vann Woodward, *The Burden of Southern History*, pp. 160–62).

40. Dallas (Tex.) *Southern Mercury*, 30 Apr. 1896.

41. Dallas *Texas Advance*, 24 Feb. 1894.

42. Richmond *Virginia Sun*, 3 Aug. 1893; also Dallas *Texas Advance*, 13 Jan. 1894; Dallas (Tex.) *Southern Mercury* in Oxford (Ala.) *Voice*, 5 Dec. 1891; Natchitoches *Louisiana Populist*, 3 May 1895; Atlanta *People's Party Paper*, 30 Dec. 1892.

43. Austin (Tex.) *People's Advocate*, 12 Oct. 1893; also Austin (Tex.) *Argus*, 30 Oct. 1894; Natchitoches *Louisiana Populist*, 10 May 1895.

44. Atlanta *People's Party Paper*, 24 Mar. 1893. The phrase "God arrayed against Magog" is the Populist's. He may have left out the word "Gog," but because of the idea of conflict between God and Magog, I doubt that "God" should have been "Gog."

Chapter 11

1. I am offering an extended examination of the Populists' experience in only four southern states for several reasons. Most importantly, sufficient sources for the other southern states are lacking. In the rest of the text I have used material from as many sources as I could locate, but it should be apparent from the following chapters that I could not make a detailed examination of my thesis in each state without a considerable amount of material covering both a temporal span of five or six years and a range of thought from radical to moderate. This kind of material cannot be found in contemporary Democratic newspapers. No substitutes exist for Populist newspapers and manuscript collections. On the more positive side, in these four states (with the possible exception of Mississippi) the reformers saw their greatest success, and the sources for the party are by far the best. These states also provide good geographic and ideological range. The North Carolina and Alabama Populists were heavily represented in the fusionist wing of the national party,

while the Texans and to some extent the Georgians supplied the mid-roaders with the bulk of their pre- and post-1896 southern support. From what I can tell, no state party displayed more antimonopoly and greenbacker sentiment than Texas, nor was any state party converted more thoroughly and more quickly to free silver than that of North Carolina. The experience of the Populists in these four southern states covers that of the rest of the South in all but detail.

2. Raleigh *Progressive Farmer*, 7 July 1891.

3. Tarboro (N.C.) *Farmers' Advocate*, 17 June, 2 and 9 Sept. 1891, 27 Apr. and 7 Dec. 1892; Raleigh *Progressive Farmer*, 31 May 1892.

4. Tarboro (N.C.) *Farmers' Advocate*, 8 July 1891 and 23 Mar. 1892; Raleigh *Progressive Farmer*, 31 May and 27 Sept. 1892; Salisbury (N.C.) *Carolina Watchman*, 17 Dec. 1891 and 10 Mar., 22 Sept., and 3 Nov. 1892.

5. Raleigh *Progressive Farmer*, 19 Apr., 26 July, and 23 Aug. 1892; Goldsboro (N.C.) *Caucasian*, 3 Nov. 1892.

6. For exceptions, see Warren Plains (N.C.) *People's Paper*, 12 June 1896; Raleigh *Progressive Farmer*, 10 July 1894, 13 and 27 Aug. 1895, and 25 Feb., 28 Apr., 8 Sept., and 27 Oct. 1896; Goldsboro (N.C.) *Caucasian*, 13 and 27 Apr. 1893; Wadesboro (N.C.) *Plow Boy*, 8 Jan. and 18 Mar. 1896.

7. Raleigh *Progressive Farmer*, 19 Apr. 1892.

8. Ibid., 23 Aug. 1892; also 26 July 1892; Goldsboro (N.C.) *Caucasian*, 3 Nov. 1892.

9. Raleigh *Progressive Farmer*, 30 Aug. 1892.

10. Ibid., 27 June 1893.

11. Ibid., 1 Mar. 1892; Goldsboro (N.C.) *Caucasian*, 2 June 1892.

12. Raleigh *Progressive Farmer*, 27 Sept. 1892.

13. Ibid., 20 Sept. 1892, 25 July 1893, and 27 Nov. 1894; Goldsboro (N.C.) *Caucasian*, 25 Aug. 1892. In early 1896, however, the *Caucasian* did see a brief resurgence of attention to black voters. See Raleigh *Caucasian*, 12 and 19 Mar. 1896.

14. See Goldsboro (N.C.) *Caucasian*, 19 Oct. 1893.

15. Raleigh *Progressive Farmer*, 11 Oct. and 1 Nov. 1892 and 18 Sept. 1894; Goldsboro (N.C.) *Caucasian*, 27 Oct. 1892.

16. Hickory (N.C.) *Mercury*, 31 Aug. and 14 Sept. 1892; Raleigh *Progressive Farmer*, 11 Oct. 1892 and 12 Mar. 1895; Raleigh *Caucasian*, 28 Mar. and 16 May 1895.

17. Beaver Dam (N.C.) *Our Home*, 26 May and 2 Aug. 1893; Hickory (N.C.) *Mercury*, 21 Sept. 1892; Goldsboro (N.C.) *Caucasian*, 31 May 1894. North Carolina's most antimonopoly greenback paper, the Tarboro *Farmer's Advocate*, used this kind of racial appeal less often than any other paper in the state.

18. The data on black voting which Kousser developed indicate just how poorly the Populists did among an active black electorate. See J. Morgan Kousser, *The Shaping of Southern Politics*, p. 183. For the North Carolina Populists' success in black belt counties, see Appendix F.

19. Raleigh *Progressive Farmer*, 14 June 1892. Lawrence Goodwyn, *The Populist Moment*, pp. 182, 198, notes the weakness of the Alliance's subtreasury campaign in North Carolina, as compared to Georgia, Alabama, and Texas. The cooperative effort had also been more conservative in North Carolina than elsewhere in the South (Lawrence Goodwyn, *Democratic Promise*, p. 341).

20. For exceptions, see letters or exchanges in Raleigh *Progressive Farmer*, 3 Jan., 23 May, and 18 July 1893; 30 Jan. 1894; and 13 Aug. 1895. On 10 Mar. 1896, in an editorial headed "The Passing of the Sub-Treasury," the editor of the *Progressive Farmer* maintained that the plan had been found "impractical" because it was "expensive and cumbersome" and because the purposes it was intended to serve—getting the farmers out of the hands of produce exchanges and futures speculators and expanding the money supply—could be

done better other ways. The editor said nothing of its original purpose, to free the farmers from the lien system and furnishing merchant, indicating how much the rudimentary class orientation of 1891 and 1892 had disappeared.

21. See, for instance, Salisbury (N.C.) *Carolina Watchman*, 8 Sept. 1892; Raleigh *Progressive Farmer*, 6 Aug. and 31 Oct. 1893; Raleigh *Caucasian*, 14 May 1896.

22. Clinton (N.C.) *Caucasian*, 18 June 1891.

23. Raleigh *Progressive Farmer*, 3 Jan. 1893.

24. Ibid., 27 Feb. 1894.

25. Raleigh *Caucasian*, 6 June 1895.

26. Ibid., 13 Feb. 1896; also 14 May and 11 June 1896.

27. Ibid., 9 May 1895 and 6 Feb. and 26 Mar. 1896; Raleigh *Progressive Farmer*, 25 Feb. 1896.

28. Raleigh *Caucasian*, 9 Apr. 1896.

29. Raleigh *Progressive Farmer*, 12 May 1896.

30. Ibid., 2 June 1896; also 14 Apr. 1896.

31. See ibid., 18 and 25 Aug. 1896; Raleigh *Caucasian*, 9 Apr., 7 May, and 17 Sept. 1896; Butler to Simms, 17 Feb. 1896, box 2, folder 22, and Schenk to Butler, 5 Apr. 1896, box 2, folder 25, Marion Butler Papers. Some evidence existed, however, of the remains of a greenback position. On 8 Jan. and 18 Mar. 1896 the editor of the Wadesboro (N.C.) *Plow Boy* wrote that free silver was an insufficient reform and greenbacks were more important. Nothing remained, however, of the other Omaha platform issues.

32. Clinton (N.C.) *Caucasian*, 6 Aug., 19 Nov., and 31 Dec. 1891; Goldsboro (N.C.) *Caucasian*, 18 Feb. and 30 June 1892.

33. Clinton (N.C.) *Caucasian*, 23 July 1891.

34. Ibid., 31 Dec. 1891.

35. For exceptions, see Goldsboro (N.C.) *Caucasian*, 13 and 27 Apr., 15 June, and 6 July 1893 and 1 and 15 Feb. 1894; Raleigh *Caucasian*, 30 May and 4 July 1895.

36. Goldsboro (N.C.) *Caucasian*, 26 May 1892.

37. Ibid., 2 June 1892.

38. Ibid., 9 June 1892.

39. Ibid., 28 July 1892.

40. Ibid., 11 Aug. 1892.

41. Ibid., 18 Aug. 1892. For a more detailed discussion of this transformation, one which argues that grass-roots Alliance pressure forced Butler to go with the new People's party or be cast aside as a leader of the political power the Alliance promised, see Philip Roy Muller, "New South Populism," pp. 65–74.

42. Richmond *Virginia Sun*, 4 May 1892; also C. Vann Woodward, *Tom Watson, Agrarian Rebel*, pp. 202–3.

43. In Apr. 1892 Polk himself wrote to James Denmark, his business manager on the *Progressive Farmer*, that "I am trying to get the Omaha platform down to the single issue of financial Reform [sic]. Nothing would so demoralize the enemy. *Keep this to your self* [sic]." (Emphasis Polk's.) The pressure to trim the Omaha platform existed in North Carolina before it was approved. Polk to Denmark, 29 Apr. 1892, box 7, folder 104, L. L. Polk Papers.

44. Raleigh *Progressive Farmer*, 3 Jan., 14 Feb., 23 May, 18 July, 12 Sept., and 5 Dec. 1893, and 30 Jan., 17 and 24 Apr., and June to Oct. 1894; Goldsboro (N.C.) *Caucasian*, 6 and 13 July 1893. Even Marion Butler on a few occasions spoke of the need for greenbacks. See Goldsboro (N.C.) *Caucasian*, 15 June and 23 Nov. 1893 and 1 and 15 Feb. and 29 Nov. 1894.

45. Goldsboro (N.C.) *Caucasian*, 7 Dec. 1893.

46. See Hickory (N.C.) *Mercury*, 29 June 1892; Tarboro (N.C.) *Farmers' Advocate*, 20

May 1891 and 13 July 1892; Salisbury (N.C.) *Carolina Watchman*, 12 Feb. and 26 Mar. 1891 and 6 Oct. 1892; Raleigh *Progressive Farmer*, 10 May and 21 June 1892.

47. See Salisbury (N.C.) *Carolina Watchman*, 14 July 1892; Tarboro (N.C.) *Farmers' Advocate*, 13 July 1892.

48. Goldsboro (N.C.) *Caucasian*, 22 Feb. 1894.

49. Ibid., 10 May 1894; also 29 Mar. and 5 and 12 Apr. 1894.

50. For Georgia, see chap. 12, below.

51. Raleigh *Progressive Farmer*, 18 July 1893; also 23 Jan. 1894.

52. Goldsboro (N.C.) *Caucasian*, 28 June 1894.

53. Ibid., 2 Aug. 1894.

54. Simeon A. Delap, "The Populist Party in North Carolina," pp. 55–56; Helen G. Edmonds, *The Negro and Fusion Politics in North Carolina, 1894–1901*, pp. 34–38.

55. Raleigh *Progressive Farmer*, 20 Nov. 1894. See also note 72, below, for Boggs's position in 1896.

56. See, for instance, Raleigh *Progressive Farmer*, 9 and 30 Apr. and 11 June 1895.

57. See Goldsboro (N.C.) *Caucasian*, 14 Sept. 1893 and May and June 1894; Raleigh *Progressive Farmer*, 10 Mar. and 14 Apr. 1896.

58. Goldsboro (N.C.) *Caucasian*, 17 May 1894.

59. Although Kitchin in a May 1895 letter did admit that free coinage of silver and gold would not increase the money supply sufficiently, he made no mention of legal tender paper currency (Raleigh *Progressive Farmer*, 14 May 1895). He apparently never again used that qualifier. (See Raleigh *Progressive Farmer*, 25 June and 26 Nov. 1895 and 28 Jan., 25 Feb., and 21 Apr. 1896.) By Oct. 1896 both he and another free silver convert, Spier Whitaker, were campaigning for the state and national Democratic ticket, claiming to be Populists while attacking any effort by the North Carolina Populist party, including the fusionist state executive committee, to do anything but fuse with free silver Democrats (see Raleigh *Caucasian*, 15 Oct. 1896).

60. C. Vann Woodward, *Origins of the New South, 1877–1913*, pp. 280–81; Stanley L. Jones, *The Presidential Election of 1896*, pp. 61–62.

61. Raleigh *Progressive Farmer*, 18 June 1895; Raleigh *Caucasian*, 20 June 1895.

62. Raleigh *Progressive Farmer*, 3 Sept. 1895.

63. Ibid., 17 Sept. 1895.

64. Raleigh *Caucasian*, 3 Oct. 1895.

65. Ibid., 4 July 1895; also Goldsboro (N.C.) *Caucasian*, 5 Oct. 1893.

66. Raleigh *Caucasian*, 17 Oct. 1895.

67. Raleigh *Progressive Farmer*, 25 Feb. and all of Mar. 1896. For a while the Omaha platform remained. See the opposition to the course Butler would follow in early 1896 in the *Progressive Farmer* (all of Mar. and 7 Apr. 1895). After early April the Omaha platform dropped out of the debate. For other references to the debate, see ibid., 3 Mar. 1896; and Wadesboro (N.C.) *Plow Boy*, 8 Apr. 1896. For a little remaining greenback sentiment, see Wadesboro (N.C.) *Plow Boy*, 8 Jan. and 18 Mar. 1896.

68. Raleigh *Caucasian*, 6 Feb. 1896.

69. Ibid., 13 Feb. 1896.

70. For the minority report of the state executive committee, see Raleigh *Progressive Farmer*, 5 May 1896.

71. Ibid., 15 Sept. 1896.

72. Delap, "The Populist Party in North Carolina," pp. 60–63; Edmonds, *The Negro and Fusion Politics*, pp. 48–59; Woodward, *Origins*, pp. 288–89. There was at least one holdout, however. George Boggs, an old antimonopoly greenbacker (see note 55, above) and chairman of the ninth congressional district Populist executive committee, pointed out in Oct. 1896 that the free silver question had been "greatly exaggerated," that it was no

panacea, and that on "the money question" the Democratic platform and the Populists disagreed. The Democratic platform endorsed a redemption, intrinsic value currency and failed to recognize that *all* money was fiat. For Boggs "capitalism is despotism" and the struggle was still between "the absorbers of wealth" and "its producers," "the plutocrats against the people." He would have been in good company in Texas. In North Carolina his was a voice in the wilderness by 1896. Boggs's speech is in Raleigh *Progressive Farmer*, 27 Oct. 1896.

73. Raleigh *Caucasian*, 12 Mar. 1896; also 30 Apr. 1896.

74. Ibid., 7 May 1896; also Raleigh *Progressive Farmer*, 5 May 1896. Frederick A. Bode, in his *Protestantism and the New South*, pp. 5–6 and chap. 3, treats in depth the North Carolina Populists' critique of the conservative role in the southern social order of the institutional church. This was a strong side of the Southern Populists' use of their own heritage and was not limited to North Carolina (see chap. 2, notes 34–37, above). Bode does not deal with the impact of evangelical Protestant metaphors and images on Populist thinking and analysis beyond the subject of religion.

75. Raleigh *Caucasian*, 29 Oct. 1896.

76. From Bryan's "Cross of Gold" speech at the 1896 Democratic national convention. William J. Bryan, *The First Battle*, p. 200. This speech is most easily available in George B. Tindall, ed., *A Populist Reader*, pp. 203–11.

77. Norman Pollack, ed., *The Populist Mind*, p. 61.

78. See Kousser, *The Shaping of Southern Politics*, p. 183. Neither candidate picked up any black belt counties. See Appendix F.

79. Edmonds, *The Negro and Fusion Politics*, p. 221.

80. William Warren Rogers, *One-Gallused Rebellion*, pp. 100–101, 115–17, 168–72; William Warren Rogers, "Reuben F. Kolb," pp. 109–19.

81. Rogers, *One-Gallused Rebellion*, p. 173.

82. Ibid., p. 190.

83. Ozark (Ala.) *Banner*, 9 Mar. 1893.

84. Rogers, *One-Gallused Rebellion*, pp. 115–18, 168–73; Sheldon Hackney, *Populism to Progressivism in Alabama*, pp. 7–8.

85. John B. Clark, *Populism in Alabama*, p. 93 and n. 34 p. 93; Goodwyn, *Democratic Promise*, chap. 8 and pp. 244–59.

86. Rogers, *One-Gallused Rebellion*, pp. 189–90.

87. Ibid., pp. 190–91.

88. Geneva (Ala.) *Record*, 15 Apr., 20 May, 17 June, and 28 Oct. 1891.

89. Ibid., 11 Mar., 8 Apr., 20 May, and 17 June 1891.

90. Rogers, *One-Gallused Rebellion*, p. 194.

91. Montgomery (Ala.) *Alliance Herald*, 19 Nov. 1891.

92. Ibid., 16 July 1891. Baltzell was standing on the Ocala platform, which demanded regulation rather than ownership of the railroads.

93. Rogers, *One-Gallused Rebellion*, pp. 181–85.

94. Ibid., pp. 214–15.

95. Ibid., pp. 212, 230, 327; Clark, *Populism in Alabama*, p. 123; Hackney, *Populism to Progressivism*, p. 249.

96. See especially letters from Aug. through Oct. 1894 and Mar. and Apr. 1895, Farley Maxwell Papers. Maxwell was also commander of the Tuscaloosa chapter of the Confederate Veterans Organization (list of CVO members, Farley Maxwell Papers).

97. Drawer 1, folders 1, 2, Oliver Day Street Papers.

98. Hackney, *Populism to Progressivism*, pp. 27–30.

99. Oxford (Ala.) *Voice*, 23 Jan. 1891.

100. Ibid., 6 Feb. 1891.

101. Ibid., 22 May and 5 June 1891.

102. Ibid., 18 July 1891.

103. Ibid., 9 Apr. 1892; also 23 Apr. 1892.

104. Ibid., 9 July 1892.

105. Ibid., 10 Sept. 1892.

106. Ibid., 24 Sept. 1892.

107. Ibid., 1 and 22 Oct. 1892. The Weaver-Field ticket, unlike the Kolb state ticket, never appeared on the *Voice*'s editorial page.

108. Hackney argues that there was no difference between the two parties (*Populism to Progressivism*, pp. 21, 67). Clark intimates that in 1892 there was, but generally treats them as the same (*Populism in Alabama*, pp. 116–17, 142–43, 148). Rogers is never quite clear, speaking of them as different (*One-Gallused Rebellion*, pp. 220, 232, 241–44, 273, 288) or essentially the same (pp. 189, 231). After 1894 Rogers treats them as identical.

109. Rogers, *One-Gallused Rebellion*, pp. 182–84; Clark, *Populism in Alabama*, pp. 102–9.

110. Rogers, *One-Gallused Rebellion*, pp. 198–204, 207–9; Oxford (Ala.) *Voice*, 5 Mar. 1892; Kolb to T. A. Street, 22 Apr. 1892, Oliver Day Street Papers.

111. Rogers, *One-Gallused Rebellion*, pp. 213–14; Clark, *Populism in Alabama*, p. 133.

112. Butler (Ala.) *Choctaw Alliance*, 14 Feb. 1894; Ozark (Ala.) *Banner*, 15 Feb. 1894; Rogers, *One-Gallused Rebellion*, pp. 272–73.

113. Butler (Ala.) *Choctaw Alliance*, 15 Aug. 1894.

114. Rogers, *One-Gallused Rebellion*, pp. 230–31.

115. Kolb to T. A. Street, 29 Mar. 1893, Oliver Day Street Papers.

116. Rogers, *One-Gallused Rebellion*, pp. 220, 273; also Ozark (Ala.) *Banner*, 23 Nov. 1893.

117. Rogers, *One-Gallused Rebellion*, pp. 221, 233.

118. Troy (Ala.) *Jeffersonian*, 17 Nov. 1893.

119. Ibid., 5 Jan. 1894.

120. Ibid., 16 Mar. and 6 Apr. 1894. For government ownership of the railroads, see also 27 July and 24 Aug. 1894.

121. See ibid., 30 Mar., 13 Apr., and 4 May 1894.

122. Ibid., 15 and 22 June 1894.

123. Ibid., 29 June 1894.

124. Ibid., 17 Aug. 1894.

125. Ibid., 24 Aug. 1894.

126. An exception to this rule was Frank Baltzell's Montgomery (Ala.) *Alliance Herald*. The *Herald* mentioned the subtreasury plan as late as May 1893 but in the same issue indicated that it felt free silver would be "sufficient monetary reform to end the currency contraction" (4 May 1893). In 1894 there were a few signs of the advocacy of a legal tender fiat currency (see 10 May 1894) and a more active role for the national government in the social and economic life of the nation (see 17 May 1894), but nothing on government ownership and little evidence of any real understanding of the implications of a greenback monetary system. Free silver and fair elections dominated the editorials and letters in those issues available after 1891.

127. Butler (Ala.) *Choctaw Alliance*, 2 Nov. 1892.

128. Ibid., 23 Nov. 1892; also 18 Jan. 1893.

129. Ibid., 26 July 1893; also 1 Mar. 1893.

130. See ibid., 21 Dec. 1892 and 31 May 1893.

131. See ibid., 15 Feb. and 19 and 26 July 1893; and 24 Jan. and 18 Apr. 1894.

132. See ibid., 8 Nov. 1893.

133. For town versus country, see Ozark (Ala.) *Banner*, 9 June and 8 and 22 Sept. 1892

and 3 Aug. 1893. For producer versus nonproducer, see 28 July 1892 and 3 Aug. and 28 Sept. 1893.

134. Ibid., 4 Aug. 1892; also 11 Aug. 1892.

135. See ibid., 11 May 1893.

136. See ibid., 19 Jan., 2 Feb., and 22 June 1893.

137. Ibid., 2 Feb. 1893.

138. Ibid., 24 Aug. 1893; also a letter in 21 June 1894.

139. See ibid., 10 Aug. 1893. R. S. Dennington became the editor of the *Banner* in mid-January 1894, and the paper became very locally oriented, with little discussion of any national issues. An exception to this was the coverage and commentary on the Pullman strike. Dennington was a longtime member of the International Typographers' Union. See, for the Pullman strike, July and Aug. 1894.

140. Rogers, *One-Gallused Rebellion*, p. 214.

141. Ibid.

142. Ibid., p. 219.

143. See Centreville (Ala.) *People's Reflector*, 13 Oct. 1892; Ozark (Ala.) *Banner*, 13 and 20 Oct. 1892.

144. Ozark (Ala.) *Banner*, 3 Nov. 1892.

145. Rogers, *One-Gallused Rebellion*, pp. 221–25.

146. Butler (Ala.) *Choctaw Alliance*, 17 May 1893.

147. Ibid., 13 Sept. 1893.

148. Rogers, *One-Gallused Rebellion*, pp. 241–43.

149. Hackney implies that the Populists made the offer, although he does not distinguish between the Jeffersonians and the Populists (*Populism to Progressivism*, pp. 46–47). Clark, writing in 1927 and relying on the Montgomery *Advertiser* and the Birmingham *Iron Age*, argues that the Populist executive committee probably concurred in the first offer (*Populism in Alabama*, p. 149). Rogers maintains that the Populists did not support it, citing the efforts of the Populist state chairman, George Gaither, and state secretary Joseph Manning, to organize for the complete overthrow of the Democratic party in Alabama (*One-Gallused Rebellion*, pp. 242–43).

150. Ozark (Ala.) *Banner*, 19 Oct. 1893.

151. Butler (Ala.) *Choctaw Alliance*, 24 May 1894.

152. Ibid., 17 May 1893.

153. Rogers, *One-Gallused Rebellion*, pp. 247–48; Butler (Ala.) *Choctaw Alliance*, 18 and 25 Oct. 1893; *Alliance News* (Ala.) in Butler (Ala.) *Choctaw Alliance*, 4 Oct. 1893.

154. Butler (Ala.) *Choctaw Alliance*, 14 and 21 June 1893.

155. Ibid., 25 Oct. 1893; also 18 Oct. 1893.

156. Rogers, *One-Gallused Rebellion*, p. 264.

157. Ibid., p. 248.

158. Butler (Ala.) *Choctaw Alliance*, 2 May 1894.

159. Ibid., 23 May 1894. William Stevens, black leader of the black and tan faction of the state Republican party, was refused the privilege of speaking to the Jeffersonian state convention in Feb. 1894 and "hurriedly and unceremoniously" hustled out of the meeting. (Rogers, *One-Gallused Rebellion*, p. 273; also Clark, *Populism in Alabama*, n. 27 p. 152.)

160. Rogers, *One-Gallused Rebellion*, pp. 242–44.

161. Butler (Ala.) *Choctaw Alliance*, 14 and 21 June 1893; also 8 Nov. 1893; Rogers, *One-Gallused Rebellion*, pp. 244, 248.

162. Ozark (Ala.) *Banner*, 23 Nov. 1893.

163. Rogers, *One-Gallused Rebellion*, pp. 283–84.

164. Ibid., p. 289.

165. Ibid., pp. 289–90.

166. Ozark (Ala.) *Banner*, 23 Nov. 1893.

167. Rogers, *One-Gallused Rebellion*, pp. 190, 245.

168. Ibid., pp. 282–83.

169. Ozark (Ala.) *Banner*, 15 Feb. 1894.

170. See Butler (Ala.) *Choctaw Alliance*, 21 Feb. 1894; Ozark (Ala.) *Banner*, 15 Feb. and 17 May 1894; Clark, *Populism in Alabama*, p. 152; Rogers, *One-Gallused Rebellion*, pp. 272–73.

171. Hackney, *Populism to Progressivism*, p. 62.

172. William Warren Rogers and Robert David Ward, *Labor Revolt in Alabama*, chap. 7, especially p. 129.

173. This is particularly true of 1892, if Kousser's figures are correct (*Shaping of Southern Politics*, p. 137 and n. 49 p. 138). The Populists were unable to attract enough black votes to win the state. In 1894 and 1896 the Sayre law helped do what the reformers, Populists and Jeffersonians both, were already doing; that is, give the bulk of the black vote in the black belt and white counties to the Democrats. The experience of the Georgia Populists indicated that it need not have been that way. If the Alabama reformers had made the effort the Georgians did, they could have won in 1892. (For Georgia figures, see Kousser, *Shaping of Southern Politics*, p. 215.) Even in 1894 they had a chance. But the Alabama reformers did not understand the need and did not make the effort. What would have happened without the Sayre law is hard to say, but 1892 indicates that it would not have been a victory for Kolb.

174. Butler (Ala.) *Choctaw Alliance*, 24 Jan. 1894.

175. Ibid., 30 May 1894.

176. Ozark (Ala.) *Banner-Advertiser*, 11 and 18 July, 8 Aug., 14 Nov., and 19 Dec. 1895; and 12 and 19 Mar. and 15 and 29 Oct. 1896.

177. Butler (Ala.) *Choctaw Alliance*, 30 June 1896; also 27 Oct. 1896. There were a few holdouts. See Ozark (Ala.) *Banner-Advertiser*, 20 June, 25 July, 5 Sept., and 10 Oct. 1895 and 9 Apr. 1896. J. M. Whitehead in the Greenville *Living Truth* and A. P. Longshore in the Anniston *Alabama Leader*, both old antimonopoly greenback Populists, continued to stress the antimonopoly greenback issues and downplay the importance of free silver in 1895 and 1896. See Ozark (Ala.) *Banner-Advertiser*, 4 Apr., 6 June, and 18 July 1895; Anniston *Alabama Leader*, 25 July, 15 Aug., 12 Sept., 3 Oct., and 19 Dec. 1895. Whitehead also tended to be better on the race issue, although he, too, had given up on the idea of a black and white coalition of the disadvantaged. See Ozark (Ala.) *Banner-Advertiser*, 10 Oct. 1895. The Ozark *Banner-Advertiser* also mentioned and discussed the old antimonopoly greenback issues some into 1896, although they completely disappeared under the free silver onslaught of that year. See Ozark (Ala.) *Banner-Advertiser*, 2 Apr. 1896.

178. Butler (Ala.) *Choctaw Alliance*, 17 Mar. 1896.

179. Ozark (Ala.) *Banner-Advertiser*, 19 Mar., 9 Apr., and 7 May 1896.

180. Ozark (Ala.) *Banner*, 9 Feb. 1893.

181. Also Butler (Ala.) *Choctaw Alliance*, 19 July 1893.

182. Ozark (Ala.) *Banner-Advertiser*, 19 Dec. 1895.

183. Ibid., 12 Mar. 1896.

184. Ibid., 23 Apr. 1896.

185. Ibid., 1 Oct. 1896.

186. Because material from Louisiana was confined almost entirely to the *Louisiana Populist*, which did not begin publication until Aug. 1894, I did not include it in the body of this section. It appears, however, that the situation in Louisiana was similar to that in North Carolina and Alabama. The *Populist* said nothing of the subtreasury. By mid-1895, at the latest, free silver had become the most important, if not the sole, national issue considered. It certainly dominated every other national demand. The only national reform

issue articulated by the Louisiana Populists at their 1896 state convention was free silver. For their 1896 state platform, see Natchitoches *Louisiana Populist*, 17 Jan. 1896.

187. In early March 1894, while it still identified with the Jeffersonian Democrats, the Troy *Jeffersonian* warned the blacks that the political struggle in Alabama was between white voters only (2 Mar. 1894). After blasting the Democrats as the party of "Clevelandism, Mugwumpism, and niggerism" on 20 Apr. 1894, however, the *Jeffersonian* printed less and less on the race issue. As the paper grew more radical, it dropped its outspoken antiblack sentiments.

188. See Appendix C; also Kousser, *The Shaping of Southern Politics*, p. 137.

189. Birmingham *People's Weekly Tribune*, 28 May 1896.

190. Ozark (Ala.) *Banner-Advertiser*, 2 Apr. 1896.

191. Ibid., 30 Apr. 1896. Kousser points out that the supporters of Kolb and the Populists voted overwhelmingly against a convention in 1900 (*The Shaping of Southern Politics*, p. 167). Disapproving of disfranchisement, however, might well have been primarily disapproval of their own disfranchisement, not necessarily that of blacks. If the two went hand in hand, as Kousser points out they did in the South (chaps. 8, 9), then white voters opposed black disfranchisement, although perhaps not out of a concern for black political rights.

192. Ozark (Ala.) *Banner-Advertiser*, 25 June and 2 July 1896.

193. Birmingham *People's Weekly Tribune*, 4 June 1896.

194. Ibid., 20 Aug. 1896; also 18 June 1896.

195. See Appendix C.

196. Birmingham *People's Weekly Tribune*, 1 Oct. 1896.

197. Ozark (Ala.) *Banner-Advertiser*, 25 June 1896.

198. Rogers, *One-Gallused Rebellion*, pp. 308–11.

199. See Centreville (Ala.) *People's Reflector*, 20 Oct. and 10 Nov. 1892; Geneva (Ala.) *Record*, 28 Oct. 1891.

200. Troy (Ala.) *Jeffersonian*, 17 Nov. 1893.

201. Ibid., 30 Mar. 1894.

202. Ibid., 11 and 25 May 1894.

203. Ibid., 7 and 21 Sept. 1894.

204. See, for examples of the sectional appeal, Oxford (Ala.) *Voice*, 1891 and 1892; Montgomery (Ala.) *Alliance Herald*, 26 Apr. 1894.

205. Butler (Ala.) *Choctaw Alliance*, 23 Nov. 1892 and 19 July 1893.

206. See n. 133 above.

207. Oxford (Ala.) *Banner-Advertiser*, 3 Oct. 1895.

208. By 1896, as Hackney points out in *Populism to Progressivism*, an individual reformer's political radicalism did not correlate with his stand on fusion, local or national (chap. 5, especially pp. 91–92, 97–98). He attributed this to the Populists' lack of ideology (pp. 85, 106–10) because he failed to understand that the Populists had lost their analytical base between 1892 and 1894. He failed to note this loss partly because, like so many other historians of Populism, he failed to recognize any difference between the financial reform, free silver Populists and the antimonopoly greenbackers (pp. 21, 67). In the case of Alabama the error was particularly striking because, unlike other southern states, the two groups of reformers were distinct in 1892. Missing the slow erosion of the antimonopoly greenback position in Alabama, Hackney could only explain what he called Populism as a search for power by a dispossessed group seeking not to change the society in which they lived but to gain power within it (chap. 4). After 1896 had separated the wheat from the chaff Hackney found a new tone to Populism in Alabama, one which emphasized an antimonopoly greenback stance (pp. 108–10). If he had looked more closely at the Alliancemen and Populists of 1890 and 1892, he would have found much the same there.

He might not have been so surprised if he had not from the start confused Populists with Jeffersonians.

209. Hackney, *Populism to Progressivism*, pp. 91–92, 97–103.

210. Rogers, *One-Gallused Rebellion*, pp. 205–7.

211. DuBose to Robert McKee, 13 Nov. 1890, Robert McKee Papers.

212. DuBose attributed Kolb's failure in 1890 to the St. Louis platform, and in 1892 to the Omaha platform (Clark, *Populism in Alabama*, p. 94 and n. 100 p. 109).

213. For who the Progressives were, and for some of their programs, see Hackney, *Populism to Progressivism*, chaps. 7, 13, and 14. For the disfranchisement convention and campaign, see chaps. 8, 9, 10, and Kousser, *The Shaping of Southern Politics*, pp. 165–71. For the developments in the steel industry in the Birmingham area, see Ethel Armes, *The Story of Coal and Iron in Alabama*, especially chaps. 19–29. On the U.S. Steel takeover, see chap. 29. For an analysis of what happened in the 1907 U.S. Steel takeover of Tennessee Coal and Iron, and what it meant to Alabama, see Woodward, *Origins*, pp. 299–302, and Gabriel Kolko, *The Triumph of Conservatism*, pp. 114–17. For the best statement on the colonial economy, see Woodward, *Origins*, chap. 11.

Chapter 12

1. Atlanta *People's Party Paper*, 31 Dec. 1891, 21 Jan., 18 Feb., 17 Mar., 21 Apr., 3 June, 16, 23, and 30 Sept. 1892; and 20 Jan. 1893. The exception to this was the *Wool Hat*, published in Gracewood, Richmond County, in which Augusta is also located. The subtreasury rarely appeared in the *Wool Hat*, although the paper mentioned it a few times, on 13 Aug. and 24 Dec. 1892, 11 Mar., 8 Apr., 24 June, and 2 Sept. 1893, and 24 Mar. 1894. The editor of the *Wool Hat* and some of its correspondents were familiar with greenback arguments. (See 29 June 1892, 4 and 25 Mar., 15 July, and 2 Dec. 1893, and 17 Feb. 1894.) But substantive development of them almost never appeared. The *Wool Hat* did not even print the Omaha platform until 31 Mar. 1894, after which it appeared quite frequently. On the other hand, the effort to create a biracial coalition in 1892 did appear in the *Wool Hat* (see below, n. 7).

2. Atlanta *People's Party Paper*, 15 July, 8 Aug., 16 and 23 Sept., and 28 Oct. 1892.

3. Ibid., 4 Feb., 31 Mar., 28 Apr., 17 June, and 15 and 29 July 1892.

4. Ibid., 17 June, 29 July, 19 Aug., and 30 Sept. 1892.

5. Ibid., 31 Mar., 29 July, and 5 Aug. 1892.

6. Ibid., 3 June, 22 and 29 July, 5 and 12 Aug., and 4 Nov. 1892.

7. Ibid., 4 Feb., 17 Mar., 21 and 28 Apr., 13 May, 15 and 29 July, 12 Aug., 16 Sept., and 23 Dec. 1892; Gracewood (Ga.) *Wool Hat*, 13 and 27 Aug. and 8 and 22 Oct. 1892.

8. Atlanta *People's Party Paper*, 14 Oct. 1892; also 25 Nov. and 23 Dec. 1892. Again, the Gracewood (Ga.) *Wool Hat* proved a partial exception; blacks sometimes were implicitly blamed for the fraud in Augusta. See 15 Oct. and 17 Dec. 1892.

9. Atlanta *People's Party Paper*, 14 Oct. 1892.

10. J. Morgan Kousser, *The Shaping of Southern Politics*, p. 215. At least this is true in terms of the percentage of the available black vote, which was smaller in Georgia than either North Carolina or Alabama. I would disagree with Kousser's contention that the black vote "probably never held the balance of power in Georgia" (p. 215). His own figures suggest that black votes could be considered important. The Populists took 49.3 percent of the white votes cast in 1894, and 39.1 percent of the black. It would not have taken many more black votes to change the result. See also Appendix D.

11. Gracewood (Ga.) *Wool Hat*, 13 and 20 Aug., 17 and 24 Sept., and 1 Oct. 1892.

12. In the *Wool Hat* this town-country conflict aspect of the politics of class was also quite sharp. See Gracewood (Ga.) *Wool Hat*, 1 June 1892; also 13 July, 17 and 24 Sept.,

and 1 and 15 Oct. 1892; Atlanta *People's Party Paper*, 10 Mar., 28 Apr., and 28 Oct. 1892; Dahlonega (Ga.) *Signal*, 6 May and 5 Aug. 1892.

13. C. Vann Woodward, *Tom Watson, Agrarian Rebel*, pp. 236–43; Alex M. Arnett, *The Populist Movement in Georgia*, pp. 153–55.

14. See Monroe (Ga.) *Populist* in Gracewood (Ga.) *Wool Hat*, 19 Aug. 1893. Also see Gracewood (Ga.) *Wool Hat*, 13 May, for opposition to Augusta boycott.

15. Atlanta *People's Party Paper*, 21 July 1893; Woodward, *Tom Watson*, p. 248.

16. Gracewood (Ga.) *Wool Hat*, 29 July 1893; also see 2 and 23 Sept. 1893; Watson speeches in Atlanta *People's Party Paper*, July to Oct. 1893.

17. Gracewood (Ga.) *Wool Hat*, 19 Aug., 16 Sept., and 7 Oct. 1893 and 6 Jan. and 28 Apr. 1894.

18. Atlanta *People's Party Paper*, 16 Feb. 1894.

19. The Gracewood (Ga.) *Wool Hat* announced the switch on 21 Apr. 1894, only a month before the state convention which nominated Hines for governor.

20. Woodward, *Tom Watson*, pp. 263–64.

21. Atlanta *People's Party Paper*, 20 Apr. 1894.

22. Gracewood (Ga.) *Wool Hat*, 14 Apr. 1894. For more of the same tone in Watson, see reports of his speeches in Augusta and Waynesboro in the *Wool Hat*, 14 and 28 Apr. 1894.

23. Atlanta *People's Party Paper*, 4 May 1894.

24. Ibid., 25 May 1894.

25. Ibid., 27 Jan., 3 Feb., 31 Mar., 12 May, 9 June, 7 July, 27 Oct., and 3 Nov. 1893.

26. See ibid., 28 Oct. 1892; 24 Feb., 25 Aug., and 22 Sept. 1893; and 23 Feb. 1894.

27. Ibid., 25 May 1894.

28. His appeal on the last focused on the failure of the state railroad commission to prevent the recent Georgia Central frauds, where small stockholders had been badly burned, and the commission's inability to end strikes and satisfy the grievances which made it "one man's interest to destroy the business and property of another." On this issue, Watson was only a few years early. See Dewey Grantham, Jr., *Hoke Smith and the Politics of the New South*, pp. 167–71, 200–201.

29. Always aware of the slightest political advantage, Watson sounded the memories of Henry Grady when speaking in Atlanta. In Atlanta he played carefully on the ideal of a racially harmonious past. "We have grown up in this land together; we have worked together, suffered together, and in the days of the war, the Southern slave took his axe and bed-quilt and slept before the door of the 'big-house' and guarded their temple with his own life." Watson also appealed to Grady's ideas for a solution. The whites must teach the blacks that "we are their natural friends," or some "scalawag carpetbagger or demagogue will tell them we are their enemies." But Watson did not stay with Grady; he never did. "If we do not talk to them in public, in the broad light of day, face to face and foot to foot, they will be talked to behind closed doors and their ears filled with falsehoods to which we have no opportunity to reply." Neither Grady nor the New South promised the solutions Watson did; the New South advocates never took the blacks seriously enough. "[T]hese people, being citizens, being taxpayers, being wards upon who we spend money for education, people whose souls and minds are lifted to the contemplation of the rights and liberties of citizenship: I say let us settle the color question by conceding to the colored man the right to decide for himself; to act for himself, vote for whom he pleases and have that vote fairly counted." Watson might use the rhetoric of the New South in Atlanta, but he did not advocate New South programs.

30. Atlanta *People's Party Paper*, 25 May 1894; Woodward, *Tom Watson*, pp. 265–66.

31. Woodward, *Tom Watson*, p. 268. See reports of Watson speeches in the Gracewood (Ga.) *Wool Hat*, 28 July and 25 Aug. 1894, and his letter accepting the tenth congressional district nomination in the *Wool Hat*, 1 Sept. 1894.

32. Atlanta *People's Party Paper*, 27 July and 24 Aug. 1894.

33. Ibid., 13 and 27 July 1894.

34. See Gracewood (Ga.) *Wool Hat*, 28 Apr. and 23 June 1894.

35. See ibid., 12 May and 27 Oct. 1894.

36. The opposition to the new trend from old Alliancemen and Populists (see, for instance, Atlanta *People's Party Paper*, 25 May 1894 and Woodward, *Tom Watson*, p. 263) was by the time of the election evidently healed over. Watson's disclaimer of an Aug. 1894 article in the Atlanta *Constitution* talking about the split was not contradicted by any Georgia Populists, and the issue disappeared from the *People's Party Paper*. Watson had not backed down, as had the North Carolina and Alabama reformers by 1894, on the radical issues and implications of the Omaha platform and antimonopoly greenbackism.

37. While the Gracewood (Ga.) *Wool Hat* maintained its appeal to black voters, however, the growing use of the sectional metaphor and the increasing emphasis on Populist moderation and an appeal to the urban middle class coincided with a decreasing appeal to a coalition of working people and farmers. Editorials and letters concerning labor problems and issues that were prominent in 1892 (see 13 July, 13 Aug., 17 Sept., and 1 Oct. 1892) began to tail off in 1893, and by 1894 were rarely present. For an exception to this, see letters from "Diogenes," of Augusta, on 4 and 18 Aug. 1894. In 1892 the Richmond County Populists nominated a "workingman's candidate" (Silas Reid, Sr., who may have been a businessman when nominated) for one of the three state legislative seats from Richmond County, and nominated no one to represent Augusta businessmen (20 and 27 July 1892). For the Augusta municipal elections in the workingclass fifth ward, the Populists in Dec. 1893 nominated H. L. Plunkitt, "an honorable gentleman, a good citizen, and a solid businessman" (2 Dec. 1893). Reid was never identified as a businessman. Finally, response to the Homestead strike in 1892 in the *Wool Hat* was all positive. The strike was Carnegie's fault, the strikers had a right to organize and resist the Pinkertons, and nothing was said of the need to strike at the ballot box rather than the workplace (see *Wool Hat*, 13 July 1892). Except for an exchange from Watson's *Daily Press*, however (21 July 1894), and some sensitive discussions of organized labor's plight by "Diogenes" (4 and 18 Aug. 1894), after an initially prostriker response (see 14 July 1894) letters and editorials in the *Wool Hat* concerning the Pullman strike tended to downplay the grievances of the strikers and advised them constantly to vote right rather than strike in order to improve their condition. (See 21 and 28 July 1894.) Some of this decline of appeal to working people in Augusta likely resulted from the inability of the Populists to prevent fraud or attract enough workingclass votes to affect the Augusta outcome. But an appeal to the new urban middle class to join the Populists would have mitigated against creating the crude class alignments the Populists tried to effect in 1892 and early 1893 with Augusta factory operatives and working people. Only in 1892 were the Democrats attacked by the Populists for "their most diabolical appeal to array the city workers against their brethren in the country" (17 and 24 Sept. 1892).

38. See Gracewood (Ga.) *Wool Hat*, 28 Apr. and 28 July 1894; Atlanta *People's Party Paper*, 25 May and 13 July 1894.

39. Atlanta *People's Party Paper*, 11 May, 27 July, 10 and 17 Aug., 7, 14, and 28 Sept. 1894; Gracewood (Ga.) *Wool Hat*, 19 May, 1 and 15 Sept. 1894.

40. Atlanta *People's Party Paper*, 17 Aug. and 28 Sept. 1894.

41. Ibid., 19 Oct. 1894.

42. Ibid., 26 Oct. 1894.

43. Ibid.

44. Ibid., 28 Oct. 1892. See chap. 5, above, for Doyle incident.

45. For Watson, see his Macon speech, Atlanta *People's Party Paper*, 13 July 1894; also 27 July and 24 Aug. 1894.

46. Ibid., 24 and 31 Aug. and 7 and 28 Sept. 1894.

47. Ibid., 20 July 1894.

48. Ibid., 31 Aug. and 19 Oct. 1894; also Gracewood (Ga.) *Wool Hat*, 1 Sept. 1894.

49. See Atlanta *People's Party Paper*, 9 Feb., 13 Apr., 29 June, 6 July, all of Sept., and 5 Oct. 1894.

50. See Appendix D and Kousser, *The Shaping of Southern Politics*, p. 215. In an absolute sense, the Republican party may have played a role in this success. In 1892 the Republicans named a state ticket but endorsed Peek for governor. In 1894 and 1896 they ran no candidates and endorsed no one, at least officially. Since the Republicans took approximately the same position in each election, especially in 1894 and 1896, the relative success of the Georgia Populists with black voters would appear to have been related to their own efforts. The election results in the black belt indicate that the Georgia reformers' efforts were rewarded, and their lack of them in 1896 punished.

51. Dallas (Ga.) *Herald*, 14 Dec. 1893; Atlanta *People's Party Paper*, 27 Apr., 4 May, 8 and 22 June, 20 July and 10 Aug. 1894.

52. Atlanta *People's Party Paper*, 3 Nov. 1893.

53. Ibid., 22 June 1894.

54. Ibid., 3 Aug. 1894.

55. Ibid., 3 Nov. 1893. Ten months later Snead was a candidate for state office on the People's party ticket in his county (ibid., 31 Aug. 1894).

56. Dallas (Ga.) *Herald*, 14 Dec. 1893; also 3 Nov. 1893. See also Bion Williams's letter in the Gracewood (Ga.) *Wool Hat*, 30 June 1894.

57. See his DiGive's Opera House speech, Atlanta *People's Party Paper*, 25 May 1894; also 20 July, 17 Aug., 21 and 28 Sept., and 23 and 30 Nov. 1894.

58. Atlanta *People's Party Paper*, 17 Aug. 1894.

59. Ibid., 17 June to 3 Aug. 1894.

60. Ibid., 14 Dec. 1894.

61. Ibid., 28 Dec. 1894.

62. See ibid., 15 Feb., 15 and 22 Mar., and 5 Apr. 1895.

63. Dallas (Ga.) *Herald*, 21 Mar. and 4 Apr. 1895; Gibson (Ga.) *Glascock Banner*, 21 Feb. 1895; Statesboro (Ga.) *Banner Watchman* in Ozark (Ala.) *Banner-Advertiser*, 25 July 1895. On the role of the socialists in the conference, see Chester McArthur Destler, *American Radicalism, 1865–1901*, pp. 228–30.

64. Potter (Ga.) *Populist* in Gibson (Ga.) *Glascock Banner*, 14 Feb. 1895; Gibson (Ga.) *Glascock Banner*, 31 Jan., 14 and 21 Mar., 18 Apr., 30 May, 20 June, 11 July, 1 Aug., and 5 Dec. 1895; Rutledge (Ga.) *Gleaner* in Ozark (Ala.) *Banner-Advertiser*, 5 Dec. 1895.

65. Dallas (Ga.) *Herald*, 4 Oct. 1894 and 3 Jan. 1895; also Cedarville (Ga.) *Advance Courier* in Dallas (Ga.) *Herald*, 21 Mar. 1895.

66. See county resolutions in *Atlanta People's Party Paper*, 9, 23, and 30 Mar., 6 and 13 Apr., 11 and 18 May, and 1 June 1894.

67. Atlanta *People's Party Paper*, letters in July, also 21 Sept., 5 Oct., and 14 Dec. 1894 and 11 Jan. 1895.

68. Gracewood (Ga.) *Wool Hat*, 1 Apr. 1893; also 21 Jan. and 11 Mar. 1893.

69. Ibid., 2 and 16 Sept. 1893.

70. Ibid., 27 Oct. 1894; also 23 June 1894. Although quite conversant with greenback theory, the editor of the Gibson (Ga.) *Glascock Banner* on 18 July 1895 maintained that free silver would end hard times.

71. Atlanta *People's Party Paper*, 29 June and 13 July 1894.

72. Gracewood (Ga.) *Wool Hat*, 21 and 28 July and 4 and 25 Aug. 1894.

73. See Atlanta *People's Party Paper*, 5 and 19 Apr. 1895.

74. Ibid., 5 July 1895.

75. Ibid., 22 Mar. 1895.

76. Ibid., 8 Feb. 1895.

77. Gibson (Ga.) *Glascock Banner*, 20 June 1895.

78. Atlanta *People's Party Paper*, 5 Apr. 1895.

79. Part of the reason for the attack was a series of letters written to the *People's Party Paper* by S. C. McCandless, a Populist from Jackson, Georgia, who defended the concept of socialism without outlining any specific program. For McCandless's letters, see Atlanta *People's Party Paper*, 16 Aug. and 13 Sept. 1895.

80. Atlanta *People's Party Paper*, 16 Aug. 1895.

81. Ibid., 2, 16, and 30 Aug. and 1 Nov. 1895. For his continued attack on socialism, see ibid., 15 and 22 Nov. and 20 and 27 Dec. 1895; and 10 and 17 Jan., 14 Feb., and 19 and 26 June 1896.

82. Ibid., 20 Dec. 1895; also 27 Dec. 1895.

83. Woodward, *Tom Watson*, pp. 284–87; C. Vann Woodward, *Origins of the New South, 1877–1913*, pp. 278–83; Stanley L. Jones, *The Presidential Election of 1896*, pp. 55–57, 61–64.

84. He may also have been influenced in this direction by the national level debate going on between the extreme free silver Populists and the mid-roaders, the free silverites—especially through N. A. Dunning's *National Watchman*—accusing the mid-roaders of being socialists. See Dunning letters in Atlanta *People's Party Paper*, 7 and 21 Feb., 27 Mar., and 3 Apr. 1896; Lawrence Goodwyn, *Democratic Promise*, chap. 14; Jones, *The Presidential Election of 1896*, pp. 78–86.

85. Atlanta *People's Party Paper*, 30 Aug. 1895.

86. John D. Hicks, *The Populist Revolt*, Appendixes B and F.

87. Atlanta *People's Party Paper*, 18 Oct. and 27 Dec. 1895. See also his editorials on the land, 10 and 17 Jan. 1896.

88. Ibid., 18 Oct. 1895.

89. Ibid., 27 Dec. 1895.

90. Ibid., 7 Feb. 1896.

91. Ibid., 27 Dec. 1895. For a similar opinion from a letter writer, see 17 Jan. 1896.

92. Ibid., 15 Nov. 1895.

93. Ibid., 24 Apr. 1896.

94. Ibid., 3 Apr. 1896; also 10 and 24 Apr. 1896.

95. See, for example, ibid., 24 Apr., 31 July, and 9 Oct. 1896.

96. Ibid., 22 May 1896; also 31 July 1896.

97. See section on Texas, this chapter, below.

98. Atlanta *People's Party Paper*, 1 Nov. 1895.

99. Ibid., 27 Dec. 1895.

100. Ibid., 29 Nov. and 27 Dec. 1895.

101. Ibid., 3 Jan. 1896.

102. Ibid., 26 June 1896.

103. Ibid., 21 Aug. 1896.

104. Raleigh *Progressive Farmer*, 20 Nov. 1894.

105. Irwinton (Ga.) *Reform World* in Atlanta *People's Party Paper*, 12 June 1896; also Rutledge (Ga.) *Gleaner* in Ozark (Ala.) *Banner-Advertiser*, 5 Dec. 1895; Atlanta *People's Party Paper*, 26 June, 10 July, and 23 Oct. 1896.

106. Atlanta *People's Party Paper*, 29 May 1896.

107. See ibid., 29 May, 12 June, and 10 July 1896.

108. Gibson (Ga.) *Glascock Banner*, 30 May, 6 June, 1 Aug., and 5 Dec. 1895.

109. Ibid., 5 Dec. 1895.

110. Dallas (Ga.) *Herald*, 21 Nov. 1895.

111. Ibid., 26 Dec. 1895.

112. Ibid., 16 July 1896.

113. Atlanta *People's Party Paper*, 25 Oct. 1895.

114. Ibid., 27 Mar. 1896. For some calls for blacks to attend Populist mass meetings, see ibid., late May and June 1896.

115. See, for instance, ibid., 4 Sept. 1896.

116. See ibid., 18 and 25 Sept. and 2 Oct. 1896.

117. Woodward, *Tom Watson*, p. 312.

118. Ibid., pp. 275–76.

119. See Appendix D. Kousser's figures also show a similar decline (*The Shaping of Southern Politics*, p. 215).

120. For exceptions to both, see Atlanta *People's Party Paper*, 11 May 1894 and 28 Feb. 1896.

121. Ibid., 11 Dec. 1896.

122. Ibid., 16 Aug. 1895.

123. Grantham, *Hoke Smith*, pp. 127, 137–47, chap. 11, pp. 219–21, 230–32.

124. Dallas *Texas Advance*, 30 June 1894.

125. Alwyn Barr, *Reconstruction to Reform*, pp. 53–54, 64–70.

126. Ibid., maps following pp. 34, 130.

127. Except for Walker County, however, which had more blacks than whites in 1890, none of these counties could be considered strong Populist counties; none of them went Populist more than twice in three elections. The center of Populist strength in the state lay to the west and north of these old greenback counties, often in areas unsettled in the 1870s. The relationship between greenback votes and reform (Populist and Jeffersonian Democratic) votes was also true in Alabama. The greenback candidate for governor of Alabama in 1880, with Republican support, received 24 percent of the total vote. In 1882 the Greenback gubernatorial candidate, again with Republican support, increased that share to almost 32 percent. In both cases the greenback vote was heavily concentrated in north Alabama, where the Agricultural Wheel and the Farmers' Alliance first entered the state, and where Kolb did best in 1892 and 1894. See, for Alabama, William Warren Rogers, *One-Galloused Rebellion*, p. 54; Allen J. Going, *Bourbon Democracy in Alabama, 1874–1890*, pp. 58–59.

128. Ernest William Winkler, ed., *Platforms of Political Parties in Texas*, pp. 180–81, 187–89.

129. Kirk H. Porter and Donald Bruce Johnson, *National Party Platforms, 1840–1968*, pp. 57–58.

130. Winkler, *Platforms*, pp. 234–37, 246–47, 256–57, 260–63, 268–71, 281–84, 293–99, 314–16, 332–34, 379–84. For the Farmers' Alliance in Texas, see Goodwyn, *Democratic Promise*, chaps. 2, 3, and pp. 125–34, 140–42, 217–25, 232–43.

131. Goodwyn, *Democratic Promise*, chaps. 2, 3, 5, 6, and 8.

132. The strength of this analysis in the state was given a visible demonstration in the late months of 1891 and the early months of 1892. In Alabama the Jeffersonian Democrats were financial reform, free silver reformers who had to be driven from a conservative Democratic party. In Texas the Jeffersonian Democrats also had to be driven from the Democratic party, but one which was committed to free silver and the abolition of national banks. The Texas Jeffersonians split with the Democratic party over the subtreasury, the centerpiece of the antimonopoly greenback Farmers' Alliance and Populist platforms. (Winkler, *Platforms*, the Democratic 1890 platform, pp. 286–90, and the Jeffersonian Democratic platform, pp. 300–301.) The Texas Jeffersonians, unlike their Alabama counterparts, were in fundamental agreement with the Populists and by April 1892 had joined them. (See Barr, *Reconstruction to Reform*, pp. 128–29; Roscoe C. Martin, *The People's Party in Texas, a Study in Third Party Politics*, pp. 42–43.)

133. Winkler, *Platforms*, pp. 315–16. Also included were planks forbidding alien landownership and demanding that the state recover all public lands possible and reserve them for homesteaders, allowing corporations only as much land as they needed to carry out their business. They also demanded the direct election of president, vice-president, and United States senators; an end to competition between free and convict labor and "intellectual and moral instruction" provided for the inmates of state prisons; fair elections and honest counts; an elective railroad commission until the ultimate solution of government ownership; an efficient lien law protecting workingmen; a state bureau of labor and board of arbitration; a salary ceiling for county officials and two demands involving the improvement of public schools, increased school terms, free textbooks, and a change in school financing.

134. Winkler, *Platforms*, pp. 332–34.

135. Ibid., pp. 379–84.

136. Dallas (Tex.) *Southern Mercury*, 8 and 22 Jan., 27 Aug. 1891 and 6 Oct. 1892; San Antonio *Truth* in Mineola (Tex.) *Alliance Courier*, 6 Oct. 1892; Lampasas (Tex.) *People's Journal*, 19 Aug. and 28 Oct. 1892; Dallas (Tex.) *Southern Mercury* in Lampasas (Tex.) *People's Journal*, 12 Aug. 1892.

137. Dallas (Tex.) *Southern Mercury*, 9 Apr. 1891.

138. Stephenville (Tex.) *Empire*, 28 May and 7 Oct. 1892; McKinney (Tex.) *Democrat* in Dallas (Tex.) *Southern Mercury*, 29 Jan. 1891; Lampasas (Tex.) *People's Journal*, 19 and 26 Aug. and 16 Sept. 1892; Dallas (Tex.) *Southern Mercury*, 6 Oct. 1892.

139. Stephenville (Tex.) *Empire*, 16 Sept. 1892.

140. See, for instance, Dallas (Tex.) *Southern Mercury*, 1 Jan. 1891 and 6 Oct. 1892. The antisectional theme dominated the Lampasas (Tex.) *People's Journal* (see Aug., Sept., and Oct. 1892). The appeal to labor was not prominent, but it was evident. (See Dallas, Tex., *Southern Mercury*, 1 and 8 Jan. 1891; Lampasas, Tex., *People's Journal*, 16 Sept. 1892.)

141. The subtreasury was mentioned or defended in Dallas *Texas Advance*, 4 Nov. 1893 and 24 Mar. and 30 June 1894; Dallas (Tex.) *Southern Mercury* in Butler (Ala.) *Choctaw Alliance*, 31 May 1893; Dallas (Tex.) *Southern Mercury*, 18 May 1893.

142. Hamilton (Tex.) *Progress*, 31 Mar. 1893; Dallas *Texas Advance*, 28 Oct. 1893 and 7 Apr. 1894; Dallas (Tex.) *Southern Mercury*, 18 Jan., 19 Apr., 11 Oct., and 29 Nov. 1894.

143. Dallas *Texas Advance*, 25 Nov. 1893 and 5 May 1894; Dallas (Tex.) *Southern Mercury* in Butler (Ala.) *Choctaw Alliance*, 31 May 1893; Dallas (Tex.) *Southern Mercury*, 27 Dec. 1894.

144. Austin (Tex.) *People's Advocate*, 12 Oct. 1893 and 18 Jan. 1894; Dallas *Texas Advance*, 25 Nov. 1893; Austin (Tex.) *Argus*, 14 Aug. and 25 Sept. 1894.

145. For the rudimentary class orientation, see, for example, Austin (Tex.) *People's Advocate*, 15 Mar. and 5 Apr. 1894; Austin (Tex.) *Argus*, 31 July and 28 Aug. 1894; Dallas *Texas Advance*, 30 Sept. 1893 and 3 Feb. and 19 May 1894; Dallas (Tex.) *Southern Mercury*, 2 Mar. and 18 May 1893 and 26 Apr. and 27 Dec. 1894.

146. Dallas *Texas Advance*, 4 Aug. 1894.

147. For discussion of laboring people's issues, see Austin (Tex.) *People's Advocate*, 22 Dec. 1893 and 5 Apr. 1894; Austin (Tex.) *Argus*, 10, 17, and 31 July, 28 Aug., and 4 and 18 Sept. 1894; Dallas *Texas Advance*, 18 Nov. 1893 and 17 Mar., 19 May, and all of July 1894; Dallas (Tex.) *Southern Mercury*, 8 Jan. 1891.

148. A most accurate perception. See Goodwyn, *Democratic Promise*, pp. 285–91; Martin, *The People's Party in Texas*, pp. 89, 93.

149. Lawrence D. Rice, *The Negro in Texas, 1874–1900*, pp. 69–71.

150. Lampasas (Tex.) *People's Journal*, 14 Oct. 1892. Gerald Gaither, *Blacks and the Populist Revolt*, p. 119, reports "substantial" Populist grass roots organizing efforts among blacks in late 1891 and early 1892.

151. Rice, *The Negro in Texas*, p. 78.

152. Lampasas (Tex.) *People's Journal*, 9 Dec. 1892.

153. Austin (Tex.) *Argus*, 21 Aug. 1894; Dallas *Texas Advance*, 30 June 1894.

154. See Dallas *Texas Advance*, 30 Sept. 1893.

155. Ibid., 30 June 1894; also Austin (Tex.) *Argus*, 4 Sept. 1894. That Tracy understood the problem was no surprise. He had been at it a long time. In the state election of 1878 he was busy in the Houston area organizing black greenback clubs (Rice, *The Negro in Texas*, p. 56).

156. Rice, *The Negro in Texas*, p. 84.

157. Dallas (Tex.) *Southern Mercury*, 15 Oct. 1896; also 8 Oct. 1896 for a defense of blacks with some paternalistic overtones.

158. Kousser, *The Shaping of Southern Politics*, especially chaps. 8, 9.

159. In the fall of 1892 the *Southern Mercury* printed a letter from James H. "Cyclone" Davis outlining the Douglass-Cleveland affair (Dallas, Tex., *Southern Mercury* in Centreville, Ala., *People's Reflector*, 13 Oct. 1892). A month and a half after Tracy's eloquent editorial in the *Advance* on the need for a black and white political coalition he, too, denounced Cleveland's appointment of the "nigger Taylor" to the office of recorder of deeds for the District of Columbia (Dallas *Texas Advance*, 11 Aug. 1894). The *Southern Mercury* four months later attacked the Southern Democrats for using fraudulent black votes to defeat the reformers in the South, implying that because of this the South, as during Reconstruction, was once again under "negro rule" (Dallas, Tex., *Southern Mercury*, 6 Dec. 1894). Goodwyn found the *Southern Mercury* under Milton Park's editorship to be rather opportunistic on the race issue (*Democratic Promise*, p. 297). He is right, but this opportunism was also better than the blacks received from the Populists almost anywhere else in the South. See also, for Texas, Gaither, *Blacks and the Populist Revolt*, p. 119.

160. See Appendix G. When southern counties are divided up by the percentage of blacks in the total population in 1890, with white counties having less than a 40 percent black population, border counties having populations from 40.0 percent to 49.9 percent black, and black belt counties being 50.0 percent black or more, in Georgia (gubernatorial elections) and Mississippi (congressional elections) the Populist party did best in all three categories in 1894. In Alabama (gubernatorial elections) it did best in 1892. In North Carolina (outside the fusion election in 1894) in the gubernatorial elections of 1892 and 1896 the Populists did best in all categories in 1892. The Populists contested too few elections in Virginia for comparison. In Texas, on the other hand, the Populists did best in the 1896 gubernatorial election, improving their showing in each kind of county in every gubernatorial election from 1892 on. For Texas Kousser's figures show the same trend (*The Shaping of Southern Politics*, p. 199). Only the radical Texas party ever attracted so close to a majority of black votes in their state. Although Texas was in some ways unusual—fewer blacks, less experience with slavery, and no serious disfranchisement barriers until well into the first decade of the twentieth century—Texas was still a southern state. It had been settled by Southerners and the great bulk of its whites continued to live in east Texas among the black population of the state. The Texas Populists clearly had the greatest success, among Southern Populist state parties, attracting black support.

161. Austin (Tex.) *People's Advocate*, 3 Jan. 1895. See also note 180, below.

162. Dallas (Tex.) *Southern Mercury*, 14 Mar., 11 Apr., 30 May, 1 Aug., and 7 Nov. 1895 and 26 Mar., 30 Apr., 11 June, 16 July, 6 Aug., 3 Sept., and 26 Nov. 1896. Also see Meridian (Tex.) *Sun* in Dallas (Tex.) *Southern Mercury*, 10 Dec. 1896; Comanche (Tex.) *Pioneer Exponent*, 2 Jan. 1896.

163. Dallas (Tex.) *Southern Mercury*, 16 and 30 Jan. 1896.

164. Ibid., 28 Nov. and 12 Dec. 1895.

165. Ibid., 23 Jan. 1896.

166. Goodwyn, *Democratic Promise*, pp. 460–63; Destler, *American Radicalism*, pp. 227–31; Hicks, *The Populist Revolt*, pp. 349–50; Jones, *The Presidential Election of 1896*, pp. 84–85.

167. Letter to Atlanta *People's Party Paper*, 1 Dec. 1893. If Barnett Gibbs, an important Democratic politician and former lieutenant governor, was any indication, however, this influx might have been easier for the Texans to handle than that further east. Gibbs came over because of Democratic perfidy and because the Populists advocated government ownership of the railroads (Dallas, Tex., *Southern Mercury*, 12 Mar. and 9 Apr. 1896). By May 1896 Gibbs was making speeches stating that free silver was an insufficient reform (Dallas, Tex., *Southern Mercury*, 7 May 1896).

168. Dallas *Texas Advance*, 2 June 1894.

169. Austin (Tex.) *Argus*, 4 Sept. 1894.

170. Barr, *Reconstruction to Reform*, p. 57; Martin, *The People's Party in Texas*, pp. 118–19.

171. Dallas (Tex.) *Southern Mercury*, 27 Feb. and 18 June 1896.

172. Ibid., 17 Oct. 1895 and 27 Feb. and 18 June 1896.

173. Ibid., 17 Oct. 1895.

174. Ibid., 18 June 1896.

175. Ibid., 7 Feb. 1895.

176. Ibid., 27 Dec. 1894, 11 July 1895, and 5 and 26 Mar. 1896.

177. Ibid., 11 Apr. 1895; also 25 Apr. 1895.

178. Ibid., 14 Mar. 1895.

179. Ibid., 9 July 1896.

180. Interestingly, the Populist paper that most clearly advocated socialism as the ultimate solution to the problems that a growing industrial and financial capitalism brought to America—the Austin *People's Advocate*, 5 Apr. 1894—was one of the weakest Texas papers on the greenback issue, running a series of articles from the American Bimetallic League written by the ABL's president, A. J. Warner, in 1894, and calling free silver and more money at one point "The One Great Issue" (Austin, Tex., *People's Advocate*, 23 Aug. 1894 and 3 Jan. 1895).

181. Dallas (Tex.) *Southern Mercury*, 7 Nov. 1895.

182. Ibid., 28 Nov. 1895.

183. See ibid., 21 Nov. 1895 and 23 Jan. 1896.

184. See, for instance, ibid., 2 Apr. and 18 June 1896. Not all of them did, however. In Jan. 1896 an Erath County mass meeting, while endorsing the Omaha platform "in general terms," favored "the elimination of the sub-treasury feature of that platform, as well as making the land plank more definite" (Dallas, Tex., *Southern Mercury*, 23 Jan. 1896). This was very similar to Watson's position, and the state platform in 1896 did not endorse the subtreasury since it was left out of the national People's party platform, which the Texans did endorse. For the Texas Populist platform, see Winkler, *Platforms*, pp. 379–83.

185. Dallas (Tex.) *Southern Mercury*, 14 Feb. 1895.

186. Palo Pinto (Tex.) *Tribune*, 17 May 1895; Dallas (Tex.) *Southern Mercury*, 21 Mar., 11 Apr., 23 May, 11 and 25 July, 22 Aug., 24 Oct., and 7 Nov. 1895; and 23 Jan., 27 Feb., 12 Mar., 9 Apr., 18 June, and 26 Nov. 1896.

187. Dallas (Tex.) *Southern Mercury*, 24 Jan., 14 Feb., 21 Mar., 30 May 1895 and 19 Mar. and 26 Nov. 1896. The tendency for the antimonopoly issue to taper off in the summer and fall of 1896 was due to the effort the Texans—editors, speakers, and letter writers alike—put into pointing out the weakness of the Democratic advocacy of a redeemable currency.

188. Dallas (Tex.) *Southern Mercury*, 6 Feb. 1896.

189. See Comanche (Tex.) *Pioneer Exponent*, 2 Jan. 1896; Dallas (Tex.) *Southern*

Mercury, 3 Jan., 7 Feb., 14 Mar., 2 and 23 May, 12 Sept., 17 Oct., 7 and 28 Nov., and 19 Dec. 1895; and 13 Feb., 2 Apr., 21 May, 11 and 25 June, 16 July, 3 Sept., and 15 Oct. 1896; Meridian (Tex.) *Sun* in Dallas (Tex.) *Southern Mercury*, 10 Dec. 1896.

190. Dallas (Tex.) *Southern Mercury*, 24 Jan. 1895.

191. Ibid., 6 Feb. 1896; also Dallas *Texas Advance*, 19 May 1894.

192. Dallas (Tex.) *Southern Mercury*, 1 Aug. 1895.

193. It is interesting in this regard to note that while James H. "Cyclone" Davis in his book, *A Political Revelation*, showed considerable understanding of the Omaha platform issues and considerable sophistication in defending their practicality and constitutionality, he never very clearly integrated the three planks of the platform into an antimonopoly whole. For as close as he came, see pp. 100–101.

194. Dallas (Tex.) *Southern Mercury*, 12 Sept. 1895. Davis's suggestions were Bland of Missouri and DuBois of Iowa, Tillman of South Carolina and Sibley of Pennsylvania, or Tom Johnson of Ohio and Judge Harry Caldwell of Arkansas.

195. Ibid.

196. Ibid., 3 Oct. 1895.

197. Ibid., 10 Oct. 1895.

198. Woodward, *Tom Watson*, p. 295; Barr, *Reconstruction to Reform*, pp. 166–67.

199. Dallas (Tex.) *Southern Mercury*, 6 Aug. 1896.

200. Ibid., 20 Aug. 1896; Martin, *The People's Party in Texas*, pp. 244–46.

201. See Dallas (Tex.) *Southern Mercury*, 30 July, 20 Aug., and 10 and 15 Sept. 1896; McKinney (Tex.) *Democrat* in Dallas (Tex.) *Southern Mercury*, 22 Oct. 1896.

202. Dallas (Tex.) *Southern Mercury*, 20 Aug. and 8 and 22 Oct. 1896.

203. Ibid., 16 July 1896.

204. Ibid., 30 July 1896; also 6 Aug. 1896.

205. Ibid., 16 July and 29 Oct. 1896.

206. Ibid., 20 Aug. 1896; also 27 Aug. 1896.

207. Ibid., 20 Aug. 1896.

208. Ibid., 27 Aug. and 3 Sept. 1896.

209. Ibid., 8 Oct. 1896.

210. Ibid., 24 Sept. and 1 Oct. 1896; also 8 and 15 Oct. 1896.

211. Barr, *Reconstruction to Reform*, p. 171.

212. For an exception, see Dallas (Tex.) *Southern Mercury*, 30 May 1895.

213. Ibid., 31 Oct. 1895.

214. Ibid., 2 July 1896.

215. Ibid., 5 Mar. 1896.

216. The appearance of material from "Coin" Harvey and the American Bimetallic League (ABL) in the South seems to have reinforced the differences between Texas and the other Southern Populist state parties, between antimonopoly greenback Populists and financial reformers, rather than created them. Both influences were toward a redemptionist monetary position, and only in Texas was greenback sentiment strong enough to criticize the free silverites who adopted this position. Harvey's material and that of the ABL appeared everywhere in the Southern Populist press, and frequently employed rhetoric very similar to that of the Southern Populists. But in most cases Harvey and the League made their appearance in these papers after the trend to free silver was already strong among the Populists of North Carolina, Alabama, and Georgia. There were only a few holdouts from Harvey's and the League's material outside of Texas, and these generally were papers which in 1892 had shown greenback tendencies or a broader, more complex and integrated idea of Populist reform than most Southern Populist papers. This was not entirely true, however. Watson's paper had a lot of Harvey and ABL material and the *Progressive Farmer* had very little.

217. In the tradition of Woodward, Key, and Cash, J. Morgan Kousser in his *The Shaping of Southern Politics* has brilliantly described another way in which the dominant classes in the South manipulated racism to maintain and extend their own hegemony.

218. C. Vann Woodward's preface to the second revised edition of his *The Strange Career of Jim Crow*, published in 1966, has a careful discussion of this problem.

219. Helen G. Edmonds, *The Negro and Fusion Politics in North Carolina, 1894–1901*, p. 10. Also Barr, *Reconstruction to Reform*, p. 220.

220. Woodward, *The Strange Career of Jim Crow*, pp. 78–80.

221. Kousser, *The Shaping of Southern Politics*, pp. 224–29.

222. The drive for a stronger railroad commission in Alabama, for instance, sprang from what Sheldon Hackney described in *Populism to Progressivism in Alabama*, p. 130, as a desire to "bring greater profits to the merchants, cheaper goods to the farmers and consumers, and greater opportunity for local manufacturers through cheaper raw materials."

223. Grantham, *Hoke Smith*, pp. 187–92, 196–203.

224. Hackney, *Populism to Progressivism*, pp. 236–37.

225. Woodward, *Origins*, pp. 301–2. That same year saw the Texas Progressives pass the Robertson law, requiring all life insurance companies operating in the state to invest at least 75 percent of their legal reserves in Texas real estate and securities. This law is one of the best examples of the new southern middle class's approach to reform. While it indirectly benefited many Texans, particularly since it was accompanied by reform of insurance practices, the law kept Texas capital at home and available to the new Texas middle class, capital that had heretofore been siphoned off to the North (Woodward, *Origins*, pp. 384–85). The Texas railroad commission, established in 1891 by a Democratic legislature, sought to do much the same thing. The commissioners, appointed by the governor rather than elected, compromised and cooperated with the roads and appear to have set their policy in terms of helping Texas shippers and merchants, setting rates favorable to shippers moving their goods through Houston and Galveston rather than overland by interstate railroad (Barr, *Reconstruction to Reform*, p. 122). Hoke Smith's drive to modify the railroad commission in Georgia, according to his biographer, lay most immediately in the effort of the Atlanta Freight Bureau and the Atlanta Chamber of Commerce in 1904 to reduce rates between Atlanta and Savannah. Smith represented the Freight Bureau in front of the existing commission, which ruled in the railroads' favor and against the so-called "port rates." This defeat led the shippers to look for a "trust buster" to run for governor and modify the commission. In Smith they found their candidate (Grantham, *Hoke Smith*, pp. 132–33). This conservative bias of the reformers helps explain how they could consider disfranchisement a reform, as Kousser in *The Shaping of Southern Politics*, pp. 260–61, points out they did. It also helps explain their tendency to oppose child labor laws, or labor reform in general, and to discourage any real effort to aid the mudsills of Southern agriculture, the tenants and sharecroppers, black and white.

226. Woodward, *Origins*, pp. 369–72; Samuel P. Hays, *The Response to Industrialism, 1885–1914*, pp. 128–29.

227. Woodward, *Tom Watson*, p. 402.

228. This and the following Watson quotations are from Woodward, *Tom Watson*, p. 350.

229. Watson's point about southern railroads was well taken. See John F. Stover, *The Railroads of the South, 1865–1900*, pp. 206–9, chaps. 12, 13; Maury Klein, *The Great Richmond Terminal*. The whole of Klein's book is the story of the creation of the Southern Railway Company in the 1890s out of previously independent and often locally owned and controlled smaller southern railroads.

230. Woodward, *Origins*, pp. 318–20, 406–8, 416–23; Paul M. Gaston, *The New South Creed*, pp. 201–5.

Conclusion

1. Robert Wiebe in his *The Search for Order, 1877–1920*, chap. 1, has a sense for this kind of a world. A good example of this kind of community in the South, its patterns of living as well as its problems of race and exploitation, is described by Nate Shaw in Theodore Rosengarten, ed., *All God's Dangers*. The particular time focused on comes a bit after the Populist period, but for all intents and purposes it remained the same world.

2. See, for instance, Atlanta *People's Party Paper*, 24 June 1892 and 12 Apr. 1895; Dallas (Ga.) *Herald*, 10 Oct. 1895; Ozark (Ala.) *Banner*, 3 Aug. 1893.

3. See Raleigh *Caucasian*, 29 Oct. 1896; Ozark (Ala.) *Banner*, 9 June 1892; Gadsden (Ala.) *Alliance Advocate*, 17 Nov. 1892. The theme, along with many others we have described, appeared prominently in Bryan's famous Cross of Gold speech at the 1896 Democratic national convention (William J. Bryan, *The First Battle*, p. 205). Here, as elsewhere, Bryan harnessed the language of reform to a conservative end. Although Bryan differed considerably from the Populists in many of their original reform positions, he *sounded* good, and without the protection of the antimonopoly greenback basis for reform many Southern Populists found Bryan's free silver and sectional politics irresistable in 1896. Bryan's speech is also available in George B. Tindall, ed., *A Populist Reader*, pp. 203–11.

4. Ozark (Ala.) *Banner-Advertiser*, 23 Jan. 1896.

5. Thomas Jefferson, *Notes on Virginia*, Querry XIX, "Manufactures," pp. 164–65.

6. Raleigh *Progressive Farmer*, 25 Dec. 1894; also 28 Apr. 1891; Tarboro (N.C.) *Farmers' Advocate*, 21 Sept. 1892; Dallas (Ga.) *Herald*, 28 Feb. 1895; Raleigh *Progressive Farmer* in Atlanta *People's Party Paper*, 6 Nov. 1896.

7. Raleigh *Progressive Farmer*, 2 July 1895.

8. Austin (Tex.) *Argus*, 31 July 1894; also Raleigh *Progressive Farmer*, 15 Jan. 1895; Atlanta *People's Party Paper*, 16 Dec. 1892.

9. Raleigh *Progressive Farmer*, 1 Dec. 1891; also Atlanta *People's Party Paper*, 18 Oct. 1895.

10. Raleigh *Progressive Farmer*, 27 June 1893; also Hardy (Ark.) *National Reformer*, Oct. 1894; Atlanta *People's Party Paper*, 10 Nov. 1893; N. A. Dunning, ed., *The Farmers' Alliance History and Agricultural Digest*, pp. 3–4.

11. Atlanta *People's Party Paper*, 30 Nov. 1894; also 21 Jan. 1892.

12. Ibid., 4 Jan. 1895.

13. Ibid., 16 Dec. 1892.

14. Ozark (Ala.) *Banner*, 15 Dec. 1892.

15. Raleigh *Progressive Farmer*, 29 May 1894.

16. Dallas *Texas Advance*, 19 May 1894.

17. Salisbury (N.C.) *Carolina Watchman*, 5 Mar. 1891; also Hardy (Ark.) *Morgan's Buzz Saw*, July 1896; Gibson (Ga.) *Glascock Banner*, 31 Jan. 1895; Austin (Tex.) *Argus*, 18 Sept. 1894.

18. Raleigh *Progressive Farmer*, 27 Aug. 1895; also 19 Nov. 1895; Dallas (Tex.) *Southern Mercury*, 12 Dec. 1895; M. W. Howard, *The American Plutocracy*, chap. 14.

19. Dallas (Tex.) *Southern Mercury*, 25 July 1895.

20. Gracewood (Ga.) *Wool Hat*, 21 Jan. 1893; also 3 Mar. 1894; Atlanta *Living Issues* in Gracewood (Ga.) *Wool Hat*, 4 Feb. 1893.

21. Dallas (Ga.) *Herald*, 11 Apr. 1895. For the point that the American industrial society

served the few when it should serve the many, see also Dallas (Tex.) *Southern Mercury*, 24 Dec. 1896; Goldsboro (N.C.) *Caucasian*, 29 June 1893; Austin (Tex.) *People's Advocate*, 22 Mar. 1894; W. Scott Morgan, *History of the Wheel and Alliance, and the Impending Revolution*, p. 701.

22. Troy (Ala.) *Jeffersonian*, 7 Sept. 1894; also *Texas Union Workman* in Troy (Ala.) *Jeffersonian*, 28 Sept. 1894; Dallas (Ga.) *Herald*, 19 Oct. 1893; Wedowee (Ala.) *Randolph Toiler*, 9 Jan. 1896; Hardy (Ark.) *National Reformer*, Oct. 1894; Butler (Ala.) *Choctaw Alliance*, 23 Nov. 1892.

23. Ozark (Ala.) *Banner-Advertiser*, 14 Feb. 1895; also Natchitoches *Louisiana Populist*, 2 Nov. 1894; Dallas (Tex.) *Southern Mercury*, 7 Feb. and 24 Oct. 1895; Hardy (Ark.) *Morgan's Buzz Saw*, Oct. 1894, Dec. 1895, and Aug. 1896; Hardy (Ark.) *National Reformer*, Oct. 1894.

24. Hardy (Ark.) *National Reformer*, Apr. 1894.

25. Austin (Tex.) *Argus*, 18 Sept. 1894.

26. Tarboro (N.C.) *Farmers' Advocate*, 6 Jan. 1892; also Anniston *Alabama Leader*, 19 Sept. 1895; Lampasas (Tex.) *People's Journal*, 7 Oct. 1892; Thomas E. Watson, *People's Party Campaign Handbook*, 1892, p. 221.

27. Gracewood (Ga.) *Wool Hat*, 18 Aug. 1894.

28. Raleigh *Progressive Farmer*, 19 Jan. 1892; also 1 Sept. 1891; Gracewood (Ga.) *Wool Hat*, 10 Mar. 1894; Dallas (Tex.) *Southern Mercury*, 1 Jan. 1891 and 11 June 1896.

29. Hardy (Ark.) *National Reformer* in Beaver Dam (N.C.) *Our Home*, 21 June 1893; also Gracewood (Ga.) *Wool Hat*, 13 May 1893; Austin (Tex.) *People's Advocate*, 22 Mar. 1894.

30. Richmond *Exchange Reporter*, 18 Aug. 1891; also Atlanta *People's Party Paper*, 11 Dec. 1896; Goldsboro (N.C.) *Caucasian*, 12 Oct. 1893; Austin (Tex.) *People's Advocate*, 17 Dec. 1893; Gracewood (Ga.) *Wool Hat*, 3 June 1893; Hardy (Ark.) *Morgan's Buzz Saw*, July 1896.

31. Dallas (Tex.) *Southern Mercury*, 11 June 1896.

32. The cooperative crusade was the heart of this experience. See Lawrence Goodwyn, *Democratic Promise*, chap. 5; Robert C. McMath, Jr., *Populist Vanguard*, pp. 17–20, 30–32, 48–58.

33. Butler (Ala.) *Choctaw Alliance*, 12 Sept. 1894; also Raleigh *Progressive Farmer*, 1 Sept. 1891.

34. Richmond *Virginia Sun*, 13 Feb. 1892; also Hardy (Ark.) *National Reformer*, Sept. 1893.

34. Gracewood (Ga.) *Wool Hat*, 14 July 1894.

36. For the clearest statement of this idea, see James Murdock in Raleigh *Progressive Farmer*, 1 Sept. 1891 and 19 Jan. 1892.

37. See Austin (Tex.) *Argus*, 17 and 31 July 1894; Austin (Tex.) *People's Advocate*, 22 Feb. 1894.

38. Austin (Tex.) *People's Advocate*, 5 Apr. 1894.

39. See, for instance, Atlanta *People's Party Paper*, 11 Dec. 1896.

40. Anniston *Alabama Leader*, 1 Aug. 1895.

41. Richmond *Virginia Sun*, 13 Feb. 1892. For other references to the "brotherhood of man," see Hardy (Ark.) *National Reformer*, Feb. 1895; Atlanta *People's Party Paper*, 14 Apr. 1893; Irwinton (Ga.) *Reform World* in Atlanta *People's Party Paper*, 6 Nov. 1896; Dallas *Texas Advance*, 28 Oct. 1893 and 6 Jan. 1894; Gracewood (Ga.) *Wool Hat*, 20 May 1893.

42. Dallas *Texas Advance*, 28 July 1894.

43. Raleigh *Progressive Farmer*, 29 May 1894.

44. Gibson (Ga.) *Glascock Banner*, 14 Mar. 1895.

45. Hardy (Ark.) *Morgan's Buzz Saw*, Nov. 1895.

46. Raleigh *Progressive Farmer*, 15 Aug. 1893; also Goldsboro (N.C.) *Caucasian*, 15 Sept. 1892 and 16 Nov. 1893.

47. Centreville (Ala.) *People's Reflector*, 22 Sept. 1892.

48. Gracewood (Ga.) *Wool Hat*, 24 Feb. 1894; also Ozark (Ala.) *Banner*, 4 Aug. 1892; Dallas (Ga.) *Herald*, 28 June 1894 and 8 Aug. and 19 Sept. 1895; Goldsboro (N.C.) *Caucasian*, 18 Aug. 1892; Troy (Ala.) *Jeffersonian*, 19 Jan. 1894.

49. Tarboro (N.C.) *Farmers' Advocate*, 25 Nov. 1891; also Cooper (Tex.) *People's Cause*, 28 Feb. 1896; Goldsboro (N.C.) *Caucasian*, 6 July 1893; Harry Tracy, "The Sub-Treasury Plan," in Dunning, *The Farmers' Alliance History*, p. 340.

50. See Dallas (Tex.) *Southern Mercury*, 2 July 1896; Atlanta *People's Party Paper*, 13 Apr. 1894, 29 Mar. 1895, and 31 July 1896; Dahlonega (Ga.) *Signal*, 3 Sept. 1892; Goldsboro (N.C.) *Caucasian*, 24 Aug. 1893.

51. Salisbury (N.C.) *Carolina Watchman*, 5 Feb. 1891; also Dallas (Tex.) *Southern Mercury*, 24 Oct. 1895 and 14 May 1896; Clinton (N.C.) *Caucasian*, 19 Feb. 1891; Atlanta *People's Party Paper*, 14 Jan., 11 Feb., and 20 May 1892, 25 May 1894, 20 Dec. 1895, and 21 Aug. 1896; Ozark (Ala.) *Banner-Advertiser*, 11 July 1895.

52. See, for instance, Oxford (Ala.) *Voice*, 5 Dec. 1891; Anniston *Alabama Leader*, 14 Nov. 1895; Butler (Ala.) *Choctaw Alliance*, 22 Mar. 1893; Atlanta *People's Party Paper*, 30 Nov. 1894.

53. Atlanta *People's Party Paper*, 8 Dec. 1893.

54. Concord (N.C.) *Standard* in Salisbury (N.C.) *Carolina Watchman*, 29 Oct. 1891; also Raleigh *Caucasian*, 21 May 1896; Austin (Tex.) *Argus*, 17 July 1894; Dallas (Tex.) *Southern Mercury*, 17 Sept. and 12 Nov. 1896; Raleigh *Progressive Farmer*, 14 May 1895; Dallas *Texas Advance*, 14 Apr. 1894; Gracewood (Ga.) *Wool Hat*, 22 Apr. 1893; Richmond *Virginia Sun*, 18 May 1892; *Faulkner County Wheel* (Ark.), 1 July 1891; Nashville *Weekly Toiler*, 21 Oct. 1891; Gibson (Ga.) *Glascock Banner*, 30 May 1895; Lampasas (Tex.) *People's Journal*, 19 Aug. 1892; Harry Tracy, Appendix, in James H. Davis, *A Political Revelation*, pp. 383–86.

55. Stephenville (Tex.) *Empire*, 28 May 1892; also Richmond *Exchange Reporter*, 17 Oct. 1891; Richmond *Virginia Sun*, 26 Mar. 1892.

56. For exceptions, see Gracewood (Ga.) *Wool Hat*, 25 Nov. 1893; Tarboro (N.C.) *Farmers' Advocate*, 29 Apr. 1891.

57. Gracewood (Ga.) *Wool Hat*, 13 Jan. 1894; also 25 Nov. 1893; Atlanta *People's Party Paper*, 28 Jan. 1892.

58. Goldsboro (N.C.) *Caucasian*, 16 Nov. 1893; also Raleigh *Caucasian*, 15 Aug. 1895; Atlanta *People's Party Paper*, 3 Dec. 1891; Tarboro (N.C.) *Farmers' Advocate*, 9 Dec. 1891 and 9 Mar. 1892; Raleigh *Progressive Farmer*, 8 Mar. 1892.

59. See Raleigh *Caucasian*, 16 July 1896; Dallas (Tex.) *Southern Mercury* in Tarboro (N.C.) *Farmers' Advocate*, 2 Nov. 1892.

60. Tarboro (N.C.) *Farmers' Advocate*, 9 Dec. 1891; also Raleigh *Progressive Farmer*, 9 May 1893; Dallas (Tex.) *Southern Mercury*, 4 Apr. 1895.

61. Raleigh *Progressive Farmer*, 7 June 1892.

62. Ibid., 6 Aug. 1895; also Bickley to Butler, 7 Aug. 1896, box 3, folder 31, Marion Butler Papers.

63. Salisbury (N.C.) *Carolina Watchman*, 12 Feb. 1891; also Butler (Ala.) *Choctaw Alliance*, 26 Oct. 1892; Raleigh *Progressive Farmer*, 24 Nov. 1891.

64. A mark of the impact of the new society was the infrequent inclusion of "brain workers" in this class, yet even then industry referred primarily to the effort of work by individuals.

65. Dallas (Tex.) *Southern Mercury*, 1 Jan. 1891, and "Don't Throw Your Vote Away,"

Populist campaign pamphlet, 38–360, William DuBose Sheldon Papers.

66. Tarboro (N.C.) *Farmers' Advocate*, 23 Mar. 1892; also Salisbury (N.C.) *Carolina Watchman*, 26 Mar. 1891; Atlanta *People's Party Paper*, 28 Jan. and 31 Mar. 1892.

67. Ozark (Ala.) *Banner*, 11 May 1893; Tarboro (N.C.) *Farmers' Advocate*, 8 Apr. 1891; Atlanta *People's Party Paper*, 22 Sept. 1893.

68. Gracewood (Ga.) *Wool Hat*, 24 Sept. 1892, 5 Aug. 1893, and 21 July 1894. For an implicit distinction between farming and the "railroad industry" by Watson, see Atlanta *People's Party Paper*, 7 Apr. 1893.

69. See, for instance, Raleigh *Progressive Farmer*, 27 Aug. 1895; *Faulkner County Wheel*, (Ark.), 1 July 1891; Nashville *Weekly Toiler*, 21 Oct. 1891.

70. See, for instance, Goldsboro (N.C.) *Caucasian*, 15 Sept. 1892; Raleigh *Caucasian*, 30 May 1895.

71. Dallas (Ga.) *Herald*, 25 May 1893.

72. Ozark (Ala.) *Banner-Advertiser*, 9 Jan. 1896.

73. See Tarboro (N.C.) *Farmer's Advocate*, 20 July 1892; Butler (Ala.) *Choctaw Alliance*, 8 Nov. and 13 Dec. 1893; Ozark (Ala.) *Banner-Advertiser*, 11 June 1896; Notes for President Pierson's speech on the currency question in the minute book of the Old Hickory Alliance, 5 Mar. 1890, Charles H. Pierson Papers.

74. Atlanta *People's Party Paper*, 12 Apr. 1895; also Greenville (Ala.) *Living Truth* in Butler (Ala.) *Choctaw Alliance*, 19 Apr. 1893.

75. For the greenbackers this may well have been an inheritance from Henry Carey and his concept of "harmony of interests." Carey was a greenbacker in the late 1860s and 1870s, at least to the extent that he favored a soft money policy by the federal government, which meant issuing legal tender fiat paper money. See David Montgomery, *Beyond Equality*, pp. 86–87, 179; Robert P. Sharkey, *Money, Class, and Party*, pp. 166–67; Unger, *The Greenback Era*, pp. 50–51.

76. From the Omaha platform. See Norman Pollack, ed., *The Populist Mind*, p. 63.

77. One interesting exception to this appeared in the Gracewood (Ga.) *Wool Hat*. In a series of articles entitled "Capital versus Labor," "Diogenes" started with the notion that labor creates all wealth and followed it to the conclusion that capitalists were unnecessary, that capital was a privilege that the laborer allowed the capitalist. He did not, however, discuss what could be done about changing the "false relations" between capital and labor, except to suggest that a "revolution" might be necessary. See 29 Apr. and 6, 13, 20, and 27 May 1893. The series "Labor versus Capital" ran through 17 June 1893.

78. Atlanta *People's Party Paper*, 6 Mar. 1896.

79. Dallas (Tex.) *Southern Mercury*, 19 Sept. 1895; also Austin (Tex.) *Argus*, 31 July and 4 Sept. 1894.

80. Atlanta *People's Party Paper*, 5 July 1895.

81. Richmond *Virginia Sun*, 31 Jan. 1894; also Tarboro (N.C.) *Farmers' Advocate*, 8 Apr. 1891.

82. Dallas *Texas Advance*, 16 Dec. 1893.

83. Wadesboro (N.C.) *Plow Boy*, 30 Jan. 1895.

84. See, for instance, Oxford (N.C.) *Granville County Reformer*, 21 June 1894; Raleigh *Progressive Farmer*, 8 May 1894 and 8 Jan. 1895.

85. See, for instance, Atlanta *People's Party Paper*, 14 Jan. 1892.

86. Ibid., 8 Dec. 1893. See paragraph accompanying note 53, above.

87. Dallas *Texas Advance*, 14 Apr. 1894; also Raleigh *Progressive Farmer*, 15 Aug. 1893; Nashville *Weekly Toiler*, 21 Oct. 1891.

88. Dallas (Tex.) *Southern Mercury*, 10 Oct. 1895.

89. Ibid., 19 Sept. 1895.

90. James Agee and Walker Evans, *Let Us Now Praise Famous Men*, pp. 76–77.

91. For comparative figures on farm tenancy, state by state, from 1880 through 1910, see Theodore Saloutos, *Farmer Movements in the South, 1865–1933*, p. 237. Sheldon Hackney found that the one factor which correlated best with the incidence of Populism in Alabama was the increase in farm tenancy (*Populism to Progressivism in Alabama*, pp. 25–26).

Bibliography

A. Manuscript Collections

Athens, Ga.
  Manuscript Division, University of Georgia
    Rebecca Latimer Felton Papers
Baton Rouge, La.
  Possession of John Price
    Hardy L. Brian Papers
Chapel Hill, N.C.
  Southern Historical Collection, University of North Carolina
    Marion Butler Papers
    Leonidas LaFayette Polk Papers
    Cyrus W. Thompson Papers
    Thomas E. Watson Papers
Charlottesville, Va.
  Alderman Library, University of Virginia
    Charles Herbert Pierson Papers
    William DuBose Sheldon Papers
Montgomery, Ala.
  Alabama State Department of Archives and History
    John Witherspoon DuBose Papers
    Robert McKee Papers
    Farley Maxwell Papers
Tuscaloosa, Ala.
  Alabama University Library
    Oliver Day Street Papers

B. Newspapers

ALABAMA

Montgomery, Ala. Alabama State Department of Archives and History
  Anniston *Alabama Leader*, 30 May to 19 Dec. 1895.
  Birmingham *People's Daily Tribune*, 8 Nov. 1894.
  Birmingham *People's Weekly Tribune*, Kolb's paper, 26 Mar., 7 and 14 May, 28 May to
    30 July, 20 Aug., 10 and 24 Sept., and 1 Oct. 1896.
  Butler *Choctaw Alliance*, a paper strongly identified with the Populists as opposed to the
    Jeffersonian Democrats, 19 Oct. 1892 to 7 Nov. 1894 and 7 Jan. to 29 Dec. 1896,
    with only a few copies missing in either series.
  Centreville *People's Reflector*, state Alliance president Sam Adams's paper, 22 Sept. to 10
    Nov. 1892.

Bibliography

Gadsden *Alliance Advocate*, 3 Nov. to 19 Dec. 1892.

Geneva *Record*, 21 issues in 1891.

Greenville *Living Truth*, 25 June, 2 July, and 24 Sept. 1896.

Montgomery *Alabama Monitor*, 30 Oct., 13 Nov., and 11 Dec. 1896.

Montgomery *Alliance Herald*, 16 July and 19 Nov. 1891; 4 May 1893; 26 Apr. to 17 May 1894.

Oxford *Voice*, a paper identifying strongly with the Jeffersonian Democrats, 9 Jan. 1891 to 5 Nov. 1892, with almost all the copies in the run.

Ozark *Banner*, 2 June 1892 to 24 Jan. 1895, when it merged with the Enterprise *Advertiser* to form the *Banner-Advertiser*.

Ozark *Banner-Advertiser*, 31 Jan. 1895 to 17 Dec. 1896, to provide a complete run for Alabama reform.

Troy *Jeffersonian*, 17 Nov. 1893 to 26 Oct. 1894, with a few copies missing.

Tuscaloosa *Journal*, 24 July 1895 and 29 July and 10 Oct. 1896.

Wedowee *Randolph Toiler*, 24 Oct. 1895 to 18 Dec. 1896, with a few copies missing.

Wedowee *Toiler*, 23 Mar. 1893.

ARKANSAS

Little Rock, Ark. Arkansas History Commission

Faulkner County Wheel, 1 July 1891.

Hardy *Arkansaw Kicker*, 14 Mar. 1896.

Hardy *Morgan's Buzz Saw*, monthly, Oct. 1894; Jan. and July to Dec. 1895; and Jan. to Dec. 1896.

Hardy *National Reformer*, monthly, July to Dec. 1893; Jan., Mar., Apr., Sept. to Nov. 1894; and Jan. to June 1895, when it merged with *Morgan's Buzz Saw*.

Little Rock *Arkansas Farmer*, 3 Dec. 1891.

Little Rock *Dollar*, 13 Dec. 1895.

Searcy *Southern Economist*, 23 May 1895 and 28 May 1896.

GEORGIA

Athens, Ga. University of Georgia Library

Dahlonega *Signal*, a strongly local, fairly nonpolitical paper, 2 Jan. 1891 to 14 Dec. 1894, a fairly complete series.

Dallas *Herald*, edited by an old greenbacker, 4 May 1893 to 27 Aug. 1896, a fairly complete series.

Gibson *Glascock Banner*, 3 Jan. to 5 Dec. 1895, with a few issues missing.

Atlanta, Ga. Georgia State Department of Archives and History

Gracewood *Wool Hat*, 1 June 1892 to 17 Nov. 1894, with a few issues missing, especially in Oct. and Nov. 1894.

Hindsville *Gazette*, 2 Dec. 1891.

Chapel Hill, N.C. Southern Historical Collection, University of North Carolina

Atlanta *People's Party Paper*, 26 Nov. 1891 to 1 Jan. 1897.

LOUISIANA

Baton Rouge, La. Department of Archives, Louisiana State University

Leesville *People's Friend*, 4 July 1895.

Natchitoches *Louisiana Populist*, 24 Aug. 1894 to 25 Dec. 1896, a complete run. The paper started on the initial date of the run.

Springville *Star*, 24 May 1894.

Bibliography

New Orleans, La. Tulane University Library
New Orleans *Issue*, which was mostly plate material, especially after 1893; 1 Aug. 1891; 4 July and 10 and 31 Dec. 1892; 8 Apr. and 10 Dec. 1893; 18 scattered issues Feb. to Dec. 1894; 6 scattered issues 1895.
Possession of John Price. Hardy L. Brian Papers
Montgomery *Mail*, 7 July 1894.
Winnfield *Comrade*, 13 Dec. 1894.

NORTH CAROLINA
Chapel Hill, N.C. Southern Historical Collection, University of North Carolina
Asheville *Mountain Home Journal*, 15 June 1892.
Beaver Dam *Our Home*, 26 May, 21 and 28 June, 26 July, and 2 Aug. 1893.
Charlotte *People's Paper*, 24 Jan. 1896.
Henderson *Vance Farmer*, 20 Sept. 1892.
Hickory *Mercury*, 2 Dec. 1891; and 9 Mar., 6 Apr., 29 June, 24 and 31 Aug., 14 and 21 Sept. 1892.
King's Mountain *Progressive Reformer*, 23 Apr. 1896.
Oxford *Granville County Reformer*, 17 May and 21 June 1894.
Raleigh *Caucasian*, Marion Butler's paper, which started in Clinton, 1 Jan. 1891 to 26 Jan. 1892; moved to Goldsboro, 2 Feb. 1892 to 20 Dec. 1894; finally moving to Raleigh, 27 Dec. 1894 to 17 Dec. 1896.
Raleigh *Hayseeder*, 22 Oct. 1896.
Raleigh *Progressive Farmer*, 6 Jan. 1891 to 22 Dec. 1896.
Salisbury *Carolina Watchman*, 8 Jan. 1891 to 23 Feb. 1893, with a few copies missing.
Tarboro *Farmers' Advocate*, 8 Apr. 1891 to 22 Dec. 1892.
Wadesboro *Plow Boy*, whose editor was opposed to Butler's course in North Carolina in 1895 and 1896; 9 Jan., 30 Jan. to 13 Feb., 27 Feb., 18 and 25 Sept., 16 and 30 Oct., 13 Nov., and 18 Dec. 1895; and 8 and 22 Jan., 12 and 26 Feb., 18 Mar., 8 Apr., and 21 Oct. 1896.
Warren Plains *People's Paper*, 20 Dec. 1895 and 3 Jan., 14 Feb., 12 June, and 16 Oct. 1896.

TENNESSEE
Nashville, Tenn. Tennessee State Library and Archives
Nashville *Weekly Toiler*, 25 Jan., 13 and 27 May, 3 June, 14 to 28 Oct., and 2 and 23 Dec. 1891; and 27 Jan., 10 Feb., 30 Mar., 4 and 18 May, 19 and 26 Oct., and 2 Nov. 1892.
Trenton *Tennessee Populist*, 8 Mar. 1894.

TEXAS
Austin, Tex. Texas State Archives
Austin *Argus*, 10 July to 28 Oct. 1894.
Austin *People's Advocate*, 12 Oct., 9 Nov., and 7 and 14 Dec. 1893; 18 Jan., 22 Feb., 1, 15, and 22 Mar., 5 and 26 Apr., 17 and 24 May, 12 and 26 July, 23 and 30 Aug., 13 Sept. to 25 Oct., 15 and 29 Nov., and 20 Dec. 1894; and 3 Jan. 1895.
Dallas *Southern Mercury*, 6 Oct. 1891; 3 Nov. 1892; 2 Mar. and 18 May 1893; scattered copies 1894; and 3 Jan. 1895 to 24 Dec. 1896.
Decatur *Times*, 22 Mar. 1893.
Graham *Young County Call*, 22 Mar. 1895.
Austin, Tex. University of Texas Archives
Austin *People's Advocate*, 22 Dec. 1893.
Burnett *Avalanche*, 10 Mar. 1892.

Bibliography

Comanche *Pioneer Exponent*, 2 Jan. 1896.
Cooper *People's Cause*, 28 Feb. 1896.
Dallas *Southern Mercury*, 1, 8, 22, and 29 Jan., 9 Apr., and 27 Aug. 1891; 19 and 26
  Apr. and 6 and 27 Dec. 1894; and 3 Jan. 1895 to 24 Dec. 1896.
Dallas *Texas Advance*, 16 and 30 Sept., 14 Oct., and 28 Oct. to 23 Dec. 1893; and 6 and
  13 Jan., 3 Feb., 24 Feb. to 5 May, 19 May, 2 June, and 30 June to 25 Aug. 1894.
Hamilton *Progress*, 31 Mar. and 24 May 1893.
Lampasas *People's Journal*, 5 Aug. 1892 to 27 Jan. 1893.
McKinney *Democrat*, 9 July 1896.
Mineola *Alliance Courier*, 6 Oct. 1892.
Runge *Karnes County News*, 8 May 1891.
Stephenville *Empire*, a Democratic paper which ran, from May to Nov. 1892, a Populist
  column written by local Populists; 28 May, 11 and 25 June, 16 Sept., and 30 Sept. to
  28 Oct. 1892.

VIRGINIA
Charlottesville, Va. Alderman Library, University of Virginia
  Richmond *Exchange Reporter*, semimonthly from 11 July 1891 to 2 Jan. 1892, weekly
    to 6 Feb. 1892, when it became the Richmond *Virginia Sun*.
  Richmond *Virginia Sun*, 25 issues between 13 Feb. and 16 Nov. 1892; 15 issues between
    18 Jan. and 2 Nov. 1893; 31 Jan. and 20 Dec. 1894; and 13 Feb. and 5 Mar. 1896.

C. Contemporary Published Material

Bellamy, Edward. *Looking Backward, 2000–1887*. New York: New American Library,
  1960. First published in New York in 1887.
Bryan, William J. *The First Battle: A Story of the Campaign of 1896*. Chicago: W. B.
  Conkey Co., 1896.
Davis, James H. *A Political Revelation*, with Appendix by Harry Tracy. Dallas, Tex.: The
  Advance Publishing Co., 1894.
Dunning, N. A., ed. *The Farmers' Alliance History and Agricultural Digest*. Washington,
  D.C.: The Alliance Publishing Co., 1891.
George, Henry. *Progress and Poverty: An Inquiry into the Cause of Industrial Depression
  and of Increase of Want with Increase of Wealth*. New York: Random House, 1930.
  First published in New York in 1880.
Harvey, William H. *Coin's Financial School*. Edited by Richard Hofstadter. Cambridge,
  Mass.: Harvard University Press, 1963. First published in Chicago in 1894.
Howard, M. W. *The American Plutocracy*. New York: Holland Publishing Co., 1895.
Morgan, W. Scott. *History of the Wheel and Alliance, and the Impending Revolution*.
  Hardy, Ark.: Published by the author, 1891.
Nugent, Catherine, ed. *Life Work of Thomas L. Nugent*. Stephenville, Tex.: Published by
  the author, 1896.
Tribune Almanac and Political Register. New York: The Tribune Association, 1893, 1894,
  1895, 1896, 1897, 1898.
Watson, Thomas E. *People's Party Campaign Handbook, 1892. Not a Revolt; It Is a
  Revolution*. Washington, D.C.: National Watchman Publishing Co., 1892.

Little Southern Populist pamphlet material remains. The Hardy Brian, Marion Butler,
Thomas E. Watson, and William DuBose Sheldon Papers have what little there is. I have
not listed it here because almost always the pamphlets consisted of reprints from newspaper

Bibliography

articles and editorials or speeches, and the flyers were party platforms or documents which the newspaper reprinted. I used the pamphlet material from the newspapers with very few exceptions.

D. Government Documents

Office of the Secretary of State for Mississippi. *Election Returns for the State of Mississippi.* Jackson, Miss.

United States Bureau of the Census. *Negro Population in the United States, 1790–1915.* Washington, D.C.: Government Printing Office, 1918.

E. Other Published Sources

Agee, James, and Evans, Walker. *Let Us Now Praise Famous Men.* New York: Ballantine Books, 1966. First published in New York in 1939.

Ahlstrom, Sidney E. *A Religious History of the American People.* New Haven, Conn.: Yale University Press, 1972.

Argersinger, Peter. "Pentacostal Politics in Kansas: Religion, the Farmers' Alliance, and the Gospel of Populism." *Kansas Quarterly* 1 (Fall 1969): 24–35.

Armes, Ethel. *The Story of Coal and Iron in Alabama.* Birmingham, Ala.: Chamber of Commerce, 1910.

Arnett, Alex M. *The Populist Movement in Georgia: A View of the "Agrarian Crusade" in Light of Solid-South Politics.* Columbia University Studies in History, Economics, and Public Law, vol. 104. New York: Columbia University Press, 1922.

Bailyn, Bernard. *The Ideological Origins of the American Revolution.* Cambridge, Mass.: Harvard University Press, 1967.

Barr, Alwyn. *Reconstruction to Reform: Texas Politics, 1876–1906.* Austin: University of Texas Press, 1971.

Becker, Carl L. *The Heavenly City of the Eighteenth-Century Philosophers.* New Haven, Conn.: Yale University Press, 1932.

Bode, Frederick A. *Protestantism and the New South: North Carolina Baptists and Methodists in Political Crisis, 1894–1903.* Charlottesville: University Press of Virginia, 1975.

Boorstin, Daniel J. *The Lost World of Thomas Jefferson.* New York: Henry Holt and Co., 1948.

Brock, W. R. *The Character of American History.* 2nd ed. New York: St. Martin's Press, 1965.

Brown, William, and Reynolds, Morgan. "Debt Peonage Re-examined." *Journal of Economic History* 33 (Dec. 1973): 862–71.

Buder, Stanley. *Pullman: An Experiment in Industrial Order and Community Planning, 1880–1930.* New York: Oxford University Press, 1967.

Burnham, W. Dean. *Presidential Ballots, 1836–1892.* Baltimore, Md.: The Johns Hopkins Press, 1955.

Cawelti, John G. *Apostles of the Self-Made Man: Changing Concepts of Success in America.* Chicago: University of Chicago Press, 1965.

Clark, John B. *Populism in Alabama.* Auburn, Ala.: Auburn Printing Co., 1927.

Clark, Thomas D. "The Country Newspaper: A Factor in Southern Opinion, 1865–1930." *Journal of Southern History* 14 (Feb. 1948): 3–33.

Conkin, Paul K. *Self-Evident Truths: Being a Discourse on the Origins and Development of*

Bibliography

the First Principles of American Government—Popular Sovereignty, Natural Rights, and Balance and Separation of Powers. Bloomington: Indiana University Press, 1974.

Crowe, Charles. "Tom Watson, Blacks, and Populists Reconsidered." *Journal of Negro History* 55 (Apr. 1970): 99–116.

Curti, Merle. *The Growth of American Thought*. 3rd ed. New York: Harper and Row, 1964.

Delap, Simeon A. "The Populist Party in North Carolina." In Trinity College Historical Society *Papers*, Ser. XIV: 40–74. Durham, N.C., 1922.

Destler, Chester McArthur. *American Radicalism, 1865–1901: Essays and Documents*. New London: Connecticut College, 1946.

Edmonds, Helen G. *The Negro and Fusion Politics in North Carolina, 1894–1901*. Chapel Hill: University of North Carolina Press, 1951.

Farish, Hunter Dickinson. *The Circuit Rider Dismounts: A Social History of Southern Methodism, 1865–1900*. Richmond, Va.: The Dietz Press, 1938.

Faulkner, Harold U. *American Economic History*. 8th ed. New York: Harper and Row, 1960.

Fine, Sidney. *Laissez-Faire and the General Welfare State: A Study of Conflict in American Thought, 1865–1901*. Ann Arbor: University of Michigan Press, 1956.

Fite, Gilbert C., and Reese, Jim E. *An Economic History of the United States*. 3rd ed. Boston, Mass.: Houghton Mifflin Co., 1973.

Foner, Eric. *Free Soil, Free Labor, Free Men: The Ideology of the Republican Party Before the Civil War*. New York: Oxford University Press, 1970.

Friedman, Lawrence J. *The White Savage: Racial Fantasies in the Postbellum South*. Englewood Cliffs, N.J.: Prentice-Hall, 1970.

Friedman, Milton, and Schwartz, Anna Jacobson. *A Monetary History of the United States, 1867–1960*. Princeton, N.J.: Princeton University Press, 1963.

Gaither, Gerald H. *Blacks and the Populist Revolt: Ballots and Bigotry in the "New South."* University, Ala.: University of Alabama Press, 1977.

Gaston, Paul M. *The New South Creed: A Study in Southern Mythmaking*. New York: Alfred A. Knopf, 1970.

Going, Allen J. *Bourbon Democracy in Alabama, 1874–1890*. University, Ala.: University of Alabama Press, 1951.

Goodwyn, Lawrence. *Democratic Promise: The Populist Moment in America*. New York: Oxford University Press, 1976.

———. "Populist Dreams and Negro Rights: East Texas as a Case Study." *American Historical Review* 76 (Dec. 1971): 1435–56.

———. *The Populist Moment: A Short History of the Agrarian Revolt in America*. New York: Oxford University Press, 1978.

Grantham, Dewey, Jr. *Hoke Smith and the Politics of the New South*. Baton Rouge: Louisiana State University Press, 1958.

Green, James R. *Grass-Roots Socialism: Radical Movements in the Southwest, 1895–1943*. Baton Rouge: Louisiana State University Press, 1978.

Grob, Gerald N. *Workers and Utopia: A Study of Ideological Conflict in the American Labor Movement, 1865–1900*. Evanston, Ill.: Northwestern University Press, 1961.

Hackney, Sheldon. *Populism to Progressivism in Alabama*. Princeton, N.J.: Princeton University Press, 1969.

Hadwiger, Don F. "Farmers in Politics." *Agricultural History* 50 (Jan. 1976): 156–70.

Hair, William Ivy. *Bourbonism and Agrarian Protest: Louisiana Politics, 1877–1900*. Baton Rouge: Louisiana State University Press, 1969.

Handlin, Oscar. "Reconsidering the Populists." *Agricultural History* 39 (Apr. 1965): 68–74.

Bibliography

Harrell, David Edwin, Jr. "The Sectional Origins of the Churches of Christ." *Journal of Southern History* 30 (Aug. 1964): 261–77.

Haynes, Fred Emory. *James Baird Weaver*. Iowa City: The State Historical Society of Iowa, 1919.

Hays, Samuel P. *The Response to Industrial America, 1885–1914*. Chicago: University of Chicago Press, 1957.

Heilbroner, Robert L. *The Worldly Philosophers: The Lives, Times, and Ideas of the Great Economic Thinkers*. New York: Simon and Schuster, 1953.

Hicks, John D. *The Populist Revolt: A History of the Farmers' Alliance and the People's Party*. Minneapolis: University of Minnesota Press, 1931.

Higgs, Robert. *Competition and Coercion: Blacks in the American Economy, 1865–1914*. New York: Cambridge University Press, 1977.

Hofstadter, Richard. *The Age of Reform: From Bryan to F.D.R.* New York: Alfred A. Knopf, 1955.

————. *Social Darwinism in American Thought*. Revised ed. New York: George Brazillier, 1959.

Hollingsworth, J. Rogers. "Commentary: Populism and the Problem of Rhetoric and Reality." *Agricultural History* 39 (Apr. 1965): 81–85.

Holmes, William F. "The Demise of the Colored Farmers' Alliance." *Journal of Southern History* 41 (May 1975): 187–200.

————. "Whitecapping: Agrarian Violence in Mississippi, 1902–1906." *Journal of Southern History* 35 (May 1969): 165–85.

Jefferson, Thomas. *Notes on the State of Virginia*. Edited by William Peden. Chapel Hill: University of North Carolina Press, 1955.

Jones, Stanley L. *The Presidential Election of 1896*. Madison: University of Wisconsin Press, 1964.

Jordan, Winthrop D. *White Over Black: American Attitudes toward the Negro, 1550–1812*. Chapel Hill: University of North Carolina Press, 1968.

Key, V. O., Jr. *Southern Politics in State and Nation*. New York: Alfred A. Knopf, 1949.

Kirkland, Edward Chase. *Dream and Thought in the Business Community, 1860–1900*. Ithaca, N.Y.: Cornell University Press, 1956.

————. *Industry Comes of Age: Business, Labor, and Public Policy, 1860–1897*. Vol. 6 of *The Economic History of the United States*. New York: Holt, Rinehart and Winston, 1961.

Kirwan, Albert D. *Revolt of the Rednecks: Mississippi Politics, 1876–1925*. Lexington: University of Kentucky Press, 1951.

Klein, Maury. *The Great Richmond Terminal: A Study in Businessmen and Business Strategy*. Charlottesville: University Press of Virginia, 1970.

Koch, Adrienne. *The Philosophy of Thomas Jefferson*. New York: Columbia University Press, 1943.

Kolko, Gabriel. *The Triumph of Conservatism: A Reinterpretation of American History, 1900–1916*. Glencoe, Ill.: The Free Press of Glencoe, 1963.

Kousser, J. Morgan. *The Shaping of Southern Politics: Suffrage Restriction and the Establishment of the One-Party South, 1880–1910*. New Haven, Conn.: Yale University Press, 1974.

Lindsey, Almont. *The Pullman Strike: The Story of a Unique Experiment and of a Great Labor Upheaval*. Chicago: University of Chicago Press, 1942.

Locke, John. *Two Treatises of Government: A Critical Edition with an Introduction and Apparatus Criticus*. Edited by Peter Laslett. Cambridge: Cambridge University Press, 1960.

Bibliography

Logan, Frenise A. *The Negro in North Carolina, 1876–1894*. Chapel Hill: University of North Carolina Press, 1964.

McCloskey, Robert. *American Conservatism in the Age of Enterprise, 1865–1910*. Cambridge, Mass.: Harvard University Press, 1951.

McLaurin, Melton Alonza. *Paternalism and Protest: Southern Cotton Mill Workers and Organized Labor, 1875–1905*. Westport, Conn.: Greenwood Publishing Corp., 1971.

McLoughlin, William G., Jr. *Modern Revivalism: Charles Grandison Finney to Billy Graham*. New York: The Ronald Press Co., 1959.

McMath, Robert C., Jr. *Populist Vanguard: A History of the Southern Farmers' Alliance*. Chapel Hill: University of North Carolina Press, 1975.

MacPherson, C. B. *The Political Theory of Possessive Individualism: Hobbes to Locke*. London: Oxford University Press, 1962.

Martin, Roscoe C. *The People's Party in Texas, A Study in Third Party Politics*. In the University of Texas *Bulletin*, no. 3308. Austin: University of Texas, 1933.

Marty, Martin E. *Righteous Empire: The Protestant Experience in America*. New York: The Dial Press, 1970.

Marx, Leo. *The Machine in the Garden: Technology and the Pastoral Ideal in America*. New York: Oxford University Press, 1964.

Meier, Gerald M. *Leading Issues in Economic Development: Studies in International Poverty*. 2nd ed. New York: Oxford University Press, 1970.

Meyers, Marvin. *The Jacksonian Persuasian: Politics and Belief*. Stanford, Cal.: Stanford University Press, 1957.

Miller, Robert Moats. "Southern White Protestantism and the Negro, 1865–1965." In Charles E. Wynes, ed. *The Negro in the South Since 1865: Selected Essays in American Negro History*. University, Ala.: University of Alabama Press, 1965: 231–47.

Mitchell, Wesley C. *A History of the Greenbacks with Special Reference to the Economic Consequences of their Issue: 1862–1865*. Chicago: University of Chicago Press, 1903.

Montgomery, David. *Beyond Equality: Labor and the Radical Republicans, 1862–1872*. New York: Alfred A. Knopf, 1967.

Muller, Philip Roy. "New South Populism: North Carolina, 1884–1900." Ph.D. dissertation, University of North Carolina at Chapel Hill, 1971.

Niemi, Albert W., Jr. *U.S. Economic History: A Survey of the Major Issues*. Chicago: Rand McNally College Publishing Co., 1975.

Noblin, Stuart. *Leonidas Lafayette Polk: Agrarian Crusader*. Chapel Hill: University of North Carolina Press, 1949.

North, Douglass C. *Growth and Welfare in the American Past: A New Economic History*. Englewood Cliffs, N.J.: Prentice-Hall, 1966.

Nugent, Walter T. K. *Money and American Society, 1865–1880*. New York: The Free Press, 1968.

Palmer, Bruce. "The Southern Populists Remember: The Reform Alternative to Southern Sectionalism." *Southern Studies: An Interdisciplinary Journal of the South* 17 (Summer 1978): 131–49.

Pessen, Edward. *Jacksonian America: Society, Personality, and Politics*. Homewood, Ill.: The Dorsey Press, 1969.

————. *Most Uncommon Jacksonians: The Radical Leaders of the Early Labor Movement*. Albany: State University of New York Press, 1967.

Peterson, Merrill D. *The Jefferson Image in the American Mind*. New York: Oxford University Press, 1960.

Pollack, Norman. "Fear of Man: Populism, Authoritarianism, and the Historian." *Agricultural History* 39 (Apr. 1965): 59–67.

Bibliography

————. *The Populist Response to Industrial America*. Cambridge, Mass.: Harvard University Press, 1962.

————, ed. *The Populist Mind*. New York: Bobbs Merrill Co., 1967.

Porter, Kirk H., and Johnson, Donald Bruce. *National Party Platforms, 1840–1968*. 4th ed. Urbana: University of Illinois Press, 1970.

Ransom, Roger L., and Sutch, Richard. *One Kind of Freedom: The Economic Consequences of Emancipation*. New York: Cambridge University Press, 1977.

Reid, Joseph D. "Sharecropping as an Understandable Market Response—the Post-Bellum South." *Journal of Economic History* 33 (Mar. 1973): 106–30.

Rice, Lawrence D. *The Negro in Texas, 1874–1900*. Baton Rouge: Louisiana State University Press, 1971.

Ridge, Martin. *Ignatius Donnelly*. Chicago: University of Chicago Press, 1962.

Riordan, William L., ed. *Plunkitt of Tammany Hall*. New York: E. P. Dutton and Co., 1963.

Robertson, Ross M. *History of the American Economy*. 2nd ed. New York: Harcourt, Brace, and World, 1964.

Rogers, William Warren. *The One-Gallused Rebellion: Agrarianism in Alabama, 1865–1896*. Baton Rouge: Louisiana State University Press, 1970.

————. "Reuben F. Kolb: Agricultural Leader of the New South." *Agricultural History* 32 (Apr. 1958): 109–19.

————, and Ward, Robert David. *Labor Revolt in Alabama: The Great Strike of 1894*. Southern Historical Publications, no. 9. University, Ala.: University of Alabama Press, 1965.

Rosengarten, Theodore, ed. *All God's Dangers: The Life of Nate Shaw*. New York: Alfred A. Knopf, 1975.

Rothstein, Morton. "The Ante-Bellum South as a Dual Economy: A Tentative Hypothesis." *Agricultural History* 41 (Oct. 1967): 373–82.

Saloutos, Theodore. *Farmer Movements in the South, 1865–1933*. University of California Publications in History, vol. 64. Berkeley: University of California Press, 1960.

Saunders, Robert. "The Ideology of Southern Populists, 1892–1895." Ph.D. dissertation, University of Virginia, 1967.

————. "Southern Populists and the Negro, 1893–1895." *Journal of Negro History* 54 (July 1969): 240–61.

Schwartz, Michael. *Radical Protest and Social Structure: The Southern Farmers' Alliance and Cotton Tenancy, 1880–1890*. New York: Academic Press, 1976.

Shannon, Fred A. *The Farmer's Last Frontier: Agriculture, 1860–1897*. Vol. 5 of *The Economic History of the United States*. New York: Holt, Rinehart and Winston, 1945.

Sharkey, Robert P. *Money, Class, and Party: An Economic Study of Civil War and Reconstruction*. Baltimore, Md.: The Johns Hopkins Press, 1959.

Sheldon, William DuBose. *Populism in the Old Dominion: Virginia Farm Politics, 1885–1900*. Princeton, N.J.: Princeton University Press, 1935.

Smith, Henry Nash. *Virgin Land: The American West as Symbol and Myth*. Cambridge, Mass.: Harvard University Press, 1950.

Spain, Rufus B. *At Ease in Zion: A Social History of Southern Baptists, 1865–1900*. Nashville, Tenn.: Vanderbilt University Press, 1961.

Spratt, John S. *The Road to Spindletop: Economic Change in Texas, 1875–1901*. Dallas, Tex.: Southern Methodist University Press, 1955.

Stover, John F. *American Railroads*. Chicago: University of Chicago Press, 1961.

————. *The Railroads of the South, 1865–1900*. Chapel Hill: University of North Carolina Press, 1955.

Thernstrom, Stephan. *Poverty and Progress: Social Mobility in a Nineteenth-Century City*.

Bibliography

Cambridge, Mass.: Harvard University Press, 1964.

Tindall, George B., ed. *A Populist Reader: Selections from the Works of American Populist Leaders*. New York: Harper and Row, 1966.

Trefousse, Hans. *Ben Butler: The South Called Him Beast*. New York: Twayne Publishers, 1957.

Unger, Irwin. "Critique of Norman Pollack's 'Fear of Man.'" *Agricultural History* 39 (Apr. 1965): 75–80.

––––––. *The Greenback Era: A Social and Political History of American Finance, 1865–1879*. Princteon, N.J.: Princeton University Press, 1964.

Weinstein, Allen. *Prelude to Populism: Origins of the Silver Issue, 1867–1878*. New Haven, Conn.: Yale University Press, 1970.

Wiebe, Robert. *The Search for Order, 1877–1920*. New York: Hill and Wang, 1967.

Williams, William Appleman. *The Roots of the Modern American Empire: A Study of the Growth and Shaping of Social Consciousness in a Marketplace Society*. New York: Random House, 1969.

Wiltse, Charles M. *The Jeffersonian Tradition in American Democracy*. Chapel Hill: University of North Carolina Press, 1935.

Winkler, Ernest William, ed. *Platforms of Political Parties in Texas*. In the University of Texas *Bulletin*, no. 53. Austin: University of Texas, 1916.

Woodman, Harold D. *King Cotton and His Retainers: Financing and Marketing the Cotton Crop of the South, 1800–1925*. Lexington: University of Kentucky Press, 1968.

––––––. "The New History and the New South." *Journal of Southern History* 43 (Nov. 1977): 523–54.

Woodward, C. Vann. *The Burden of Southern History*. Baton Rouge: Louisiana State University Press, 1960.

––––––. *Origins of the New South, 1877–1913*. Vol. 9 of *A History of the South*, ed. by Wendel Holmes Stephenson and E. Merton Coulter. Baton Rouge: Louisiana State University Press, 1951.

––––––. *The Strange Career of Jim Crow*. 3rd rev. ed. New York: Oxford University Press, 1974.

––––––. *Tom Watson, Agrarian Rebel*. New York: Rinehart and Co., 1938.

Wright, Benjamin Fletcher, Jr. *American Interpretations of Natural Law: A Study in the History of Political Thought*. Cambridge, Mass.: Harvard University Press, 1931.

Wyllie, Irving G. *The Self-Made Man in America: The Myth of Rags to Riches*. New Brunswick, N.J.: Rutgers University Press, 1954.

INDEX

Index

Blacks, 50–66 passim, 141, 145, 160, 161, 162, 165, 170, 179, 180, 198, 217; vote by, 50, 149, 153, 161; voters, 52, 53, 145, 173, 174, 184, 186, 196; Georgia, 52, 170, 171, 172, 174; equal political and legal rights for, 58, 145, 169, 171–73, 180; political alliance with rural poor whites, 143, 144, 167, 170, 172, 176, 182, 185, 186, 187; Alabama, 166, 170; North Carolina, 170; newspapers of, 173; poor, 179; Texas, 184, 185, 186, 187

Bland Act, 102

Blount County, Ala., 160

Boggs, George, 149

Bowman, P. G., 156, 160

Brian, Hardy, 54

Brotherhood of Locomotive Engineers, 11

Brotherhood of Locomotive Firemen, 206

Brown, Joe, Jr., 181, 197

Bryan, Willam Jennings, 36, 103, 104, 117, 128, 142, 193, 218; Cross of Gold speech, 152; 1896 nomination of, 190, 192

Burke County, Ga., 175

Butler, Marion, 20, 31, 33, 77, 144–49, 151–54, 159, 171, 189, 195, 211

Butler County, Ala., 156

Calvin, John, 22

Campbell, Alexander, 12, 89

Capitalism, 3; industrial, 6, 8, 17, 18, 92, 184; financial, 7, 19, 30, 36, 38, 47, 81, 89, 112, 114, 124, 133, 144, 168, 173, 182, 195, 197; American, 28, 47, 81, 89, 93, 100, 104, 109, 114, 135, 182, 195, 197; Populist critique of, 199–221; Populist definition of, 213

Carnegie, Andrew, 35, 199

Carr, Elias, 147

Cartledge, J. L., 213

Caucasian (N.C.), 14, 25, 114, 146, 147, 148, 149

Choctaw Alliance (Butler, Ala.), 53, 159, 161, 162, 164, 167; editor, 160, 161, 163

Choctaw County, Ala., 53, 161; Populists, 163

Christianity, 24–26, 33, 62

Chronicle (Augusta, Ga.), 171

Church, 7; rural, 6, 22; institutional, 24, 25, 36, 65, 128; Holiness, 128; Pentecostal, 128

Civil War, 35, 42, 71, 83, 97, 98, 99, 100, 107, 108, 128, 204, 213, 219

Clayton, Henry D., 155

Cleveland, President Grover, 4, 27, 54, 55, 62, 76, 83, 116, 132, 147, 148, 156, 157, 158, 173, 190, 194; and Douglass "affair," 58, 145, 160; New York City school decree, 145, 173; administration, 180

Coeur d'Alene, Idaho, strike, 4

Committee on the Monetary System, 88

Communism, 32

Congress, 34, 45, 79, 170, 179

Conservatism, 149; southern, 198

Conservatives, 115, 153

Constitution, 31, 43, 44, 56, 78, 79, 80

Constitution (Atlanta, Ga.), 92

Cooperative movement: failure of, 7, 118

Cotton mills, 6, 18, 30

Coxey, Jacob, 149, 177, 179. *See also* Coxey's Army

Coxey's Army, 166. *See also* Coxey, Jacob

Credit, 3, 89, 91–94, 106, 107, 109, 124, 199, 214; system, 93; rural, 100

Crime of '73, 98

Crop lien system. *See* Lien system

Cross of Gold speech, 152

Culberson, Charles, 191, 193

Currency, 43, 69, 82, 83, 88, 92, 94, 98–108 passim, 116, 118, 119, 174, 175, 178, 179, 191, 214; national, 33, 43; fiat, 97; greenback, 97, 136; "intrinsic value," redeemable, 103; supply, 120; redeemable system, 137; expansion, 148, 158; issue, 155; legal tender fiat system, 156, 157, 159, 160, 172, 176, 177, 185, 189, 191, 195; system, 167. *See also* Free Silver; Money

Curry, J. L. M., 61

Darwinian theory, 204, 207

Davis, James H. "Cyclone," 44, 45, 46, 79, 80, 191, 192

Davis, Jefferson, 55

Debs, Eugene V., 35, 76

Declaration of Independence, 46

Democratic party, 48, 50, 54, 81, 147, 148, 154, 155, 167, 168, 172, 192, 195; 1896 national plank on free silver, 104; Na-

Index

Index

Index

Index

Index

Index